Miami University, 1809–2009

ASSOCIATE EDITORS

Andrew Cayton

Kate Rousmaniere

Robert S. Wicks

Peter W. Williams

ILLUSTRATIONS EDITOR

Robert S. Wicks

ARCHIVES EDITORS

Robert F. Schmidt

Valerie E. Elliott

MIAMI UNIVERSITY

1809–2009

Bicentennial Perspectives

Curtis W. Ellison, EDITOR

OHIO UNIVERSITY PRESS
in association with Miami University

Ohio University Press, Athens, Ohio 45701

www.ohioswallow.com

© 2009 by Miami University

All rights reserved

To obtain permission to quote, reprint, or otherwise reproduce or distribute material from Ohio University Press publications, please contact our rights and permissions department at (740) 593-1154 or (740) 593-4536 (fax).

Printed in China

This book is printed on Oji recycled paper, which is acid-free with 100% post-consumer waste.

Designed by Kachergis Book Design.

15   14   13   12   11   10   09   5   4   3   2   1

Front endsheet: Map of Miami College, 1810. Manuscript. Miami Special Collections.

Back endsheet: Student map of Miami campus, 1934. Amy M. Swisher and Virginia Steinmann. McGuffey Museum.

ILLUSTRATION CREDIT KEY

IT Services = Miami University Information Technology Services

McGuffey Museum = William Holmes McGuffey Museum, Miami University

Miami Art Museum = Miami University Art Museum

Miami Archives = Miami University Archives

Miami Physical Facilities = Miami University Physical Facilities Department

Miami Special Collections = Walter Havighurst Special Collections Library

Smith Library = Smith Library of Regional History, Oxford, Ohio

Western Archives = Western College Memorial Archives, Miami University

LIBRARY OF CONGRESS CATALOGING-IN-PUBLICATION DATA

Miami University, 1809–2009 : bicentennial perspectives / editor, Curtis W. Ellison.

   p. cm.

   ISBN 978-0-8214-1826-0 (hardcover : alk. paper) — ISBN 978-0-8214-1827-7 (pbk. : alk. paper) — ISBN 978-0-8214-1857-4 (deluxe : alk. paper)

   1. Miami University (Oxford, Ohio)—History.   2. Miami University (Oxford, Ohio)—Anniversaries, etc.   I. Ellison, Curtis W.

   LD3241.M52M53 2008

   378.771'75—dc22

2008043570

CONTRIBUTORS

James Patrick Ambuske, Director of Special Projects for University Advancement

Daryl W. Baldwin II, Director, Myaamia Project

Terry A. Barnhart, Professor of History, Eastern Illinois University

Marcia B. Baxter-Magolda, Distinguished Professor of Educational Leadership

J. K. Bhattacharjee, Professor Emeritus, Microbiology

Gerardo Brown-Manrique, Reg. Arch. and Professor of Architecture

Bobbe Burke, Coordinator of Off-Campus Affairs and Coordinator of Miami Tribe Relations, Student Affairs

Andrew Cayton, Distinguished Professor of History

Jerome U. Conley, Interim Assistant Dean and Associate Librarian, University Libraries

Michael L. Carrafiello, Associate Dean, Miami University Hamilton, Director, Michael J. Colligan History Project and Associate Professor of History

Valerie E. Elliott, Miami University Assistant Archivist and Head, Smith Library of Regional History, Lane Public Libraries, Oxford

Curtis W. Ellison, Professor of History and American Studies and Director, William Holmes McGuffey Museum

Osama M. Ettouney, Chair and Professor of Mechanical & Manufacturing Engineering

David A. Francko, Dean of the Graduate School, University of Alabama

Mary E. Frederickson, Associate Professor of History

Ann Fuehrer, Associate Professor of Women's Studies

Raymond F. Gorman, Senior Associate Dean, Farmer School of Business and Professor of Finance

Stephen C. Gordon, Curator, William Holmes McGuffey Museum

William J. Gracie, Jr., Professor Emeritus, English

Mary Jane Gregg, PhD Candidate, Educational Administration

C. Lee Harrington, Chair and Professor, Department of Sociology and Gerontology

B. Derrell Hart, Dean of Students, 1980–89, and Associate Vice President for Student Affairs, 1989–93

Carolyn Haynes, Director, University Honors Program and Professor of English

John M. Hughes, Provost and Senior Vice President, University of Vermont, and Professor Emeritus, Geology

George Ironstrack, Assistant Director, Myaamia Project

Robert C. Johnson, Associate Provost and Dean of the Graduate School, 1992–94, 1995–2003, and Professor Emeritus, English

Robert G. Keller, University Architect and Campus Planner

Susan Cross Lipnickey, Associate Professor of Kinesiology and Health

Peter Magolda, Professor of Educational Leadership

Frances McClure, Assistant to the Curator of Special Collections, 1976–94

William J. McKinstry, Professor Emeritus, Economics

Karl R. Mattox, Dean of the College of Arts & Science, 1990–99 and Professor Emeritus, Biology

Christopher R. Minelli, JD Candidate, University of Illinois College of Law

Bradley J. Mollmann, MA Candidate, History

Richard W. Momeyer, Professor of Philosophy

Gerri Susan Mosley-Howard, Associate Vice President for Student Affairs and Dean of Students, and Associate Professor of Educational Psychology

Christopher A. Myers, Professor of Zoology

Roderick E. Nimtz, Director, Voice of America Learning Center

Glenn J. Platt, C. Michael Armstrong Professor of Network Technology and Management

William Pratt, Professor Emeritus, English

Laura Rhoades, PhD Candidate, Educational Leadership

Kate Rousmaniere, Chair and Professor, Department of Educational Leadership

Randolph Runyon, Professor of French & Italian and Miami University Carillonneur

Robert F. Schmidt, University Archivist

David Shaffer, Director, University Marching Band and Visiting Assistant Professor of Music

Richard V. Smith, Professor Emeritus, Geography

Aaron Andrew Spetz, Architect, Cincinnati, Ohio

Rob Tolley, Senior Lecturer in Anthropology, Indiana University East

John Hoxland White, Jr., Adjunct Professor of History and Mechanical & Manufacturing Engineering

Robert S. Wicks, Director, Miami University Art Museum and Professor of Art

Heanon M. Wilkins, Director, Educational Opportunity Program, 1969–71; Director, Black World Studies Program, 1987–90; Professor Emeritus, Spanish and Portuguese

Eugene E. Willeke, Director, Institute of Environmental Sciences, 1977–2005 and Professor Emeritus, Geography

Peter W. Williams, Distinguished Professor of Comparative Religion and American Studies

Douglas M. Wilson, Alumni Secretary, 1966–68; Director of Alumni Affairs, 1968–79; Vice President for University Relations, 1982–88

Allan M. Winkler, Distinguished Professor of History

Edwin M. Yamauchi, Professor Emeritus, History

Morris Young, Associate Professor of English, University of Wisconsin–Madison

Contents

Preface

Few stories review the fragility, transience, and strength of our institutions more vividly than the inspection of two hundred years in the life of a public university. This book, a Miami bicentennial legacy project, makes that effort. Its aim is to imagine how the future emerges with trappings of the past, keeping some and discarding others. The editors hope it provokes thought and encourages writing about Miami University as it showcases a fraction of the rich material in archival collections, where we can see the choices of predecessors building the complex world we inhabit.

This work relies on the efforts of many contributors whose ties to Miami yield diverse perspectives on its past. Their contributions raise awareness of change as a factor in our future and challenge us to join a conversation about Miami history that began with its first president and faculty and continues into Miami's third century.

Here we weave an account of Miami's past that draws on events, eras, people, places, themes, programs, and plans, accompanied by images of our evolving campuses and the people who gave them meaning. The story connects local events and national trends across five distinct historical eras. A Miami history Web site hosted by the Miami University Libraries provides access to more work by contributors to this volume, and to other resources on Miami history and culture.

In 2004 Provost Ronald Crutcher asked a Miami University committee to identify potential bicentennial projects. This book took shape with the support of that group. We are grateful to Vice Provost John Skillings and Bicentennial Coordinators Steve Snyder, Executive Assistant to the President, and Jerome Conley for thoughtful and essential assistance at many points since that time. Vice President Jayne Whitehead and the Division of University Advancement provided financial support that made this book possible.

We relied on University Archives and its accomplished staff, Archivist Robert Schmidt, Assistant Archivist Valerie Elliott, and Program Associate Gayle Brown. Students Amy Bergseth, Dharitri Bhattacharjee, David Childs, Ann Cox, and Fatuma Boru Guyo provided research services. Erika Nelson made the index. Joshua Avery converted cumulative data into graphical presentations. Information Technology Services staff Jeff Sabo and Scott Kissell provided photographic services. Registrar Laura Henderson coordinated photography of historical paintings in the Miami University Art Museum. Staff of the McGuffey Museum, Smith Library of Regional History (Lane Public Libraries), and Western College Memorial Archives provided important assistance, as did Janet Stuckey, Havighurst Special Collections. Jim Bricker of Special Collections assisted in locating and scanning historical documents. Celia Ellison gave the manuscript valuable readings at various stages.

David Sanders, director of Ohio University Press, and his highly capable staff provided assistance and patience for which we are quite grateful. We have been pleased to work with the professionals of this distinguished press.

We especially thank contributors, who freely gave their time and expertise, and call attention to their names at the front of the work. We express deep gratitude to colleagues, friends, and family members whose assistance and encouragement have been important and greatly appreciated.

Curtis W. Ellison
OXFORD, OHIO
OCTOBER 2008

Myaamiaki neehi Myaamionki

The Miami People and Their Homelands

George Ironstrack

Little Turtle. Graphite drawing of Miami war leader Mihšihkinaahkwa (ca. 1747–1812) by Julie Langford Olds, 2007. Based on early engravings and on a painting by Gilbert Stuart destroyed when the British burned Washington, D.C., in 1814. Collection of the artist.

The half-century following the end of the American Revolution brought deep changes to indigenous peoples living south of the Great Lakes. During this time the Miami and their relatives, the Shawnee and Delaware, resisted the invasion of their homelands, confronted military defeat, reluctantly relinquished much of their home territories, and finally faced forcible removal from them.

Myaamiaki, the Miami, were originally a village-centered people who spoke a common language (Miami-Illinois) and shared the same culture. Miami people located villages along the *Waapaahšiki Siipiiwi* (Wabash River valley in northern Indiana) and the *Inoka Siipiiwi* (Illinois River valley in northern Illinois), at *Šikaakonki* along the southern shores of Lake Michigan (near Chicago, Illinois), and at *Pinkwi Mihtohseeniaki* or Pickawillany along the Great Miami River in western Ohio, which was so named because it was a route used to reach the Miami living along the Wabash. From spring to late fall the lives of Miami people centered on these villages and focused on agricultural pursuits. They raised vast fields of *Myaamia miincipi* (Miami corn) and traded with their neighbors. In winter months Miami people would disperse to smaller camps to concentrate on hunting. Elderly and some younger people often remained in the more permanent village sites to maintain dwellings. In the spring, the people of the village would return to begin planting and preparing for the agricultural cycle. This rhythm of seasons and life cycles formed Miami people's lives for thousands of years.

These cultural rhythms were inherently connected to the lands the Miami called home. *Myaamionki,* or the homelands of the Miami people, ran from the Mississippi River east to the Scioto River and from the Ohio River north to the Fox River in Wisconsin and the St. Joseph River in southern Michigan. It was a shared landscape, overlapping with homelands of numerous indigenous peoples such as the Shawnee, Delaware, Illinois, Potawatomi, Ottawa, and Wyandot. After arrival of the French in the mid-1600s, indigenous groups also began to share this landscape with Europeans.

In the mid-eighteenth century Pennsylvanians and Virginians began to move west of the Scioto and into *Myaamionki* as invited guests of Miami, Shawnee, and Delaware peoples. In 1787 Congress enacted the Northwest Ordinance, outlining the future of territory northwest of the Ohio River. In the Northwest Ordinance this was spoken of as property of the United States.

During the period leading up to the Northwest Ordinance, Miami village leaders like *Pakaana, Pinšiwa,* and Le Gris refused to attend treaty negotiations that recognized sole American ownership of lands north of the Ohio River. Meanwhile, thousands of Pennsylvanians, Virginians, and Kentuckians were pressing farther west down the Ohio. Many of these settlers, regarded by the Miami and others as invaders, moved north onto "open" land used seasonally by indigenous peoples. Some Miami villages and their allies organized attacks on American settler communities, and Americans attacked Miami villages.

In 1790, the government of the United States, under the leadership of General Josiah Harmar, organized an attack on the Miami for their "depredations" against Americans and their refusal to "treat with the United States when invited." Harmar not only attacked Miami warriors but devastated the Miami's towns and crops to destroy their ability to feed themselves as winter approached. Harmar's force was defeated in disastrous fashion by the Miami war leader *Mihšihkinaahkwa* (Little Turtle). However, the victory was far from joyous for the Miami people of *Kiihkayonki* (today's Fort Wayne, Indiana), because Harmar's forces burned their village and destroyed nearly twenty thousand bushels of corn. The following spring, as the Miami prepared to plant their crop, they also had to prepare for a second American assault. The Miami were joined now by their neighbors the Delaware, Shawnee, Ottawa, Potawatomi, Wyandot, and Kickapoo. While smaller American forces ravaged Miami villages farther down the Wabash River Valley, the Miami of *Kiihkayonki* prepared for the invasion of General Arthur St. Clair's larger force, based near Cincinnati.

St. Clair began his invasion in the fall of 1791. Since destruction of the autumn crop two years in a row would have been a death sentence to the *Kiihkayonki* villagers and to Miami resistance, the Miami and their allies attacked the invading Americans while they were at a distance from the village. In the ensuing battle the combined Indian force killed 634 and wounded another 274 American soldiers. According to historian Harvey Lewis Carter, the Miami-led alliance's victory was "the most overwhelming defeat in American military history." From a Miami perspective, the damage done to the Americans was far greater than any their own villages could have sustained. But the invaders were not indigenous villagers, and their will to destroy the resistance was greater than that of any previous group the Miami had encountered.

In the fall of 1793, a third invasion of *Myaamionki* was attempted under the leadership of General Anthony Wayne. After major defeats Wayne was cautious about his strategy. By advancing slowly and utilizing a string of forts stretching from Cincinnati north to the Wabash River valley, he was able to take away local advantages of the Miami-led alliance. Miami leaders, including *Mihšihkinaahkwa* (Little Turtle), understood this strategy and attempted to get the alliance to negotiate for peace. When this effort failed, the Miami pulled back. They would participate in the final battle for military defense of their homelands, but no longer lead it. At the Battle of Fallen Timbers in summer 1794, General Wayne needed less than two hours to defeat an

Miami Chief Brewett. Lithograph by James Otto Lewis, Aboriginal Portfolio, *1835–36. Miami Special Collections.*

alliance that had been victorious over two previous American armies. Following defeat of the indigenous alliance, Wayne's troops proceeded to seize or destroy vast quantities of corn and vegetables for the second time in four years.

Even before Fallen Timbers, the Miami had begun to plan a path for resisting American invasion by negotiation rather than force of arms. At the Treaty of Greenville, Ohio, in the summer of 1795, leaders of the Miami, Shawnee, Delaware, Ottawa, Ojibwa, Kickapoo, and Wyandot met with General Wayne to establish peace between the indigenous alliance and the United States. After days of speeches, negotiation, and argument the leaders agreed to peace, and to sell their lands only to the United States in the future. The Treaty of Greenville began a period of negotiation that resulted in surrender of most of *Myaamionki*. Between 1795 and 1840 the Miami negotiated thirteen treaties with the U.S. government, each treaty confining them to ever-smaller "reserve" lands. Within these parcels, Miami people found it increasingly difficult to follow seasonal lifeways. They lacked space to grow the corn their villages required, and found that movement into winter hunting camps was increasingly restricted, leading to reliance on government food sources and poor communal health. Paralleling the experience of most of indigenous America, the combination of disease and the introduction of alcohol by American traders decimated Miami communities and set the stage for what would be the bleakest period in their history.

The Miami also observed an incredible transformation of their landscape. Forested land, where the Miami hunted deer and fowl, was cleared of most of its trees. Swamps and wetlands, where they gathered wild plants, were drained and filled in. Canal channels were dug along the courses of rivers. And the rivers themselves swelled in size, swallowing whole islands and drowning important sites along their banks. These radical changes in the landscape of *Myaamionki* sent shockwaves through Miami culture that were just as culturally destructive as the later education programs that sought to "kill the Indian and save the man." Then, as the Miami struggled to maintain their footing on lands that were shifting beneath them, the federal government decided that they would have to leave their homelands altogether.

In 1840, Miami leaders signed a treaty that apparently agreed to removal from their homelands to lands west of the Mississippi River. Although many Miami claimed they had no intention of leaving, the 1840 treaty marked the fulfillment of United States federal policy established by the Indian Removal Act of 1830. While Miami leaders had skillfully resisted the U.S. government through negotiated delay, by 1846 further delay became impossible as more than three hundred Miami people were forcibly loaded onto canal boats. The Miami were taken to a place north of Fort Wayne, Indiana (former site of the largest Miami village of *Kiihkayonki*), and then south toward Cincinnati along the very canal system that had scarred the landscape of their home.

On the southern part of this route the Miami canal boat was pulled parallel to the course of the *Ahseni Siipiiwi* (Great Miami River) and past former village sites like *Pinkwi Mihtohseeniaki* (Pickawillany), past the sites of their victories over Harmar and St. Clair, within twenty miles of the treaty grounds at Greenville, and within thirteen miles of the grounds of a university that had taken its name from the nearby river and the surrounding valley named for the Miami.

After nearly a month of travel the Miami reached the Kansas Territory and set about slowly rebuilding their lives. They were allowed to remain in Kansas for less than twenty-four years before being forced to move yet again to the south, to what would become northeastern Oklahoma. At each point in this journey the Miami were fractured. In Indiana around three hundred Miami remained behind on communal family reserve lands granted to certain leaders, and in Kansas many Miami chose to remain in their homes rather than follow the political center of the Tribe to Oklahoma.

Thanks partly to the success of their leaders and partly to the tenacity of the people as a whole, the Miami people survived removals, dislocations, divisions, and population decline, as well as the radical transformation of their homelands. Today, Miami people can be found in every state of the United States and in more than a few other countries. The highest population concentrations remain in the Wabash River valley of north-central Indiana, near the former reserve lands in eastern Kansas, and near the modern political center of the Miami Tribe of Oklahoma in northeastern Oklahoma. Miami people still return to Greenville, Pickawillany, and numerous places in the Wabash River valley, upon which is layered so much of their history. These communities of Miami people have not survived by remaining an unchanged people of the distant past, but by adapting to change while maintaining a distinctive sense of being Miami.

act 1

Old Miami, 1809–1885

Inventing College Life

An *"Old Miami" Timeline, 1787–1885*

1787	July 13, Northwest Ordinance passed by Continental Congress
	September 17, United States Constitution written; ratified 1788
1794	September 30, President George Washington signs patent for Symmes Purchase
1795	August 3, Miami Tribe signs Treaty of Greenville
1803	September 1, commissioners of the legislature locate the Miami College township on public lands in the Cincinnati district
1809	February 17, the Miami University chartered by State of Ohio
1810	Village of Oxford laid out in the college township; Miami University campus surveyed
1811	Log schoolhouse erected on University Square to serve Oxford Township
1816	Construction of first classroom building, Franklin Hall (later part of Old Main), begun
1822	Proposed relocation of Miami University to Cincinnati defeated in legislature
1824	President Robert Hamilton Bishop inaugurated; classes begin
1825	Erodelphian Literary Society and Union Literary Society organized
1828	First residence hall, North Hall (later Elliott Hall), constructed
1835	Chapter of Alpha Delta Phi fraternity established
1836	William Holmes McGuffey publishes his first *Eclectic Reader*
	Second residence hall, South Hall (later Stoddard Hall), constructed
1838	Oxford Theological Seminary established
1839	Alpha chapter of Beta Theta Pi fraternity founded
1841	President George Junkin inaugurated
1842	President Junkin issues *Laws of Miami University for Government of the Faculty and Students*
1844	President Junkin resigns following student disruptions
1845	President Erasmus D. MacMaster inaugurated

1846	Conflict among literary societies, president, board, and faculty
	Miami Tribe removed from traditional lands to western territories
1848	January 12, Old Main sealed with snow, seventeen students dismissed or depart
	December 27, Alpha chapter of Phi Delta Theta fraternity founded
1849	President MacMaster resigns
	President William C. Anderson inaugurated; joins Phi Delta Theta fraternity
	Oxford Female Institute (later Oxford College) chartered; John W. Scott, principal
1852	Chapter of Delta Kappa Epsilon fraternity established
1853	Western Female Seminary (later Western College) chartered; Helen Peabody, principal
1854	Oxford Female College chartered; John W. Scott, principal
	President John W. Hall inaugurated
1855	Alpha chapter of Sigma Chi fraternity founded
1859	Junction Railroad reaches Oxford
1861	April 12, American Civil War begins
	Ozro Dodds, student, and Professor Robert W. McFarland form volunteer companies for Union
1866	President Robert L. Stanton inaugurated; seeks new funding sources for Miami
1871	Andrew D. Hepburn named president
1873	National financial panic, low enrollment, no endowment; trustees suspend operation
1873–85	Miami Classical School and Miami Classical and Scientific Training School operate on campus
1885	President Robert W. McFarland takes office; Miami reopens classes

"Old Miami" Themes

In the wake of the American Revolution, Anglo-European settlement surges west from the original American colonies across the emerging United States. After the defeat and removal of the Miami and other Native Americans in the late eighteenth and early nineteenth centuries, land agents survey the Ohio River valley for economic development by a rising white middle class engaged in farming, trade, urbanization, and industry. The national government, however, reserves land to support institutions of higher education that will prepare leaders for the expanding nation. In 1803, commissioners of the Ohio legislature locate a township on public lands near Hamilton in the Cincinnati district where land rent will support a future university, and the Miami University, chartered by the State of Ohio in 1809, is laid out at the new town of Oxford in 1810.

Attracting students from the Midwest and South between 1824 and 1873, "Old Miami" offers the classical curriculum of ancient languages, mathematics, science, and religion characteristic of early American higher education for men. Literary societies founded by students debate both literary and political issues. In 1836 William Holmes McGuffey, an early faculty member, publishes the first volume of an Eclectic Reader series that will be used for schooling millions of Americans and institutionalizing ideals of republican citizenship throughout the nineteenth century.

Led by ministers of the Presbyterian Church, Old Miami experiences periodic waves of Protestant evangelism as well as growing conflicts over interpretation of church doctrine and student discipline. After strict rules for student behavior are adopted in the early 1840s, unrest grows among both faculty and students. Greek-letter fraternal organizations are founded on an impulse to free student life from faculty control, and the faculty divides over tolerance of this novelty. The revolutionary year of 1848 brings a campus crisis when many students are expelled for filling the main building with snow and debris, and in 1849 an embattled president resigns.

The academic climate changes when Miami's third president joins a fraternity. The town's social atmosphere adjusts again when three institutions for the education of women are established and prosper. In the early 1850s Oxford's social life diversifies, student restlessness subsides, and Miami enrollment grows.

Controversies over the abolition of slavery intensify in the late 1850s, and in 1861 the outbreak of the Civil War takes a heavy toll on Miami's enrollment. Miami survives the war years intact, free of debt, and with growing enrollment, but in the next decade all strategies pursued by the president and trustees to create continuing financial stability fail to keep the tuition-dependent university open. The era of "Old Miami" ends with a twelve-year suspension of classes after an economic downturn following the national panic of 1873. The campus, however, remains in continuous use as a thriving classical and scientific training school, and the village invented to host it proves resilient as well.

Oxford, 1848

First there was a snowstorm. Then on the evening of January 12, a group of students rolled snowballs into the entrance of Old Main, and the front door of Miami University was sealed shut with snow. Scholarly President Erasmus D. MacMaster, forty-one years old, a strict Old School Presbyterian minister and an unamused disciplinarian, was at home sick with a cold. When he came out, he vowed to conduct an investigation that would reveal every guilty party and promised to expel them.

Challenged by authority, entrepreneurial young men of Miami replied by returning to Old Main the following evening, nailing shut the doors and windows, filling the lobby with several cords of wood from the university woodpile; adding stoves, planks, tables, benches, and then more snow; and dropping the chapel bell into the college well. A hard freeze followed. It took three days to open the building.

President MacMaster and his colleagues set up hearings in the reopened university on January 17 and began systematically questioning every student. All appeared for the proceedings, but at first no one admitted guilt. Forty-six students were declared guilty nonetheless and were expelled. Undeterred, students built a bonfire near the east end of Old Main, where they loudly celebrated their colleagues' fate as discipline was handed down. Eventually most of the students reconsidered, admitted wrongdoing, and were reinstated, but a few, still inflamed, declined the terms for readmission. Some hired a brass band and marched in demonstration through Oxford, and some left to enroll at Centre College in Kentucky. In all, seventeen

Erasmus D. MacMaster, president of Miami University, 1845–49. Miami Archives.

View of Miami University campus. Map of Oxford, 1852. *Miami Special Collections.*

students were dismissed or suspended, or left voluntarily—including half the senior class.

The Old Miami campus had been more prosperous a decade earlier. Enrollment, at a new high of 250 men in 1839, had fallen to 162 by 1842. In 1846 it was 140. By August 1848 there were only 112 students. And in August 1849 enrollment dropped precipitously to 68 students—33 of whom were in the preparatory grammar school. Two years after removal of the Miami Tribe to western territories, the young college bearing its name in Ohio was proving to be a fragile place, vulnerable to the mood of its students.

The traumatic event known in Miami lore as the Snow Rebellion arose in response to currents of change evident in both local and broader contexts. The most immediate was a growing spirit of student revolt as Miami University moved toward midcentury, spurred on by willful presidents and faculty who believed it a sacred obligation to instill discipline in the young. MacMaster had been named president in 1845. That year the Union Literary Society, one of several student debating associations formed early at Miami, invited Robert Dale Owen to speak on campus. Owen, son of the leader of a utopian community at New Harmony, Indiana, and a "free thinker," was running for reelection to Congress. President MacMaster, no fan of religious novelty, would later describe Owen as "a man who had signalized himself by systematic and outrageous assaults, not merely upon the institutions of Christianity, but upon the fundamental doctrines of Natural Religion, and the relations of domestic life, and by publications of vilest obscenity and in defense of the grossest Atheism." He blocked Owens's appearance.

The literary societies rebelled. In 1846 the Erodelphian Society told Miami's board of trustees it would not in the future submit names of invited speakers for approval. In their turn, Miami's faculty, all Presbyterian ministers mindful of prerogatives, affirmed that they had the right to approve campus speakers. In this contest of authority the board at first waffled, then in 1848 declared that the literary societies must submit names of proposed speakers to the faculty.

After the Snow Rebellion, what earlier may have been random acts of student disruption, such as letting cows into the chapel, evolved into full-scale agitation. "Scarcely a night passes without some disorder," Professor Robert H. Bishop Jr. wrote to his father, a former Miami president, and added, "there is a very evident spirit of insubordination and want of respect to superiors."

The following year President MacMaster resigned. The final blow to his presidency may have been an event described by historian James Rodabaugh as "a bold and violent assault on the board of trustees on the night of March 6, 1849."

At about midnight, a number of students, blacked and masked and dressed in fantastic costumes, marched with horns and bells to the college where the trustees were in

Miami University. First known photograph of campus, ca. 1858. Cyanotype. Miami Archives.

session. When they were refused an entrance to the meeting, they forced the doors and dispersed the board, "after the manner," wrote a newspaper correspondent, "in which Cromwell dissolved the Long Parliament." The trustees escaped and ran for the grove, where the boys herded them up and drove them into town through mud all the way. In town a battle ensued between citizens and students and two of the boys were captured. The board immediately asked the civil authorities to prosecute the students and the faculty to expel them. The two who were caught by citizens of the village were dismissed on March 8, 1849.

The late 1840s were rife with rebellion. In 1848 multifaceted change unfurled across European and American culture. In that year the United States won an aggressive war against Mexico and acquired Arizona, Nevada, Texas, Utah, and parts of Colorado, New Mexico, and Wyoming, as well as California, where a gold rush would soon begin. The first convention for women's rights, organized by Lucretia Mott and Elizabeth Cady Stanton (sister-in-law of a future Miami president), met in Seneca Falls, New York, in 1848, and in this year the Free Soil Party was formed to oppose the extension of slavery to territories of the United States. Dramatic changes in the country's urban landscape were occurring. In New York, air conditioning was installed in the Broadway Theatre, and the first building frames of cast iron rose to five stories, both in 1848. European politics were in turmoil. In 1848 workers revolted in France, the king abdicated, and Louis Napoleon was elected president of the French Republic. Revolutions also occurred in Prague, Vienna, Venice, Berlin, Milan, Denmark, and Hungary. Serfdom was abolished in Austria. In Britain, economics and class structure were famously explored in J. S. Mills's *Principles of Political Economy* and *The Communist Manifesto* by Karl Marx and Frederick Engels, both published that year.

The student revolt at Miami followed a pattern of collegiate disorder in the United States. Helen Lefkowitz Horowitz has written that "college life" was born in "a wave of violent collective uprisings in the late eighteenth and early nineteenth centuries against the combined authority of college professors and presidents." In the typical scenario, college authorities suppressed youthful pranks and other demonstrations, and in reaction, "college men forged a peer consciousness sharply at odds with that of the faculty." Princeton was a case in point. In 1800, after three students were dismissed for disturbances during morning prayers, students rolled barrels of stones through the hallways of the main building, Nassau Hall. In 1807, Princeton students rioted again after three more suspensions. This time they occupied Nassau Hall and prepared to fight villagers called on for aid by the president; he ended the conflict by closing the college. In 1817, Princeton students "nailed up the entrances and also the doors to the rooms of tutors and religious students." There were demonstrations elsewhere. Students "horsewhipped the president, stoned two professors, and threatened the other members of the faculty with personal injury" at the University of North Carolina. "Yale students in the 1820s bombed a residence hall. In a later Yale conflict, a student killed a tutor who tried to break up a melee."

At issue were the form of discipline, the character of leadership, and ideological convictions about what religion demanded of collegiate authority. Miami president Robert Hamilton Bishop (1824–41) set forth clear prohibitions on swearing, intoxication, riot, fighting, immoral company, and games of chance; he required study hours, morning and evening prayers, and attendance at two religious services on Sunday. But he did more than this. He embraced the idea, relatively novel among college leaders, that "every young man who wishes to be a scholar, and expects to be useful as a member of a free community, must at a very early period of life acquire the power of self-government." For Bishop, this did not mean learning to acquiesce. He permitted students to organize governments in their buildings and elect their officers. He encouraged the formation of literary societies in which students developed both fellowship and rhetorical skill as they debated social and political issues of the day. Near the end of his presidency in 1840, before trustees removed him partly for holding such attitudes, Bishop reflected on his approach to learning.

I for one, at least, freely declare—that I on many occasions am pleased with the opinions of young men freely and honestly expressed, though they should contradict some of my settled and favorite opinions. And I am more than pleased when the matter with respect to myself is still a matter of doubt. I love to see in young men a disposition to think and to act in all things for themselves and on their own responsibility, and to require a satisfactory reason for everything which they are required to do.

Three of Miami's early presidents embraced these educational values, but at least two who did not held office during the tumultuous 1840s. The Snow Rebellion of 1848 was more significant than merely the pranks of raucous boys or the reactions of their frustrated teachers at a small Ohio college. In its aftermath, students gained unprecedented levels of authority over college life outside the classroom through the official sanctioning of Greek-letter fraternal organizations, whose early members had played roles in disruptions of the 1840s. A new president, William C. Anderson, arrived in 1849. Like all his predecessors, he was a Presbyterian minister, but one inclined toward Bishop's educational values. He publicly endorsed the cause of independent campus organizations by joining a fraternity. Perhaps partly to promote a spirit of community, some faculty now lived in residence halls with students.

A related sequence of events that would also affect the character of student life in Oxford well into the twentieth century began in 1849. Former

Miami professor John W. Scott opened the first of three schools for women established in Oxford in the next five years. By 1855 female students enrolled at institutions for women outnumbered Miami male students, a pattern that would continue for almost all of the Old Miami years. As Miami's fraternal community thrived, Oxford's men and women students could socialize at "gala visitations" on ceremonial occasions, even if in formal Victorian ways.

By the early 1850s student life in Oxford turned less confrontational. In 1854 "Old Miami" enrollment reached its zenith at 266 men. The Snow Rebellion and its aftermath had played their part in the nineteenth-century transition of American college life, and the village of Oxford, Ohio, was on its way toward becoming a special place for students.

scene one

A New University in an Emerging Nation

CLEARING THE LAND

When the Treaty of Paris ended the American Revolution in 1783, Anglo-American culture already had a firm hold on the Eastern seaboard of North America and was preparing for a dramatic expansion. Even before the Constitution was adopted, the Continental Congress outlined terms for governing territories north and west of the Ohio River by enacting the Northwest Ordinance of July 13, 1787. This important legislation created citizenship and equal rights for all white male inhabitants, endorsed religious freedom, and abolished slaveholding in the region. It set out guiding principles for admission of future states—Ohio, Indiana, Michigan, Illinois, Wisconsin, and Minnesota—and so provided a model for even further expansion.

The Northwest Ordinance followed previous congressional acts aimed at economic development of land acquired by the new nation. Revolutionary War soldiers, for example, were awarded land grants in a variety of areas, and in 1785 an ordinance for this purpose stipulated, "There shall be reserved the lot No. 16 of every township for the maintenance of public schools, within said township." This set a precedent that would later allow the reservation of entire townships from which land rent collected on property would endow educational institutions, a system imported from Europe and used to support the early colonial colleges, beginning at Harvard at least as early as 1652. The 1787 provisions, however, made broader policy statements about values of the public welfare in connection with the land grant strategy. "Religion, morality, and knowledge," it said, "being necessary to good government and the happiness of mankind, schools and the means of education shall forever be encouraged."

17

John Cleves Symmes. Oil painting by
Charles Wilson Peale, 1793. Miami Art
Museum.

General Rufus Putnam, who surveyed lands along the Ohio River in the eastern part of the territory, formed the Ohio Company in 1786 to petition Congress for a major grant. Manasseh Cutler, one of Putnam's partners, soon became a prime agent, and may have played a part in drafting the Northwest Ordinance. Only two weeks after it was adopted Congress granted the Ohio Company close to five million acres for development. Within this land grant would be chartered in 1804 the Northwest Territory's first institution of higher education, the Ohio University.

At this time John Cleves Symmes, a former member of the Continental Congress serving as a judge in New Jersey, formed a partnership with Jonathan Dayton and Dr. Elias Boudinot to speculate in western lands. Following passage of the Northwest Ordinance, Symmes made a trip down the Ohio. In August 1787 Symmes petitioned Congress for a grant of land between the Great Miami River and the Little Miami River. Noting the educational provision of the Ohio Company grant, he asked that "instead of two townships for the use of a University, that one only be assigned for the benefit of an academy." At first he proposed to locate that township near Cincinnati at the junction of the Ohio and Licking rivers. In October 1787 he was granted two million acres, reduced one year later at his request to one million acres. As a period of financial difficulty and political squabbling about terms of the grant and its viability ensued, the land available for a college township was moved ever farther to the north and away from populated districts. Finally, in 1803 the Ohio legislature resolved to establish "a College Township in the District of Cincinnati" and appointed Jeremiah Morrow, Jacob White, and William Ludlow to find a location for it, "having regard to the quality of the land, the situation for health, the goodness of water, and the advantage of inland navigation." They chose an uninhabited area in western Butler County not far from the Indiana border, near a tributary of the Great Miami River and about sixteen miles northwest of the county seat at Hamilton.

Because that decision would place the college township outside the Symmes Purchase, a five-year waiting period was required before the state could formally acquire the property for this purpose. It took six years. The Ohio legislature passed "An Act to Establish The Miami University" on February 17, 1809. The legislators' intent was to create a place "for the instruction of youth in all the various branches of the liberal arts and sciences, for the promotion of good education, virtue, religion and morality, and for conferring all the literary honors granted in similar institutions." They added, "The benefits and advantages of the said University shall be open to all the citizens within this state." These provisions were entirely in accord with the revolutionary hopes of Ohio's early white settlers that in the spirit of Jeffersonian democracy they could build a new republic on a foundation of civic literacy.

DESIGNING HIGHER EDUCATION
IN OHIO AND THE MIDWEST

Early nineteenth-century colleges and universities were revolutionary institutions, and no one knew exactly what they would become. English immigrants had created colleges in the 1600s and 1700s, including Harvard, Yale, Princeton, and the College of William and Mary, mainly to train ministers and polish the manners of colonial gentlemen. As in Europe, only a handful of men attended these institutions, studying Greek, Latin, and history in a somewhat desultory fashion. The overwhelming majority of American colonists worked constantly to support themselves and their households, and received no more than a rudimentary education in the basic skills of reading, writing, and mathematics. College, reserved for sons of the elite, was far from a prerequisite for survival.

After creation of the United States in 1776, interest in the role of education in a new republic exploded into calls for institutions of higher learning open to a wider array of white men. In a monarchical government, literacy had been a sign of status accorded to those with the time and money to learn how to read and write. But in a democratic government, which was about making choices on issues as well as leaders, people needed to function as responsible citizens. They had to be able to read newspapers, pamphlets, and letters; to assess arguments, correspond with others, and manage complex commercial transactions. They also needed to learn how to participate in politics with civility and decorum. Leaders of the country talked incessantly about the importance of education. The provision for perpetual encouragement of schools in the third article of the Northwest Ordinance stated this directly. The Ohio Constitution of 1802 added that education should be encouraged "by legislative provision not inconsistent with the rights of conscience." Ohio governor Thomas Worthington spoke common wisdom in 1818 when he called for a state system of public education in Ohio. Without it, people would be "unable to manage with propriety, their private concerns, much less to take any part in the management of public affairs," and would be "unacquainted with those religious and moral precepts and principles, without which they cannot be good citizens."

Although it was widely agreed that education was critical to the success of the republic, early residents of the Midwest could not agree on either its specifics or how to pay for it. In principle, religion was important; in practice, religion meant different things to different people. In principle, education made better citizens; in practice, people differed on proper values. In principle, the state government should support education at all levels; in practice, no one wanted to pay for anything from which they could not see direct financial benefit to themselves and their community. In principle, the citizens of fledgling settlements north and west of the Ohio River wanted a college in order to boost their collective economic prospects as well as their general respectability and public visibility; in practice, the residents of small towns were often uncomfortable with rowdy students and stiff-necked faculty.

Because states of the Midwest did not regularly support higher education financially until the last decades of the nineteenth century, public institutions such as Ohio University (1804), Miami University (1809), the University of Michigan (1817), and Indiana University (1820) were anomalies. Chartered by state or territorial legislatures, they were for all practical purposes left to their own devices. Ohio University and Miami University were managed by boards of seven to fourteen trustees who were elected by the Ohio General Assembly until after the Civil War, then appointed by the governor. But the state did not appropriate money regularly to either university until the 1880s, and to Miami, not until 1896. In reality, both Ohio and Miami were local institutions constantly teetering on the edge of financial disaster.

The State of Ohio was doing what other American states, the federal government, and European nations were doing in the early nineteenth century—using the practice traditional in cash-poor monarchies of granting special privileges to an association of men empowered to carry out a public good at their own expense. Their charters essentially farmed out public responsibilities to private groups. Over time American courts began to regard these charters as contracts and argue, most famously in *Dartmouth College v. Woodward*, 1819, that states had no right to interfere in the operation of colleges. The trustees, not the General Assembly, operated Ohio University and Miami University.

Small colleges established by religious denominations were more common than quasi-public universities. Most also had state charters. Ohio had over twenty colleges in 1860, more than any other state, primarily religious institutions whose public role was to advance the interests of their local communities. Run by a handful of faculty supervised by local trustees in an arrangement not unlike contemporary public school districts, early colleges emphasized a broad-based classical curriculum. Most were exclusively for white men. There were, however, institutions devoted to women, as well as a handful for African Americans, and Oberlin, positively radical, opened its doors after the 1830s to women and African Americans as well as white men.

Whether public or private, midwestern colleges tended to be more practical and pietistic than their counterparts in other regions of the United States. Their students tended to be in their mid-twenties, a little older than students in the South or New England. Some midwestern colleges substituted Hebrew for Latin to facilitate study of the Bible, and some required manual labor. Religious revivals occurred with frequency. Faculty members were often ministers or priests. Few questioned the overlap between the sacred and the secular, and most associated higher education with the study of morality, philosophy, ethics, religion, and the wisdom of the ancient Greeks and Romans.

Most colleges quickly became bulwarks of regional social order. They smoothed the rough edges of the sons of middle-class citizens and added a veneer of culture to small-town life. Colleges trained young men in the professions of law and ministry and brought business to local shopkeepers. Whatever their misgivings, entrepreneurs frequently took pride in donating large sums of money to colleges, both to immortalize themselves as respectable citizens and to help occasionally floundering institutions survive. Colleges were often named after benefactors (Carleton, DePauw, Kenyon), hometowns (Wilmington, Franklin, Marietta, Wooster), or pillars of the church (Knox, Loyola, Notre Dame, Otterbein, Ohio Wesleyan, Xavier).

The notion that the state had an obligation to provide funding for public universities emerged slowly in the nineteenth century because legislators continued to assume that chartered institutions could serve the public good with private money and local control. A turning point came in 1862 when Justin

Smith Morrill, a Republican congressman from Vermont, exploited the absence of Southerners from Congress during the Civil War to win passage of an act giving each state thirty thousand acres of public land for every U.S. senator and congressman it had in 1860. Profits from sale of this land were invested in a permanent fund for support of agricultural and mechanical institutions. The Morrill Act shifted emphasis away from a classical curriculum for gentlemen and toward more practical training with the goal of benefiting a broader range of citizens.

In Ohio, the General Assembly rejected the intense appeals of poverty-stricken Ohio and Miami universities to be designated the state's land-grant institution. Under the leadership of Republican governor Rutherford B. Hayes, the Ohio Agricultural and Mechanical College, founded in 1870, became a more broadly based school with a liberal arts curriculum. In 1878 its name was changed to "The Ohio State University." (Land-grant schools in other states include Michigan State University, Purdue University, Iowa State University, and the University of Illinois.) By the turn of the twentieth century, normal schools were established for training primarily women to become public school teachers. With the expansion of higher education that followed, many of these institutions, including Bowling Green and Kent in Ohio, became state universities.

BUILDING A COLLEGE IN THE WOODS

Miami University originated in an eighteenth-century insistence on the importance of educating male citizens for the civic, economic, and cultural leadership of a revolutionary republic. Early colleges and universities were to be moral as well as intellectual centers that nearly everyone assumed would be supported by efforts of the good people of their church or community rather than by state appropriations. And those people were expected to prosper. The entrepreneurial land agents who saw in Ohio a frontier of commercial opportunity were not disappointed, as immigrants, mostly from the East, expanded the state's population dramatically. In 1800 Ohio's population was 45,365. A decade later, the year after Miami was chartered, the state had grown to 230,760 people. The population more than doubled again before Miami offered its first college classes in 1824, and a decade before the Civil War, Ohio was the new country's third-largest state. By 1850, Cincinnati, Ohio's largest city, was also the largest city of the West.

During this frenzy of settlement, land speculation, and nation building, civic engagement abounded. Local political rivalries affected Miami's early prospects, as urbanizing commercial centers of the Miami Valley competed to build the actual university campus—which did not have to be placed in the township designated to support it—in their hometown. Cincinnati, Dayton, Hamilton, Lebanon, and Yellow Springs all offered proposals, and the

Early Nineteenth-Century Ecology of Southwest Ohio

When early European settlers arrived in the area that would become Oxford and Miami University, they stepped into a temperate deciduous forest landscape that had been shaped by the Wisconsin glacier, which reached its most southerly advance a few miles south of Oxford some nineteen thousand years ago. The retreating glacier left a land dominated by glacial limestone-based soils and a varied, rolling topography of river valleys and hills. Geological and biological factors—including a climate that features aspects of both the Midwest and the Upper South—made the natural vegetation of Butler County a mosaic of different forest types.

Surveyors who mapped the Northwest Territory and the state of Ohio marked the corners of one-mile square section lines with "witness trees," generally large trees of striking appearance that were blazed with a surveyor's mark and then recorded on maps. From the species distribution of witness trees, notes made on vegetation associated with witness trees, and other topographic details recorded by surveying crews, botanists can determine that beech-maple forests dominated the northeast corner of what is now the Oxford area. A remnant of this original old-growth forest can be found today in Hueston Woods State Park.

Farther south and east was a mixed mesophytic forest dominated by oaks, hickories, and ash trees with few, if any, maples and beeches. Low areas along creek and river channels featured bottomland forests dominated by ash, elms, sycamore, buckeye, and other moisture-loving species. These forest types can still be observed to the east and south of Oxford and Miami University, although only second- and third-growth forest remnants now lie among urban developments and farmland.

trustees chose a site in Lebanon, a centrally located and well-established community founded in 1802 that also boasted Ohio's oldest weekly newspaper. However sound the logic of this location, representatives of rejected communities complained about procedural irregularities, and on February 6, 1810, the legislature rejected the trustees' choice. It directed instead that the trustees lay out an entirely new town to be "known by the name of Oxford" on undeveloped wooded land within the college township, a township that had been sited seven years earlier outside Symmes Purchase and to the west of all contending towns. Although situating the new university where there were no towns may have been a setback to its rapid prosperity, commercial arguments favoring this location claimed it would appreciate land values by providing a new market for township farms, which would in turn increase Miami's land rent income.

In 1810, when the town of Oxford was surveyed, no roads led to Oxford, and mail took two weeks to arrive from the established town of Lebanon, 37 miles away. Miami's trustees had first met in Lebanon on June 7, 1809, soon after the university's charter was granted. The board set to work conscientiously, selecting officers, securing surveys to ascertain the location of the town and university lands, and raising money.

In 1810 the trustees employed Congregational minister John W. Browne to raise funds for building a campus. He traveled as Miami's first fundraiser for more than a year and a half, but when his expenses were calculated, he

David Purviance, president pro tempore of Miami University, 1822–24. From Levi Purviance, The Biography of Elder David Purviance, *1848.*

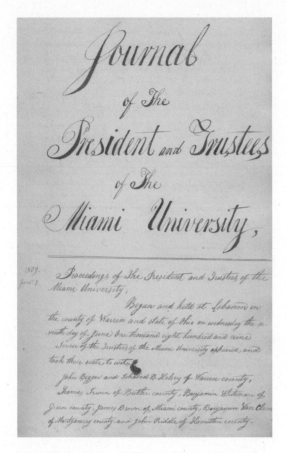

Miami University Board of Trustees Minutes, June 7, 1809.
Miami Special Collections.

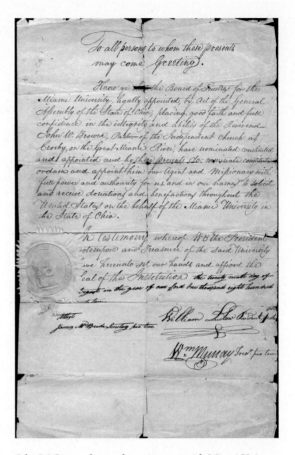

John W. Browne letter of appointment with Miami University seal, August 29, 1810. Only known impression of original seal. Miami Special Collections.

had actually lost money. He did, however, secure about a thousand books for a college library through the generosity of Miami's first corporate donors—booksellers and printing houses.

A single-story log building of 20 x 30 feet was the first structure built on university land in 1811. With permission of the trustees, and responding to a petition by local settlers, James M. Dorsey taught the first classes in this building to schoolchildren. Later it would become the first home of President Bishop. Seven years later trustee James Hughs was asked to offer college preparatory grammar school classes on behalf of Miami University in its first classroom building, a new twelve-room brick structure, first named Franklin Hall, that included a library, meeting room, and housing for twenty-one students. Grammar school classes began there November 3, 1818, with Hughs and a Prussian assistant named Nahum Myers, who taught Hebrew while learning to speak English.

Miami's first academic calendar offered grammar school classes continuously through the year with vacations in April and October. Students were

Seven presidents served Miami before Robert Hamilton Bishop took office in 1824. The first of these was John Bigger of Warren County, who was named "President pro tempore" at the first trustees' meeting. Among Bigger's actions was the hiring of James Heaton to survey university lands.

Bigger's successor, Joseph Van Horne of Hamilton County, was named "President to serve during the present meeting" at a meeting in Hamilton on March 26, 1810. His tenure was short. During the meeting, rules for "the President and Trustees of the Miami University" were adopted—taking the chair, calling to order, and deciding questions of order. The president could vote in case of deadlock, and could appoint committees. A presidential signature was required to validate resolutions. Upon ratifying the new rules, trustees elected William Ludlow from Hamilton president pro tempore, Van Horne having served barely a day.

Ludlow would be the most active early president. At a meeting on June 2, 1810, trustees learned of a discrepancy between Heaton's survey of college lands and earlier surveys. The board decided "it shall be the duty of the said President of the Miami University within 3 days after the present meeting" to ask the United States Surveyor-General to resurvey the boundary lines of the college township. At this meeting they also authorized the "President of Miami University" to appoint John W. Browne to solicit donations for Miami. Then they contracted for the making of one hundred thousand bricks for building construction.

Ludlow served until 1813, when John Reily of Butler County was elected president. The board paid Ludlow $82.00, plus $25.50 "as full compensation for all his services and expenses, whilst acting as President of the Board." Reily—who at various times taught school, managed a pack-horse business, and fought Indians—served until 1819, when his absence prompted election of the Reverend Matthew Wallace as "President pro tem" for one meeting. The next day Reily was reelected and served until David Purviance of Preble County was named President pro tempore in April 1822. A prominent Presbyterian divine and an Ohio legislator, Purviance led the board in planning the opening of the university.

A committee had been named in 1821 "to look out for a suitable person to take the Presidency of this institution." The search for Miami's first academic president took nearly three years. On July 6, 1824, the board elected Robert H. Bishop "President of the Faculty of Miami University" with an annual salary of $1,000. On September 15, 1824, Bishop began his seventeen-year presidency. Today Miami's early presidents are largely forgotten. But while they lacked a degree-granting college to oversee, they took essential steps to create one.

John W. Browne solicitation booklet, 1810.
Miami Special Collections.

"My success in Cash was small yet in Books I found encouragement..."

The Origins of Miami University's First Library

John W. Browne was publisher of the Cincinnati newspaper *Liberty Hall*, a member of Ohio's constitutional convention in 1802, sometime recorder for Hamilton County, and minister of the Congregational Church in Paddy's Run (now Shandon), Ohio. In 1810 trustees commissioned Browne to raise funds for constructing buildings. He departed on a nineteen-month mission in February 1811, crisscrossing Maryland, Delaware, New York, New Jersey, Massachusetts, and Connecticut on horseback in search of support. In the nation's capital he met with President James Madison, with Ohio and Kentucky state representatives, and with other prominent figures.

Although Browne often received a sympathetic hearing, the nation was at war with Great Britain and hard currency was scarce, so he found it difficult to raise even the $50 allowed him for a monthly salary, let alone funds adequate for constructing buildings. Yet Browne persevered. To maintain his spirits and pay for lodging he often preached the gospel to local congregations. He soon found that many people were more willing to part with their books than to open their purses. Through Cincinnati connections, Browne received introductions to major eastern publishers, from whom he requested "at least a copy of every publication which has been made by the differed Printers & Booksellers within my reach—and so as to maps, charts plans &c of any part of the globe." By this means Browne succeeded in securing more than one thousand volumes that would form the nucleus of the university's library.

He did not live to read them. In January 1813, crossing the Little Miami River on his way to fulfill a preaching engagement at Newton, Ohio, Browne lost control of his horse and fell into frigid waters. Rescued by a friend, he died hours later from exposure.

Today few volumes from Browne's original bequest can be identified with certainty. Important examples include a copy of Thomas Reader's *Remarks on the Prophetic Part of the Revelation of St. John: especially the Three Last Trumpets* (London, 1778) and *Clavis Pentateuchi* (Edinburgh, 1770), James Robertson's Latin study of the Hebrew Bible. Quite likely, many of the titles in Miami's earliest library catalogue, published in 1833, were volumes collected by Browne. That list reveals an impressive range of interests among Browne's contacts: medicine; poetry; translations; biography; geography; mathematics; philology; theology; law and politics; Greek and Latin classics; logic and rhetoric; periodical works; voyages and travels; statistics and chronology; chemistry and natural history; natural, mental, and moral philosophy; and miscellanies.

Miami's earliest library was placed in the university's main building in 1824. Hours of use were Saturdays between two o'clock and five o'clock p.m. Only members of the senior class were allowed to borrow books—and even they could request no more than two books at a time and keep them for a period no longer than two weeks. Fines for delinquent materials were 6¼ cents per week. Underclassmen could not use the library when Miami opened. They would soon, however, be able to avail themselves of the student literary society collections, chiefly novels and poetry.

examined at the beginning and end of each class meeting, no absence was permitted, and morning prayers and Sunday worship were required. As a strategy for instilling civic virtue, there was a list of prohibitions—among them profanity, alcohol, gambling, noise, immoral literature or pictures, and keeping company with "persons of notoriously bad character." The trustees closed the first grammar school in 1821 due, they said, to excessive expense, but reopened it as a preparatory school within the university when college proper classes began on November 2, 1824—fifteen years after Miami had been chartered by the state.

In 1822 there had been a concerted effort to move Miami University to

Cincinnati, relocating it within the Symmes Purchase. That proposal was sty-mied in the legislature by Oxford's Joel Collins, who had first surveyed the town, and by James McBride of Hamilton. McBride, who surveyed an early road into Oxford Township, served as a trustee and later as president of the board. He was elected to the legislature in 1822 on a pledge to keep the uni-versity in Oxford. Together, Collins and McBride assured that Butler County remained the location of Miami University.

In 1824 the persevering trustees turned over daily management of the now operational college to three faculty members, one of them its first aca-demic president, Robert Hamilton Bishop (1824–41). Educated in Scotland by liberal Presbyterian theologians, Bishop came to Miami from Transylva-nia University in Lexington, Kentucky. A tally of July 1825 reveals a total of 58 students enrolled, 26 of them admitted to the college curriculum, 23 in the grammar school, and 9 in the English and Scientific Department, a course of study outside the college curriculum. On the second day of Miami's campus life, the trustees ordered a bell for the tower of the college building.

By 1839, fifteen years after it began collegiate instruction, during waves of dramatic population growth across its region, Miami had risen to prominence in the new West. One account of enrollment in leading institutions that year has it ranked sixth. The only western school in this group enrolling more stu-dents in that peak year for Old Miami was Oberlin College—the youngest, and the earliest to admit women and African Americans.

Grammar Schools

In the nineteenth century the delineation between "elementary," "secondary," and "higher education" was not so clear as it is today, and attendance at different levels of schooling was not aligned with specific age groups. There were no universally standardized grades, no requirements to begin a next level, no common assumptions about an appropriate age for enrolling in different levels of education, and no public regulations for school attendance. Young children received rudimentary education in reading and writing at publicly funded primary schools, also called "district schools" or "common schools." A higher level of education took place in public "grammar schools" or privately funded "academies"—both emphasizing a more classical academic orientation. Although "high schools" began to replace grammar schools and academies beginning in 1821, there were no compulsory attendance laws or other regulations to standardize public education until the early twentieth century, and not until the mid-twentieth century would over fifty percent of American youth attend high school.

As a result, many institutions of higher education—including Miami University—offered coursework and study in classical languages that counted as both secondary and higher education and prepared students to enter the "college proper." This curriculum was confined to the university's "preparatory department" or "grammar school." Admission by test devices was not systematic until the mid-twentieth century, and many nineteenth-century college students were of an age group today assigned to high school. Miami's grammar school operated from 1811 to 1821, reopening when college classes began in 1824. The university maintained some legacy of the practice continuously until it closed the McGuffey Laboratory School in 1983.

James McBride

At various points in his life, James McBride, of Hamilton, Ohio, embraced merchandizing, architecture, banking, engineering, and public service. A chronicler of early settlement in the Miami Valley and a surveyor of prehistoric Indian mounds, McBride made original contributions to both local history and archaeology. His position as a community leader in Hamilton and his wide-ranging associations enabled McBride to become a zealous and effective officer and trustee of the fledging university at Oxford.

McBride was born November 2, 1788, on a farm near Greencastle, Pennsylvania. He arrived in Hamilton at age eighteen, and in a few years his prosperity and that of his adopted community became entwined. He surveyed the first county road through Oxford Township in 1808, when the future village of Oxford and its university were nothing more than a stand of blazed trees and a flowing spring of water. He served as secretary pro tempore of Miami's board of trustees from 1810 to 1820; in this role, McBride assiduously recorded all transactions, and between 1815 and 1818 prepared annual reports for the Ohio legislature.

In 1814 McBride assured township residents that the university—not yet built—had been irrevocably planted on the banks of Four Mile Creek, where it would remain "till time shall be no longer." He was a prominent agitator against a legislative bill to move the university to Cincinnati, which was defeated in January 1822. After he joined the legislature in the fall of 1822, McBride was vigilant in frustrating further attempts to relocate Miami.

James McBride. Engraving by A. H. Ritchie, A History and Biographical Cyclopedia of Butler County, Ohio, 1882.

McBride's stewardship continued as the institution grew in size and respectability. He planned the construction of new buildings in the 1820s and 1830s, served on trustee committees between 1821 and 1852, and was president of the board from 1852 until his death in 1859. His distinctive handwriting stands out boldly in early records of Miami University, documenting the distinguished record of a figure intimately connected with its fortunes for nearly fifty years.

In 1839 Miami students attended college in a well-established setting. Built on a gentle hill clear-cut from the forest, the university's physical facilities centered on a main building of whitewashed brick. This structure, known to future generations of Miamians as "Old Main," was added to and renovated numerous times until it was demolished in the late 1950s. In 1839 it had a three-story addition (constructed for the opening of college classes in 1824), with the 1818 building now forming a west wing. Two brick multistory dormitories, built in 1828 and 1836, were located east and south of the main building, facing west. "Old North," today's Elliott Hall, was a living facility for students that would be "plain but strong with funnels instead of fireplaces." Rooms were heated with wood-burning stoves, also used by students for cooking their meals. "Old South," today's Stoddard Hall, was constructed on the site of a low mound left by people who inhabited the Miami Valley in prehistoric times. Intended to house junior and senior men, "Old South" offered single rooms, some with fireplaces and mantels; featured corridors running the length of the building served by a center stairway; and was officially described as "plain," "substantial and neat." All three structures had neoclassic proportions, yet none was ornamented with Georgian decorative elements. Their symmetrical alignment foreshadowed Miami's first quadrangle that would emerge almost a century later. A functional science laboratory of 24 x 40 feet, featuring a telescope on a stone pier, was built southwest of the main building in 1838, completing the Old Miami campus.

MIAMI'S PRESBYTERIAN HERITAGE

Like other churches in the Reformed tradition, early Presbyterians placed a premium on a learned clergy, steeped in biblical languages and historical theology as well as liberal arts. In an era when formal theological education was becoming the rule, Old Miami played a significant role in providing it. Lane Theological Seminary was founded in Cincinnati in 1828 for the education of clergy, which Lyman Beecher, its first president, promoted on the grounds that the West was likely to fall under Roman Catholic influence if Protestants failed to provide a strong alternative. President Bishop persuaded Lane Seminary to designate Miami as Lane's literary department, with theological studies to be completed at the Cincinnati institution. Consequently, Hebrew and systematic theology, intrinsic parts of ministerial training, were included in the Old Miami curriculum.

Presbyterianism had strong ties to Scotland. John Knox (1517–1572) has been credited with transforming the Scottish people from medieval Celtic bands into a modern nation by converting them to Presbyterian Christianity. In later centuries, Scots fought both the English and among themselves, generating splinter groups around doctrine or politics. This was reflected in the tradition transported to North America. The first presbytery in the colonies was formed in 1706 in New Jersey, New York, and Pennsylvania. After splits that occurred during Great Awakening revivals of the 1740s had healed, and American independence was achieved, a body known as the Presbyterian Church in the U.S.A. (PCUSA)

1838–1839
Enrollment at Leading Institutions

Institution	Charter Date	Enrollment
Yale	1701	411
Oberlin	1833	404
Dartmouth	1769	301
Union	1795	286
Miami	1809	250
Virginia	1819	247
Transylvania	1780	269
Princeton	1746	237
Harvard	1636	216
Kenyon	1824	203

Miami Bell at Old Main. Photograph, 1868. Miami Archives.

Robert Hamilton Bishop was born in Whitburn, Scotland, near Edinburgh, in 1777. After early studies with a Presbyterian minister, he enrolled at the University of Edinburgh, then a center of Enlightenment thought. Following theological education in Selkirk, he was licensed as a Presbyterian minister in 1802 in a nation and denomination prone to religious quarreling and schism. That year he married Ann Ireland and left Scotland for a career as an Associate Reformed (Presbyterian) Church minister in Ohio and Kentucky, then frontier territory.

In 1804 Bishop became professor of philosophy at Transylvania University in Lexington, Kentucky, with Henry Clay and Daniel Drake as colleagues. Although he served briefly as acting president, Bishop's tenure there was less than tranquil. His simultaneous service with two local churches led to a dispute with his denomination over the propriety of serving as both teacher and preacher. The rift delayed his ordination until 1808; eventually he resigned his pastorates and established one of the first "Sabbath Schools" for African Americans. (In 1819 he left the Associate Reformed Church to join the more mainstream Presbyterian Church in the U.S.A.)

When a Unitarian was named president of Transylvania University in 1818, Bishop led an attack upon the newcomer's theological liberalism, incurring the ill will of faculty and trustees. He was pleased to accept an invitation to become Miami's president in 1824, an offer tendered by a board on which several Transylvania alumni served.

As trustees expected, Bishop transformed Miami from a preparatory school into a university, and although Presbyterians had been organized by the Reverend James Hughs in Oxford as early as 1818, Bishop reorganized Oxford's Presbyterian church and allowed it to meet in Miami's chapel. He soon became known for permissive views on student behavior, was embroiled in controversies because of his antislavery activism in the church, and undertook a futile attempt at mediation within a denomination on the brink of schism. Removed as Miami's president in 1841 by the Board of Trustees, he remained at Miami as professor of history and political science.

Robert H. Bishop, president of Miami University, 1824–41. Engraving. Miami Archives.

In Bishop's era the modern notion of academic specialization was not yet the rule, but the lively education he received in Edinburgh under Dugald Stewart and Adam Ferguson served him well as a pioneer in teaching what is now called the social sciences, including the incipient discipline of sociology. Bishop's publications included books on the variety of subjects he taught, as well as numerous contributions to regional periodicals. After he lost his Miami faculty position in 1845, he taught at Farmers' College in Cincinnati, where he remained until his death in 1855.

Bishop and his wife had eight children. All five sons attended Miami, and Robert Hamilton Bishop Jr. taught at Miami for his entire career. After initial burial in Cincinnati, the remains of President Bishop and his wife were reinterred in Miami's Formal Gardens in 1959. As they had been at Farmers' College, and according to his request, they were placed in a low, unmarked mound.

organized in 1788 and pledged to support President Washington. Associate Reformed Presbyterians, however, refused to join this group, kept exclusive membership requirements, and abstained from political activity. Bishop joined the more inclusive PCUSA.

The following decades were not harmonious for Bishop or the PCUSA. In 1801 Presbyterians and Congregationalists adopted a Plan of Union for frontier evangelism, providing that their churches could not be within five miles of one another and that clergy of either denomination could be called to the pulpits of either. Presbyterians dominated in southern Ohio while Con-gregationalists, many from Connecticut, abounded in northeastern Ohio. In 1832 Lyman Beecher, a Connecticut Congregationalist reformer and revival preacher (and father of novelist Harriet Beecher Stowe) accepted a call to be president of Presbyterian Lane Seminary in Cincinnati and minister of Cincinnati's Second Presbyterian Church. But ecumenism would not last. At stake were the basic traditional teachings of Calvinism, especially the doctrine of predestination, which

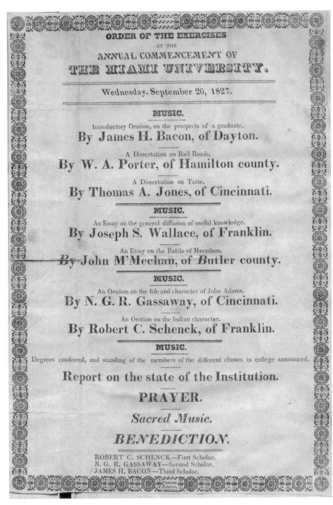

Commencement program, 1827. Miami Archives.

held that since the beginning of time God ordained that some would be saved and others eternally damned. Theologians such as Beecher's ally, Nathaniel William Taylor, began to chip away at this teaching, and Beecher was tried on heresy charges in 1835 but acquitted. An "Old School" and "New School" emerged, which formally divided after the Old School majority ended the Plan of Union in 1837.

Oxford's earliest Presbyterian congregation was gathered by Rev. James Hughs, principal of the grammar school, in 1818. He died in 1821. The church, revived by Bishop in 1825, worshipped at Miami's chapel until its building was completed in 1835. In 1834 Rev. Samuel McCracken, Miami's mathematics professor, organized an Associate Reformed Presbyterian church and served as its pastor while also carrying out instructional duties—a career path shared by several colleagues. In 1838 the Oxford Theological Seminary was established by the synod of this denomination. It trained nearly a hundred clergy over the next twenty years in a building shared with the local congregation on Church and Poplar streets, then was moved by the synod to Monmouth, Illinois, in 1858.

The Old School–New School schism generated Oxford's Second Pres-

Miami University.

GOD willing, the second year of the *MIAMI UNIVERSITY* will commence on the first Monday of November next. During the year which ends with this date, the classes in the College have been formed to suit the state of the country with respect to Grammar Schools, rather than according to any course prescribed in any of the older institutions. Next year a more rigid adherence to the course of instruction adopted in the older institutions will be attempted; and with the blessing of Heaven, and the continued support of the Miami Country, the public may expect by the commencement of the third year as full a course of instruction in the Miami University as is given in most of the Colleges in the United States.

The qualifications necessary for entrance into the Freshman Class at the commencement of the second year, will be—Common Arithmetic as far as the Extraction of Roots—two Books of the Æniad—and as much Greek as may be necessary to get a moderate lesson in the Greek Testament with tolerable ease.

The requirements for admission into the Sophomore Class will be, in addition to the above, the whole of Pike's Arithmetic—modern Geography—Algebra—Mair's Introduction—G. Minorca—the whole of Virgil and Sallust, and some portions of Horace and Cicero.

No student when once admitted as a member of any of the regular classes, will on any account whatever be permitted to proceed from a lower to a higher class, till he has mastered the studies of the lower one.

With the second year a course of instruction will commence in its features somewhat distinct from what has hitherto formed any part of the regular instruction in Colleges, but which it is believed will be adapted to the situation and the prospects of a very large portion of the young men of the States of Ohio and Indiana. It will comprehend English and Latin Grammar—Geography—Arithmetic—Mensuration—Surveying—Rhetoric—Composition—Moral Philosophy—Political Economy—and the elements of Ancient and Modern History. No person will be admitted to this course who is under sixteen years of age—nor will it be for the advantage of any one to commence unless he has made his arrangements to continue at least one year. The whole of the course will probably be completed in two years.

Arrangements have been made to have the essential parts of a Philosophical Apparatus in Oxford, in the course of two or three months hence. The College year is divided into two sessions of five months each. The whole expense of the year including tuition, boarding, lodging and washing, will not exceed eighty dollars. Tuition in every case to be paid five months in advance. It is of vast importance that those who intend to enter, be on the spot at the commencement of the year.

ROBERT H. BISHOP, President.

September 15, 1825.

James B. Camron, Printer

Advertisement for Miami University, September 15, 1825. Miami Archives.

byterian Church in 1841, and in 1850 a Third Presbyterian Church was organized. These quarrels had serious ramifications for Miami, as the faculty divided along factional lines. The Scottish McCracken and McArthur and the Scots-Irish William Holmes McGuffey, professor of languages, were staunchly Old School, which put them at swords' points with Bishop and John Witherspoon Scott, who taught the sciences. Bishop antagonized the Old School further by inviting Lyman Beecher to preach at the Miami chapel. Though harassed by students at the instigation of McArthur and McCracken, Beecher spent two weeks in Oxford, visiting with student antagonists and winning support for the New School cause. Bishop and Scott did seek to mediate the division they accurately foresaw as leading to formal schism. To this end Bishop began publishing in 1838 the *Western Peace Maker and Monthly Religious Journal*, but his attempt at reconciliation alienated both parties. These efforts ended in 1845 when Bishop and Scott were removed from the Miami faculty.

A broader impact of Presbyterianism on popular culture is seen in the career of William Holmes McGuffey, compiler of the *Eclectic Readers*, who served Miami as university librarian and professor from 1826 to 1836. Although his *Readers* do not teach specific Presbyterian doctrine, they are filled with an evangelical Protestant ethos that informed Old Miami and many early American colleges. This popular doctrine embraced the authority of the Bible, the need for literacy to interpret the Bible, the reign of God's Law, a strict moral code of personal conduct, and the idea that self-discipline and rigorous study lead to both worldly success and otherwoorldly redemption. In these teachings, McGuffey, Miami, and the Presbyterian Church spoke as one.

JOHN WITHERSPOON SCOTT, EDUCATOR

President Bishop's principal faculty ally was John W. Scott. Born in Pennsylvania, January 22, 1800, the son of a well-to-do Presbyterian minister, Scott was known as "the worst and wildest boy in Beaver County" yet was an exceptional student and graduated from Washington College in 1823. He

The Oxford Theological Seminary

Miami University had been open for almost fourteen years when the Oxford Theological Seminary was chartered in January 1838. At a meeting in Chillicothe the previous fall, the Associate Reformed Synod of the West resolved to move its theological seminary from Pittsburgh to Oxford. It purchased an acre of ground at the northeast corner of Poplar Street and what would later be named Church Street.

In an unusual move, the Associate Reformed congregation in Oxford offered to relocate in order to share a new building with the seminary. The synod and the congregation each paid half the cost of constructing the two-story brick building and, when completed, the space was apportioned equally. Seminary students used the first floor for their library, and classrooms. The local congregation worshipped in the sanctuary on second floor, reaching the space via a packed earth ramp that enabled congregants to enter and exit the upper level without disturbing male students in the lower level. For many years before the embankment was removed, the building was known as the "bank" church.

The Reverend Joseph Claybaugh of Chillicothe was appointed professor at the seminary and also served as pastor of the church until his death in 1855. Miami professor Samuel McCracken taught Hebrew when the first session began in the fall of 1839. Enrollment averaged about ten students each year during the 1840s, the only decade for which records survive, and Claybaugh was remembered by many of those students as a man of deep piety, an energetic minister, and a good instructor.

The seminary did not survive long past Claybaugh's death. The decision to move the seminary from Pittsburgh to Oxford had been so controversial that the Synod of the West divided in 1839, creating a second seminary in Allegheny, Pennsylvania. By the late 1850s, however, the Associate Reformed Church had four theological seminaries east of Indiana but none west of it. The Second Synod of the West moved the Oxford Theological Seminary to Monmouth, Illinois, where it opened in the fall of 1858 under the stewardship of the Reverend Alexander Young, Claybaugh's successor. The building that once housed Oxford's only theological institution served as the United Presbyterian Church for over a century, and is today owned by the Presbyterian Church (USA) and called simply the Seminary Building.

Oxford Theological Seminary (1838–57), ca. 1890. Smith Library.

Few nineteenth-century Americans surpassed William Holmes McGuffey in finding novel ways to promote civic engagement. In 1836 he published the first of the most widely read public school textbooks in American history. Used, reused, and venerated by children and adults, the McGuffey Reader series introduced literary study to millions of Americans and served as a nationalizing agent while teaching children how to read, write, and think. The *Eclectic Readers* galvanized ideologies of America's expanding middle class.

Born in Washington County, Pennsylvania, in 1800 into a family with eleven children, McGuffey was reared by Presbyterian parents who believed good work to be evidence of faith, and religion the foundation of proper thinking. In 1802 his family moved to Trumbull County, Ohio, where the largely self-educated McGuffey learned mathematics and Latin. By age fourteen, after attending academy, he taught subscription school in frontier settlements. He then went to Washington College in Pennsylvania, where he graduated with honors in ancient languages and philosophy in 1826.

A year earlier Robert Hamilton Bishop had invited McGuffey, whom he met in Kentucky, to come to Miami. Upon his graduation McGuffey rode to Oxford on horseback with his ten-year-old brother, Alexander. For the next decade, as professor and university librarian, McGuffey taught Miami students a frontier version of civic humanities; in the 1830s he also offered Miami's course in moral philosophy. Married in 1827, in 1833 he constructed a six-room house to accommodate the needs of a growing family. The first brick structure on the wooded lots south of campus, his Federal vernacular home was also symbolic of his aspiration.

In 1836 McGuffey, increasingly critical of Bishop's disciplinary policies, left Oxford to take a brief presidency at Cincinnati College, then moved on to Athens, where he served as president of Ohio University until 1845. He left Ohio University amidst controversy, returning to Cincinnati to teach in Woodward College for a year before assuming a professorship of moral philosophy at the University of Virginia, where he remained until his death in 1873. In later years he turned down presidential offers from Miami, the University of Missouri, and Washington College.

Although a professor for more than forty-five years, McGuffey probably considered the plain manner of a country preacher his most important achievement, believing that using accessible language sharpened one's intellect and helped reveal applications of the Bible to personal conduct. Ordained in 1829, he may have given more than three thousand sermons during his long career. His oratorical skill also served him in reform societies such as Cincinnati's Western Literary Institute, and brought him into contact with cultural elites. In 1834 Lyman Beecher's daughter Catharine Beecher, a well-known educator and writer, was asked by Winthrop B. Smith of Truman and Smith publishers to write a new standard school textbook. She suggested they contact Professor McGuffey.

McGuffey signed a contract to compile four "graded" readers and a primer. Eventually six readers were published, arranged by levels of difficulty for ages five to eighteen. They featured compilations of "eclectic" selections borrowed from many subjects, but especially from American and English literature. The phonics-based primer and *Eclectic Readers* were designed to teach children rudiments of spelling, reading, enunciation, and writing. Unlike somber school

William Holmes McGuffey. Oil painting attributed to Horace Harding, 1836. McGuffey Museum.

Harriet Spining McGuffey. Oil painting attributed to Horace Harding, 1836. McGuffey Museum.

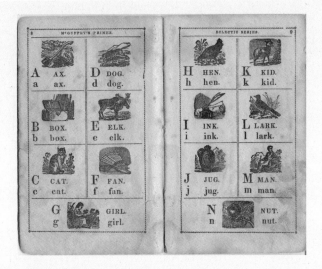

The First Eclectic Reader for Young Children *(1836) by William Holmes McGuffey. Miami Special Collections.*

Alphabet page from McGuffey Smaller Eclectic Primer (1849). Miami Special Collections.

texts such as *The New England Primer* that employed religious stories, McGuffey saw his *Eclectic Readers* as vehicles for instilling civic virtue, personal responsibility, and self-improvement through stories of everyday life. Often pedantic, the *Readers* stressed the importance of good behavior, proper manners and good character, and the belief that personal ambition would always need to be tempered by humility and social responsibility. By adhering to a strict moral code and leading a Christian life, one could rise into the middle class, where "the way to success is the path of duty."

The unparalleled success of McGuffey's *Eclectic Readers* can be attributed in part to skillful promotion and marketing by Cincinnati book publishers, beginning with Winthrop Smith and continuing through several firms. Even though the first reader was published a quarter century before the Civil War, McGuffey and Smith understood that by the 1830s, in order to capture a rapidly developing middle-class market in both the Midwest and upper South, the *Readers* would need to avoid sectional partisanship. The stories rarely mentioned African Americans, avoided mention of immigrants, and portrayed women in stereotypical roles. While not exonerating the *Readers* from charges of insensitivity to the diverse cultures then forming the United States, their marketing goals suggest why their stories strike many as homogenized artifacts of their time.

The *Readers* went through many editions, but after 1853 McGuffey had little involvement with them. His younger brother, Alexander Hamilton McGuffey (1816–1896), was involved in issuing a sixth *Reader* in 1857, while

pursuing a law career in Cincinnati and gaining renown as a patron of the arts. A substantially revised 1879 edition, published by Cincinnati's Van Antwerp, Bragg & Company, set a high standard for school texts. Moreover, illustrations in the readers were sketched by some of the most talented artists of the day, and set to print using state-of-the-art engravings. Even so, by the second quarter of the twentieth century the moralistic messages of the *Eclectic Readers* lost resonance in an increasingly pluralistic and industrial nation, and their use declined compared to progressive texts such as Scott Foresman's "Dick and Jane" *Basic Reader* series, first published in 1930.

In 1836 McGuffey had set to print the republican aspirations of his age in a book that would continue to sell thousands of copies annually into the twentieth century, and that even into early years of the twenty-first century would never be out of print. He took on the nineteenth-century challenge of blending the strict personal behavior said to be necessary for prudent democracy with the values of a relentlessly expanding commercial marketplace. His search for an internal discipline of mind and emotions in an era of revolutionary change haunted all Old Miami years and personalities, and would play a part in its most intense difficulties. Yet from his home in Virginia, perhaps remembering how a wild landscape had been cleared during the earliest days of Miami University to make a campus for teaching reason and mannered culture to the young, McGuffey must have easily selected the opening alphabet page image for his 1849 *Eclectic Primer*. "A" it showed, was for "AX."

35

completed graduate work at Yale under Benjamin Silliman, a leading scientist, receiving a master's degree in 1826. He taught at Washington College for two years, married, and accepted an offer from Miami, where he became professor of mathematics, geography, natural philosophy and astronomy, and political economy.

Students recalled Scott as a model teacher who treated them with both kindness and candor. He shared many views on education, religion, and politics with Bishop, and was ordained for the ministry in 1830. Although McGuffey helped bring Scott to Miami, their relationship soured over student discipline, when McGuffey began complaining privately about Bishop's laxness with troublemakers. No doubt Scott welcomed McGuffey's departure in 1836. Scott also had a flair for invective. When trustees removed Bishop from the presidency and replaced him with the Old School Presbyterian George Junkin, Scott wrote to a former student.

We have just this day had a glimpse of our Prest. elect, the redoubtable Dr. Junkin. Bah! . . . The truth is after seeing him, my mind has been struck still more forcibly with the want of generosity with which Dr. Bishop has been treated; and especially the absurdity of putting him as a Professor under the Presidency of such a man,—a Sampson under a pigmy.

After Junkin resigned in 1844, trustees removed both Scott and Bishop from the faculty as well, prompting Scott to publish a scathing response portraying trustees as a tribunal of liars, religious bigots, and proslavery fanatics. When former student Freeman Cary invited Scott and Bishop to join the newly established Farmers' College in Cincinnati, they accepted. Scott also taught at a new college for women located nearby.

This had apparently been a long-held dream. In 1839 Scott had helped establish Miss Bethania Crocker's Oxford Female Academy, whose "aim was to develop the minds rather than merely polish the manners, to give girls intellectual training that compared favorably with that given to young men." By 1847 the female seminary in Cincinnati where Scott taught had thirty students; twelve of them boarded in the Scott family home. Meanwhile, the demise of Oxford Female Academy led prominent Oxford citizens to create a joint stock company for support of a permanent women's school in Oxford. They asked Scott to take charge of it. Chartered as the Oxford Female Institute in 1849, it soon outgrew its small building, but the possibility of moving caused dissention that resulted in the chartering of a separate Oxford Female College in 1854. This school professed a national ambition. It would, said its promoters, "in moral literary, and scientific grade, and in all its facilities for a thorough intellectual and moral training . . . take rank with the first institutions in the country." Oxford Female Institute stockholders, however, viewed Oxford Female College as a competitor and were angry with Scott,

John Witherspoon Scott and Caroline Scott Harrison (seated), with daughter Mary Harrison McKee and children, in the White House, 1889. Miami Archives and Smith Library.

whom they considered its guiding hand. By winter 1855, Scott and a number of Institute students withdrew to the vacant Oxford Hotel until a new Oxford Female College building was completed in 1856.

Scott's tenure as president of Oxford Female College was unhappy. He began in debt, and efforts to raise money were unsuccessful. To save money on instructors and equipment, he arranged for some women to attend Miami science lectures. These were the first coeducational classes ever held at Miami, but the experiment was not universally admired and ended abruptly when Scott, fed up with financial woe and criticism, left Oxford for Hanover College in 1859. Yet Scott deserves a place among early pioneers of female education in the United States. His effort to establish a women's college that could stand on an equal footing with institutions for men had preceded Matthew Vassar's enterprise by over a decade.

Caroline Lavinia Scott was born in 1832 in a handsome brick house on the southwest corner of High Street and East Street, today's Campus Avenue. Her father, John Witherspoon Scott, was a Miami professor from 1828 to 1845, when the university terminated his employment. Scott took a teaching position with Farmers' College in Cincinnati, where the family lived for several years.

In 1849, Scott became principal of the Oxford Female Institute, and Carrie returned to Oxford with her parents to enroll in her father's school. The family moved into an old frame house across from the institute's new building on West Street, today's College Avenue. Some of Scott's students were also boarding there. During her first year back in Oxford, Carrie corresponded with a young man she had met in Cincinnati, and by the following fall, he had transferred from Farmers' College to Miami University.

Her suitor was Benjamin Harrison, from North Bend on the Ohio River. The grandson of a U.S. president, Harrison spent his last two academic years at Miami and was a member of Phi Delta Theta fraternity. He lived in the college dormitory later named Elliott Hall, but also roomed at times in village homes and ate at Mrs. Hughs's boardinghouse near campus. Stories are told of the couple's trysts on her parents' lattice-enclosed porch, of buggy rides on country roads, and of parties at friends' homes. When they graduated from Miami and the Oxford Female Institute in 1852, Ben and Carrie were engaged to marry.

The young couple spent a year apart while the bride-to-be taught music in Carrolton, Kentucky, and her future husband studied law in Cincinnati. In October 1853 they were married in the Scott home by the bride's father. For the first year of their marriage, the couple lived in North Bend; then Benjamin opened a law office in Indianapolis, where they lived for almost three decades. The first of their three children, however, was born in Oxford, where mother and baby stayed with the Scotts for a short time.

After serving in the Civil War, Harrison began a political career that culminated in a term as president of the United States from 1889 to 1893. First Lady Caroline Scott Harrison introduced exotic plants and established the White House china collection. She helped raise funds for Johns Hopkins University's medical school—but only if it would admit women. She also was a charter member and the first president general of the Daughters of the American Revolution. Carrie died of tuberculosis in the White House in 1892, just weeks before her husband lost his bid for a second term.

Caroline Scott Harrison as a young woman, ca. 1850. Smith Library.

Benjamin Harrison as a college student, ca. 1850. Miami Archives.

YOUNG MEN OF OLD MIAMI

Colleges for men in the growing nation were hopeful places with high aspirations for the success of their graduates in leadership roles of the emerging republican society. Old Miami was no exception, and would graduate many illustrious men. William S. Yeck, Class of 1936, compiled in 2006 a detailed account of Old Miami graduates between 1824 and 1840.

One eminent Old Miami graduate not included in these years is Benjamin Harrison, Class of 1852. Harrison earned his place in Miami history as a Presbyterian of high-minded civic purpose with unusual national ambition.

1824–1840
Careers of Miami Graduates

Five U.S. Senators
One Confederate Senator
Twenty U.S. Representatives
Three Confederate Representatives
Seven U.S. Ministers to a Foreign Country
Four Generals of the U.S. Army
Three Confederate Generals
Two Admirals of the U.S. Navy
Seven Governors
Thirteen College Presidents
Nine College Founders
Eleven Newspaper Editors

THE CAREER OF BENJAMIN HARRISON

The twenty-third president of the United States (1889–93) was named for a great-grandfather who signed the Declaration of Independence. Born August 20, 1833, near North Bend on the Ohio River west of Cincinnati, Benjamin Harrison was tutored at home and in a one-room log schoolhouse. Between 1847 and 1850 he attended Farmers' College, where his professors included Bishop and Scott. He entered Miami as a junior in 1850, was elected president of the Union Literary Society, was inducted into Phi Delta Theta, and joined the Presbyterian Church. An excellent student, Harrison developed a keen interest in history and politics and aimed for a legal career. Participation in literary society debates helped him develop into a superb speaker who, it was said, could move an audience to tears. At the 1852 commencement he was chosen to give an address that he titled "England's Poor."

Two years later Harrison began a lucrative law practice in Indianapolis and became involved with the fledgling Republican Party. During the Civil War, he served in the 70th Indiana Infantry Regiment and rose to brigadier general. After the war, following two unsuccessful tries for the Indiana governorship, he was elected by the Indiana legislature to the U.S. Senate in 1881. For the next six years Harrison championed pensions for Civil War veterans, high tariffs, civil service reform, and naval expansion. In an age characterized by corruption in both major political parties, he remained a reliable party man while maintaining a reputation for unquestioned personal integrity. That record, in addition to his family background, stellar military service, and ties to an important state, led the 1888 Republican Convention to select Harrison to run against Democratic President Grover Cleveland. The campaign, largely fought over the tariff, was low key, with Harrison limiting himself to delivering a few speeches from the front porch of his Indianapolis home. When results were in, Harrison trailed Cleveland in the popular vote by nearly

Benjamin Harrison and Whitelaw Reid presidential campaign ribbon, 1892. Richard M. Sollmann Collection.

ninety thousand votes but won the Electoral College by a large margin.

Harrison was inaugurated in a torrential rainstorm on March 4, 1889. He had no intention of being an activist president, yet played roles in passage of a Veterans' Dependent and Disability Pensions Act, the Sherman Anti-Trust Act, and the Land Revision Act that created the national forest system. A champion of better treatment for African Americans, Harrison lobbied unsuccessfully for bills prohibiting southern states from denying the vote to blacks. In foreign affairs he continued an ambitious naval modernization program and aggressively defended American interests in disputes with Britain, Canada, and Chile.

Although Harrison was a hard-working chief executive and one of the best public speakers of his day, he was never genuinely popular. At a time when personal relationships were the stuff of politics, Harrison was dubbed the "Human Iceberg," for he did not suffer fools gladly. One observer noted, "Harrison can make a speech to ten thousand men, and every one of them will go away his friend. Let him meet the same ten thousand men in private, and every one will go away his enemy."

Neither Harrison nor his party was enthusiastic about his nomination for a second term. A major economic downturn was under way and Harrison was preoccupied with his wife's declining health. Republican opponents replaced Vice President Levi Morton with Whitelaw Reid, a Miami alumnus, making the Harrison-Reid ticket allegedly the only one ever featuring graduates of the same college. However, the two were not close and the president was unhappy that Morton had been dropped. Harrison campaigned little against his Democratic opponent and when Caroline died in October of 1892, campaigning by both sides virtually ceased. Democrat Grover Cleveland won a decisive victory.

In 1896, the sixty-two-year-old Harrison married his late wife's niece, thirty-seven-year-old Mary Lord Dimmick, for a brief and happy union that ended in 1901 when Harrison died of pneumonia. Few would agree with nineteenth-century observer Henry Adams's judgment that Harrison was the greatest president since Lincoln, yet historians credit him with performing ably in office. That would probably please Harrison, whose life seemed to embody the Miami motto *Prodesse Quam Conspici*—to accomplish without being conspicuous.

By the mid-nineteenth century Anglo-American culture was solidly established in Ohio's Miami Valley. It featured lively commerce, civic pride, piety, and faith in human progress secured by disciplining the mind for useful citizenship and habits of industry. At Oxford the land had been cleared to build a small campus of orderly structures to educate youth in the traditions of Europe and New England, and Miami University had become an attractive place for young men to begin shaping careers in the ministry, education, law, politics, and military affairs. While Miami steadfastly remained a college for men, Oxford's thriving educational institutions for women were also distinguishing the community. In shaping the expansion of white middle-class culture across what would be called the American Midwest, Miami had become a leader.

scene two

Life at Old Miami

TRAVEL IN THE EARLY MIDWEST

Miami's first trustees were charged with putting the university where there were no towns. The first settlers walked to what would become Oxford along Four Mile Creek. Others came on horseback along woodland trails. The absence of bridges or ferries meant fording or swimming creeks and rivers. By 1809 some animal traces had been widened so that horse-drawn vehicles might pass, and ferries were available at busy river crossings. The area's first major bridge was opened over the Great Miami River at Hamilton in 1819.

Roads came slowly. Work on the National Road from Maryland to St. Louis (U.S. 40) did not reach Ohio until 1825, and took eight more years to reach Columbus. Private toll roads were expected to produce a system of all-weather roadways. In 1832 the Colerain, Oxford and Brookville Turnpike took the path of present U.S. 27. Stock sold slowly, and the State of Ohio tried to encourage the project by buying shares. Chief Engineer Albert S. Gilbert pushed his men to cut a roadway across rolling countryside using a ten-ton roller pulled by sixteen oxen to compress a stone surface. The turnpike was mostly finished in 1843, nineteen years after classes began, but tollhouses and gates took two more years. Open to all travelers, each toll road had gatehouses at regular intervals where an attendant took payment. A horse and rider paid 6¼ cents, a double-team carriage 25 cents. A trip over the turnpike could be expensive. For an unskilled worker a forty-mile carriage ride would cost a day's wages—one dollar—in toll fees. Smaller tolls were charged for taking animals to market, and the Colerain Pike was solid in the fall with hogs heading to Cincinnati pork packers.

Highway travel was uncomfortable, slow, even unsafe. Most roads were cheaply built and poorly maintained, offered a rough ride, and were nearly impassable seas of mud in the spring. Passengers could be injured when bro-

Stagecoach from Cincinnati. Illustration by Henry F. Farny from A Boy's Town *by William Dean Howells, 1918.*

ken wheels caused coaches to roll over. Stages stopped to change horses every ten miles, yet rarely tarried, so those who left the coach risked being left behind. A speed faster than five miles an hour was rare, and only the busiest lines ran daily. If a coach was full, passengers had to wait a few days. But coach travel could be entertaining. Charles Cist (1793–1868), a Cincinnati newspaper editor, published a story about Miami students around 1845. He boarded a coach in Cincinnati at Dennison's Hotel. All was serene as it rolled slowly toward Oxford with Cist the sole occupant. Near Hamilton a half-dozen college boys climbed aboard, all puffing vigorously on cigars. The smoke made Cist ill, but he said nothing. When the coach stopped in Hamilton to change horses, Cist slipped into a drug store to purchase a small piece of asafetida, a foul-smelling skin balm. Students were happily blowing smoke as the veteran editor reentered the vehicle. When horses clattered ahead and Cist began to rub the new purchase on his hands, the boys began to exclaim, "Whew! What a horrid smell! What is it? Oh! Awful!" Cist at first offered no explanation, enjoying their distress. Then he said, "Young gentlemen, we have all our especial tastes. You are fond of tobacco smoking, to me it is excessively disagreeable; I have just made a purchase, which I am rubbing in my hands as an antidote to your smoke, and I must confess I rather enjoy it." At first the students seemed dumbfounded, then burst into laughter and threw their stogies out the window. Cist pitched out his lump of fetid resin and the remainder of the journey was presumably made in harmony.

After creating a transportation revolution in England and France, the canal came to the United States in the 1820s. The Miami and Erie Canal between Toledo and Cincinnati, surveyed in 1822, linked to a water route from New York City connecting to interior cities via the Hudson River, New York's

Oxford Railroad Depot (1859), Elm and Collins streets, first depot in Oxford. Photograph, ca. 1880. Miami Archives and Smith Library.

Erie Canal, and the Great Lakes. Dayton and Cincinnati were united by 1828, but the state-sponsored canal system took until 1845 to reach Toledo. Since the canal passed through Hamilton, Miami students from upstate or out of state could travel by boat to a point not far from the university and then take a stagecoach to Oxford. The canal packet glided along smoothly, if painfully slowly. Day travel was pleasant, but the cabin, where multilayer bunks were held by ropes and tended to creak and sway in an annoying manner, was considered by many to be congested and too public at night. Meanwhile, steamboat service on the Ohio River developed remarkably. Large, comfortable boats, offering very low fares and excellent meals, had taken much of the inland travel business. The river system reached up the Missouri into the far west, down the Mississippi to New Orleans, and up to St. Paul. Tributaries such as the Kentucky or Red rivers were navigable. Steamboats worked well when traveling from one river town to another, but then travelers were back to the stagecoach. Another drawback was low water. Larger boats could not operate in late summer and fall, a problem not addressed until 1929, when a federal system of locks and dams kept water at a steady nine feet.

The steam railroad originated in England as a public carrier in 1825, and the Little Miami Railroad was begun in 1836 to connect Cincinnati and Springfield. Completion took a decade, but by the time it opened more railroads were addressing the state's transportation needs. The railroad was superior to other forms of transport. It could go anywhere, unlike canal and river carriers. Unlike highway travel, it did not depend on animal power. Steam locomotives never grew tired and could operate long distances. For the first time, average people could travel at sustained speeds never possible before—twenty-five miles per hour was common. Trains operated regularly except in the most severe weather. In the summer of 1851 a student from Tennessee, T. C. Hibbett, reached Miami by various means, then returned home partway by the "steam cars," as railroads were called. On his way to school he left Lavergne, Tennessee, for a journey of five days that began with a long, dusty stagecoach ride from his home to Louisville. Then he boarded a riverboat for Cincinnati. From there a stagecoach carried him on to Oxford. By the time he was ready to head home, the C.H. & D., the first railroad in Butler County, was nearing Hamilton and open for part of his trip.

While Hibbett was in school, work began on the Junction Railroad that eventually would pass through Oxford heading to Indianapolis. Groundbreaking was in September 1853, almost five years after the railroad's charter was granted. Plagued by financial distress and the death of its president during the early stages of construction, this railroad was late starting and finishing. Since other lines already connected Indianapolis to Cincinnati, the route served only small communities with modest traffic potential unable to support its expense. However, the Junction line was opened from Hamilton to Oxford in June 1859 and progressed slowly to the west. In November 1859, rails reached College Corner, Ohio, where a connecting stagecoach carried passengers to Connersville, Indiana. Six years later the Junction line reached

Diary of T. C. Hibbett,
1852. Miami Special Collections.

Cambridge City, and new owners headed by Cincinnati industrialist Lewis Worthington raised the capital to push the railroad to Indianapolis.

The Junction Railroad could not pay its bills, much less reward stockholders. It was foreclosed in 1872 and, except for a few years early in the twentieth century, became a vassal of larger railroad companies. However, most Oxford students and residents were only vaguely aware of these corporate woes, for trains continued to run as mandated by state and federal regulators. They were both efficient and inviting. Sleeping and parlor car accommodations were available for an extra charge. Although economy-minded coach passengers tended to avoid costly dining cars, sandwiches and other light fare could be purchased from news butchers. Many travelers took a box lunch. Some trains stopped for twenty minutes at depot dining rooms, but this practice was largely abandoned by 1900. Special theater trains carried passengers to Cincinnati for evening performances, and returned them to Oxford and other nearby towns afterward.

In Oxford, eight passenger trains daily were common in pre-automobile times, and a few of the better trains carried Pullman sleepers and parlor and reclining-chair cars. Some cars were taken, via transfers, to more distant points over a 250,000-mile U.S. rail network. Direct trains to Detroit or Cincinnati operated from Hamilton. Cincinnati offered service to New York, Chicago, and New Orleans. Once in Chicago, passengers could easily make connections to all major western cities. Through tickets to all these destinations could be purchased at the Oxford Depot. By the end of Old Miami, the national railroad transportation network had linked the university to the nation.

SCHOOL DAYS

Classroom pedagogy in Old Miami bore little resemblance to that in later eras. Students spent much time either preparing for or giving recitations before their professors. The *Catalogue* for 1832 indicates that freshmen enrolled in the four-year "College Proper" curriculum were expected to recite twice daily on the subjects of Latin, Greek, geography, and Roman antiquities, plus once daily on algebra, geometry, and plane trigonometry. Sophomores were to recite once daily in Latin, Greek, and Antiquities; once daily in Spherical Trigonometry and Applications of Algebra to Geometry; and once daily in Elements of Rhetoric and Criticism. Sophomores were also expected to study a modern language. In the first term juniors recited once daily in Mathematics and twice daily in Greek and Modern Languages, and attended two lectures weekly on Chemistry and Natural Philosophy (natural science). In the second term, juniors were to recite twice daily in Mental Philosophy and Hebrew Grammar, once daily in Mathematics, and once daily in Natural Philosophy. Seniors, in the first term, recited once daily in Astronomy, Chemistry, and Botany and in Hebrew Language; they spent two hours daily with the presi-

dent on History and Philosophy of Social Relations. In the second session, seniors recited once daily in Mineralogy, Geology, and Mathematics; in Mental
Philosophy and Greek Classics; and in Latin Classics; and three times weekly
for the president on Logic and Philosophy of Social Relations.

Every faculty member conducted recitations. There were five professors in
1835, undoubtedly well worked. The catalog states that over the entire curriculum every student would spend two and half years each with the antiquities
professor, the rhetoric and criticism professor, and the science professor; three
years with the mathematics professor; and one year with the president on history and social relations. The catalog added, perhaps redundantly, "The general principle of the whole course is that every young man shall be fully and
profitably employed."

To achieve compliance with this regime, during the Bishop presidency the
faculty set the students' daily calendar. Study hours were from 6:00 to 8:00
a.m. and 6:00 to 9:00 p.m. Meals and recreation were assigned to 8:00 to 9:00
a.m., noon until 2:00 p.m., and 4:00 to 6:00 p.m. Students themselves, with
the approval of the president and trustees, adopted rules for governing life in
the dormitories. In 1824 those were:

1. Perfect silence shall be observed in all the rooms and passages during the whole
of the study hours.

2. The Senior student in each room shall be answerable for the good conduct of
all his mates.

3. A regent shall be chosen by ballot who shall continue in office one month and
whose duty it shall be to see that perfect order is observed during study hours, and for
this purpose it shall be his duty to visit all the rooms or any one of them as often as he
may find it necessary, and see that every student is in his place. He shall give notice of
the beginning and ending of study hours by having a trumpet sounded. He shall make
a report to the monthly meeting of students of every species of disorder which may
come under his observation.

4. There shall be a regular meeting of all the students who may lodge in college
once each month, for the purpose of adopting any new regulations which may be
found necessary.

5. Those students who may study in college, but not lodge there, shall retire to
their lodging rooms every evening by nine o'clock.

In addition to recitations, daily attendance at chapel services conducted
by the president or faculty was also required, and faculty fined students 25¢
per infraction for visiting another student's room during study hours. As the
century moved forward this regimen was punctuated by occasional adjourn-
ment of required recitations for participation in religious revivals being held
in one or more of Oxford's churches.

Literary societies quickly became a prominent feature of campus life. Here

Erodelphian Debating Hall, Old Main, with bust of Robert H. Bishop by Hiram Powers in niche. Photograph, ca. 1880. Miami Archives.

Miami Union Literary Society Hall, Old Main. Photograph, ca. 1890. Miami Archives.

Announcement of second anniversary, Union Literary Society, 1827. Miami Special Collections.

students could gather to debate social and political issues of the day as well as literary topics. The Erodelphian Society, organized by thirteen students in 1825, was followed soon by the Union Literary Society. These two were the most prominent at Old Miami and were given dedicated rooms in Old Main for their debates. Other groups included the Epanthean Society, created in 1837, then Miami Hall in 1838. In 1840 the literary societies were incorporated by the state legislature as independent and self-governing.

Greek-letter fraternal organizations came early. The second chapter of Alpha Delta Phi in the United States was established at Miami in 1835. The Alpha chapters of Beta Theta Pi (1839), Phi Delta Theta (1848), and Sigma Chi (1855) were founded in Oxford. A chapter of Delta Kappa Epsilon was established in 1852. New chapters emerged as schisms over social regulations, including tolerance of alcohol use, divided older groups.

THE MIAMI TRIAD

Visitors to the Cincinnati Reds' Great American Ball-park can cross a bridge over Interstate 471 at Third and Main, where an historical marker notes the life of Salmon P. Chase, a lawyer, governor of Ohio, and religious authority who had a law office at this site in the early nineteenth century. Events leading to the founding of the first college fraternity chapter west of the Allegheny Mountains, the catalyst to many Miami fraternities and sororities that would attain national prominence, began in 1835 on this corner.

America's first fraternity was founded in December 1776 in Williamsburg, Virginia. Students from the College of William and Mary met secretly in the Raleigh Tavern on Duke of Gloucester Street to discuss topics considered taboo by the classically minded faculty, and to find fellowship and distraction. Led by student John Heath, they created rituals and secret signs to protect their proceedings from outsiders, and Phi Beta Kappa, derived from initials of the motto "Philosophia Biou Kubernetes," or "Love of learning is the guide of life," was born. Members of Phi Beta Kappa spread the organization to colleges throughout the middle Atlantic and New England by the turn of the nineteenth century, and soon organizations with features similar to Phi Beta Kappa emerged.

At Union College in New York, a variety of fraternal organizations were created on this model, including Alpha Delta Phi. A founder of that fraternity, Samuel Eells, graduated from Union in 1834 and came to Cincinnati to apprentice at Chase's law office with other recent graduates, including William S. Groesbeck of Miami, to whom Eells disclosed the existence of Alpha Delta Phi. Groesbeck, who had been active in the Union Literary Society at Miami, wrote to friends Charles Telford and John Temple, still Miami students. Eells initiated the three of them in Cincinnati in 1835.

When classes began that year Telford and Temple increased the membership of the fledging Miami chapter to nine. At first Alpha Delta Phi meetings were entirely *sub rosa* activities confined to dormitory rooms. That winter the organization made itself known to students when President Bishop announced the "Alpha, Delta, and Phi Society" at chapel, and members began wearing their badges. The reaction was immediately hostile, and within the month both literary societies had banned Greeks from their membership rolls. Their anger was based partly in misunderstanding and partly in fear. In many ways literary societies and early fraternities seemed identical. Both had defined membership, similar structures for organizational leadership, and a focus on academic discussion and oratory. Literary societies held weekly debates and an annual public exposition, while the earliest fraternity also held weekly debates and brought speakers on topics ranging from "The Inheritance of English Literature" to "The Progress of Reform." To a non-Greek, however, the fraternity appeared to be a subunit of the literary society that might take control of the organization's internal politics. John Riley Knox, president of the Union Society, supported expulsion of Alpha Delta Phi members, but in time Knox himself would create a fraternal organization. Later claiming that he had "imagined that an association might be formed which would embrace the good without the ingredient of evil," Knox gathered eight trusted friends in Old Main to discuss a new society; on August 8, 1839, the group met in the Union Society hall, where they developed a constitution and symbology for Beta Theta Pi.

President George Junkin (1841–44) strongly opposed secret fraternities and asked trustees to ban them. Consequently, Beta

Marker commemorating Phi Delta Theta founding in 1848, Elliott Hall. Miami Archives.

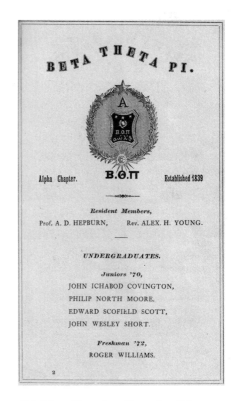

Beta Theta Pi members. Recensio, 1868. Miami Archives.

Adams Drug Store, 20 East High Street, Oxford, site of Sigma Chi founding in 1855. Photograph by Frank R. Snyder, 1915. Miami Archives and Smith Library.

Theta Pi remained *sub rosa* until 1846, when the literary societies once again accepted Greeks. Membership slowly rose in both types of organizations, but the intricate system of rushing, pledging, and initiation that modern Greeks know was wholly absent in the nineteenth century. Early fraternity members "examined" possible candidates for membership when they matriculated, and rushed them into an immediate initiation as soon as they had proven worthy of membership. Hazing was rare before the Civil War, when fraternities were essentially extensions of the academic curriculum and not yet formally independent extracurricular organizations.

Reaction to the 1848 Snow Rebellion was a blow to Miami fraternities. Many assumed that Greeks were masterminds, instigators, and leaders of the mayhem that occurred on campus when Old Main was filled with snow. Following a week-long tribunal of interrogation, all members of Alpha Delta Phi either were expelled or voluntarily quit, and only two members of Beta Theta Pi were left to graduate in 1849. However, Beta Theta Pi had already spread to other colleges. In 1840 a chapter was established in Cincinnati, and three years later the fraternity was operating as far away as Princeton, Harvard, and the University of Michigan. This ensured that the secrets of Beta Theta Pi would remain alive even during a period of inactivity by its Alpha chapter.

In the aftermath of the Snow Rebellion an entirely new fraternity was formed at Miami. In those days college classes were held through the Christmas season because winter travel was slow and unpredictable. During Christmas 1848, Miami student Robert Morrison met with five other students in what is now Elliott Hall. The Phi Delta Theta fraternity was founded there in a spirit of brotherhood, excitement, and continuity—*esto perpetua*. The "Bond of Phi Delta Theta," written and signed in a second-story room, is still recited at Phi Delta Theta chapters across this country and Canada. This fraternity, however, worked to bring harmony between students and faculty by taking several professors as members—including Miami president William C. Anderson in 1849.

Future U.S. president Benjamin Harrison moved to Oxford in 1850 and was soon accepted into Phi Delta Theta. He rapidly gained influence in the organization and, with David Swing, pushed for a fraternity-wide ban on alcohol consumption. This led to a rift that ended with expulsion of three members and the resignation of three more. About that time Jacob Cooper was visiting friends and talking about a fraternity he was in at Yale. In 1852 six former members of Phi Delta Theta, led by Gideon McNutt, formed the Miami chapter of Delta Kappa Epsilon. By the end of the year its membership doubled.

Delta Kappa Epsilon was heavily involved in the Erodelphian Literary Society. A controversy emerged in 1854 over election of a "Chief Poet" of that society, a position akin to student body president today. Delta Kappa Epsilon was fractured over the affair when six rebels, led by Benjamin Piatt Runkle, formed Miami's third new fraternity in 1855. In Runkle's second-floor room of a brick building on High Street and East Park Place, they wrote a constitution for Sigma Phi. When they learned of a Union College organization with that name, they renamed their fraternity Sigma Chi. With this action the three fraternities created as alpha chapters at Miami, the "Miami Triad" of Beta Theta Pi, Phi Delta Theta, and Sigma Chi, were established.

The 1850s were the high point of fraternity life at Old Miami. By 1858 Alpha of Sigma Chi was no longer functioning due to membership difficulties, but the fraternity lived on in chapters at other colleges. Miami's involvement in the Civil War drained the membership of fraternal organizations, and occasional student animosity did nothing to replace it. When Miami closed in 1873, the last nail in the Old Miami Greek coffin was pounded in.

William C. Anderson, president of Miami University, 1849–54. Oil painting, ca. 1850s. Miami Art Museum.

Miami reopened in 1885 debt-free and with a more progressive curriculum, and Miami Triad chapters were revived before the turn of the century. That led to an explosion of Greek organizations in the twentieth century. Coeducation brought sororities to campus, and minority enrollment brought traditionally African American and Latino fraternities. Other fraternities and sororities were founded at Miami in the spirit of the Miami Triad, but remained local and disappeared by the late 1960s. Exceptions were Delta Zeta sorority (1902) and Phi Kappa Tau fraternity (1906), both now international organizations. Because generations of students had a gift for inspiring one another to share fraternal secrets, the Miami Triad sparks fond memories for alumni the world over.

EARLY STUDENT ACTIVITIES

In addition to studying, joining fraternal organizations or literary societies, and attending church services or class recitation, Old Miami students could participate in groups designed to promote missionary activity. The Society of Inquiry on Missions was organized in 1833, and soon after, the Missionary Society of the Associate Reformed Church. These groups sponsored missionaries to foreign countries and to Indian tribes. The classes of 1828, 1840, and 1845 produced missionaries to Syria; classes of 1834, 1835, and 1847 included missionaries to India; and the Class of 1840 had a missionary to Africa. A missionary went to the Creeks in 1837, and beginning in 1840, an apparently unsuccessful effort was made to open a school for children of Miami people living near the Wabash River in Indiana.

Publishing became a fond commitment. The *Literary Focus,* a newspaper printed by the literary societies, was begun in 1827 (and followed the next year by the biweekly *Literary Register,* published by the faculty until 1829). Three student publications were short lived in the 1830s, and four more in the 1850s. In 1867 the literary societies started the *Miami Student,* and in 1869 the sophomores released the first *Recensio.*

There were many necessary ways to spend one's time as well. Cutting wood for fireplaces and stoves was a routine task mentioned often in student diaries. Acquiring candles, whale oil for lamps, or provisions was a frequent

The Literary Register, 1829. *Miami Archives.*

The Miami Student, *first issue, 1867. Miami Archives.*

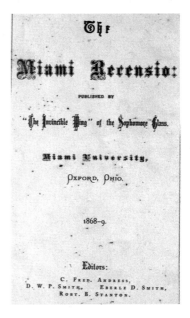

Recensio, *1869. Miami Archives.*

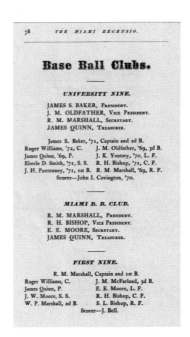

Organized baseball competition. Recensio, *1869. Miami Archives.*

chore. Cooking food in the dormitories on a wood stove, eating at the Mansion House hotel, or taking meals in local homes were options. Boarding was popular at the home of Mrs. Hughs, still standing today at the southwest corner of Campus Avenue and Walnut Street.

Recreation was inventive. Students could swim and fish in Four Mile Creek or hunt in deep woods surrounding the village. Variations of football, cricket, marbles, and holes, a game somewhat like golf that was dug and played on campus, entertained students, as did learning to ride velocipedes, predecessors of bicycles, in the 1860s. Students had a glee club and a "serenade band." The favorite student activity, however, may have been what would become the "national pastime," for by 1869 students had formed nine baseball clubs. Saloons were also a matter of interest to both

Bicyclists in front of Old Main, ca. 1890. Miami Archives.

Organized bicycling. Recensio, 1869. Miami Archives.

students and faculty, and at times Oxford, and the township, had several of them. Drinking, although forbidden by university and civil authorities in the early 1850s, was described often in accounts of daily life. In the middle 1850s saloons were legalized. The president organized a temperance society.

By the mid-1850s there were numerous women students at the seminaries and colleges established for them in Oxford, and often the total enrollment of Oxford's women students exceeded that of Miami men. A litany of complaints came from officials of the women's schools, asserting that Miami men were frequently an unwelcome and disruptive presence. The president of the Oxford Female Institute, located at the west edge of the village, spoke with Miami trustees about the activities of Miami men, but could not secure, in his view, proper disciplinary action or preventive restraint. In the 1870s the Western Female Seminary allegedly hired armed guards to deter trespassers bent on mischief. Miami men, for their part, assailed authorities of the women's schools for their straitlaced protectionism. Their larger interest in the women's schools was probably clarified by Abner Jones, Class of 1858, who recorded in his journal a Thanksgiving visit to the Western Female Seminary. "I was introduced to about fifty girls—they are the finest,—prettiest, and most intelligent girls I ever saw—they talked with the greatest freedom—I think there is *the* place to choose a good wife."

In *The Miami Years* Walter Havighurst writes that "Miami in the 1850s was ringed in women's colleges." This development resulted from the efforts of professors and other parents who wanted their daughters to have educational opportunities comparable to those of young men. Early attempts at a women's high school (started in 1831) and an Oxford Female Academy (chartered in 1839) ended when the female teachers married.

The first long-lasting institution of higher learning for women was the Oxford Female Institute, chartered in 1849 with John Witherspoon Scott as its first principal. Professor Scott had taught at Miami and more recently at Farmers' College in the Cincinnati area, where he was involved with the Ohio Female College; when Scott returned to Oxford to head the new women's school, some of his students accompanied him.

Oxford Female Institute, West Street, later College Avenue, Oxford (1850–67). Smith Library.

Because the institute's building was not yet completed, students lived in houses in town, while local enrollees lived at home. Classes were conducted at the Oxford Theological Seminary until its own male students returned for the fall term. Institute classes were then conducted in rented space above Mollyneaux's store on Main Street and West Park Place. Construction of the new building was completed in 1850 with a chapel and classrooms but no living quarters. Out-of-town students lived in Scott's home directly across the street from the school. An old frame house once known as the Temperance Tavern, it was soon filled with young women, and the principal's wife, Mary Neal Scott (with hired help), managed it as a rooming and boarding house.

Although the institute did not confer bachelor's degrees, it offered a curriculum beyond that of the local public school and within three years had an enrollment of 172. Success led to the need for additional space—and controversy. When Ebenezer Lane, one of the benefactors of Lane Theological Seminary in Cincinnati, offered thirty-four acres of wooded land near his Oxford home, the opportunity to move the institute eventually split its supporters into two factions: those in favor of the new site just northeast of town and those opposed to abandoning their investment in the property within the village limits.

Oxford Female College, northeast of Oxford (1856–82). Miami Archives.

This division led to the formation of a second institution, the Oxford Female College, which was chartered in 1854 with Scott's support. Within a year, Scott resigned from the institute and took up quarters in the vacant Oxford Hotel on the northeast corner of High and Poplar Streets. There he held college classes until the opening of the grand new edifice on its spacious campus in 1856. The new building, designed by leading Cincinnati architect James K. Wilson, was the most prominent structure in Oxford at the time, with steam heat, gas lighting, and an eight-hundred-seat chapel in addition to a dining hall, classrooms, and servants' quarters. Only part of the money for construction had been raised ahead of time, however, so the school opened with two hundred students and a very large debt.

Oxford Female College that became Oxford College for Women, West Street, later College Avenue, Oxford (1882–1928). Miami Archives and Smith Library.

(continued)

Western Female Seminary (1855–60). Western Archives.

Western Female Seminary after first fire (1860–71). Western Archives.

The Oxford Female College and the Oxford Female Institute existed independently until financial problems forced their merger in 1867, when the combined school occupied the larger college facility on the hillside above the Tallawanda Creek. After the college property was sold to the Oxford Retreat Company in 1882, its students and faculty moved back to the original institute site, which had been enlarged by a dormitory annex in 1856. Retaining the name Oxford Female College, the school began conferring bachelor's degrees in 1886. The word *female* was dropped from the college name in 1890; when the school was rechartered in 1906 it changed its name again, to Oxford College for Women. Remodeling over the years increased the size of the main building, and adjoining property was purchased to enlarge the campus to include a house for the president, a separate building for home economics, and an athletics field.

The Female Institute and Female College faced continuous financial challenges. They relied heavily on Oxford's Presbyterian churches (particularly First and Third). The National Society, Daughters of the American Revolution raised money for a new dormitory to honor the most famous member of that organization, Female Institute graduate Caroline Scott Harrison, but it was never constructed.

When Oxford College for Women closed in 1928, it had a long-standing reputation as a school that emphasized Christian values, provided scholarships to ministers' daughters, and prepared women to be teachers. Its property was acquired by Miami and its alumnae were added to Miami's rolls.

Another school for women, the Western Female Seminary, located just east of the village, was chartered in 1853 and opened in 1855. Its name was chosen because it was to be a western daughter institution of Mount Holyoke

Seminary in Massachusetts, and it was from Mount Holyoke that the principal and first five faculty members came. The Reverend Daniel Tenney, of the Second Presbyterian Church, was responsible for soliciting funds to help establish a new institution meant to have evangelical Christian instruction in its curriculum. He gave up his church pastorship to oversee construction of the five-story building that graced a hilltop overlooking the road to Cincinnati. Helen Peabody, a graduate of Mount Holyoke Seminary, served as principal of "The Western" for twenty-two years. Under Miss Peabody's leadership, the seminary remained firmly in the mold of her alma mater, including use of the "domestic system" that required students to take turns performing domestic chores—preparing meals, washing dishes, and sweeping floors—so the seminary need not pay outside workers. In exchange for about an hour of work daily, each student was charged comparatively low fees to attend school.

The seminary was beset by disasters. A fire destroyed its only building in early 1860; a new edifice was completed in time for the school year to begin in 1862 with an enrollment of 120 students. The seminary survived the Civil War, the resulting economic repercussions, and even typhoid fever, which took the lives of several students and teachers. But another fire in the spring of 1871 forced students into temporary shelter at the Oxford Female College or in the homes of Oxford residents. Because the exterior brick walls of the previous building were incorporated into a new building, construction proceeded so rapidly that the seminary opened for the fall term less than six months after the fire.

Its most daunting challenge, however, would be change. By the latter half of the 1800s true degree-granting women's colleges such as Wellesley, Vassar, Smith, and Bryn Mawr were established in the East, and

Western Female Seminary and Western College for Women after second fire (1871–1974). Smith Library.

in Ohio women had been admitted to Oberlin and Antioch. The Western Female Seminary was forced to choose between modernization and the possibility of obsolescence. The seminary began granting bachelor's degrees in 1895 and changed its name to the Western College for Women in 1904. The campus expanded with the construction of Sawyer Gymnasium and the donation of 70 acres of adjacent land and a home for Western presidents, Patterson Place, in 1914; Kumler Memorial Chapel in 1918, designed by Carrère and Hastings, the New York firm who were architects of the New York Public Library; and the Ernst Nature Theatre, an outdoor performance facility carved into a hillside east of the main building. Scenic stone bridges and lampposts created by Cephas Burns, a local African American stonemason, were added to the campus between 1917 and 1925.

The college offered more than a striking campus, however—it was a pioneer in education. Alumnae Hall was constructed in 1892 for science laboratories, art studios, and a library. A new residence hall was dedicated in 1904 and later named for Leila McKee, the last principal of the Seminary and first president of the College. In addition to participating in basketball, tennis, and baseball, the women students played golf on what is believed to be only the third course laid out on any American college campus. It was the first college in the nation to give a resident fellowship for creative work, to composer Edgar Stillman Kelley in 1910; he would remain at Western for over two decades. A music auditorium in Presser Hall (1931) was named for him. Working farms on property near the college were a source of income, and during World War I Western students helped butcher livestock and harvest produce; during World War II Western women worked in victory gardens to help the war effort on the home front. Also during World War II, the college opened its own

studios to broadcast programs through a radio station in Hamilton; Western is believed to be the first women's college in the country to broadcast daily on a commercial radio station.

The college also established itself as a center for international commitments. Many graduates in early days became missionaries or ministers' wives, and their letters from Christian outposts were read aloud to the student body. Although women from other countries attended Western by 1902, their numbers increased after World War II. Beginning with summer travel seminars, foreign study for Western students was systematically incorporated into the academic calendar year. By the mid-1950s, Western was developing a truly multicultural student body by promoting a highly distinctive international agenda.

In June 1964, with the civil rights movement well under way, Western College rented its campus for a national civil rights project later known as "Freedom Summer." Before traveling to Mississippi to teach in Freedom Schools and assist in registering African Americans to vote, idealistic college-age volunteers came to train in nonviolent techniques for coping with white resistance to their efforts. Three of these young people—Michael Schwerner, James Chaney, and Andrew Goodman—were murdered in Mississippi soon after leaving Oxford, an atrocity that attracted national attention and influenced passage of the Voting Rights Act of 1965.

In the late 1960s and early 1970s, despite its attractive campus, respected faculty, and diverse student body, Western College enrollment declined. To attract more students, it restructured its curriculum, built new facilities, and admitted men in its final years. The college, however, was forced to close in 1974 and its campus was acquired by Miami University.

While this ended the last of Oxford's private schools for women, some of their legacies continued. The greatly enlarged building of the Oxford Female Institute was nicknamed "Ox College" during its years as a Miami residence hall and was listed in the National Register of Historic Places in 1976. In 2001 it was leased to become the Oxford Community Arts Center. The original Oxford Female College was used as a private hospital for the mentally ill before being acquired by Miami in 1925. After use for many years as a men's residence hall named Fisher Hall, then by the Department of Theatre, it was listed in the National Register of Historic Places in 1971 before being razed in 1978 to make way for the Marcum Conference Center. Most Western College buildings were renovated for Miami programs that moved onto its campus, and the Western College for Women Historic District was listed in the National Register of Historic Places in 1979.

West half of Oxford Public Square, north side, ca. 1865. Miami Archives and Smith Library.

Mansion House Hotel, Main and High streets, Oxford, 1851. Miami Archives and Smith Library.

West half of Oxford Public Square, west side, ca. 1865. Miami Archives and Smith Library.

CROSSROAD OF CONFLICT

Images of Miami's campus in the 1830s and 1840s depict a tidy seat of orderly learning picturesquely situated on a hill cleared from the surrounding forest. In one picture all the buildings are whitewashed. Photographs of the town in the 1860s, however, show it to be less austere. Although streets are unpaved, they are busy with people, animals, and drawn conveyances. The town square is fenced to deter grazing animals, and there is an imposing three-story hotel with a cupola at the intersection of Main and High streets. Two views of businesses on the west square near the end of the Civil War reveal that in this area alone Oxford could boast of establishments for groceries, furniture, lumber, dry goods, shoes, and boots, as well as a saddler, a tailor, a barber, and an undertaker. There was a saloon, too. After the railroad arrived in 1859, a hotel named for the line, the Junction House, opened across from the depot on South Elm Street, where its building still stands today. There were two more hotels on High Street. This level of antebellum development suggests that the village was welcoming visitors and meeting the entrepreneurial commercial hopes of the republic.

Oxford's earliest religious congregations were Baptist, Methodist, and Presbyterian. By the 1850s the First, Second, and Third Presbyterian churches plus an Associate Reformed church had appeared, reflecting doctrinal and financial difficulty in that denomination of the early Miami flock. There was a Universalist church in 1839, and an African Methodist Episcopal church in 1842. Catholic services began in 1853. Religious zeal entwined with disputes over student discipline in the 1840s. As clouds of sectionalism loomed darkly in the 1850s, that zeal did not dissipate. Since the 1830s or before, the hard issue had been slav-

Bethel African Methodist Episcopal Church, South Beech Street, Oxford, ca. 1920–30. Smith Library.

Oxford Methodist Church, Church and Poplar streets, before 1872. Miami Archives and Smith Library.

ery—what to do about it, and what stand was moral in the eyes of God. Miami students and faculty would divide into several factions over this matter.

No Miami figure argued outright for enslaving African American laborers, but few were immediate abolitionists either. Neither can be said with certainty of Miami students. Most students were partisans of their state and region, and most came from north of the Ohio River, but some did not. In 1842, for example, when 162 students were enrolled, 33 were from states that sanctioned slavery. There were strong differences of political opinion on campus as well. Joseph R. Davis, a nephew of Jefferson Davis who would become a Confederate brigadier general and lead troops at Gettysburg, the Wilderness, Spotsylvania, Cold Harbor and Petersburg, was a Miami student, Class of 1841. So were two sons of James G. Birney, a Cincinnati journalist and abolitionist who was elected Secretary of the American Anti-Slavery Society in 1837 and became the Liberty Party candidate for president in 1840 and 1844.

The faculty divided as well. McGuffey's ally in criticizing Bishop's disciplinary methods, Albert T. Bledsoe, like McGuffey spent the war years at the University of Virginia. While no evidence has been found that McGuffey supported slavery or the Confederacy, Bledsoe served in the Confederate army and was assistant secretary of war for Jefferson Davis, commissioner of the Confederacy to England, and a postwar literary apologist for the Southern cause. When President George Junkin left Miami in 1844, he made his way to Washington College in Lexington, Virginia. Although Junkin departed Virginia for Pennsylvania at the outbreak of war, one of his daughters, Eleanor, had married the man soon to be celebrated by the South as Confederate general "Stonewall" Jackson. She died following childbirth. Her sister Margaret married Major John T. L. Preston, a major at Virginia Military Institute. During the war Margaret Junkin Preston published "Confederate nationalist"

Joseph R. Davis, Class of 1842, nephew of
Jefferson Davis and brigadier general, Army
of Northern Virginia. *From Web site of Mikel
Uriguen,* The Generals of the American Civil
War, http://www.generalsandbrevets.com/index.
htm, May 9, 2008

Robert C. Schenck, Class of 1827, brigadier
general, United States Army, and minister
to Great Britain. Brady's National Photographic Portrait Galleries, ca. 1865. *Miami
Archives.*

poetry; in the war's aftermath she wrote poems, essays, and reviews validating a "lost cause ethos."

In the early days of controversy over slavery, many Miami faculty and trustees favored a form of compromised abolition and
sympathized with the American Colonization Society, which advocated ending slavery by deporting freed slaves to Liberia. The
Ohio State Colonization Society was organized in 1827, with Robert Hamilton Bishop as vice president, and its Miami chapter was
also established that year. Jeremiah Morrow, governor of Ohio
(1822–26) and an early Miami trustee, was president of the State
Colonization Society. Individuals who disagreed on other matters—McGuffey, Scott, and Junkin—were all initially attracted to
colonization.

Some of the faculty, like many worried people in the Ohio
borderland, were looking for a compromise on slavery that might
avoid open sectional hostilities. Not all were. The American Anti-
Slavery Society was founded in Boston in 1833 to advocate for
no compromise with slavery, and in the following year an Anti-
Slavery Society chapter was founded at Miami. Abolitionists
counted in their number prominent fugitive slave orators such
as William Wells Brown and eminent New Englanders such as
William Lloyd Garrison, who argued that moral clarity required
nothing less than immediate repentance of national sin. A contingent of Cincinnati's Lane Theological Seminary withdrew from
the seminary in 1833 to found Oberlin College after an intense debate at Lane on abolition stirred righteous indignation across the
Miami Valley and throughout the Presbyterian Church.

Thomas E. Thomas, a Miami student who helped found Miami's Anti-Slavery Society, served after graduation as a minister
in Hamilton, where he was highly visible in church politics and
an ally of Bishop in doctrinal disputes. Perhaps Bishop had moved
toward an antislavery stance as early as 1837, when he attempted
to fill McGuffey's newly vacated chair with the quite visible abolitionist Thomas. Perhaps Bishop's willingness to welcome debate on immediate abolition in both the college and the church
so alienated Old School Presbyterians on the Miami board that
he was removed. His successor, George Junkin, was an Old School
"heresy hunter" who in 1843 delivered an eight-hour address in
Hamilton by the title "The Integrity of Our Union vs. Abolitionism," in which he argued for suppression of abolition radicalism
because it was destructive to law and order. A version of that address was printed for wide circulation, precipitating a book of

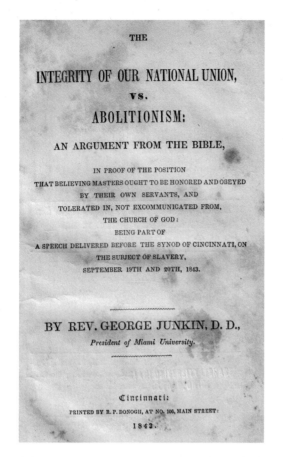

THE

INTEGRITY OF OUR NATIONAL UNION,

vs.

ABOLITIONISM:

AN ARGUMENT FROM THE BIBLE,

IN PROOF OF THE POSITION
THAT BELIEVING MASTERS OUGHT TO BE HONORED AND OBEYED
BY THEIR OWN SERVANTS, AND
TOLERATED IN, NOT EXCOMMUNICATED FROM,
THE CHURCH OF GOD:
BEING PART OF
A SPEECH DELIVERED BEFORE THE SYNOD OF CINCINNATI, ON
THE SUBJECT OF SLAVERY,
SEPTEMBER 19TH AND 20TH, 1843.

BY REV. GEORGE JUNKIN, D. D.,

President of Miami University.

Cincinnati:
PRINTED BY R. P. DONOGH, AT NO. 106, MAIN STREET:
1843.

"The Integrity of Our National Union vs. Abolitionism,"
George Junkin, 1843. Miami Archives.

Thomas E. Thomas, Class of 1840, abolitionist, minister. Correspondence of
Thomas E. Thomas, 1909.

George Junkin, president of Miami University, 1841–44. Oil
painting by Samuel B. Waugh. Miami Art Museum.

opposing views, among them Bishop's "Bible Arguments Against Slavery."

While Miami faculty became ever more confrontational in the slavery debate, the town of Oxford became a stop on the Underground Railroad. Quite a few Oxford houses are said to be possible sites, and several are probable. Ebenezer Lane built a home east of Oxford near the Four Mile Creek about 1829, to which runaways may have had access by following the water route. The best-documented site is the home of African American John Jones, due south of Oxford near the line of the Junction Railroad. Jones's father was a known conductor in Hamilton, and both aided runaways heading for Richmond, Indiana. Lewis Place on High Street, today Miami's presidential home, was built in 1838 as the home of Jane

Ebenezer Lane home, Oxford. From A. C. Stewart, Oxford Town: The Village on the Hill, 1920.

Ebenezer Lane, benefactor of the Lane Theological Seminary, Cincinnati, ca. 1850. Cincinnati Historical Society Library.

John S. Jones, Oxford Underground Railroad conductor. Photograph, ca. 1870. Smith Library.

[PUBLISHED BY REQUEST.]
COLORED CONVENTION.

Pursuant to notice a Convention of the colored people of Butler county, was held in Oxford, on the 7th inst., for the purpose of appointing a delegate to the State Convention, to meet in Columbus, on the 19th day of January, 1853. The meeting was organized by appointing Alfred J. Anderson, chairman, and Andrew Simpson, secretary.

A committee of five was then chosen to prepare business, and they submitted the following as expressive of the sentiments and objects of the Convention.

WHEREAS, The signs of the times show clearly that a crisis in the history of the colored race, in this country, is rapidly approaching—that to remain passive and disinterested spectators, withholding our co-operation and support, while the strife at issue is relative to our own rights and our own interests, is to acknowledge, in the fullest sense, our unfitness to enjoy any of the rights and privileges we claim.

Resolved, That we will on all proper occasions and to the fullest extent of our limited abilities, do all we can to promote the emancipation of our enslaved brethren and our own political equality.

2d, Resolved, That for the successful accomplishment of these ends, we must be consistent advocates of the principles here published, and that we think our State Conventions should not, in advance, pledge the colored people to the performance of more than it can reasonably be expected they will accomplish, regarding, as we do such pledges, highly injurious, and should, therefore, be discontinued.

3d, Resolved, That this meeting, holding American slavery to be degrading to humanity and contrary to every principle of justice and

Butler County Black Convention, 1853, held in Oxford. Hamilton Weekly Telegraph, January 20, 1853.

North Lewis, an abolition sympathizer who is thought to have operated there a stop on the Underground Railroad.

In the early twenty-first century interest in the Underground Railroad in southwest Ohio was high, stimulated by the opening of the National Underground Railroad Freedom Center in Cincinnati. This was a good location for it, because southwestern Ohio became a well-known destination for African Americans before 1860. In 1830 the village of Oxford had 7 black residents. Oxford census data of 1850 showed a white population of 1,031 and a black population of 80—7.2 percent of the total. By 1860 Oxford had 1,676 whites and 190 blacks—10.3 percent. In this same decade Butler County increased from 1.2 percent black to 2.0 percent black. On January 7, 1853, eight years before the Civil War began, a Butler County Black Convention was held in Oxford. It passed a resolution declaring slavery "a sin against God and a crime against man."

Then, in April 1861, came war.

CONTESTING LIBERTY AND POWER IN THE LITERARY SOCIETIES

On the Miami campus, political debates since the spring of 1860 had already transformed the students. As the United States began to unravel in sectional conflict, young men studying the classics in Oxford were confronted with the fate of their country, and many, including those from Southern states, were forced to examine the foundations of American democracy.

In earlier years the Erodelphian and Union Literary societies had been accustomed to examining such questions as which profession better enhanced oratorical skills, the bar or the pulpit; or whether women should confine themselves to the domestic sphere. The spring of 1860 shifted those debates to issues of liberty, power, and loyalty. In March 1860 the Union Literary Society began debating whether or not the French Revolution aided the cause of liberty. A week later, students resolved to determine if a limited monarchy was preferable to a republican government. These questions suggest tentative engagement with their country's deteriorating political dialogue, a product of western expansion in the wake of the Mexican-American War. The acquisition of half of Mexico in 1848 launched a race between those advocating slavery's expansion and those wanting to stop it. Competition for new states meant control of Congress, leading Erodelphians to ask more directly on March 20, 1860, if "a dissolution of the Union would be preferable to the annexation of another slave state." They decided, as they would again a month later on the same question, that the addition of slave states was a necessary cost of keeping the Union intact.

In 1857 the Supreme Court in *Dred Scott v. Sanford* had stripped Congress of the ability to prohibit slavery in federally managed territories, nullifying the prohibition of slavery in the Northwest Ordinance and voiding the Missouri Compromise of 1820. On June 15, 1860, however, Erodelphians concluded that Congress, contrary to the Supreme Court's ruling in *Dred Scott*, did have authority to regulate slavery in the territories. But despite their approval of congressional regulatory power, Erodelphians were still shy of using presidential power to control the expansion of slavery. In mid-October they questioned whether the "Republican platform adopted at Chicago is preferable to the Douglass Democratic platform adopted at Baltimore." In nominating Lincoln, the Republican party resolved to tolerate slavery where it existed but allow its spread no further. The northern Democratic Party, nominating Stephen A. Douglass, granted concessions to the South by promising to abide by *Dred Scott* and work for acquisition of Cuba, where slavery might be exported. Erodelphians found in favor of the Democrats.

Abraham Lincoln's election on November 6, 1860, finally put the issue of secession directly in front of the nation, and Miami's literary societies took it up. On November 23, four weeks before South Carolina withdrew from the Union, the secession question produced heated debate among members of the Erodelphian Society. Meeting minutes do not record exactly what was said or which side of the debate individuals chose. They do show that arguments against secession prevailed. However, clues in the logbook suggest there was conflict at the meeting. Near the end of the entry appears a list of members marked as recipients of 25-cent fines, most imposed for "disorder." That word conveys tension flowing through the chamber. This was also true for the Union Society, which considered secession in early 1861, after the Palmetto State voted to dissolve the Union. "After a lengthy and interesting discussion," the Union minutes record, judges of the debate found in favor of the argument against secession. They also note that some were fined for "disorder."

Around noon on April 12, first reports of the Confederate attack on Fort Sumter reached Oxford. Professor David Swing, a gifted orator popular with students, amended his private journal entry for the day by adding "WAR!!!" in large letters to the margins. "The firing on Ft. Sumter," wrote Stephen Cooper Ayers, "produced a profound sensation. Lectures and lesson were forgotten, the excitement was intense." Meeting minutes for Erodelphians are missing after December 1860. The Union log indicates that records for April 12 "have been lost." Given the commotion, it is doubtful either group met.

War slowed the pace of campus life. "A great many of the students have already [left] for war and for their homes," wrote Union member David Stanton Tappan to his sister, "and more are talking of leaving." Tappan, the nephew of future U.S. Secretary of War Edwin M. Stanton and a future president of Miami University, speculated that "College will hold out until the end of the term unless there are more causes of suspending operations." The quick loss of about 45 percent of Miami's 143 students to war service, or home, left Oxford "exceedingly dull for the past few days, so few students are here, and nothing is going on." Many Southern students returned to their families.

In early May, despite dwindling numbers, remaining students persisted in efforts to understand the unfolding drama. They debated the right of Virginians living in the pro-union western portions of that commonwealth to secede and form a new state. In September 1861 the Union Literary Society debated Lincoln's expansion of presidential power when he declared martial law in Baltimore to maintain control of railways connecting Washington, D.C., to the North, prompting arrest of citizens suspected of aiding the Confederacy. Their effort to analyze Lincoln's decision became part of a long national conversation about preserving civil rights in wartime.

By December 1861 the immediacy of war took precedence as a string of Confederate victories dashed hopes of a speedy resolution. In their Winter Exhibition, Erodelphian Stuart Fullerton invoked the new mood by challenging his listeners to ignore the past. "We are too ardent lovers of antiquity, and forgot, in the inspiration of its history, the real life in which we are actors." If Americans dwell in the past, he said, they "lose sight of the present, and fail to make our age what it should be. The historian never wrote a more thrilling page than that which we are now acting." After 1861, Union logbook entries are less detailed, failing at times to record even the question under debate. This may suggest waning enthusiasm for rhetorical conflict as students became more involved in actual conflict. The importance of the period between January 1860 and December 1861, however, should not be overlooked. During that time the Erodelphian and Union societies struggled with fundamental principles underlying the republic. While the American Civil War was fought on the battlefield, it was also contested in the halls of Old Main. Wrestling with divergent notions of loyalty and authority, Miami students laid their own foundation for a new birth of freedom.

VOLUNTEERS!

After the attack on Fort Sumter, volunteers immediately sprang to the Union cause in response to President Lincoln's call for troops. Charles Barrows, a former Miami student and Oxford artist who created the area's most memorable landscape paintings, became an illustrator for Union General Rosecrans in the Ninety-third Regiment, Ohio Volunteer Infantry (OVI). He died of typhoid in camp at Murfreesboro, Tennessee, on April 15, 1863. Ozro J. Dodds, a Miami student who earlier had military training from Lew Wallace at Wabash College, raised Company B,

Charles Barrows, Oxford artist, enrolled at Miami 1852–54, died in military service, 1863; ca. 1860. Ralph McGinnis, The History of Oxford, Ohio, *1930.*

Four Mile Creek and Bonham Road. Oil painting by Charles Barrows, 1860. McGuffey Museum.

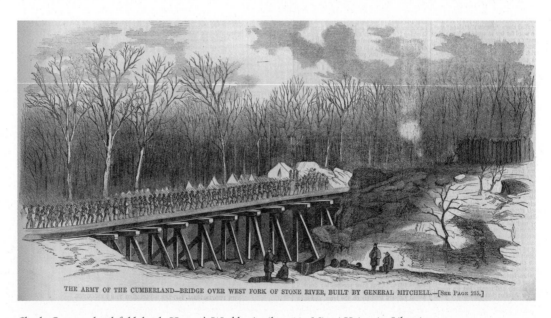

THE ARMY OF THE CUMBERLAND—BRIDGE OVER WEST FORK OF STONE RIVER, BUILT BY GENERAL MITCHELL.—[See Page 215.]

Charles Barrows, battlefield sketch, Harper's Weekly, *April 4, 1863.* Miami University Libraries.

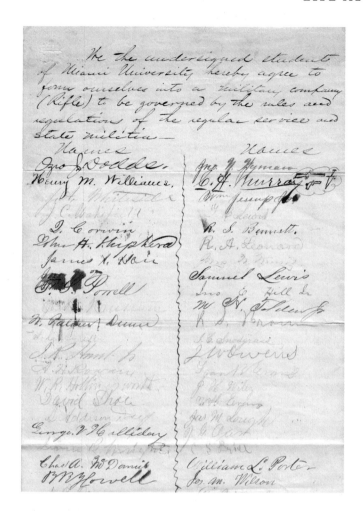

Ozro J. Dodds. Miami student, 1861, Captain of "University Rifles." Miami Archives.

Muster list, Company B, Twentieth Regiment, Ohio Volunteer Infantry, "University Rifles," 1861. Miami Archives.

Twentieth Regiment, OVI, consisting initially of thirty-one Miami students known as the "University Rifles." On April 21, 1861—nine days after Fort Sumter—amid considerable ceremony, they departed Oxford by train for Camp Jackson in Columbus. Later, this company would see service guarding railroads in West Virginia.

Company A, Eighty-sixth Regiment, OVI, drew 104 Oxford volunteers, 66 of them Miami students. Mathematics and astronomy professor Robert McFarland, who taught at Miami from 1856 to 1873 (and would serve as Miami's president from 1885 to 1888) raised this company and commanded it from 1861 to 1865. It participated in the capture of Cumberland Gap in Kentucky and escorted captured Confederate raider John Hunt Morgan to prison after his daring raid across Indiana and Ohio in July of 1863.

McFarland was incendiary on the matter of defending the Union. In 1862 Hamilton Mayor's court found him guilty of assault and battery on a student who expressed sympathy for a biblical justification of slavery during an encounter with McFarland in Oxford. McFarland corresponded with a trustee

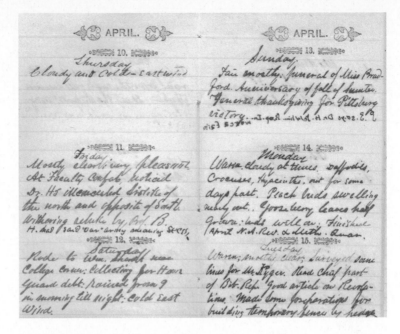

Robert W. McFarland. Tintype, ca. 1860.
Murstein Alumni Center, Miami University.

Robert W. McFarland Daybook, April 10–15, 1862. Miami Archives.

Muster list, Company A,
Eighty-sixth Regiment, Ohio
Volunteer Infantry, Oxford,
comprising 104 volunteers,
including 66 students. Miami
Archives.

Charlotte "Lottie" Moon, ca. 1870. Ophia D. Smith, Oxford Spy Wed at Pistol Point, 1962.

Virginia Moon, ca. 1865. Ophia D. Smith, Oxford Spy Wed at Pistol Point, 1962.

about alleged disloyalty in the college during the war, and wrote in his day-book a suspicion that President John W. Hall, Miami's wartime president, who had come to Oxford from Alabama, had an "ill concealed Dislike of the north and opposite of South."

There were Confederate sympathizers in Oxford. The Moon sisters, Charlotte "Lottie" Moon and Virginia Moon, were rumored to be smugglers, even spies. Their brothers served in the Confederate army. Their father was a physician who came to Oxford from Virginia in the 1830s. Charlotte Moon married Judge James Clark of Hamilton, a leader of the "Copperhead" movement of Southern sympathizers in southwest Ohio. Virginia Moon was a student at the Oxford Female Institute when war erupted in 1861, where, it was said, she boldly proclaimed her support for the South before she and her mother left town for Memphis. Virginia later corresponded with Jefferson Davis, and was detained in Cincinnati in 1863 for an attempt to smuggle contraband, probably medical supplies destined for Confederate soldiers, into Kentucky.

Actual hostilities had a deeper impact on campus than did Oxford Confederates. A study by James Rodabaugh estimated that "somewhat more than fifty percent of the students of the sophomore, junior, senior and normal school classes were drawn into the Civil War some time during the years when they were in school." Many died in battle. Minor Millikin, a Miami graduate from Hamilton, was killed in 1863 while commanding a cavalry regiment at Stones River. He was eulogized in Oxford by David Swing, in oratory that vividly suggests the tenor of wartime.

David Swing would live well beyond the Civil War to become one of the nineteenth century's best-known urban preachers. For twelve years while principal of Miami's preparatory department he had studied at Oxford Theological Seminary and preached widely in regional churches. In 1866 he accepted a call from Chicago's Westminster Presbyterian Church, soon to become Fourth Presbyterian. There his pulpit eloquence, drawing on classical writers he taught at Miami, attracted wide coverage through reprints of his enormously popular sermons in the Chicago press. In the wake of the Civil War, Swing paid little attention to traditional Presbyterian doctrine, maintaining that Christianity had to be relevant to the concerns of present-day Americans and helping shape a nondoctrinal, ethically oriented, practical religion that appealed to a secular urban elite skeptical of traditional dogma. Not all Presbyterians were happy about it. After his vindication in an 1874 heresy trial, Swing's numerous supporters built his new nondenominational Central Church, where for twenty years weekly audiences of five to seven thousand people became the norm, making him a leading national proponent of the coming century's liberal Protestantism.

Swing's elegant wartime eulogy was not, however, the only memorable war rhetoric by a Miamian. In 1863, at the Gettysburg battlefield cemetery dedication at which Abraham Lincoln gave his famous remarks on the meaning of wartime sacrifice, one of the major speakers was future Ohio governor Charles Anderson, Miami Class of 1833.

After the war, there were memories. L. E. Grennan, a schoolteacher who came to Oxford in 1866 following completion of his own war service, would publish more than forty years later a book of poetry that included several accounts of Miami war experiences. In "The War Governors" he celebrated Miami students who served as governors of Ohio, Illinois, and Indiana during the conflict. He recalled them as gallant men without whom victory was not assured, and described this homage as "A Tribute to Miami University."

David Swing. Oil painting by F. P. Day, ca. 1870. Miami Art Museum.

David Swing's War Eulogy for Minor Millikin

At dawn on the last day of 1862, Confederate forces smashed into the right flank of the Union army near Murfreesboro, Tennessee. As it gave ground during the second Battle of Stones River, the First Ohio Cavalry Regiment under the command of Colonel Minor Millikin led a desperate attempt to cover the Union retreat. Millikin, a native of Hamilton and an 1854 Miami graduate, lost his life in this effort. He had volunteered his service, he wrote, "because I loved my country. I thought she was surrounded by traitors and struck by cowardly plunderers." His personal charisma and belief in the Union cause made Millikin popular among many members of the Oxford community. Indeed, his loss weighed so heavily on Miamians that on February 8, 1863, the Reverend David Swing, professor of classical languages and a classmate of Millikin's, could transform his friend into a martyr.

Swing's oratorical genius lay, as one biographer observed, in "a felicity of simplicity without commonness." Frail in appearance, Swing compensated for a lack of physical presence with an eloquence of speech few could rival. As he stood before the congregation of Oxford's Third Presbyterian Church, Swing channeled the frustration and heartache of many Americans. He opened his eulogy, "The Spirit of Sacrifice," with a reminder that just as "Christ died for the greater good of humanity, Millikin gave his life so that his nation might live." Yet as one student observed, Swing's address "did not pretend to be a Eulogy but was a strong war sermon." Swing used Millikin's death as a vehicle to preach a larger message on the destructive evils of slavery. "Our gigantic war," he argued, was the product of a Southern desire to create "a monarchy, a slave republic" by cleaving the United States in two. "This dogma of secession is the one to which the loyal American is invited to give his heart," Swing thundered, "a dogma which if it were not in the hands of madmen would read like a joke. But curious as it is, it is passionate and brutal and bloody." As the serpent tempted Adam and Eve with the apple, "the advocates of secession hold out to use every calamity in the simple offer of death itself."

The preservation and spread of slavery, said Swing, "ruined the souls of men." Moreover, its debilitating effects left Southern literature, the Southern legal system, and the Southern pulpit years behind the North. Indeed, slavery inhibited the moral, intellectual, and religious development of all Americans, leaving slaves under a merciless lash. "Oh, why," cried Swing, "has God hesitated so long to sweep from existence a nation so infamous, that dared not even check the progress of such a destroyer?" Fortunately, he argued, Minor Millikin was among those with "noble hearts enough to say to the monster slavery, 'Thus far shalt thou come; here shall thy march be stayed.'" Learn from Millikin's example, the preacher urged his flock, for it was the "holiest Christian duty to take up this cross of war. And to bear that cross still patiently is the duty of each man worthy of the name of an American." Millikin had earned his rest because he chose the path of righteousness. "We can never come to a rest so sweet," Swing said in paying final compliment to the honored dead, "unless we approach it by the path he trod—the path of sacrifice."

David Swing had remembered his friend in transcending imagery that he surely saw as a personal evaluation of Millikin. His eulogy also reveals the extent to which slavery had radically transformed Christianity in the North into a powerful militant force. Evangelical abolitionism modified the purpose of the war. It was no longer a political struggle between the states, but a significant battle against the forces of evil. Millikin was a soldier of Christ, Swing argued, sent to destroy the great cancer left over from the American Revolution. Later at Gettysburg, Abraham Lincoln could afford, perhaps, to be more circumspect. But when Swing buried Millikin, he did more than simply honor the memory of a fallen Miamian. He also issued a call to arms, and to glory.

The Miamian Who Spoke at Gettysburg

Charles Anderson entered Miami in 1829. After graduating in 1833, he went on to be a lawyer, statesman, soldier, developer, and governor of Ohio. He was wounded leading the Ninety-third Ohio Volunteer Infantry at the Battle of Stones River in 1862. One of his contributions to a national historical event, however, has often been forgotten.

Consecration events at Gettysburg National Cemetery took place November 19, 1863. Miamians figured in them prominently. Former Ohio governor William Dennison, General Robert Schenck, and Anderson were in the platform party. They listened to Edward Everett's two-hour speech, and heard Lincoln's legendary Gettysburg Address. Anderson, however, had his own important role. As lieutenant governor-elect of Ohio, he was the featured speaker at the day's concluding evening event held in Gettysburg Presbyterian Church. President Lincoln, Secretary Seward, and most of the dignitaries attended.

Anderson arrived at the lectern of Gettysburg Presbyterian Church with skills honed by Bishop and McGuffey and a thirty-year history as an orator; his Miami graduation speech was an argument for building the Washington Monument, "An Oration on the Influence of Monumental Records on National Morals." All key elements of Anderson's graduation oration were represented in what he said at Gettysburg. His speech was filled with vivid verbal images, flowery language, and classical references. While Lincoln's entire speech required only 272 words, Anderson's speech had *one sentence* that used 252 words. Anderson honored the Union dead and confirmed the Union position. He was regularly interrupted by "thunderous applause," and some newspaper accounts suggest that Anderson delivered "the best speech of the

Charles Anderson, Class of 1833, governor of Ohio, 1865–66. *Miami Archives.*

day." One said that President Lincoln applauded the speech and invited Anderson to return to Washington on the presidential train.

Later, Lincoln's Gettysburg speech became famous and Anderson's oration remained obscure. But when Anderson took the national stage that evening he had an Old Miami education behind him. Throughout his life he remained a loyal Miamian, regularly publishing remembrances of McGuffey and Bishop. Today Charles Anderson too can be remembered, as the Miamian who spoke at Gettysburg.

Grennan also told a story well known in Miami lore. Joel Allen Battle, in Confederate service as adjutant of the 20th Tennessee Infantry, was found dead on the Shiloh battlefield by Union soldiers John C. Lewis, adjutant of the 40th Illinois, and Clifford Ross, adjutant of the 31st Indiana. They showed the body to John R. Chamberlin, 2nd Lt., 81st OVI. All three recognized the body of Joel Battle, for Chamberlin knew him as a fellow member of the Erodelphian Society, and Lewis and Ross were his Miami roommates. These three Miamians, for the Union, buried their fallen mortal opponent, "loved

Joel A. Battle of Tennessee, ca. 1860. Buried at Shiloh battlefield by Miami classmates in 1862. Miami Archives.

Civil War detail. From Edwin Fulwider's mural, The Biography of a University, *1959.* Miami Archives.

by foemen like a brother." In Grennan's vignette it was the power of college life, as much as any family division, that made of the nation's turmoil a brothers' war.

AN ERA ENDS

History readily yields up irony. During the Civil War, Miami's president was an affable Southerner who had come to Oxford from Huntsville, Alabama. Located in the Tennessee River Valley, Huntsville was the first capital of that state and had a tradition of intellectual crosscurrents, so perhaps ironically, Miami's first leader to arrive from the South was also its first New School Presbyterian. Among other subjects, President John W. Hall (1854–66) taught political economy and moral and intellectual philosophy. His views of the Constitution revealed a states' rights bias—although like abolitionist James G. Birney, who had practiced law in Huntsville, Hall supposedly left Alabama because of his moral opposition to slavery. Hall was also an ardent Unionist, but one dearly seeking sectional compromise. Through at least February of 1861,

John W. Hall, president of Miami University, 1854–66. Miami Archives.

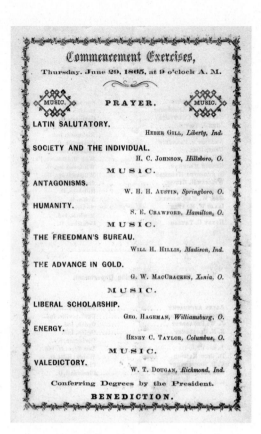

Commencement program, June 29, 1865. Miami Archives.

when on Washington's Birthday Miami students first marched to each of the women's institutions where they rallied for the Union, then passed formal resolutions declaring "unqualified devotion" to it, Hall's influence seemed to prevail. On April 13, the day after the bombardment of Fort Sumter, he prayed in morning chapel.

Spare us, O God of Jacob, we beseech Thee, from the great calamity which now threatens our Nation. Dispel these gathering clouds of civil strife and put into their hearts the spirit of compromise. Let not the dire calamity of fratricidal war distract our so long happy, prosperous and united people. Forgive us, O God of Jacob, our national sins and let all this sectional strife end in peace, and in a more strongly cemented union without the shedding of blood.

In less than ten days, sixty-three of Miami's students had gone to war, leaving eighty male students and troubled times in Oxford.

Although classes continued, news from war fronts was followed closely. More local concern may have been stirred by Ohio politics. Dayton Copperhead Clement Vallandigham was sent behind Confederate lines by President Lincoln for disloyal agitation after he violated Union General Burnside's General Order No. 38 forbidding sympathy for the enemy. Untiring in zeal, from exile in Ontario in 1863 Vallandigham ran as Ohio's Democratic Party nominee for governor of Ohio. He had followers in the Miami Valley, where sympathy for the South remained, even while patriotic sentiment for the Union ran high. In this contentious atmosphere Hall's loyalty to the Union became suspect. No formal charges were filed, but agitation by McFarland and others led trustees to investigate Hall's administration of student discipline and his management of the university. Hall was vindicated after a defense that included generous letters from alumni supporting him. During the war years Hall kept Miami's books balanced and presided over a slight rise in enrollment, but in an echo of Bishop's fate, in 1866 trustees replaced him with an Old School Presbyterian. New president Robert Livingston Stanton (1866–71), however, was also a Yankee from Connecticut, a student of Lyman Beecher, and an abolitionist.

By the time Stanton came to the presidency the war had ended and the nation was a different place than it ever had been. What lay ahead for Miami was as uncertain, perhaps, as in the earliest days of the university. It was clear, however, that entrepreneurs were rising and deep change was coming. Stanton set about to put Miami University on a sound financial footing. It needed it. Although fiscal books were balanced at the moment, Stanton described the physical condition of Old Main in 1866 as "a dilapidated pile" that was "repulsive to every gentleman who brings his son to the University, and a standing reproach and shame—I say it respectfully—to everyone who claims the University as his alma mater." Without an endowment, and dependent on tuition, Miami needed both new students and new money to compete for them. If the facilities could not be improved, Stanton said, Miami would be "largely deserted of its patrons, and drag out a lingering existence, or expire of inanition."

Before taking on building repair, Stanton attempted to reform the curriculum. A man with a practical eye, he elevated the status of the bachelor of science degree by substituting a German requirement for study of the classics. Between 1869 and 1871 he secured, with the aid of the Grant administration, a

Robert L. Stanton, president of Miami University, 1866–71. Miami Archives.

Elizabeth Cady Stanton, advocate of women's rights, sister-in-law of Robert L. Stanton, with Susan B. Anthony, ca. 1900.
Library of Congress.

military officer paid by the federal government to offer military training at Miami. He continued an initiative begun by Hall to secure endowments from the Presbyterian Church, without success. The Morrill Act of 1866 provided land to the states for sale, the proceeds to create an endowment for agricultural and mechanical colleges. In 1866, 1870, and 1872 Miami attempted to gain a share of this aid—once in cooperation with Ohio University, once with a promise of resignation by Miami's trustees in return for Morrill Act support, and twice involving legislative site visits to Oxford. All efforts failed. Instead, Ohio's Morrill Act funding went to an institution in the state capital that would become the Ohio State University.

For a while Stanton remained faithfully entrepreneurial. To build a new wing and make other improvements to Old Main, he raised $26,000 from Oxford and Oxford Township citizens and from alumni. Enrollment continued to decline, however, while debt rose. In 1870, when enrollment was 139 men, a convention of alumni at commencement adopted a resolution asking the state to turn over operation of Miami to them. A committee to incorporate the alumni was formed, and pledges made to raise a $100,000 endowment. The trustees agreed to this, but the legislature took no action. In 1871 enrollment dropped again, to 106. Stanton resigned, declaring that he had been misinformed about Miami's financial situation; that rival colleges Wabash, Antioch, and Marietta had significant endowments; and that in his view Miami could no longer compete with them.

The trustees would not capitulate. They convened with the faculty to discuss Miami's future in a "full and extended conversation." Out of that conference came modernizing changes. A governance model from the University of Virginia was adopted, providing that the faculty would choose one of themselves as its chair. They elected McGuffey's son-in-law, Andrew Dousa Hepburn (1871–73). In 1872 Hepburn presented the board with a formal plan for postwar reorganization of Miami University. The trustees accepted it, and confirmed Hepburn as Miami's president.

Hepburn's reorganization plan embraced an elective system for the curriculum that was moving across the nation. It may have gone beyond the trend by redesigning Miami into eight independent schools—Latin language and literature, Greek language and literature, modern languages and English

Andrew D. Hepburn, president of Miami University, 1871–73. Miami Archives.

philosophy, mathematics, natural philosophy, chemistry, mental philosophy, and literature. Each school was to feature both undergraduate and graduate offerings, and the catalog for 1873 declared, "Any student may enter any school, or any class in a school, that his special tastes, his aims in life, or the wishes of his friends may lead him to prefer." This startling pragmatic revolution, in the wake of Miami's unwavering half-century commitment to a classical core curriculum, had a very specific rationale. "It is found," stated the catalog, "that wherever the principle of option has been introduced greater diligence and contentment on the part of the students have been secured."

In addition to renovating Old Main, President Stanton had built a substantial home at the southwest corner of Spring and Oak streets that would be a symbolic bridge between Old and New Miami. Both Stanton, who held dinners for students in this home, and President Robert W. McFarland, who later lived there and held receptions with glee club entertainment in the 1880s, understood the power of independent student life to retain and attract students. But it was President Hepburn who first grasped the idea that after the Civil

> **INDEPENDENT SCHOOLS.**
>
> The customary division into four classes with a compulsory course of studies is abolished, and for it is substituted the system of independent schools. The University, for the present, is composed of the schools of *the Latin Language and Literature, the Greek Language and Literature, Modern Languages and English Philology, Mathematics, Natural Science, Philosophy, and Literature.*
>
> The students will be registered as members of the different schools in which they recite. Each school is divided into classes as the Professor in charge of it may deem advisable, and grants its own diploma to those who complete its course of studies.

Independent schools description, Catalogue, 1872–73. Miami Archives.

RENSSELAER POLYTECHNIC INSTI-
TUTE, Troy, N. Y.—Full Courses of Instruc-
tion in Civil, Mining, and Mechanical Engineering,
Chemistry, and Natural Science.   Appropriate de-
grees conferred. Reopens Sept. 14. For the Annual
Register, giving full information, address Professor
CHARLES DROWNE, Director.   au8-26t

MIAMI UNIVERSITY.

THE Forty-sixth Collegiate Year will open
SEPTEMBER 21, 1870, with a full Faculty.
Students will be received into the Academic, Collegiate or Scientific Department. Soldiers admitted
free. For further information, send for Catalogues,
or address the President, at Oxford, Butler County,
Ohio.   au27-3t8

Harvard University,
CAMBRIDGE, MASS.,

COMPRISES the following departments:
Harvard College; year begins Sept. 29.

Classified advertisement for Miami University, indicating "Soldiers admitted free." Cincinnati Gazette, September 3, 1870.

Graduating senior Horace Ankeney (seated), Class of 1872, with unidentified classmate. Miami Archives.

War, student choice outside the classroom had to be matched with choice in their course of studies. In 1872 Miami enrollment rose to 131 men. Hepburn could not, however, imagine the enrollment of women. That profound change would come later and bring with it the financial stability of regular state support for professional education. But as a final strategy for saving Old Miami, the trustees closed it.

In 1873, when the nation was mired in severe financial panic and only eighty-seven students enrolled, the trustees met again. They declared the president of the trustees to be the president of the university, and suspended university operation until land rent and other income could, through investment, build an endowment of $50,000. That strategy worked. In two years Miami's debt was retired. By 1880 the endowment had grown to $25,300. Four years later Miami's annual income, without students, was reported to be $9,000. The trustees would reopen college classes in 1885.

By 1885, the era of Old Miami was over. Its rigid curriculum and strict student discipline would pass away, and the charms of student life and professional education would mark Miami's future. But even during its final twelve years, when university classes were suspended and no college students lived in Miami halls, the campus did not close.

The Miami Classical and Scientific Training School

The decision of Miami trustees to suspend classes in June 1873 was not intended to be permanent. Administrative operation continued—annual trustee meetings and committees charged with meeting current expenses, paying debts, and accumulating sufficient funding to enable the university to reopen. Trustees wanted Miami's facilities and equipment to be occupied. They first authorized former Latin professor Robert H. Bishop Jr. to open the Miami Classical School in 1873. Its surviving description indicates that it was a preparatory

Artist's rendering of Miami University. Main building had only one wing and one tower at this time. From L. H. Evert, Combination Atlas Map of Butler County, Ohio, *1875.*

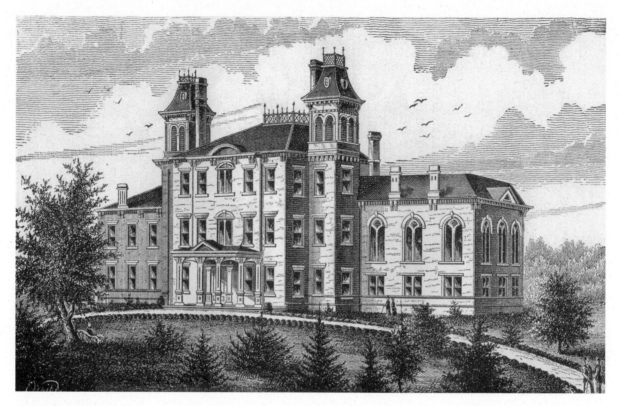

Miami Classical and Scientific Training School, ca. 1880. Miami Archives.

school intended to groom students for a traditional liberal arts curriculum in college.

In the spring of 1877 Bishop told the board he would close in June. Then two Eastern educational entrepreneurs, Isaac Trufant and Bryon Marsh, contacted the board with a proposition to lease the grounds, buildings, and educational apparatus to establish a training school. Although Trufant and Marsh supplied excellent references from employers in New Jersey, New York, and Pennsylvania, their proposal was at first rejected. They needed a loan, and wanted the board to make repairs that would improve the facilities. In June 1877 trustees authorized Trufant and Marsh to open a school, on condition that they maintain the facilities. The trustees offered a loan of $1,500 repayable at nominal interest in five years, and agreed to spend $2,500 on renovation.

Marsh later recalled that his impulse on seeing the state of the campus was to take the first train back to New York. However, now that he had "pledged to conduct a school in Babylon," Marsh supervised the needed repairs and in September 1877 the Miami Classical and Scientific Training School opened with fifteen students. It quickly became a thriving enterprise. A board committee charged with overseeing its operation reported in June 1878, "they are fully justified in speaking . . . in terms of highest commendation."

According to the school's 1878–79 *Circular,* enrollees could choose between classical, scientific, or English courses of study, each "carefully laid out" to qualify students for entering any institution of higher learning. In addition, a Telegraphic Training Department catered to boys wishing to pursue careers as telegraph operators, railroad agents, or accountants. Trufant, who served as instructor of Latin, Greek, and English, was "a short, stout bearded man, called 'Potty' by the schoolboys." Marsh, who taught Latin, math, elocution, and the natural sciences, was "a younger man, still in his thirties, with a boyish face hidden by a full beard." He was an expert sharpshooter who impressed students by his expertise with a rifle. The *Circular* listed fourteen other "Lecturers," including the musical composer and educator Karl Merz, on special loan from Oxford Female College. "Sam" Allen, moonlighting from his job as an Oxford railway attendant, headed the Telegraphic Training Department.

To the Alumni and other Friends of Miami University.

The Collegiate Department of Miami University was opened in November, 1824, with a President, one Professor, and twelve pupils in the lower classes. The first class, consisting of twelve members, was graduated in September, 1826. During a period of forty-nine years nearly one thousand young men were graduated, and more than twice that number received a large part of their education within her walls. The income from the Permanent Fund having been found, owing to the rise in prices, inadequate to meet current expenses, instruction in the Institution was suspended in July, 1873. At that time there was a debt of nearly $10,000. This has been paid, and $50,000 added to the Permanent Fund. Encouraged by this increase, the Trustees have determined to re-open the Institution, and, as a preliminary step, a Freshman class will be formed Sept. 18, 1884, under the instruction and government of Prof. R. H. Bishop. Additional Instructors will be employed as they may be needed. The aid of the Alumni and other friends is solicited in this attempt to revive Miami University; and it is hoped that in conversation and through the press, they will use their influence to raise her to her former state of prosperity and usefulness.

BOARD OF TRUSTEES.

Hon. JOHN W. HERRON, President, Cincinnati.

THOMAS MILLIKIN, Esq., Hamilton,	Hon. SAMUEL F. HUNT, Cincinnati,
Hon. J. H. THOMAS, Springfield,	Hon. J. McLAIN SMITH, Dayton,
Rev. J. W. McGREGOR, Oxford,	H. W. HUGHES, Esq., Cincinnati,
WALTER A. DUN, Esq., Cincinnati,	RICHARD SMITH, Esq., Cincinnati,
Hon. JAMES W. OWENS, Newark,	Hon. JOHN F. NIELAN, Hamilton,
Hon. JAMES E. NEIL, Hamilton,	WILLIAM BECKETT, Esq., Hamilton,
Rev. J. Y. SCHOULER, Fair Haven,	J. RILEY KNOX, Esq., Greenville,
JOHN B. PEASLEE, Esq., Cincinnati,	Hon. DURBIN WARD, Lebanon,
Rev. B. W. CHIDLAW, Cincinnati,	PALMER W. SMITH, Esq., Oxford,
L. N. BONHAM, Esq., Oxford,	ADAM McCREA, Esq., Circleville,
CALVIN S. BRICE, Esq. Lima,	Hon. M. W. OLIVER, Cincinnati,
EDWARD L. TAYLOR, Esq., Columbus,	NELSON SAYLER, Esq., Cincinnati,
Hon. WILLIAM J. GILMORE, Eaton,	IRA A. COLLINS, Esq., Hamilton.

THE ACADEMICAL YEAR

Extends from the third Thursday in September to the second Thursday in June.

The Summer Vacation is from the second Thursday in June until the third Thursday in September.

The Winter Vacation, of not more than two weeks, includes Christmas and New Year's days.

Tuition Fee: $30,00 per session, covering all incidental and other fees—to be paid in advance.

Board in private families from $3,00 to $4,50 per week.

For further information inquire of Professor Bishop, at Oxford.

By Order of the Board,

L. N. BONHAM,
PALMER W. SMITH, } Committee.

Oxford, August 5, 1884.

Printed circular, August 5, 1884.
Miami Special Collections.

Classes were conducted primarily on the first floor of Old Main, with students residing in the dormitories, now renamed Washington and Franklin Halls. Although Old Main had only a central section and one wing at this time, most school publicity depicted it with two wings, perhaps anticipating that another wing would be built. Discipline, described as "parental," was very strict. Individuals with a history of troublemaking were told not to apply, as were young men who used "tobacco in any form." This did not discourage applicants, and the school eventually reached an enrollment of 102 students. Notable alumni included "Kid" Tweed, son of New York's infamous "Boss" Tweed, and three sons of a prominent Sandwich Islands sugar farmer. Llewellyn Bonham, who would marry future President McFarland's daughter and acquire the presidential home of Stanton and McFarland at Spring and Oak Streets, was an 1884 graduate of the Classical and Scientific Training School. He went on to a thirty-year career as a prominent engineer, perfecting the Liberty Motor used by flying ace Eddie Rickenbacker in World War I, and inventing the streetcar fare register as well as a signaling device for motorists.

From the beginning, the fate of the Classical and Scientific Training School was tied to that of the university. When Miami reopened, coexistence would be difficult. In June 1882, Trufant and Marsh requested a five-year loan extension, which was refused, but trustees agreed to forgo interest and spread out repayments over five years, indicating a hope to reopen sometime after 1887. Pressure from the Oxford community and alumni forced quicker action. Trustees decided to reopen in the fall of 1884, but permitted the Trufant-Marsh School to remain as a preparatory school. This arrangement pleased no one. President Robert McFarland wrote trustees that he would not tolerate it the following year, and Trufant and Marsh wrote that the university class was incompatible with the school. They resigned in September 1885. Trustees, citing their excellent record and care of university facilities, forgave the unpaid balance of their loan.

Marsh ended his days in Daytona Beach, Florida. In a 1910 letter he fondly recalled the Classical and Scientific Training School and expressed appreciation to the Oxford community for supporting it. Fortune did not smile on his partner. In 1888 Trufant expressed interest in rejoining Miami, but was not appointed. Ever the entrepreneur, he solicited funds from Oxford citizens, traveled west to buy land in the Kansas land boom, and went broke.

act 2

New Miami, 1885–1941

Embracing Professionalism

A "New Miami" Timeline, 1884–1941

1885	Miami reopens; Robert White McFarland (1885–88) assumes the presidency
1886	Oxford Female College confers baccalaureate degrees
1887	Five women admitted as "special students" by trustee resolution of June 21
1888	Ethelbert Dudley Warfield (1888–91) assumes the presidency
	First football game played, against University of Cincinnati
1891	William Oxley Thompson (1891–99) assumes the presidency
	Miami admits seventeen women students
1892	Brice Hall, first donated building, constructed for science instruction; Calvin Brice, donor
	Alumnae Hall built at Western College, James Renwick Jr., architect; Olivia Meily (Mrs. Calvin) Brice, donor
1895	Miami builds a baseball field
	Western College and Seminary confers baccalaureate degrees
1896	Miami Field constructed for football
	Sleeper Bill provides first regular annual appropriation from State of Ohio
1897	Herron Gymnasium (later Van Voorhis Hall) constructed
1899	David Stanton Tappan (1899–1902) assumes the presidency
1900	Three of sixteen women at Miami awarded bachelor's degrees
1902	The Ohio State Normal College established in Oxford
	Guy Potter Benton (1902–11) assumes the presidency
	Delta Zeta, a fraternal organization for women, founded
1903	Nellie Craig, first African American woman, enrolls; earns Normal College diploma in 1905
1905	Hepburn Hall constructed as first residence hall for women
1908	New Administration/Auditorium Building (later Benton Hall, Hall Auditorium) constructed
1909	First Alumni Campaign matches Carnegie Award to build Alumni Library
	South Pavilion, Normal College (later McGuffey Hall), constructed

1910	Earl Kelley, first identified male African American enrolled (1908), earns Normal College diploma
1911	Raymond Mollyneaux Hughes (1911–27) assumes the presidency
1912	Bishop Hall constructed as residence for women
1917	United States enters World War I
1919	Miami "No-Horse Rule" replaced by "No-Car Rule"
1923	Wells Hall constructed as residence for women
1924	University Hospital (later MacMillan Hall) constructed
	Ogden Hall constructed as residence for men, and student center
	New Freshman Dormitory (later Swing Hall) constructed as residence for men
1925	Oxford Retreat main building (former Oxford Female College) purchased, renamed Fisher Hall
	Irvin Hall, first fully neo-Georgian classroom building, constructed as recitation building
1928	Alfred Horatio Upham (1928–45) assumes the presidency
	School of Business Administration (later Farmer School of Business) founded, located in Irvin Hall
	Oxford College for Women acquired; main building renovated for women's residence
1929	School of Fine Arts founded
1931	Center section, Hughes Hall (later Kreger Hall), constructed for chemistry
	Withrow Court constructed for men's athletics and physical education, and assembly hall
1937	North and South dormitories renovated in neo-Georgian style, named Elliott Hall and Stoddard Hall
1939	New Freshman Dormitory Number One (later Symmes Hall) constructed for men
1940	North Residence Hall (later Hamilton Hall) constructed as residence for women
1941	South Hall (later Richard Hall) constructed as residence for women
	Beta Theta Pi Campanile constructed

"New Miami" Themes, 1885–1941

After the Civil War, the nation expands geographically, immigration increases, urban centers grow dramatically, and the postwar prosperity of manufacturing industries generates new markets for consumer goods. While workplace specialization gathers momentum, a parallel specialization in higher education emerges to address new economic and cultural agendas. Public schooling expands and with it the demand for classroom teachers, now primarily women. At previously all-male university campuses the admission of women transforms the character of student life, and cocurricular organizations become more visible.

Soon after reopening in 1885, Miami admits women students in small numbers. Seventeen years later the State of Ohio establishes the Ohio State Normal College for the education of public school teachers. This new curriculum attracts many women, who by 1910 outnumber Miami's men students. With the advent of coeducation, university enrollment rises to about three thousand students and remains relatively stable until the trauma of World War II brings the New Miami era to a close.

Leaving behind the small men's college atmosphere, Miami begins to resemble a substantial liberal arts college; men mostly enroll in liberal arts programs and women mostly in teacher education. The campus diversifies further as African American students are admitted to the Normal College soon after it opens. Miami's rapid enrollment growth at this time, driven by a new level of state support for the matriculation of women, underwrites an unprecedented period of financial stability, curricular modernization, and campus construction. This era introduces Miami's first buildings constructed in a neo-Georgian "colonial" style made popular nationally by historic restorations of eighteenth-century Virginia, and older campus structures are remodeled to harmonize with that aesthetic.

Intercollegiate athletics and campus sports emerge as major attractions of college life, and social fraternities replace literary societies. Organized fundraising, formal campus planning, and creation of new professional schools in business administration and fine arts lend momentum to specialization and yield divisional and departmental organization. Miami survives World War I and the Great Depression reasonably intact, but World War II ends this period of coeducational stability as military service sharply depletes the number of male students.

prelude

"...sharp cure for all our ills"

New Miami, which in the next half century would become a place radically different from Old Miami, began its life with one last fight among Old Miami men. The presidency of Robert White McFarland (1885–88), as described by Bertha Boya Thompson, was "entangled in the great national struggle of the function of higher education in which new sciences challenged the authority of a religiously-sponsored liberal education of a classical and linguistic nature." On June 21, 1888, graduation day for New Miami's first class of three proud degree recipients, twenty-seven members of the university's hard-working board of trustees met on campus to celebrate, and to hear contending claims about tumultuous quarreling among the faculty. Surprising some partisans, they took a step trustee William McSurely told his diary "was sharp cure for all our ills, but we felt it was necessary." By a vote of seventeen to five they declared every faculty position, including that of President McFarland, "vacant at the end of the college year." Then they elected Ethelbert Dudley Warfield as president and appointed a trustee committee to revise the curriculum.

The dramatic board action on New Miami's first graduation day marked a turning point in a period of transition for both Miami and its region. Even without counting students, United States census figures revealed significant population growth in Butler County, Hamilton, and Oxford by 1890. In 1830 the county reported 27,142 people, the county seat 1,079, and Oxford 736. In 1890 corresponding populations were 48,597, 17,565, and 1,922. The county had almost doubled in population, its main urban center had grown almost 17 times over, and Oxford had more than doubled. Urbanization was rapid in Hamilton, where in 1895 a 440-foot iron-truss bridge described by its builder as "the longest single-span highway bridge in the world" replaced two outmoded predecessors spanning the Great Miami River.

Robert W. McFarland, president of Miami University,
1885–88. Miami Archives.

Oxford's local economy suffered during the twelve years that the Classical Training School occupied Miami buildings and no college men came to
town. On July 1, 1884, a petition of 444 Oxford citizens was read to the board,
calling for full reopening of the university. The board assessed the progress of
the university endowment, agreed with the petitioners, and set the official reopening for September 1885.

In 1884 the board unanimously elected Robert White McFarland, an Old
Miami professor of mathematics and astronomy, president pro tempore. Since
the suspension of classes in 1873 he had taught mathematics, astronomy, and
civil engineering at Ohio State. Now he would be paid $2,000 annually for
a two-year contract, twice the salary of Miami's first academic president in
1824. McFarland, however, may have been attracted more by the challenge
than by its compensation, for he took a $500 pay cut to accept the position.

The board of trustees, Oxford citizens, influential donors, political leaders,
and the new president aggressively supported the launch of New Miami. A
trustee committee appealed to the legislature for funds, and a group of trustees and Oxford citizens went to Columbus to lobby for that appeal. In 1885
the legislature responded with a one-time allocation of $20,000 for building
repairs, $5,000 for current expenses, and $1,000 for a new building. While

this appropriation did not necessarily predict future state funding, it encouraged higher expectations.

On June 17, 1885, Miami University alumni gathered in Oxford to celebrate. The C. H. & D. Railroad offered transportation to Oxford at half fare, Oxford streets were decked with flags, guests arriving by train were given carriage tours of the decorated town, and elaborate preparations were made for a parade, public speeches, a banquet, and an evening symposium. Afternoon platform speakers included Old Miami stalwarts Charles Anderson and eighty-five-year-old Professor John W. Scott, and the symposium featured addresses by distinguished Miami alumni, including Senator Benjamin Harrison of Indiana and the Reverend David Swing of Chicago. Railroad magnate Calvin Brice made a public commitment to endow two professorships.

When classes opened in the fall, McFarland reported building repairs still under way that, according to Thompson,

meant dust, lime, mortar, sticks, chips, mud, bats, bricks, beams, boards, teams, oils, paints, glass, gravel, picks, shovels, iron, slate, men, boys, animals, all at once, and in a whirling vortex of involved confusion, scarcely equaled by the evolutions and contortions of a bevy of gnats on a summer evening.

Miami officially reopened on September 17, 1885. One week later another celebration occurred, when "a procession of students and citizens, with every conceivable noise-maker—bells, horns, tin cans and so forth—formed and proceeded to West Park" to hear speeches by the president of the board, the president of the university, and prominent local citizens including L. E. Grennan and Llewellyn Bonham.

At the center of this activity was President McFarland, a progressive activist who took on the diverse roles of "administrator, professor, librarian, general superintendent of grounds and buildings, student solicitor, fund procurer, and the performer of many tasks of lesser importance which became his responsibility only because no one else had attended to them." McFarland had finished his public schooling at age thirteen. As a demanding teacher with a strong intellect, he earned the loyalty of his students and supported them outside the classroom as well. A public-minded figure who served as state inspector of railways between 1881 and 1885, McFarland was said to delight in "long, laborious and complicated mathematical computation." He also made contributions in history and archaeology, and published an edition of Virgil. As an Old Miami faculty member McFarland had been an ideological Unionist who in 1862 pled guilty to assault and battery on a student. He also became a military officer in the Union army. As president he had a clear view of his authority: "In all cases of executive action, civil or military, it is not always helped but always hindered by the many-voiced multitude."

Although McFarland had been classically educated in the antebellum era,

*Elizabeth (Lizzie) McFar-
land, daughter of Robert W.
McFarland, admitted in 1887
as one of Miami's first women
students. Miami Archives.*

*Ella McSurely, daughter of
William J. McSurely, admitted in 1889 as one of Miami's
early women students. Miami
Archives.*

after the Civil War he became a forward-thinking progressive who
tried to move the university beyond the Old Miami classical curriculum. He permitted optional chapel attendance, favored a pedagogy
of deduction over memorization, personally carried a heavy teaching
assignment, and taught a practical class in civil engineering. He supported the development of physical sciences, a bachelor of arts degree
that allowed substitution of German for Greek, and a bachelor of science degree that accepted modern languages and science in place of
Latin and Greek.

Moreover, in a town long noted for Presbyterian piety, McFarland
came from a solid Methodist background. He held the BA, MA, and
LLD degrees from Ohio Wesleyan University. In Oxford he found it
prudent, he said, to attend Presbyterian services, but he had detractors. The wife of a trustee wrote to her husband: "Mrs. Fullerton says
Dr. Byers told her that Prof. McFarland was not only an infidel, but
tried to make infidels of the boys. He knew him to say, 'boys, you know
that we don't take stock in Moses like our fathers did,' and like expressions. I am afraid a great mistake has been made in making him Pres.
of M. U."

Even more damaging in some eyes, President McFarland favored
the admission of women to Miami University. The Civil War had accelerated the exodus of male instructors from public schools, opening
teaching opportunities for women, and after the war they presented
a growing demand for advanced education. The University of Michigan opened to women in 1870, Ohio State and Cornell in 1873, and by
1880 more than half of American colleges and universities were said to
be coeducational. Although Miami was closed as a collegiate institution for twelve years while this movement was building, in 1882—three
years before it reopened—trustee Nelson Saylor "proposed that no applicant be refused on the ground of sex." Five years later, on June 21,
1887, the trustees adopted a resolution opening Miami to women. On
October 10, two women were admitted—Elizabeth E. McFarland, the
president's daughter, and Daisy M. McCullough—as special students
who could attend classes but not earn degrees. Three more women
were admitted that year, all Oxford residents. It took two more years
to enroll another—Ella McSurely in 1889.

McFarland's progressivism was contested. While he had supporters in chemistry professor Henry Snyder, botany and paleontology professor Joseph Francis James, and German and French professor Oliver
Hoben—all advocates of liberalizing the curriculum as well as admissions—his opponents were John Robert Sitlington Sterrett, professor
of classical studies and earlier a student of William Holmes McGuffey

Daisy McCullough (front row, center, with purse), admitted in 1887 as one of Miami's first women students. Miami Archives.

at Virginia; Alfred Emerson, professor of Latin and Greek; and the Reverend Andrew Dousa Hepburn, DD, professor of literature and history, husband of McGuffey's daughter Henrietta, and final president of Old Miami.

A Pennsylvanian who during antebellum days and the Civil War associated himself with the South, Hepburn attended the University of Virginia in the early 1850s, graduated from Princeton Theological Seminary in 1857, and then ministered to a church in Virginia. From 1859 to 1867 he was professor of mental philosophy at the University of North Carolina and, according to his daughter, "served for a time as chaplain to the Confederate soldiers." In 1868 Hepburn became professor of logic and English literature at Miami. He succeeded Robert L. Stanton in the presidency, and after Miami closed in 1873 he taught at Davidson College in North Carolina, where he also became president. Brought back to Miami as a professor by McFarland in 1885, Hepburn and his family were given lodging in North Hall. Hepburn made no secret of his opposition to the admission of women, but offered Ella McSurely accommodation with his family if she decided to enter Miami. Described as "suave and diplomatic," Hepburn was an active member of Beta Theta Pi fraternity.

When McFarland's initial two-year contract expired, the trustees extended it one year but determined to select a continuing president in 1888. In January of that year McFarland and Professor Sterrett quarreled over the authority to assign a third-story room in North Hall to Sterrett's servant. Their exchange of hostile letters was given to the executive committee of the board, who removed responsibility for dormitory assignments from the president and gave it to Hepburn. In firsthand reports to the board, faculty members Sterrett,

Andrew D. Hepburn, president of Miami University, 1871–73, and professor of English, 1868–73 and 1885–1908. Photograph by Frank R. Snyder, 1906. Miami Archives and Smith Library.

Emerson, and Hepburn charged McFarland with general disorganization, neglect of discipline, and even students' poor penmanship. They petitioned for a revised curriculum that would return classical studies to required status, and sought revisions of rules—among them, probably, the one permitting optional chapel attendance. They complained that the president favored the physical sciences. After giving their reports, Emerson and Sterrett resigned and left for Chicago and Texas.

The board of trustees in 1888 included ministers, lawyers, physicians, bankers, and investors. In a short time the university had moved from fifty to seventy-two students, renovated its physical plant, admitted women, and laid a new curricular foundation that was to prove prophetic of the coming scientific influence in everyday life. But change came hard. Having released McFarland and the entire faculty, the board promptly rehired Snyder and Hepburn. Students and townspeople alike protested these actions, some vigorously. Thomas Millikin, a trustee from 1878 to 1887, complained boldly that it was the result of "too much Presbyterian church."

Undoubtedly religion was a factor, since doctrinal partisanship lingered from Old Miami. Curricular modernization and the admission of women—steps supported by the board's majority—possibly loomed larger. But two decades after the war, change was accelerating across the nation. In 1888 Burroughs patented the adding machine, Tesla invented an alternating current motor, Eastman invented amateur photography, and Pullman built an electric locomotive. The election of Benjamin Harrison to the U.S. presidency brought Miami a sense of national importance in an era when politics, commerce, and great fortunes intermingled freely. In this milieu Miami's trustees were an activist lot, determined to make a success of their reborn institution. They named standing committees on finance, law, accounts, alumni, endowment, and legislative aid, as well as an executive committee to review Miami personnel. They had a strong sense of direct responsibility. The Trustee Committee-on-Examinations even read the questions and answers on all final tests given to students. The trustees appointed a variety of short-term committees to address smaller subjects and generally proved to be a group in no mood for a disabling controversy on campus.

Financial tycoon Calvin Brice was perhaps the most colorful figure among them, as well as a key benefactor at a critical moment. He had entered Miami at the age of thirteen and three years later, when war erupted, signed up for Ozro Dodd's University Rifles. He fought with McFarland's company in West Virginia, and when hostilities ended, studied law at the University of Michigan. He practiced in the railroad town of Lima, Ohio, specializing in corporate law and transportation. Early in his career Brice borrowed funds to purchase a stake in the Lake Erie and Western Railway from Sandusky, Ohio, to Peoria, Illinois. He became its president in 1879, parlaying this position into syndicate financing for new railroads carefully routed to compete with successful ones. When his group of investors built the Nickel Plate Railroad connecting New York, Chicago, and St. Louis, it threatened the position of the New York Central. Its owner William H. Vanderbilt, said to be the richest man in the nation, purchased the Nickel Plate for $7,200,000 in 1882. Thereafter Brice would be a prominent investor in industrial enterprises and become Miami's first major private donor. He made a $5,000 contribution to endow the salary of the Miami president in 1888 and pledged to support two professorships for two years. In 1889, the year after Miami trustees administered their "sharp cure," Brice offered to match any funds the State of Ohio would provide. He made good on this promise by matching appropriated dollars to construct Miami's first modern science laboratory, dedicated as Brice Scientific Hall in 1892. From 1889 to 1892 Brice was chairman of the Democratic National Committee, and from 1890 to 1896 served as Democratic senator from Ohio. He died unexpectedly of pneumonia in 1898. Perhaps to recognize Brice's support of his alma mater, his son was named to the board of trustees.

Calvin S. Brice, Class of 1863, railroad entrepreneur, U.S. senator, and Miami University benefactor. Miami Archives.

Olivia Meily Brice, wife of Calvin S. Brice and benefactor of the Western Female Seminary. Western Archives.

The arrival of Ethelbert Dudley Warfield marked a second phase in the complex beginning of New Miami. Only twenty-seven years old when he assumed the presidency, Warfield saw an emerging national agenda in higher education. "No effort has been spared," he said, "to secure the application of the most approved methods adopted in the best European and American colleges" for the total reorganization of the university. He added, "It is confidently believed that the opportunities now afforded are equal to the best to be obtained in the West." Among them would be a faculty committed to modernizing college life.

scene three

Institutionalizing New Miami

WARFIELD AND THE "DUDE FACULTY"

Although Ethelbert Dudley Warfield, president from 1888 to 1891, served for barely three years, life at Miami and Oxford would never be quite the same after his tenure. Warfield came to Oxford from a law practice in Lexington, Kentucky, to lead Miami following the board's traumatic realignment of its faculty the previous spring. He brought unprecedented youthful energy to the institution.

With an outstanding academic background at Princeton and Wadham College, Oxford, Warfield had earned a law degree from Columbia. Determined to make Miami the equal of prestigious eastern universities, he populated the faculty with young men of educational attainments similar to his own, including Yale graduate Walter Ray Bridgeman as professor of Greek, and three Princeton graduates—Arnold Guyot Cameron as professor of German and French, Robert Bruce Cash Johnson as professor of mental and moral science, and Thomas Marc Parrot as principal of the Preparatory Department. Professors Hepburn and Snyder remained. Charles Wesley Hargitt, with a PhD from Ohio University, was named professor of biology and geology; Amherst graduate William Augustus Merrill, professor of Latin language and literature; and Joseph V. Collins, holder of a doctorate from Wooster, professor of mathematics and astronomy. They were all young; Collins was only twenty-four, and only Hargitt had previous teaching experience. Several were described as brilliant: five were Phi Beta Kappa, and most studied at least briefly at prominent eastern or European universities. Later they would move on to such places as Yale, Princeton, Syracuse, and the University of California.

Ethelbert Dudley Warfield, president of Miami University, 1888–91 (seated second from left), with the "dude faculty." Miami Archives.

Warfield's faculty was professional in spirit as well as preparation. Turned out smartly in formal attire, they imparted to male students an understanding that wearing a "dress suit" was expected. Warfield, whose wife had died two years before he joined Miami, drew a handsome salary for the time and could afford both a butler and a cook for entertaining at his Victorian home, which still stands at the northwest corner of Church Street and Campus Avenue. Moreover, Warfield and his young colleagues were bachelors whose social behavior was noticed. Western Female Seminary, under the new leadership of Principal Leila McKee, employed a number of women faculty from prestigious women's institutions, and some Miami faculty struck up acquaintances with them that were much discussed in town. Warfield, Cameron, and Bridgeman all married Western faculty before they left Oxford a few years later, but their courtships reportedly caused a stir. More than fifty years later Warfield's son recalled his father's account of those days.

He said that on occasion the good people of Oxford were duly horrified to see a horse-drawn buggy coming down the street containing two hitherto irreproachable young ladies with the President and the Mathematics Professor of Miami University [actually the modern languages professor] sitting on top of the buggy, with their feet dangling. This, in 1889, was clearly compromising, and the next spring the men made honest women of them, to wit Mrs. E. D. Warfield and Mrs. Guyot Cameron.

Even more delicious, perhaps, was an incident at the "very acme of their indiscretions." It occurred "one autumn evening when the young professors and their sweethearts were discovered broiling beefsteaks over a picnic bonfire in the lower campus."

WESTERN COLLEGE FOR WOMEN AND NEW MIAMI

Warfield advertised that Miami was "open to both sexes with equal advantages to each," but during his brief presidency only a few women attended classes and none earned a degree. However, Oxford Female College on College Avenue was attracting a steady enrollment of women, and the Western Female Seminary was entering a period of dramatic modernization that would earn much attention at Miami.

In 1888 Leila S. McKee, a Wellesley College graduate and daughter of a vice president of Centre College in Danville, Kentucky, was elected principal of the Western Female Seminary, replacing founding principal Helen Peabody. Miss McKee, eleven years out of college, was a sociable, vigorous, forward-looking woman with ambition. In the spring of her first year in office she toured eastern schools including Mt. Holyoke, Yale, Smith, Amherst, and Wellesley with the intent of transforming Western into a four-year college and broadening its liberal arts curriculum to include laboratory sciences and creative arts.

By June 1889, when Western trustees authorized construction of a modern building to house a library, a science laboratory, and an art studio, Western's library in Peabody Hall held ten thousand volumes, almost exactly as many as Miami's library in Old Main. Western's new building, heated by steam and lighted by electricity, was sited next to Peabody on the brow of a hill overlooking a pond where it would become a prominent feature of the Oxford landscape. The president of Western's alumnae association, Olivia Meily Brice, wife of Calvin Brice, donated $5,000 toward the new building, and with the support of alumnae, trustees, and friends of the school, raised the substantial sum of $50,000 to give it the name "Alumnae Hall."

Miss McKee would serve Western for sixteen years, establish its four-year degree, rename the institution "The Western College for Women," and become its first president in 1894. The library in Alumnae Hall would grow to thirty thousand volumes. McKee initiated the office of college dean and witnessed the creation of laboratory classes in natural sciences and requirements in physical training, music, and other arts. Two literary clubs, a YWCA, and a college magazine, the *Western-Oxford*, emerged during her tenure. She encouraged and took direct part in ceremonial events meant to enrich social as well as intellectual life, such as an annual college pageant, class plays,

Peabody Hall. Oil painting by C. E. Fay, 1871. Western Archives.

Tree Day at Western College, 1911. Photograph by Frank R. Snyder. Miami Archives and Smith Library.

Valentine parties, chaperoned carriage parties and hayrides, mock presidential campaigns in election years, field trips to arts institutions, and from Wellesley, the tradition of Tree Day. In 1894 Western's first maypole was set up near Alumnae Hall, where students danced to fiddle, banjo, guitar, and mandolin music. She started a tradition of senior class flags designed by students and chose the Western colors, blue and white. She also sent missionaries to China, Japan, Persia, and India and enrolled Western's first students from other countries. By its fiftieth anniversary—celebrated in 1905—Western had 36 faculty and staff, 204 students, a greatly expanded campus, and a new dormitory under construction that was later named for President McKee.

The McKee era transformed Western Female Seminary into what would become Oxford's longest-running women's college by revolutionizing its curriculum, social life, and aspirations. Alumnae Hall and its facilities made this possible and offered a symbol of visible achievement by women. Formal dedication of the building in 1892 emphasized that it was a gift *of* women *to* women to be dedicated *by* women. Commencement week that year was called "Women's Week." Miss McKee received an honorary doctorate from Centre College. Former principal Helen Peabody made a farewell visit before moving to Pasadena, California. Following commencement in the main building, Alumnae Hall was dedicated by presentation of a memorial stained-glass window placed in the library by Mrs. Brice's Class of 1866.

Helen Peabody, principal of the Western Female Seminary, 1855–88. Western Archives.

INVENTING INTERCOLLEGIATE ATHLETICS

Stimulated perhaps by a debonair president and faculty, social organizations for men proliferated in New Miami. The YMCA, with overtones of religious devotion, may have been the most popular nonfraternity group. It had rooms in North Hall and a formal name reminiscent of literary societies, "The Society of Inquiry of the Young Men's Christian Association." There was a banjo club and groups for horseback riding, ocarina playing, kodaking, and cubeb smoking. Nonclass activities were not exclusively social, for since the departure of McFarland, chapel attendance had been required daily at 7:45 a.m. and Sunday at 4:30 p.m. Students were also expected to attend a village church service of their choice Sunday morning—on penalty of demerits affecting their class standing.

Leila McKee, principal of the Western Female Seminary, 1888–94, and president of the Western College and Seminary for Women, 1894–1904. Western Archives.

When Leila S. McKee and the librarian of Western Female Seminary visited progressive New England schools in 1890 to get ideas that presumably included plans for a new library, they could have found one or several buildings an inspiration. Architectural activity in the East certainly affected the building of Alumnae Hall, which opened in 1892, nearly two decades before Miami opened its own Alumni Library in 1909.

Alumnae Hall was designed by Renwick, Aspinwall and Russell of New York, working with J. W. Yost of Columbus, Ohio. Constructed of rusticated random ashlar stone and brick, it featured a twelve-sided, double-height room at the north end that would be a stunning library. Its Romanesque revival qualities were accented by an arched entry, a beautifully articulated French Gothic bell tower, an Italianate low-sloped hipped roof for the library, exposed rafter ends, and classically inspired arched windows. An upper floor, lit by skylights, contained a sequence of art galleries. From a square upper gallery, other galleries could be seen. After passing through one of three arched openings while descending several steps, one entered a short but wide space lit by windows at either side, then moved into what was presumably the main gallery, again lit by skylights, near which studios were tucked under eaves and in dormers. With the Main Building (1871, named Peabody Hall in 1905), and McKee Hall (1904), Alumnae was the centerpiece of three monumental buildings along the edge of a ravine around which Western College would cluster. Those with an eye for it might imagine the impact in 1905 of this row of highly visible women's college buildings on Miami students who entered Oxford by coach from the south and saw them first before arriving at Miami's more modest campus of that day.

Alumnae Hall (1892). Western Archives.

Because of its impressive architectural pedigree, Alumnae Hall was a structure of national importance. The principal of its design firm, James Renwick Jr., enjoyed an especially long and distinguished career. Alone and in partnership he designed numerous religious structures including Grace Church (1843–1846) and St. Patrick's Cathedral (1858–1888) in New York City, as well as the original building for the Smithsonian Institution (1847–1855); the Main Building of Vassar College (1861–65); the Corcoran Gallery, now the Renwick Gallery of the Smithsonian in Washington, D.C. (1859–1871); and hospitals, hotels, commercial buildings, and residences. Reviewing Vassar's Main Building, one critic observed, "There was an inherent flaw: the incompatibility of the monumental, urbane building with its rural, picturesque site." Renwick corrected that difficulty with Alumnae Hall, by achieving an excellent balance of monumental form and picturesque setting.

While Henry Hobson Richardson popularized the style within which Renwick worked, his strong and often idiosyncratic forms differed from Renwick's more delicate and varied ones. By the 1890s Leila McKee was certainly aware of Richardson's work, for his Chamber of Commerce Building in Cincinnati opened in 1888. When Miss McKee went east in 1890 she may have seen Richardson's Sever Hall at Harvard (1880) or some of the five memorial libraries Richardson designed in Massachusetts that are similar in function and form to Alumnae Hall. Renwick worked in a variety of styles but preferred Romanesque and Gothic, and Alumnae Hall was evidence of his skill at blending stylistic elements, with medieval ones dominant. J. W. Yost, serving presumably as local representative for Renwick, was probably responsible for placing the building sympathetically on Western's topography. Yost's Orton Hall at Ohio State opened a year after Alumnae as that institution's library and shared features with it, including a strikingly similar cylindrical tower.

The main window for Alumnae Hall library—which honored Western's class of 1866 and the building's primary donor, Olivia Brice—was designed by Mary Elizabeth Tillinghast, the nation's first significant woman stained-glass artist. She had an early artistic partnership with the noted interior painter John LaFarge, and designed a window for Renwick's Grace Church in New York City. Tillinghast is credited with being the first art glass window designer to exploit the impact of modern electrical lighting on stained-glass windows in churches. One critic called her "the foremost woman artist of the American School, both in stained glass and in general." Soon after the opening of

Alumnae Hall, the Brice Window was removed by workmen sent to Oxford by Tillinghast so it could be exhibited in 1893 at the Columbian World's Exposition in Chicago. It was placed in the Woman's Division of the Manufacturers and Liberal Arts Building, testifying both to the artist's reputation and to cultural restrictions placed on women at the time. It won a gold medal at the exposition.

After 1892 Alumnae Hall became the centerpiece of the Western campus and symbolized the accomplishments of Western alumnae. Illustrations of it were used to publicize Western's modern curriculum and resources to potential students. Other buildings took cues from it. The geometric forms of Boyd Science Hall and Alexander Dining Hall refer directly to Alumnae. The stonework and some detailing of Mary Lyon and Edith Clawson halls recall Alumnae's style. Even modernist Thomson, clad mostly in brick veneer, turns a stone face toward the college drive. When Alumnae Hall was razed in 1977, an important marker of stylistic coherence at the heart of the campus was lost.

In the New Miami era, when Western College and Miami University were colleagues in modernizing higher education, Alumnae Hall opened a new world of knowledge to women. In the early twenty-first century devoted former students, acting on behalf of the Western College Alumnae Association, Inc., and Miami's Western College Program, outlined the foundation of Alumnae Hall with perennial flowers—making it the only place at Miami where an exact footprint of the past is formally remembered.

Aaron Andrew Spetz, M.Arch., 2003

Tillinghast Window (1892), Kumler Chapel. Mary Elizabeth Tillinghast. Scott Kissell, IT Services, 2008.

By 1899 both the literary societies and fraternities had been revived, yet despite efforts to encourage literary society membership with significant prizes for oratory and extemporaneous speaking, they steadily lost ground to social fraternities. By 1889, 44 percent of Miami's students belonged to either Phi Delta Theta or Beta Theta Pi. In that year the oldest of the "Miami Triad" of fraternities, Beta Theta Pi, celebrated its fiftieth anniversary.

It was on the first Commencement day of President Warfield's administration that a reception was given at Western in honor of the *Beta Theta Pi* fraternity. At Miami's formal dinner following the reception, announcement was made that the *Beta* fraternity, which had been founded at Miami, had chosen a national symbol, the rose. Miss McKee had helped to select it and was a guest at the banquet when three roses were presented to John Covington, the toastmaster, who shared them with the founder and co-founder of the fraternity. These roses had been picked from a bush which climbed over the south end of the porch at Western, a bush cherished through many years as "The *Beta* Rose."

The novelty of college life in this era, however, was formally organized sports. Concern about pranks and drinking may have contributed to a "wholesale endorsement" of athletic programs by Miami's young president and faculty. Warfield permitted tennis courts to be built on campus "to break up the students' habit of loafing up town," and faculty and students played together. A football playing field was laid out with its south end in the vicinity of today's Irvin and Alumni Halls, and professors played there with students and townspeople. Apparently the first organized game pitted Miami against an independent Dayton team, the Stillwaters, featuring players who had learned the game at eastern colleges. Miami lost. The first organized intercollegiate game was played December 8, 1888, with the University of Cincinnati.

Baseball had been revived from Old Miami and with tennis, gymnastics, and football also under way, an athletic organization said to include all students in the university elected officers and charged its president and team captains to arrange games. The first annual meeting of the Miami University Athletic Club was held June 5, 1889. Walter Ray Bridgeman, graduate of Yale, professor of Greek, member of Delta Kappa Epsilon, and umpire in Miami's first intercollegiate football game, suggested to a student committee composed of two men and one woman that Miami's athletic colors be red and white. That suggestion was adopted.

Artist's rendering of the first Miami-Cincinnati football game, 1888. C. F. Payne, 1988. Miami Archives.

Miami baseball team, 1909. Miami Bulletin, July 1909. Miami Archives.

Ethelbert Dudley Warfield and "The First Football Game," 1888

The first intercollegiate football game was played between Rutgers and Princeton on November 6, 1869, at New Brunswick, New Jersey, with Rutgers winning 6 to 4. Both teams fielded twenty-five men. Players advanced the ball only by kicking or hitting it with their hands, heads, or sides, so this game resembled what Americans called soccer and the rest of the world called football. As the game developed, teams were reduced to eleven, with seven forwards, a quarterback, two halfbacks, and a fullback. The ball could be kicked or carried, and it could be thrown backward or laterally but not forward. There were no special uniforms or padding, and no substitutions.

This is the brand of football brought to Oxford by a graduate of Princeton, Ethelbert Dudley Warfield. He was the younger brother of famed Princeton theologian B. B. Warfield. With him came several other eastern Ivy Leaguers who played football, including Walter Ray Bridgeman, who had played at Yale. For entertainment in Oxford the faculty, including twenty-seven-year-old President War-field, played football in a field between Old Main and the future site of Alumni Library. They insisted that students join them. Clarence Dickinson, a fifteen-year-old freshman, recalled, "President Warfield, who was six feet four inches tall, broke through the line, knocking men right and left—till I was the only one between him and the goal! I can still hear the spares yelling 'Hold him, Dickie! Hold him!'—but he knocked me sprawling."

A knee injury incurred during a game prevented War-field from playing on Saturday, December 8, in the first of a long-running series of football contests between Miami University and the University of Cincinnati. The Cincinnati team, along with three fans, arrived shortly after noon at the railroad station. Their team averaged 162 pounds, whereas the Miami team averaged only 142 pounds. Professors Bridgeman and Parrott chose the players, and Parrott played left end.

Unfortunately, it began to rain. One observer wrote, "The rain did not slacken during the entire game and the players were soaked to the skin while the water oozed out of the spectators' shoes." Because of the downpour the game was called at 2:57 p.m., while still a scoreless tie (Cincinnati having nearly missed a goal as judged by Bridgeman, the umpire). The *Miami Student* reported, "Had the game been played to a finish it is safe to say that Miami would have been victorious." It also noted, "Foot-ball is getting in its deadly work. Some have bruised faces, some limp, some carry their arms in slings, and some walk as if they were weary of life."

The following year Miami played four games, winning all of them and outscoring opponents 100 to 4. Three opponents were held scoreless. The glorious football tradition of the Red and White had begun. Miami vs. Cincinnati is said to be the oldest frequently played rivalry west of the Alleghenies.

SCIENCE STIRS

Perhaps despite personal misgivings that scientific education lacked the rigor of requirements in ancient languages, President Warfield recognized that modern life required investment in the sciences. Although the trustees had eliminated the bachelor of science option on Warfield's arrival, he sought its reinstatement alongside the bachelor of arts, arguing that "popular appreciation" of natural science required it. Chemistry professor Snyder was more direct.

For there is no calling in modern life that is not being vitalized and energized, either indirectly by the scientific spirit of the age or directly by the adoption and use of scientific principles and methods. Furthermore, this fact is becoming generally recognized and often determines the place where a student will pursue his course of study.

In addition to a chemistry laboratory, two rooms in North Hall were given in 1888 to a new course in biology, and it was immediately overenrolled. Warfield began seeking state assistance to construct a new scientific laboratory building.

TRANSITIONS

Robert Hamilton Bishop Jr., who had been associated with Miami University for almost seventy years, died in 1890. That same year Warfield was offered the presidency of Ohio State University, which he declined. In 1891 he accepted the presidency of Lafayette College, a private institution, and three of his young faculty accepted offers at Yale, Lake Forest, and Syracuse. Bishop was memorialized during the 1891 commencement week in June. At the graduation ceremony, Ethelbert Dudley Warfield was awarded an honorary LLD degree.

About a month before Warfield's final Miami ceremony, LaFayette Walker, principal of Oxford College, gave an angry interview to a Hamilton newspaper, reprinted in the *Miami Student,* charging that "discipline at the University amounts to nothing." Walker accused Warfield and what he called Miami's "Dude Faculty" of permitting, even encouraging, Miami students to frequent seven saloons and a gambling house in Oxford. According to Walker, a Miami trustee had confided that his son was kept away from Miami "because he was afraid his boy would go to the devil." Walker suggested that Warfield and his faculty be replaced by "the sort of a man who would go across a field, talk education with a farmer's son and induce him and others to attend the University." At this time Miami students not living in North and South halls roomed in the town. "The boys," Walker added, "should room in dormitories under the supervision and care of married professors, whose wives could exert

LaFayette Walker, president of Oxford Female College, 1882–90, and Oxford College, 1890–1900. Photograph by Frank R. Snyder. Miami Archives and Smith Library.

a good moral influence over them. Students should not be allowed out of the building at night after 7:30 or 8:00 o'clock." This earned a response. The *Miami Student* denied all charges about Miami's condition, calling them "bosh." President Warfield was out of town. Upon his return he was greeted at the train station by a brass band and an assembly that paraded through Oxford to Warfield's home, where a rally was held with speeches by the president, members of his faculty, and Western Female Seminary principal Leila McKee.

Soon Warfield would be gone. Miami's next president, William Oxley Thompson (1891–99), had some of the personal traits that LaFayette Walker hoped for. He would preside for almost a decade during an even more rapid modernization of Miami and Oxford, institutionalizing by the turn of the nineteenth century a clear precursor to the modern university.

TOWARD 1899

Thompson had been president of Longmont College in Colorado, and viewed the job professionally. An ordained minister with an MA from Muskingum College, diplomatic rather than doctrinaire, he had great physical energy and was described by Trustee McSurely as "a frank, straightforward man," "free from crankiness," "substantial," and "well-rounded." Already widowed twice at the age of thirty-five when he came to Oxford, he married a Western Seminary instructor in 1894. At a point when Miami needed to

William Oxley Thompson, president of Miami University, 1891–99. Photograph by Baker's Art Gallery, Columbus, Ohio. Miami Archives.

increase enrollment, Thompson actively recruited students by touring southern Ohio, preaching and attracting young men to the university. When he took office in the fall of 1891, only 60 students were enrolled; by the next fall enrollment had jumped to 122. Nonetheless, he felt that in an era of expanding higher education, Miami should remain a relatively small college that gave personal attention to students.

President Thompson was a businesslike manager. Historian Bertha Boya Thompson compiled a record of his actions: He assessed a $5 fee to every student as a "Guarantee Fund" to cover costs of student pranks. He spoke against fraternity hazing; proposed the creation of a student government with responsibility for discipline in the dormitories; and oversaw completion in 1892 of Miami's first scientific laboratory building, Brice Hall, as well as a fully fenced athletic field on four acres of the botanical gardens. It had space for a baseball diamond, football field, half-mile track, and ticket office. Brice Hall was Miami's first building fully fitted with gas and heated by steam. It could generate its own electricity: "The electric system was a complete plant in itself, furnishing each room with light and supplying a current for charging a storage battery. The entire wiring of the building was done by Professor Snyder's students as a part of their laboratory work."

In 1892 the master of arts degree was professionalized by requiring both a period in residence and a specific course of study to earn the degree. Requirements for honors were added in 1897, and in 1899 a trustees committee completed a revision of the curriculum to accommodate additional elective options. The new curriculum made all subjects elective in the senior year. In 1899 the credit-hour requirement for graduation was set at 128, and a thesis requirement implemented. In 1898 Thompson proposed a probationary period of three to five years for new professors. In 1899, enrollment had grown to a New Miami high of 149, still almost all men.

Thompson was an effective political leader. He lobbied successfully for an 1896 bill introduced by Ohio Speaker of the House David L. Sleeper of Athens, Ohio, establishing a state tax to underwrite financial support of Ohio University and Miami University. In return, these universities were required to admit all qualified residents of Ohio free of tuition charges—a step Thompson had convinced the trustees to take four years earlier in order to attract more students. Miami's income increased by $8,000 after the first year of the new levy. At the urging of students, Thompson proposed, and the board built, a structure the president believed would be valuable in recruiting more students—a new gymnasium. "The growth of modern college life," said the *Miami Student*, "has made such an accommodation for students a necessity."

Miami's new gymnasium, augmenting its athletic field, arrived just in time to support new levels of intercollegiate competition. The Ohio Inter-Collegiate Athletic Association, formed in 1896, adopted uniform regulations established by college presidents meeting in Columbus: players had to be degree candidates; lists of competing participants were to be exchanged ten days prior to a game; umpires could not have affiliation with contesting institutions; and foul play and profanity were forbidden, as was any form of compensation to participants. Miami's new gymnasium, built on High Street north of North Hall, included a reading room, space to seat two hundred people for student meetings and the YMCA, a dressing room, lockers, showers, bathtubs and washbowls, an office for the physical director, and a 171 x 100-foot gym with an elevated track, twenty-one laps to the mile. The building was heated by steam and lighted by electricity; Professor Snyder and his physics students again supervised the wiring. This second New Miami building was officially named John Williamson Herron Gymnasium for the president of the board (who would serve as a trustee for fifty-two years). Commonly known as Miami Gymnasium, it

Laboratory class, 1908. Photograph by Frank R. Snyder. Miami Archives.

Herron Hall (1897). Miami
Archives.

opened for exhibitions in March 1897. By 1898 Miami welcomed there the popular sport of basketball. That same year an indoor athletic carnival was inaugurated, featuring class drills, work on gymnastic apparatus, short-distance races, jumping, vaulting, handball, and other events.

The year 1899 was an exemplary one for Miami. Marking seventy-five years since Old Miami classes opened in 1824, it was an opportunity to celebrate both the history of the university and the promise of its future. The desire to do so may have been stimulated by the quickening pace of change, or by the approaching turn of the century. In any event, markers of New Miami progress were showcased that year.

A thorough renovation of Old Main was undertaken for the diamond anniversary celebration during commencement week in June 1899. The West Wing was lengthened and a new East Wing and tower were added in 1898. Remodeling included the installation of central heating and electric lighting. Recognizing that literary societies were waning, the elocution teacher introduced the campus to its first dramatic entertainment—staged in Old Main's newly renovated chapel. Water, sewers, and steam heat were run to North and South halls, ending the students' seventy-five-year tradition of burning firewood, and bathrooms were installed there along with electric lighting. The board identified an area of campus north of the slant walk that bisected the campus from the northwest to the southeast to be protected from buildings not strictly for the university, such as fraternities. They also placed a new pump in the college well. In 1899 the first telephone came to South Hall. Thompson's final major project was initiated that year—raising money from trustees and alumni to build a new "fireproof" library that would protect Miami's document collection and allow expansion of its book holdings.

During commencement week, Phi Delta Theta, fifty years old in 1898, held public exercises. Board president Herron presided at an all-class reunion of Miami alumni in the renovated Old Main chapel. There were Class Day exercises, an oratorical contest, literary society reunions, an alumni dinner, a band concert, and an Oxford fireworks display. Whitelaw Reid, Class of 1856, a national political figure, former candidate for vice president, and editor of the *New York Tribune,* delivered a commencement address on twentieth-century foreign policy. He believed it would demand a departure from American isolationism.

William Oxley Thompson's eight-year presidency had been a success. For

Professor Henry Snyder, an outspoken partisan of scientific education, was a champion of the future who would not live to see it. On September 13, 1898, Snyder arrived to begin his thirteenth year at Miami. The following day his body was found next to an empty beaker in a Brice Hall chemistry laboratory.

Snyder was a Springfield, Ohio, native who attended Ohio State and was superintendent at Ohio Institute for the Blind in Columbus when McFarland recommended his appointment as the first New Miami professor of chemistry and physics. Snyder was industrious and well liked, and the husband of Minnie Snyder. As flamboyant as her husband was plain, Minnie enjoyed wearing gypsy attire, fancied herself a musician of the first order, and loved to display her talents before crowds. She organized an Oxford Quartette that included Daisy McCullough, one of Miami's first female students. Henry and Minnie lived in South Hall, where they were wary of students prone to playing pranks.

Minnie was determined to pursue a musical career. To reconcile professorial and domestic lives, Henry tried combining his science lecture and his wife's musical recital into a single performance. For one such event held in the Old Main chapel, the hall was said to be "filled with people, some having come to praise and some to scoff." Soon the Snyder show was on the road to surrounding towns, and Henry began a series of lectures at Oxford College. On stage, Minnie was decked out in colorful garb while

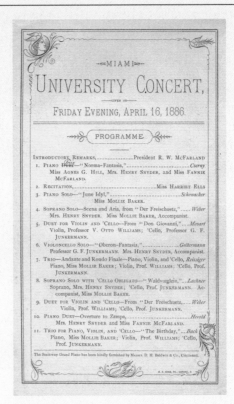

Miami University concert program, April 16, 1886. The tenth performance features a piano duet with Minnie Snyder and Fannie McFarland. *Miami Archives.*

Henry Snyder, professor of physics and chemistry, 1885–98. Recensio, 1894. Miami Archives.

Henry wore a drab formal coat and nonmatching gray trousers. Yet Henry warmed to the performance, becoming adept at using props and a slide projector. He could manipulate one of his devices, the "electrophorus," said to resemble "a pie pan filled with sealing wax," to emit large, mysterious sparks that thrilled audiences.

Oxford was shocked by Henry's sudden passing. The consensus was suicide, but not everyone accepted that explanation. Some suspected he had ingested the contents of a beaker found next to his body. Speculation on what it contained varied from potassium cyanide to a brew of poisons. In letters written to President Upham many years later, Minnie attributed Henry's demise to a combination of overwork—trying to please President Thompson—and kidney trouble. She said he worked so hard "he forgot his wife, his health and all pleasure working for Miami—Miami first—Miami always was his life." A November 1960 article in *Miami Dimensions* implied a more sinister scenario, noting that Minnie married again after Henry's death, and that her second husband, William Pugh, who played guitar in Minnie's orchestra, had also been Henry's laboratory assistant.

his focused and effective leadership, he was admired by the board of trustees, by Miami students, and by the public. In 1895 the *Miami Student* said:

The Doctor is an all around man. Among college professors he is a boy; among teachers he a hale fellow well met; among farmers you would imagine he was a granger; among students he is a friend of young men, inspiring hope in many a breast and imparting his own wonderful energy to others.

Thompson's popularity extended beyond Oxford. His predecessor, Warfield, would be the last Miami president to depart for a private institution. In 1899 Thompson declined an offer to become president of Wooster College and instead accepted the presidency at the Ohio State University. Miami trustees countered, offering to raise his salary from $3,500 to $5,000 if he would remain, but after the diamond anniversary celebration was behind him, Thompson announced his resignation. Trustee William J. McSurely, who assumed the interim presidency, wrote in his diary that as a result of Thompson's administration, "Miami University stands in a better position today to fulfill the high purposes of her organization than at any time in her long and honorable history."

"PREXY"

Guy Potter Benton was born in Kenton, Ohio, May 26, 1865. He attended schools in the Ohio countryside and demonstrated a first-class mind. A devout Methodist, he earned bachelor's, master's, and doctor of divinity degrees from Ohio Wesleyan University and Baker University in Kansas and was licensed as a Methodist Episcopal minister. In 1887 Benton's family relocated to Ft. Scott, Kansas. In 1889 he married, and began establishing a reputation as a talented school administrator. The next year, at age twenty-five, Benton became superintendent of Ft. Scott Schools, one of the five largest systems in the state. In 1895, he was named assistant superintendent for public instruction for Kansas, and in 1897 took a professorship of history and sociology at Baker University. Only a year later he was named president of Upper Iowa University. A born salesman and optimist with an uncanny ability to instill enthusiasm for his vision in others, he was temperamentally suited to an era when college presidents served their institutions as chief lobbyists and student recruiters. Benton reportedly never put on intellectual airs; he had a steady, warm, and outgoing nature and left an impression that he really meant what he said. Upper Iowa's student enrollment and endowment increased steadily, and Benton secured Andrew Carnegie's second unconditional gift for construction of a college library.

At Miami, meanwhile, President David Tappan (1899–1902) was not having a happy time. Despite the beginnings of regular state financial assistance and

The life of Peter Bruner was similar in some ways to those of other African Americans who came to Oxford after the Civil War; however, it was uniquely preserved in an autobiography, *A Slave's Adventures toward Freedom*, dictated to his daughter and published two decades before his death. Bruner was born near Winchester, Kentucky, in 1845. His mother was a slave and his father was their white owner. Bruner recounts whippings, beatings, and other injustices that led him to several unsuccessful attempts at escape. When the Union army came to central Kentucky in 1864, Bruner left his master. He enlisted, with other escaped slaves, in the Twelfth U.S. Heavy Artillery at Camp Nelson, Kentucky, but was assigned to ditch-digging and other menial duties. After being discharged in 1866 he moved to Oxford, where relatives resided. Bruner attended classes with other former slaves at a school taught by L. E. Grennan, but soon took employment in farm jobs, cutting wood, building fences, and harvesting crops. Within two years he had a house and a wife, Fannie Procton, with whom he eventually had five daughters.

When fire destroyed the Western Female Seminary in 1871, Bruner and others were hired to clear debris from the site and help rebuild. He worked there briefly as night watchman and tended the Western boiler. He soon returned to farming, but was hired again at Western, then at Oxford Female College, where he was responsible for everything from shoveling coal for the furnace to reminding students to wear their boots. Bruner's wife had worked for Oxford College, and they were married in its chapel. On their twenty-fifth wedding anniversary students and teachers presented the couple with gifts of silver and heartfelt congratulations.

During Tappan's presidency Bruner was hired as a custodian and bicycle messenger at Miami, where for thirteen years he earned the respect of students and faculty alike. Professor Robert Johnson reportedly gave Bruner a silk top hat, and Principal LaFayette Walker of Oxford College reportedly gave him a tuxedo in which he waited on President William Howard Taft during one of Taft's visits to Miami in 1905 or 1918. Miami president Thompson was so impressed with Bruner's sensible, practical view of life that he sometimes referred wayward students to Bruner for advice.

By the 1930s Peter Bruner was Oxford's last living Civil War veteran. He was enjoying retirement at his home on West Withrow Street when he was named "Mayor for a Day" in early 1938. His photograph, taken in the mayor's office, appeared on the front page of the local newspaper shortly after he died at the age of ninety-three on April 6 of that year.

Peter Bruner (1845–1938), after 1871 an employee of the Western Female Seminary, Oxford College, and Miami University. Photograph ca. 1890s. Miami Archives and Smith Library.

Train 41

The diary of Henrietta Hepburn, daughter of William Holmes McGuffey and wife of Professor A. D. Hepburn, provides a small window revealing early twentieth-century Oxford travel. In July 1902 Mrs. Hepburn celebrated her birthday with her son and grandchildren in College Hill, a Cincinnati suburb. Today such a trip might take an hour, but in her time most travel, even short excursions, was by railroad. Her plan was to go by train on the CH&D line from Oxford to Northside, a suburban stop five miles north of the downtown Cincinnati depot, and there take an electric streetcar to College Hill. Her son, Charlie, was to join her by boarding the same train at Winton Place. Generally, trains ran on time, but on the day of Mrs. Hepburn's journey the 5:00 a.m. train was an hour and a half late arriving in Oxford because the engine broke down somewhere up the line. However, it took only about twenty minutes to reach Hamilton, for no intermediate stops were made unless a passenger was boarding or detraining. Although there were thirteen small stations between Hamilton and Cincinnati, only local trains routinely stopped. Some terminated at Hamilton, so passengers desiring transit south were obliged to change trains. The station or ticket agent would have advised Mrs. Hepburn, since few laymen could decipher the printed timetable with its codes and symbols. It is likely that Mrs. Hepburn knew from experience that Train 41 worked best for her needs. On the single-track lines, sidetracks every few miles allowed mail and express passenger trains to pass local freight and passenger trains. Passengers were accustomed to sitting on a sidetrack. Mrs. Hepburn's travel time was about two hours, door to door.

Henrietta Hepburn was a child of the antebellum United States who lived to see remarkable modernization in the twentieth century, including an ability to make day trips to Cincinnati that would have been impossible in her childhood. Even so, as her birthday excursion suggests, train travel in 1902 was more complex than travelers today can readily imagine.

Oxford depot of Cincinnati, Hamilton & Dayton Railroad. Postcard ca. 1910s. *Miami Archives and Smith Library.*

Tappan's recruiting efforts, Miami's enrollment had stagnated. Then a typhoid epidemic struck in 1900. At least 40 of Miami's 150 students, and 100 townspeople, fell ill. South Hall was used as a hospital, but Tappan's youngest daughter died, along with two students. This epidemic was traced to shoddy plumbing in Old Main that contaminated the college well. The single bright spot for Miami early in 1902 was the announcement that the university would be the site of one of two state teacher training schools. Yet even these good tidings seemed lost on Tappan, who was unenthusiastic about having even a few women on campus. The prospect of having to deal with a normal college and its likely influx of women was partly responsible for his resignation after a three-year presidency.

In June 1902 Miami trustees unanimously offered the presidency to Guy Potter Benton (1902–11). Although Benton was comfortably situated, he could not resist returning to Ohio. Even before

David S. Tappan, president of Miami University, 1899–1902. *Miami Archives.*

his formal inauguration, Benton became a familiar figure in Oxford. Viewing students as members of a family, he set out to meet as many of them as possible. Benton always addressed students by their first names rather than the more formal "Mr." or "Miss." They responded by affectionately dubbing him "Prexy," a moniker he accepted as an honor.

Despite Benton's informality, his inaugural on September 18, 1902, was the first at which all participants wore academic robes—a move reflecting the new president's love of ceremony and tradition. His inaugural address was particularly notable for its enthusiastic endorsement of the Normal College. This was a watershed moment in Miami history, one that reflected Benton's conviction

Thobe

In 1930 Harry S. Thobe, master bricklayer, built a home in Oxford described by an observer as "the most remarkable piece of construction in this part of the country." His "Spanish bungalow, high-lighted in cut stone, the only one of its kind in America," was indeed a novelty. Built for sale next door to Thobe's own home—also of stone and featuring an array of innovations—his new seven-room masonry showcase had tile baseboards, floors, roof, porch, and awnings; copper drains; a built-in garage; a raised-hearth fireplace with a built-in nook and a "cathedral window"; cut-stone flowerboxes in exterior walls; a sunken garden, a fountain, and a lily pool; and "a chimney with a 300-apartment bird house." The luxuries of hot-water heat and cedar-lined closets lured "hundreds" of visitors who "marveled at the wonderful craftsmanship."

Born in Covington, Kentucky, in 1870, Thobe studied at Cincinnati's Ohio Mechanics Institute, one of the nation's first technical schools. He moved from Middletown to Oxford in 1895 to build a new railroad depot. He laid brick for Miami's first residence for women, Hepburn Hall, in 1905. He donated and built nearby the rough stone "Thobe's Fountain" that served as a memorable campus gathering spot for students well into the second half of the twentieth century. As Oxford expanded, Thobe built stately brick homes identifiable today by strikingly precise corners and "silver-dollar thin" mortar lines. He built an imposing fireplace in the main parlor of Peabody Hall at Western College, and a classic train station for Oxford that served generations of students, faculty, and townspeople. His work can be seen in Hall Auditorium, originally Benton Hall, an administration building and assembly hall built in 1908.

Thobe bred fanaticism for Miami sports. He attended every athletic event, decked out in a red-trimmed white suit with one red and one white shoe, carrying a signature red and white megaphone and umbrella. He did a "hula dance" and displayed a string of

(continued)

"The Spanish Bungalo," 205 West Chestnut Street, Oxford, built by Harry S. Thobe, 1930. Ralph J. McGinnis, History of Oxford, Ohio, 1930.

Harry S. Thobe, late 1940s. Miami Archives.

firecrackers. He predicted scores from visions he said came in dreams, and claimed that he was admitted free to every event as part of the pageantry of the occasion, often marching into football games with the band. He had detractors, and some officials tried to eject him, but Ralph McGinnis remembered him fondly.

A half dozen times a year Thobe and Dean Brandon have put on an act which alone was worth the price of admission at football games. This act was a remarkable exhibition of dignified pursuit on the part of the good Dean and of naïve innocence on the part of Thobe. Mr. Brandon, fully conscious of the dignity his position demanded, and Thobe with no dignity at all but an unlimited zeal for the home team, curving around the track in front of the east stands was a sight few can forget. Both alike, Dean Brandon with his cigarette getting shorter and shorter and his neck getting redder and redder, and Thobe with his feet getting more and more out of control were oblivious to the wide variety of advice, encouragement and just plain abuse emanating from the delighted crowd.

Harry Thobe died in 1950 at the age of eighty. He claimed to have attended fifty-four consecutive Homecoming games wearing his flamboyant garb, at times with diamond studs in his teeth. As a bricklayer, he was literally a builder of New Miami. As an intense follower of Miami athletics, so effective at crowd appeal that he was hired to perform at professional games for the Cincinnati Reds, he was a forerunner of modern sports fans.

Thobe's Fountain, early twentieth century. Photograph by Gilson P. Wright. Miami Archives.

Administration building (1908). Later named Benton Hall, then Hall Auditorium. Photograph by Frank R. Snyder. Miami Archives.

that Miami needed to grow in order to survive, and that the enrollment of women intending to become teachers would assure that positive future.

Soon after taking office, Benton announced an ambitious goal of 1,000 students by 1905 and offered students a holiday when enrollment reached 300. He devoted much of his time to personally recruiting new students throughout Ohio or corresponding with potential enrollees. It was soon evident that Benton could succeed, and while Miami did not reach his lofty goal during his presidency, enrollment by 1911 had surpassed 600. More students brought more faculty. During Benton's tenure their number nearly doubled, reaching 46 in 1911. The curriculum was expanded; departments of history, sociology, and economics were created; and the first full-time music instructor was employed. Electives were increased, though students had to select courses within groupings that corresponded to majors and minors.

This professionalizing era was built on practices crafted by President Thompson and fueled by success of the Normal College. With institutional growth came bureaucratic specialization, and the responsibilities of some positions became too complicated for a single person to manage easily. When the Normal College was created with its first dean, Franklin B. Dyer, in 1902, A. D. Hepburn was named Miami's first vice president and dean of the College of Liberal Arts. When Hepburn retired in 1908, Benton took a step that would recur many times as Miami grew—he split the position. He appointed Raymond M. Hughes as dean of Liberal Arts and Edgar E. Brandon as university vice president. Both proved to be highly effective, as did other appointees chosen by Benton, particularly the first dean of women, Elizabeth Hamilton, and Normal College dean Harvey Minnich.

One of Benton's most popular appointments was colorful gymnasium director and physical education professor Frederic "Cap" Stone, who joined the faculty in 1902. "Champion Athlete of America" from 1874 to 1884, Stone looked like a pint-sized, bald version of former heavyweight boxing champion John L. Sullivan. He was an international authority on physical fitness who rescued the athletic and physical education programs from unpopularity. Physical culture classes became mandatory for all, and, reflecting the

Cephas Burns, 1871–1935

During the presidency of William W. Boyd, ten stone footbridges and more than a dozen stone lampposts were built by Cephas Burns on the campus of the Western College for Women between 1917 and 1925. An African American stonemason who lived in Oxford and worked with a team of African American masons, Burns carefully selected "cannonball" stones from nearby creeks to replace earlier wooden bridges with picturesque spans that lent great charm to the rolling landscape. Harry Thobe also worked at Western College. Fireplaces and chimneys of Western Lodge and the Edgar Stillman Kelley Studio, however, are credited to Burns, as is some of the stonework for Kumler Memorial Chapel.

Western College bridge built by Cephas Burns (1920s). Scott Kissell, IT Services, 2007. *Miami Archives.*

Cephas Burns, builder of Western College bridges. *Smith Library.*

Guy Potter Benton, president of Miami University, 1902–11. Photograph by Frank R. Snyder. Miami Archives and Smith Library.

Promotional card for Miami University, ca. 1906. Miami Archives and Smith Library.

coeducational reality of New Miami, athletic teams were formed for both men and women. The men's football program had an undefeated season in 1907 under Coach Amos Foster, whom the *Miami Student* saw as "a man who inspires men."

Benton built facilities for the modernizing university: Hepburn Hall in 1905, a Brice Hall addition in 1906, a central heating plant in 1907, and an auditorium in 1908. Yet he recognized that an institution of higher learning was only as good as its library. In 1906, elaborating on a strategy first proposed at Miami by President Thompson, Benton approached Andrew Carnegie for a matching grant to build a new library. Carnegie agreed to fund about half the $80,000 cost, with the stipulation that Oxford residents be allowed to use the library along with Miami students and faculty. Benton spent the next three years raising money from alumni and private donors, and Miami's Alumni Library opened its doors in April 1910. That year the first wing of a new home for the Normal College, eventually known as McGuffey Hall, was also completed. In 1911 work began on a second women's dormitory, which opened as Bishop Hall shortly after Benton's departure from Oxford.

Benton holds a place among Miami's most successful lobbyists. The state funded many physical improvements during his presidency, and in 1906 Benton brought great skill to a lobbying effort against the Lybarger Bill. Under the provisions of that bill, only the normal colleges at Miami and Ohio universities would have continued to receive support. All state funding for liberal arts would have gone to the Ohio State University, where William Oxley Thompson was president. Outraged by what he considered to be Ohio State's arrogance and Thompson's betrayal of Miami, Benton rallied faculty, students, trustees, and alumni to Miami's defense. He traveled to Columbus to meet at length with legislators. Partly because of his efforts the Lybarger Bill was defeated and a compromise measure adopted that secured Miami and Ohio universities' liberal arts colleges from legislative attacks. When Benton returned to campus, he was acclaimed the "Savior of Miami."

When Benton began preparing to celebrate the centennial of Miami's chartering in 1809, he had a clear goal—he wanted to showcase Miami's progress and achievements. The Centennial Week celebration in June 1909 would mark the high point of his presidency. From June 12 to 17, Miami and Oxford took on a holiday atmosphere, with hundreds of visitors and alumni treated to a nonstop regimen of receptions, parades, conferences, and class reunions. Centennial Week culminated in the eighty-fifth commencement exercises, staged with all the formal trappings and academic regalia possible. The 1909 graduating class of thirty-five men and twenty women was the largest yet in Miami history.

By 1910, Benton was being courted by other institutions. He turned down an offer to become president of Boston College, but after nine years of unprecedented activity, even this energetic man had tired of the constant traveling, lobbying, and recruiting associated with the New Miami presidency that he had significantly shaped. Feeling that the university's future was now ensured by a modernized campus, steadily growing enrollment, and state support, he longed for a quieter environment, and when he was offered the presidency of the University of Vermont, he resigned from Miami in June 1911.

Guy Potter Benton (seated, second from left) with students, ca. 1905. Miami Archives.

Alumni Library (1910). Photograph by Frank R. Snyder, 1911. Miami Archives and Smith Library.

The Miami University Band. Miami Bulletin, 1909. Miami Archives.

The third week in June was marked by a highly significant and somewhat unusual occasion down in the southwest corner of Ohio. Miami University, old mother Miami, was celebrating the completion of her first centenary of corporate existence; and her children, unto the third and fourth generation, came from the corners of the earth bringing tribute of congratulation and good wishes. The village of Oxford was in holiday attire; but festooned bunting seemed tawdry and commonplace against the rare old-fashioned beauty of the wide, shady streets, the green inviting door-yards, and the leafy vistas of the University grounds. The weather was nearly—if not quite—perfect, making it possible to do most of the celebrating out among the trees.

The elaborate program for the week was carried out with most of the accessories that convention had attached of late to such affairs. One night the students made merry at the expense of the faculty, and paraded themselves about the campus burning quantities of red fire. On other nights a select few of them did Shakespeare and the like before sweltering audiences, as a relief from the interminable speech-making. There were various processions of black gowns and mortar-boards, at which certain of the old-timers stood aghast, protesting vigorously that they didn't trifle with such things in their day. His Excellency the Governor was on hand to represent the Commonwealth, attended by his imposing retinue in tight uniforms and gold braid. There was music by the band and music by the glee club; then there were some more speeches. Honorary degrees were distributed with the somewhat liberal hand characteristic of such events. There was also a graduating class, much the largest in the history of the institution, but in the excitement it had the habit of slipping modestly into the background and being lost to view.

Thus wrote Alfred H. Upham, professor of English and later president of Miami, at the beginning of an essay for the *Ohio Archaeological and Historical Quarterly.* He added a brief sketch of Miami history and ended with a tabulation of Miamians in professions or public service. These included one president of the United States, 7 senators, 10 governors, 30 college presidents, 274 teachers, 327 lawyers, 313 ministers (presumably no priests or rabbis), and 122 physicians—impressive for a total alumni count of 1,826 at the time.

Miami's centennial celebration began by taking up the question of when the university actually began. At issue was whether the genesis of Miami was at its charter in 1809 or at the opening of its first classes in 1824. A formal action by the trustees eliminated this problem. Despite the fact that Miami, citing 1824 as its first year of operation, had formally celebrated its seventy-fifth anniversary only ten years earlier, the trustees now ruled that Miami offi-cially began in 1809 and therefore its centenary would be celebrated in 1909—the same year, in fact, that they issued their dictum.

This ruling may have been prompted by recognition that since 1907, President Benton had been planning an ambitious celebration for 1909. A committee of faculty, trustees, and alumni had been appointed with Upham as chairman. Minutes of their meetings over two years reveal considerable optimism and ambition as well as occasional disappointment. For example, invitations went out to civic and educational leaders across the country, but the response from distant regions was not always positive. Hopes that President Taft or his vice president might make an appearance were in the air until the last moment, but attendees had to make do with Ohio governor Harmon and the U.S. commissioner of education. Taft's father-in-law, John W. Herron, had been president of Miami's board of trustees since 1880, but this familial link was apparently not enough to lure Taft to Oxford, although he had delivered Miami's 1905 commencement address when he was secretary of war. University presidents representing major regions of the nation were invited; however, the presidents of Princeton, Yale, and Columbia all sent regrets. Professor Charles Wesley Hargitt of Syracuse, who had been a member of the Miami faculty from 1888 to 1891, gave an address on behalf of colleges in the East. The work of the committee and responses to its invitations suggest that after one hundred years Miami was aspiring to national status, but was not yet nationally compelling.

The centennial committee ambitiously promoted the recovery and preservation of Miami history. It recommended that a room be set aside for a Miami history museum, but it is not clear that this was achieved. It proposed that Alumni and Field Secretary B. S. Bartlow send "blank sheets of writing paper of uniform size and quality with the request that [each alumnus] write thereon in duplicate a brief account of his life, together with such incidents connected with his university career as he may think well to record." This scheme evolved into a four-page questionnaire Secretary Bartlow mailed to alumni inviting responses on fraternity membership, military service, holding of civil office, and special questions addressed to clergy, attorneys, and physicians. The result was Bartlow's *General Catalogue of the Graduates and Former Students of Miami University including Members of The Board of Trustees and Faculty during its First Century, 1809–1909.* This is a rich source of information on early Miamians, including one hapless alum who was "unintentionally killed by a party of masked men, August, 1873."

Two other publications that resulted from centennial planning were Alfred Upham's *Old Miami: The Yale of the Early West* and President Benton's *The Real College. Old Miami*, despite its subtitle, rarely if ever mentions Yale, nor does it refer frequently to Miami's academic, intellectual, or religious life, instead opting for a nostalgic paean to undergraduate bonhomie written in a hale-fellow-well-met tone. President Benton's book was a more philosophical defense of the liberal arts college, an institution that in his view was threatened by the rise of the research university and a national tendency toward professional education at both graduate and undergraduate levels. Benton held up Miami as the prototype of a "real college" whose faculty were "virile" as well as learned, shaping students who were scholars, patriots, and men of character.

The formal centennial celebration ran from Saturday, June 12, through Thursday, June 17. Saturday began with a farewell chapel service in the morning and a "Students' Night" later in the day, which included historical pageants, a torchlight parade, and a campus concert. Sunday began with a baccalaureate sermon delivered by Benton on "The Permanency of the Kingdom." Even in New Miami the presidential function at times took on religious dimensions, and the exercise for Sunday evening was similarly titled "Annual Sermon before Christian Associations."

Monday events consisted of the Annual Gold Medal Oratorical Contest, a reunion of Normal College alumni, and the class day program and play of the Normal College. The next afternoon the Normal College held its commencement exercises, conferring degrees on twenty-seven graduates—including three men. That same day, the College of Liberal Arts held its class day exercises, then all of Miami's living former presidents—Hepburn, McFarland, Tappan, Thompson, and Warfield—attended receptions for alumni who graduated during their administrations. President and Mrs. Benton, the initial First Family to live in Lewis Place, hosted a reception there for current graduates. In the evening, Liberal Arts seniors presented Shakespeare's *Twelfth Night*.

The Centennial Procession began Wednesday morning at a quarter to nine. After an invocation, the main address was delivered by the Reverend Henry Mitchell MacCracken, Class of 1857 and chancellor of New York University. Congratulatory addresses were then delivered by the U.S. commissioner of education (apparently by proxy); Governor Harmon; and presidents of colleges representing the different sections of the nation: Syracuse for the east,

Missouri for the west, Central University (now Centre College) for the south, and Oberlin for Ohio. The presidents of nearby Western and Oxford colleges contributed further congratulations, as did representatives of Miami faculty, alumni, students, and former presidents (delivered by William Oxley Thompson of the Ohio State University). There was a musical interlude, then President Benton and Dr. John M. Withrow, a trustee, offered formal responses. A *Centennial Ode*, delivered by General Benjamin Piatt Runkle, and a benediction brought the morning's exercises to a close. Runkle began his verses by proclaiming:

> We sing not the "Yale of the West," Name most fair,
> Nor the Harvard nor Princeton, renowned as they are,
> But Miami the earnest, the pure and the strong,
> With her record of deeds, is the core of our song.

Thursday was devoted to the week's climactic event, commencement exercises of the College of Liberal Arts. After a procession, prayer, and chorale, addresses were delivered by Columbia's Brander Matthews, the first American to hold a professorship of dramatic literature, and by Lyman Abbott, Henry Ward Beecher's successor at Pilgrim Congregational Church in Brooklyn and a major voice of religious liberalism. Bachelor of arts degrees were conferred on fifty-five young men and women—the largest class in Miami's history—and Edna Laura Forrey and Walter Scott Fogarty received the master of arts in German and history, respectively. The ceremony ended with the singing of "Old Miami." Not yet officially Miami's alma mater, the words of "Old Miami" had been composed by Professor Upham while he was an undergraduate in the 1890s. It was probably sung to the tune of "Oh My Darling, Clementine" on this occasion. A reception hosted by President Benton brought an end to the week of celebration.

Miami's centennial celebration revealed a college whose culture had become more secular and collegiate than Calvinist, although an atmosphere of generic Protestantism still shaped it. Miami leaders, though proud of the university's achievements and character, eagerly aspired to broader national recognition and hoped these commemorative rites would draw favorable attention. It was, in short, in a state of self-commendation, self-evaluation, aspiration, and transition—much as it would be at the time of its bicentennial.

Miami Centennial Celebration, "Procession of Administrations." Miami Bulletin, 1909. Miami Archives.

Academic procession at 1905 Miami commencement. Commencement speaker Secretary of War William H. Taft, is in the second row next to President Benton. Photograph by Frank R. Snyder. Miami Archives.

The peace and quiet Benton hoped for in Vermont proved temporary. When the United States entered World War I in 1917, he became the nation's first college president to serve in overseas war work. Between 1917 and 1920, he held a number of posts, including general secretary of the YMCA for the city of Paris and chief educational director of the American Army of Occupation at Coblenz. For his war efforts, Benton received the Distinguished Service Medal and the French Academy's Medal of Honor. After briefly

Slant Walk with Centennial Gate, ca. 1909. Miami Archives.

flirting with a business career in New York, Benton went to the Philippines in 1920 as an educational consultant. True to form, in 1921 he became the third president of the University of the Philippines, but his life was cut short by a disease contracted in 1923. He returned to the United States and died in 1927, in Minneapolis.

As Guy Potter Benton wished, he was buried in the Miami University plot of Oxford Cemetery. During his presidency he had succeeded in breathing new life into an institution that was yet uncertain of its identity and future prospects. He had sold Miami on the idea that prosperity depended on becoming something more than a college looking nostalgically to Old Miami. Under his leadership the university became capable of withstanding a great depression and another world war, and foreshadowed the institution we know today.

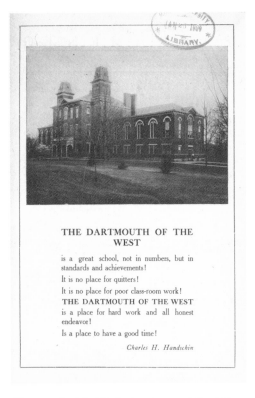

THE DARTMOUTH OF THE WEST

is a great school, not in numbers, but in standards and achievements!

It is no place for quitters!

It is no place for poor class-room work!

THE DARTMOUTH OF THE WEST is a place for hard work and all honest endeavor!

Is a place to have a good time!

Charles H. Handschin

"Dartmouth of the West" advertisement. Miami Student, January 1909. Miami Archives.

The Emergence of Professional Schools

TEACHING TEACHERS AND CHANGING SOCIETY

Creation of the Ohio State Normal College in 1902 changed Miami University. As Miami's first twentieth-century professional school, the Normal College dramatically expanded the preparation of teachers and came to include related fields in physical education, family life, manual arts, health care, and school administration. It introduced new teaching practices in applied studies and broadened Miami's boundaries by working with local school districts and bringing educators into new summer school and degree programs. In the years immediately following 1902, the most visible impact of the professional school was to make Miami truly coeducational, as hundreds of women enrolled and others took new positions as Miami's first women faculty. Normal College programs also attracted older professional students and Miami's first African American students. From its distinctive building on the southwest corner of the Oxford campus—today's McGuffey Hall—the Normal College played a key role in modernizing Miami University.

The designation "normal college" is derived from the French term *école normal,* indicating a broad nonspecialized education to prepare teachers for general instruction. In the nineteenth century most normal programs were two-year courses of study in general academic work, classroom pedagogy, and an early form of psychology, usually offered as part of secondary education, in summer institutes, or weekend programs. Nineteenth-century teachers often had no formal training, and particularly in the Midwest and West, where educated citizens were few, many new teachers had been students in the same schools only days before.

Teachers' conference, Ohio State Normal College, 1910. Photograph by Frank R. Snyder. Miami Archives.

Drawing from Recensio, 1911.

The Ohio State Normal College of Miami University. Miami Bulletin, 1909. *Miami Archives.*

Normal College practice teaching class, 1916. Photograph by Frank R. Snyder. Miami Archives.

Before 1902 some Miami graduates had entered careers in education, and a nondegree program for teacher preparation, the Normal Department, enrolled sixty-three men in 1854. Some who completed the program became professional tutors, while others taught for a few years as they prepared for other professional studies or more lucrative careers in law or medicine. Still others linked teaching with religious or reform impulses. For example, Mitchell Brown earned an AB at Miami in 1840, was ordained as a minister in Illinois in 1846, and after the Civil War, moved to Nashville to teach in a United Presbyterian school for freed slaves.

Teaching became principally a woman's occupation after the Civil War, because of the reduced male population and an effort by school reformers like

Horace Mann and Henry Barnard to promote the growth of public education by hiring women. Women, they argued, were good candidates for teaching because they had a humanizing influence in the classroom—and they could be paid less than men. By 1880 over half of all American teachers were women.

Since Miami had suspended college operation for much of the postwar period during which the gender shift in teacher education occurred, calls for the admission of women came later at Miami than elsewhere. Even though Miami prohibited enrollment of women until 1887, they could study at the Oxford Female Institute, Oxford Female College, or Western Female Seminary. Western offered the most rigorous academic work and some teacher training. Like its model, Mt. Holyoke College, it promoted teaching as a means for spreading Christian values and culture. As pressure to educate women rose, the presence of relatively large numbers of women students in Oxford significantly affected the community. Although annual enrollments fluctuated, in 1856, for example, 487 women were enrolled in Oxford's women's schools, more than double Miami's student population of 206 men.

In the late nineteenth century, the now-familiar methods of school organization and instruction—separating students into grades, standardizing buildings and classrooms, and developing district schooling and administrative structures—became common. By the early twentieth century, states had begun systematic regulation of college teacher preparation and certification programs. The creation of common readers or textbooks such as the McGuffey *Eclectic Readers* allowed teachers to design common assignments for students, systemizing methods of instruction.

Despite the increasing demand, Miami offered no formal teacher preparation program between 1865 and 1902. Ohio lagged behind all other states in creating institutions for teachers, and by 1902, Ohio and Arkansas were the only states without a state teacher training college. At Miami one barrier was opening the university to women. In 1887, the trustees admitted five women as "special students" who could attend classes but not work toward a degree, but only in 1891, the first year of Thompson's presidency, when twenty-four women entered the university, did the faculty vote to permit two of them— Mary S. Paxton, age twenty-one, and Margaret A. Hewett, age seventeen— to enroll as freshmen in the baccalaureate curriculum. The following year, the board of trustees affirmed a resolution stating that "all persons, regardless of sex, who make application, may be admitted upon the same terms into the university classes, to wit: Freshman, Sophomore, Junior, and Senior years and that all applicants may pursue, as well, studies in the regular college classes." Official permission notwithstanding, attrition was high for women in their early years at Miami. The first three to graduate—Elizabeth Beaton, Fannie Smith, and Mary Ada Gerber—earned bachelor's degrees in 1900. Beaton and Smith went on to distinguished careers in the classroom; Beaton taught in Oxford public schools for twenty-eight years. None of these early women graduates was enrolled in a teacher training school.

In 1902, state representative Charles F. See proposed a bill allocating $67,000 to establish normal colleges at Ohio University and Miami University. Miami's opened September 10, 1902, under the name Ohio State Normal College, a name it held until 1915. The college was immediately popular—seventy-one students, most of them women, arrived for its first classes in 1902. By May 1903, attrition had reduced that number to forty, about evenly divided between men and women.

Most Normal College students were high school graduates from Ohio, but there were some college graduates and experienced teachers who came to further their education. Miami provided them with new library books and outfitted a classroom for the instruction of nature study. Following state regulations, curricula were developed for elementary and secondary teachers, school administrators, and special teachers of drawing, music, industrial education, and domestic science. Yet for almost a decade there was no separate education building, so Normal College students shared facilities with other Miami students at Old Main, Brice Scientific Hall, Herron Gymnasium, and, after 1908, Benton Hall and Alumni Library. At first, women students rented rooms in the homes of townspeople. Because the number of females on campus in this late Victorian age raised questions about social propriety, the trustees soon decided to construct a dormitory to house them. Between 1903 and 1905 Normal College enrollment leapt from 161 to 261 students. In 1903, the university began a summer school that, within a few years, offered more than a hundred classes, mostly for education students and teachers from districts in southwest Ohio. Women constituted much of this enrollment. By 1910 women students outnumbered men in the entire university by 311 to 295, and in the Normal College there were 206 women and 51 men.

The first African American students working toward a degree at Miami came through the Normal College doors, and in 1905, education student Nellie Craig became the first African American to complete a Miami program of study. A native of Oxford, she taught elementary school in Oxford and in Union County, Indiana, before moving to Cleveland, where she became a leading member of the city's Black Women's Club. Lametta Granger was the next African American graduate, in the Class of 1907. After receiving her diploma, Granger taught in Farmersville and Xenia. A number of male African American students attended industrial education classes, following the conventional wisdom that African American men should perfect skills in manual labor rather than enter professions.

Fannie Smith, Class of 1900, ca. 1930. One of the first women to receive a Miami bachelor's degree. Miami Archives.

Male Normal College students, ca. 1910. Miami Archives.

Normal College senior class, 1906, including Lametta Granger, Miami's second African American Normal College graduate (second row, on left). Photograph by Frank R. Snyder. Miami Archives.

An entry in the student newspaper in December 1908 read: "Did it ever occur to you to what extent Miami has become a teachers' college? Some time ago the editor heard a few Miami boys calling a baseball team from a neighboring university 'a bunch of school-teachers.'" But in fact, the author reflected, Miami itself was taking on that very identity, and not merely in the Normal College. Of the living alumni of the College of Liberal Arts in 1908, one-third were teachers, confirming Miami's important early role as an educator of educators.

Almost immediately the Normal College developed a distinctive culture. In daily life its students interacted with other university students. While some students could eat in boarding establishments, most Miami freshmen

The earliest reference to a possible African American student at Miami was a mention in the November 1895 *Miami Student* of a "colored minister now taking some work at the University." The minister's name and exact status are unknown, but he was most likely a "special" or "irregular" student not pursuing a degree.

Miami's first known full-time African American student was Oxford native Nellie Craig, who enrolled at the Ohio State Normal College in 1903 and received her diploma in 1905. Miami's female African American population increased 100 percent the next year when it accepted Lametta Granger. The first known male African American student admitted to the university was Earl Kelley, who graduated from the Normal College in 1910 with a diploma in manual arts. Miami's first African American bachelor's degree recipients were William Hargraves and Eleanor Reece, who received a bachelor of arts and a bachelor of science, respectively, in 1925. Reece previously had earned an associate degree from Ohio University, which graduated its first African American student in 1828.

Despite growth in African American enrollment prior to World War II, Miami policy prohibited African American students from residing in its dormitories, with the exception of male athletes—who were assigned to the basement of Swing Hall. Other male African American students (all from Oxford) apparently lived with their parents. African American women students resided in university-sanctioned "cottages," the homes of Oxford families, just as did many white female students.

Miami's residence halls for women were not integrated until 1945, when Myldred Boston and Arie Parks became the first female African American students allowed to live on campus. They were assigned to a basement room in Oxford College between the smoking lounge and furnace room. Appalled by the location, Boston contacted the assistant dean of women, who provided her with names of African American families in Oxford with whom she could room. The next year Boston was assigned to Tallawanda Apartments, and her last two years to North Residence Hall (later Hamilton). Parks remained alone in the Oxford College room but did not return to Miami the following year.

Athletic competition was an arena where African American men played a prominent role in Miami's early twentieth century history. Miami's first known African American varsity athlete was Amsden Oliver, who lettered in track from 1934 to 1936, became an NCAA All-

Myldred Boston, Class of 1949, one of the first two African American women assigned to a residence hall. Recensio, 1947.

American, and was eventually inducted into Miami's athletic Hall of Fame. Oliver was the first African American to live in a dormitory, New Freshman Dormitory (today's Swing Hall), in 1933–34. Miami's first African American football star, halfback Jerry Williams, made the All-Buckeye conference team in 1938. Before coming to Miami, Williams had been a member of a national championship track team that included the immortal Jesse Owens.

Although fraternities and sororities provided social activities for members during the early twentieth century, such events were for white students only. African American students were, however, allowed to work at these events and thus glimpsed the houses and activities that were unavailable to them. As more minority students enrolled, they formed support groups. By 1939, Les Travailleurs had emerged to encourage "better feeling between the races . . . to aid its members along intellectual and cultural lines."

Before World War II, many facilities in the Oxford community were segregated. In the postwar years, returning veterans demanded better treatment, and the local chapter of the National Association for the Advancement of Colored People took on strength. Eventually remaining formal barriers in theatres, restaurants, and barbershops fell away, and the public swimming pool was finally opened to all.

ate together in the Commons at Old Main, and all were required to attend daily chapel and church in town the third Sunday of every month. In other ways the Normal College functioned largely as an institution independent of the university, with its own departmental clubs, singing groups, and a literary society, as well as athletic associations, including a women's basketball team, and chapters of the YWCA and YMCA. Chapters of national honorary societies in education, Kappa Delta Pi and Kappa Phi Kappa, were established in 1922 and 1925. Social and professional connections among students did not end with graduation—the first meeting of the Normal College alumnae association met in Hartwell, Ohio, in October 1913.

Normal College students faced social restrictions that reflected society's expectations of schoolteachers. A 1916 regulation stated that Normal College female students were permitted to go to town any night of the week, but could be accompanied by men on only two nights. The dean's report in 1928 noted with alarm an increase in cigarette smoking; because the public schools opposed smoking by women teachers, the dean announced that any woman student preparing to be a teacher would be suspended if she was found smoking.

The Normal College introduced pedagogical variety to Miami classrooms. Teacher education relied on innovative activities as future teachers studied new ideas in educational psychology and pedagogy and practiced their future occupation. In some classes students taught their classmates while the professor stood back and observed the interaction; others were known for discussion and debate; another role-played possible classroom scenarios for engaging young children in learning.

Manual Arts Club, including Earl Kelly, first African American male to graduate from the Normal College (back row, sixth from left). Recensio, 1910.

The McGuffey Laboratory School, founded in 1910, enrolled an average of four hundred school-age students annually in the 1920s and served as the training site for about one hundred student teachers each year. "Practice teaching" distinguished education schools from other academic programs, and many developed laboratory or model schools to offer practical experience prior to graduation. Miami students also completed student teaching in public schools in Oxford, Hamilton, and Middletown. The Laboratory School was an open-admission school run by the university, although African American students were not admitted until 1965. It offered kindergarten through fourth grade in its first semester of operation, and through twelfth grade by the

Normal College basketball team, 1904. Miami Archives.

end of its second year and thereafter. It eventually occupied the entire south wing of McGuffey Hall, and had both a cafeteria and a gymnasium where, in the 1930s, the office of its head football coach, Wilbur "Weeb" Ewbank, was located. He would become a legendary winner at all levels of the sport, the only coach to win championships in both the National and American professional football leagues.

The Normal College quickly earned a reputation for preparing good teachers. Of the sixty-four graduates of the class of 1913, for example, fifty-four immediately received jobs in schools, mostly in Ohio. Some graduates had distinguished careers. Josephine Leach, later Mrs. William B. Guitteau, graduated in 1907, after which she taught in Urbana, Ohio, and in North Carolina.

Costumed students in McGuffey High School play, 1912. Photograph by Frank R. Snyder. Miami Archives and Smith Library.

Weeb Ewbank on the McGuffey High School faculty, 1930–43. Photograph by Frank R. Snyder. Miami Archives.

Thomas Cheeks, Class of 1929, Bishop Medal recipient, 1976. Recensio, *1929.*

Later she studied at the University of Chicago and taught at the Francis Parker School, which was renowned for its progressive educational philosophy drawing on the ideas of John Dewey. Leach taught at Bowling Green State Normal School before moving to Toledo to become director of teacher training in that city, then assistant superintendent, and later a member of the board of education. In the 1930s she entered the legal profession, and in 1938 became the first woman appointed to Miami's board of trustees.

Thomas Cheeks, another notable graduate of the Normal College, earned a bachelor's degree in education in 1929, and became the first African American to graduate from Miami with a major in physical education. Cheeks's grandfather was Peter Bruner, an escaped slave who had become a prominent Oxford resident after the Civil War. With his encouragement, Cheeks followed his dream of attending Miami University and making a difference in society. He had a distinguished high school coaching career in Evansville, Indiana, where his team won two national basketball championships in a racially segregated high school league. In the early 1950s Cheeks moved to Milwaukee, where he became that city's first African American public high school teacher. In 1964 Cheeks was named Coordinator of School and Community Relations for Milwaukee Public Schools.

In the early years of the Normal College, there were nine full-time faculty who taught academic courses and physical education. By 1911 that number had increased to twenty-five, and in 1928 there were sixty faculty, thirty-four of them women. The first dean of the Normal College left after one year to become superintendent of Cincinnati public schools. The second, Harvey C. Minnich, reshaped the character of the college over the next twenty-six years. Minnich was a former teacher from rural Darke County and a former

Harvey C. Minnich, dean of the Ohio State Normal College, using dictaphone, 1912. Photograph by Frank R. Snyder. Miami Archives and Smith Library.

superintendent. During his tenure he introduced coursework in biology and nature study, manual arts, and domestic science, founded the laboratory school, and taught educational administration. He oversaw construction of the Normal College facility. Built in three stages, McGuffey Hall emerged between 1909 and 1924 to be one of the largest buildings on campus. Minnich modernized the teacher education program by increasing its reliance on formal credentials and supervision. By 1913 he had created a systematic four-year bachelor's degree in education, and in 1915 he supervised a name change to "Teachers College." In early years he roamed the state as a goodwill ambassador, trying to interest teachers and potential teachers in further studies, and supported the creation of the American Association of Teachers Colleges in 1920.

Twenty-six years after the beginning of Miami's professional school for teachers, a second professional school, the School of Business, was founded in 1928. Three years after that the creation of the School of Fine Arts completed a pre–World War II triad of Miami professional schools. Teacher education, however, continued to be the cornerstone of university enrollment. In 1930 the School of Education represented 42 percent of total university enrollment—not counting more than 1,500 additional students who took summer and extension classes—and throughout the 1930s it comprised one-quarter to one-third of Miami's total. The arrival of teacher education and women had solidified Miami's financial standing, and by the 1950s Miami was a strong coeducational institution with powerful links to teachers in communities across the state. That network would remain solid through the twentieth century and prove valuable as Miami began selecting talented students for admission.

Naming an Evolving School

The Ohio State Normal College, 1902–1915
Teachers College, 1915–1928
The School of Education, 1928–1977
The School of Education and Allied Professions, 1977–2007
The School of Education, Health and Society, 2008–

The School of Business

Recognizing student desire for business studies and alumni support to develop them, the College of Liberal Arts offered business courses as early as 1923. A separate School of Business Administration was created in 1928; it immediately enrolled 12 percent of the student body. Enrollment climbed to 20.6 percent of the university by 1930–31, peaking at 29.4 percent in 1940–41. Although enrollment declined during World War II with the absence of male students, it surged to 33.1 percent by 1948–49 as veterans flooded the campus.

The antibusiness ethos of the Vietnam War era drove enrollment down to 12 percent of the student body. Yet by 1975–76 enrollment had rebounded to 22 percent of all undergraduates, and the school was experiencing intense pressure on resources as an unrelenting demand for business courses threatened funding for programs in other divisions. To limit enrollment in the school, stronger requirements for both admission and retention were developed in 1975. The share of Miami enrollment attributed to the School of Business rose to 37.7 percent in 1985–86, and averaged about 25.5 percent over its history.

By the twenty-first century the Farmer School of Business had six departments: accountancy; decision sciences and management information systems; economics; finance; management; marketing; and, at Hamilton and Middletown, business technology. Master's degrees in business administration, accountancy, and economics were offered, and faculty and students flocked to the Institute for Entrepreneurial Excellence; Center for Governance, Risk Management and Reporting; and Interactive Media Studies. In 2007, thanks to a $30 million leadership gift from Richard and Joyce Farmer and the Farmer Family Foundation, the school broke ground on a new world-class facility for the school, with occupancy expected in 2009.

Harrison C. Dale, dean of the School of Business Administration, 1928–38. Recensio, 1935.

The School of Fine Arts

Miami's devotion to the arts was evident as early as 1903, when the campus hosted its first theatrical performances. By 1905 the university had an orchestra, a mandolin club, a saxophone quartet, and a choral society, the forerunner of the Collegiate Chorale.

To accommodate students who wished for formal arts studies, the trustees approved President Upham's recommendation to establish a School of Fine Arts in 1929. It began with departments of music and art drawn from the College of Liberal Arts. Architecture was added a year later, followed by theatre, which moved from the College of Arts and Science in the early 1980s. In 1999, Miami's Performing Arts Series, established in 1937, and the Miami Art Museum, 1978, were added to the school. By 2007, the school enrolled nearly one thousand students majoring in theatre, music performance and music education, art education, history of art and architecture, architecture and interior design, and graphic design and studio art, with concentrations in ceramics, metals, painting, photography, printmaking, and sculpture. The Men's Glee Club, Marching Band, and Pep Band consistently attracted musicians from all courses of study at Miami. The popularity of the steel drum band and Global Rhythms testified to growing interest in world music in the twenty-first century.

Fine Arts Building, Maple Street, temporary home of arts instruction, 1946–59. Miami School of Fine Arts Collection.

Off-campus opportunities enriched the school's offerings. Students looking for broader horizons could participate in domestic and international traveling studios and exchanges and interdisciplinary opportunities in Europe, the Middle East, Africa, and Asia. Saturday Art, a youth theatre program, and the Talawanda Schools Partnership provided local options, as did a design/build residential program in Cincinnati's Over-the-Rhine neighborhood. CraftSummer and the Yeck Young Painters and Sculptors Competitions drew participants and entrants nationwide.

Miami orchestra and choral groups in performance at Withrow Court with Edgar Stillman Kelley and Theodore Kratt. Miami School of Fine Arts Collection.

Oxford and Miami African Americans

A Timeline of Change, 1885–1941

adapted from Miami University Libraries *African American Timeline*

1885 Peter Bruner became Miami's best-known early African American employee, although unknown laborers and domestics were employed earlier.

1887 The Ohio Supreme Court upheld a lower court decision desegregating Oxford Public Schools. Brought by African American parent Perry Gibson, the decision officially desegregated school board–administered education systems in Ohio.

1896 Miami received its first regular appropriation from the State of Ohio, making it subject to state regulation in admissions. The 1896 Ohio statute provided that "said Miami University shall admit . . . all residents of this state who shall conform to the standards of admission."

1902 The Ohio State Normal College opened as part of Miami. Later to become the School of Education, it would admit many of Miami's early African American students.

1929 A group of African American students formed the Kappa Sigma Delta Club "to promote scholarship, to broaden our literary and social activities, to foster the spirit of fraternalism among its members, and in general to bring about a closer relationship with the school." This was the first known African American organization on campus.

1932 In April Kappa Sigma Delta unsuccessfully petitioned for official recognition as a fraternity but continued unofficially for five years.

1933 Amsden Oliver, All-American in track, became the first African American allowed to live in a residence hall.

1938 A group of African American students organized "The Colored Students Club" in order "to be an intellectual incentive to the Negro students at Miami University, and to extend our program in such a manner as to supply correct and sufficient social activities." In December 1938 the group successfully petitioned for recognition, and shortly afterward was renamed Kappa Sigma Delta. During 1939–40 Kappa Sigma Delta became "Les Travailleurs," then disappeared from university records.

scene five

Women in Student Culture

"THE AGE OF GARDEN FLOWERS
IS GONE . . ."

On January 28, 1910, Raymond M. Hughes, dean of the College of Liberal Arts, wrote to a correspondent about the pending creation at Miami of a chapter of Phi Beta Kappa. He reported that thirteen chapters had endorsed the idea, that more endorsements were coming, and that steps were well under way to gain approval at a United Society convention in September. The dean was optimistic. Almost as an aside, however, he mentioned a reservation. "A recent investigation of the standing of our students," he said, "has lessened my interest slightly, I must confess, when I find that the majority of the probable members will be girls."

Miami's hundred-year tradition of higher education for men only would not disappear quietly at the turn of the twentieth century. Perhaps the rapidity with which female enrollment increased after the opening of the Normal College stimulated anxiety about social change. There is anecdotal evidence of this. Just sixteen months after Normal College classes began—in December 1902 and January 1903—the *Miami Student* printed an exchange of poems by anonymous students implying that men were concerned about the number and influence of women on campus. "C" published his lines under the title "Topsy-Turvy."

> A new Miami's risen, the Co-ed's right on hand,
> To the old Miami fellows it's all Topsy-Turvy land.
> There are women on the Faculty,
> "No Smoking," in the halls,
> An array of millinery, on the old hooks on the walls.
> And a Steinway Grand piano, (the old organ's out of style),

And a nod from the Prexy means to two-step down the aisle.
But the thing that's topsy-turviest,
As every one will say,
Is the girls jumping hurdles,
While the boys do crochet.

Just rubber in "Construction" at the boys braiding mats,
And peep in the gymnasium at the girls "skinning cats."
Attend a game of basketball,
The girls are in the fray,
The fellows cheer them from above
And wave their colors gay.
The boys are "perfect ladies,"
And the girls are athletes strong,
Can all these topsy-turvy things
Continue very long?
'Tis hard to tell and yet it looks a bit as if they may,
That the girls will jump more hurdles
And the boys do more crochet.

"C" may have regarded his verse as an amusing role reversal exaggerating a
social scene novel to Miami men. The rebuttal poem that followed in January,
however, suggested a tone of irritation, if not defiance, toward the reaction of
Miami men to the presence of women. In "A Reply to 'Topsy Turvy,'" a con-
tributor signing "X" wrote:

What if to the old Miami fellows
It is all "Topsy-Turvy land."
Since the Co-ed, bag and baggage
Has strayed into their band?
Let them howl out brave and loudly,
And fume as much they may
For the state says she'll support us,
So we're coming here to stay.
What if we jumped your hurdles?
What if we have "skinned cats"?
What if we played at basket ball,
While you were braiding mats?
All this is but the beginning
Of a not too distant day,
When we shall enter larger fields,
For the state now says we may.
There'll be women on the football team,

Raymond M. Hughes, president of Miami
University, 1911–27. Recensio, 1914.

Who'll for old Miami play,
While you upon the bleachers sit
And wave her colors gay,
The tower will have an extra coat
Of paint of brightest hue,
While female fingers guard above,
Below, you'll rush their breakfast through.
There are women on "The Student" board.
They soon will issue it along,
For new woman's like the banyan tree,
The age of garden flowers is gone.
It used to be that girls went first
When chivalry was in style,
But now Miami boys must take the lead
In the "two step" down the chapel aisle.
E'en now we see the first effects
Of our journey in your midst;
The faculty wears cap and gown,
To imitate our dress;
The "Western" girls you've left alone
The "College" too, you shun,
While to Miami's walls you haste
The Co-ed's dance to join.
So while you howl and fret and fume,
And raise an awful fuss,
Away down in your hearts, at least,
We know you think of us.
So let topsy-turvy things remain,
And learn to like them as you may,
For the state says she'll support us,
And we're coming here to stay.

While women stood up for opportunities to participate in college life alongside men and publicly defended their right to do so, they also formed organizations for social support that paralleled those existing for men. In 1902, the same year the Normal College began, the founding of Delta Zeta sorority extended Old Miami's tradition of mothering social fraternities, now giving birth to one for New Miami women.

In the same year the Normal College opened, 1902, six women students organized Delta Zeta sorority. Following the lead of Miami's male fraternities, they identified the name, colors, and goals of the organization, and planned to establish chapters at other educational institutions. By the end of the academic year they had written a constitution, initiated new pledges, and secured the endorsement of President Benton, whose support earned him the title "Grand Patron of Delta Zeta."

The new sorority quickly gained respect from Miami's three fraternities, and its growth warranted renting a sorority house by 1905. Delta Zeta was admitted and installed in the National Panhellenic Conference in 1910, and its national growth was active. Early sorority members established chapters at Cornell University in 1908, DePauw University and Indiana University in 1909, and the University of Nebraska and Baker University in Kansas in 1910.

In 1922 Delta Zeta established a national headquarters and designated its location as the city of the president's residence, moving the office as the presidency changed hands. This tradition was a long one, but in 1981 the sorority's council approved the purchase of a hundred-year-old Victorian home at 202 East Church Street in Oxford to serve as a national headquarters, an historical museum, and a facility for its national council. This building was restored and furnished in 1993 through donations from chapters in all states.

Early in its history the sorority committed to a philanthropic program in speech and hearing, and its relationship of more than forty years with Gallaudet University has provided scholarships for hearing-impaired students.

At each of its major anniversaries, the sorority had presented Miami a historical token, including a portrait of Elizabeth Hamilton (first woman dean at Miami), a portrait of Lucille Crowell Cooks (a founding member of Delta Zeta and the first woman to serve as chair of the Miami University Board of Trustees), a tuition scholarship for women students, and chimes for the Sesquicentennial Chapel. The annual "Woman of the Year Award" recognized notable American women and successful executives, scientists, and artists. By the twenty-first century Delta Zeta had become one of the largest Greek organizations, with 161 chapters. The centennial celebration on the Miami campus in October 2002 drew a record attendance of 1,200 Delta Zeta alumnae.

Founding members of Delta Zeta sorority, 1902. Back Row: Julia Bishop, Anne Simmons, Anna Keen, and Alfa Lloyd. Front Row: Mary Collins, Mabelle Minton. Photograph by Frank R. Snyder. Miami Archives and Smith Library.

*Hepburn Hall, first Miami
residence hall for women
(1905). Miami Archives.*

NEW HOMES FOR WOMEN

Although Hepburn Hall was barely three years old in 1908, it already had a
colorful history. The design of Miami's first residence for women was reminiscent of the New England women's colleges already represented at Oxford Female College and Western Female Seminary. Located atop a prominent slope
to the southwest of Old Main, just northeast of where an imposing Normal
College building would rise in 1909, Hepburn Hall had become a main feature
of the New Miami campus. With a circular drive from Campus Avenue leading to an inviting porch on its west façade, it created a new front door to the
campus. And it was all about women.

Standing approximately on the site of today's King Library, Hepburn was
built at a cost of $42,000. It was the first item in President Benton's extensive
construction plans. By 1907 Hepburn housed ninety-six women, most of them
Normal College students. The housing shortage forced some residents to live
in an attic above the third floor. Early in the year there were complaints that
lights in the north attic were defective and that residents sometimes had to
strike matches to find their way. It was rumored that some women used the
attic as a smoking lounge. Both circumstances would be cited later as possible
causes of a major fire on January 14, 1908.

At about 4:30 in the afternoon a crew working at the auditorium construction site saw smoke and flames coming from the north end of Hepburn attic. According to the *Oxford News,* a professor in Brice Hall and some Hepburn residents discovered the fire about the same time. An alarm was sent to Oxford volunteer firemen. Meanwhile, students, faculty, and women from the nearby Phi Tau sorority house went to Hepburn to assist in evacuating residents, belongings, and movable items. Newspaper accounts of the event differed. Some described female residents as "huddled like sheep on the stairways" and "paralyzed with fear and unable to make an effort for life and safety." According to these versions, the best efforts of "sturdy athletes" who "fearlessly went through smoke and fire" were required to drag unfortunate helpless women from smoke-filled rooms and stairways to safety. Such stories were disputed by the *Miami Student* and the *Oxford News.* A *Student* editorial writer said:

We fail to understand why the fiction that women in time of danger are incapable of rational action is so persistently adhered to, when the truth is that under such circumstances women often show a degree of self-possession and courage equal to that of men if not greater.

The *Oxford News* observed that Hepburn Hall matron Mrs. C. W. Tudor "showed great coolness and courage" when the fire was discovered, attempting to fight it alone with a fire extinguisher until she was driven back by smoke. Mrs. Tudor then ably assisted with evacuating the building and salvaging student possessions.

Although no one perished and most Hepburn furniture was saved, early efforts to control the fire were unsuccessful because the Oxford Fire Department lacked manpower and an adequate water supply. Oxford's steam fire engine, unused for weeks, broke down. Firefighters were hard pressed to keep the blaze from spreading to Brice Hall. Dean Minnich contacted City of Hamilton officials for assistance, but it was over an hour before a train with Hamilton's fire engine, hoses, and men could depart for Oxford, and when they arrived the fire engine would not function properly. Yet, by 8:30 in the evening, the fire was under complete control.

Both President Benton and Dean Hamilton were away from campus. In their absence responsibility for responding to the disaster fell

Women at Hepburn Hall sharing food from home. Roderick Nimtz Collection.

Hepburn Hall after 1908 fire. Miami Archives.

to Dean Hepburn, Dean Minnich, and education professor Anna Logan. Logan found shelter and food for displaced women. Her appeal for housing got a ready reception from Western and Oxford colleges, from Oxford citizens, and from Miami fraternities; all displaced students were said to be housed before the fire was finally extinguished.

Although Ohio newspapers reported that Hepburn Hall was destroyed, like the Western College building in 1870, its exterior walls remained intact and interior floors were repairable. President Benton predicted that replacement could cost as much as $60,000, but later estimates shrank to $18,500, and there was fire insurance coverage. In appreciation of the Oxford Fire Department, Benton sent a $5 check to each firefighter and a $10 expression of gratitude to the chief. Recognizing the pressure to house women students, in late January Benton promised that Hepburn Hall would be rebuilt immediately, and by June 1908 it was again fully operational. Dean Hepburn, longtime opponent of coeducation, celebrated the reopening of the women's residence hall bearing his name in his own way. He retired from the university.

COTTAGES AND RESIDENCE HALLS

The reconstructed Hepburn Hall could not house all women now coming to Miami. Trustee records for January 1912 reveal a major debate in the board about new housing for women. Raymond Mollyneaux Hughes (1911–27), the first physical scientist to hold Miami's presidency, proposed limiting the admission of women to the number that could be accommodated in existing dormitories, and board president Walter L. Tobey polled board members about it. Their responses were revealing. Some strongly opposed the Hughes plan, arguing that the university must expand its enrollment of women, and some favored it, even implying opposition to existing levels of enrollment by women. Also at issue was whether to allow women students to live with families in private homes where they would pay rental charges comparable to those for university housing. The trustees divided over this matter as well, some arguing that direct control and supervision would be important and others not commenting. Three of the trustees who voted with the majority questioned whether the board had the power, or even the legal right, to limit enrollment. The final tally was marginally indecisive: in Tobey's estimation, five trustees supported an enrollment limit, four did not, and two were undetermined.

Throughout the New Miami era, the housing shortage for women was addressed by purchasing private residences to house students, by building temporary housing, by building residence halls on campus, and by utilizing the "cottage" system, which placed women in private residences selected from a list of owner-occupied homes approved by Miami. Cottages were required to meet Miami standards and provide "a sitting-room for callers." Students paid room rent to Miami to defray costs, and Miami reimbursed cottage owners for rent, telephones, water, coal, light, cleaning, repairs, incidentals, and services of a "furnace boy." Students were to observe the social regulations and restrictions applicable to those living in dormitories.

While the president and trustees debated admitting more women, Dean Hamilton focused on the welfare of those already enrolled. In June 1910 she articulated to the board an *in loco parentis* philosophy for educating women.

It is possible, I believe, for the girl in a co-educational school of the present day to be broadly educated, to bear her share of representation in all phases of college activity, to give intelligent consideration to the development of her body as well as her mind, and still to retain something of that old-fashioned gentleness that belongs to the womanly woman; but the price of it is eternal vigilance.

To help accomplish this, Dean Hamilton created a "Faculty Women's Club" composed of "faculty women and faculty wives" who she believed had "wonderful possibilities in the help and sympathy and counsel which they may bring to bear upon the consideration of many of the problems of our women students." She reported that student government had created a "Big Sisters" program that "helped solve many problems in the cottages and thereby materially aided in fostering better observance of study hours, regularity of social plans, and greater harmony between house matron and students." She advocated "vocational information" advising for the student's sophomore year, and by 1929–30 inaugurated a novel freshman adviser system to "provide close personal contact in living quarters between adviser and student, the fortnightly conference of advisers," and "the interpretation to faculty members of the individual problems of backward students." This innovation, she said, was viewed by other colleges with "great interest in the experiment as one that may be of great value in the induction of freshmen into college life."

All this reflected the concept of academic community fostered by the women's colleges, from one of which—Oxford College—Miss Hamilton had been recruited to shape coeducation at Miami. Her approach valued structured supervision in university residential housing on campus grounds, but women were enrolling too rapidly to make that possible. On May 1, 1911, Dean Hamilton reported to the board that seventy-five women lived in the cottages, where they were grouped to provide "community life" and "the same principles of self-government that obtain in the dormitory on the campus."

Ogden Hall, residence for men (1924). Built with 1915 bequest of Laura Ogden Whaling as a memorial to her brother George C. Ogden, Class of 1863. Miami Archives.

Yet cottages were never the preferred housing mode. Anticipating completion of Bishop Hall, in 1911 she told the board, "It is a matter of congratulation that in another year the beautiful new dormitory, now in rapid process of erection on the campus, will be ready to receive the large majority of our women students now scattered through the homes of the town." This will "bring all our students into uniform conditions of community life where the stimulus of living together will bring an inspiration for working together with more earnest cooperation than has ever been possible before."

Although the issue of where to house Miami's growing enrollment of women would not go away, the next residence hall project would be for men. In 1915 Laura Ogden Whaling of Cincinnati willed the largest bequest in Miami history, $400,000, partly to build a residence hall as a memorial to her brother who graduated in the Class of 1863. This was litigated, and by 1923 when work began the amount was $260,000. That sum was enough to move Herron Gymnasium to the east so that the wooded area north of the slant walk could be preserved and yet meet a bequest stipulation that George C. Ogden Hall be built west of Herron Hall along High Street.

Four years later, in his annual report, President Hughes again took up the subject of limiting the enrollment of women. Female enrollment in 1926–27, he said, was 935 for the year, and he added, "The largest number enrolled at any one time was about 880 girls." About 60 of these were living at home, and 820 were either in dormitories or "in the village." Even though acquisition of the former Oxford Female College to create a residence for men (named Fisher Hall) had expanded campus housing, the president had a warning on this matter.

It has seemed to me that we should use every reasonable effort to prevent the number of girls increasing further until the number of men enrolled should equal the number of women. Heretofore, the actual limitations on the rooming facilities available for girls has proved a natural and proper limitation. Now with the occupancy this fall of Fisher Hall by freshman men, we withdraw from the rooms in town about 150 men and therefore vacate possible places for additional women. As more freshman dormitories for men are erected and as the town grows, the quarters which could be provided for women will grow, and unless some definite policy is developed and worked toward there is a large possibility that the number of women will considerably exceed the number of men within the next five years.

His remedy was building a temporary "frame and stucco" dormitory for entering women, and limiting the number to those who could be accommodated there and in East and West halls—also built as temporary housing for women south of Spring Street where Warfield Hall stands today. Upperclass women would be "rooming out in town but it would mean that every freshman woman would either be in her own home or in a college dormitory and that no girl would be out in town more than one year." This would "take care of the problem of the limitation of University women in a rational and effective way."

After Wells Hall was completed in 1923, the majority of enrolled women were in residence on campus, yet the cottage system continued into the 1950s. At the point of highest use it involved fifty or more village homes. More than a hundred separate homes were used at one time or another, some housing up to twenty-five women. After World War II, returning veterans were the favored village renters, and Miami began a residence hall building program. By 1948 only fourteen cottages were available. By 1955 Miami had twenty

East Hall and West Hall (late 1920s). Photograph by Frank R. Snyder, ca. 1940. Miami Archives.

Wells Hall (1923) in the late 1920s. Miami Archives.

residence halls. Fifteen of them, including two that originated in Old Miami, were redesigned, built, or acquired during the New Miami expansion. That year Dean of Women Helen E. Page could report the success of Miami's holistic residence hall program.

Since our University is a residential one, there is ample opportunity for providing means for the molding of whole persons. Our staff feels an obligation to make possible the facilities for intellectual, civic and social development for each student. The halls serve as laboratories for teaching consideration of others in a group living situation, to promote a respect for and an understanding of the rules necessary in group living, and to emphasize the importance of serious academic effort.

SHAPING A NEW CAMPUS CULTURE

Elizabeth Hamilton, born August 23, 1873, at Gallipolis, Ohio, had a long and distinguished career as Miami University's first dean of women. She assumed her post in 1905, and was the only dean of women the university knew until she retired forty years later at the end of World War II. Miami colleagues who worked with Hamilton over many years remembered her as a dean "unusually gifted in sensing changes in student thought" and a scholar with a "direct and decisive" mind.

Hamilton moved to Oxford with her mother and sister in 1890. Recently widowed, her mother decided to support her children by opening a boardinghouse. She chose Oxford because it was a college town where her daughters would have a good chance of getting an education. They both enrolled in Oxford College, and Elizabeth graduated in 1895 with BA and BS degrees. She taught Greek at Oxford College from 1897 to 1903, and served one year as Oxford College dean.

President Benton spent considerable effort persuading Elizabeth Hamilton to leave Oxford College and become Miami's dean of women in the spring of 1905. Hamilton's appointment made news: she was the first woman dean at Miami and among the first deans of women in the United States. Years later she recalled tension in the air when she made her first annual report to the board of trustees in 1906. "When a woman's voice was heard for the first time in that heretofore man's college meeting," she remembered, "there was a noticeable rustle as they sat up and looked me over!" In her new position Dean Hamilton shaped the academic and social lives of Miami's growing number of women students from her office and apartment in Hepburn Hall. She also taught Greek and one or more sections of freshman English every semester until shortly before she retired.

Before World War I coeducation on American college campuses was viewed as an experiment. Hamilton saw Miami as a civic community in which students should be encouraged to learn self-government, develop a sense of personal liberty, and practice individual responsibility. After Hamilton's first five years at Miami, President Benton commended her "rare common sense, her infinite tact, her strong character and her high ideals." Her reputation grew stronger over the years as she was repeatedly praised for exceptionally fine service. Her work, Benton said at one point, "means everything to the women enrolled in this institution."

Hamilton served four decades with dignity, distinction, and apparently a high degree of tolerance, for throughout her career she consistently earned less than other deans and leading Miami administrators. She gained a reputation beyond Miami for research on women's colleges and the higher education of women, helped organize the National Association of Deans of Women and the Ohio Association of Deans of Women, established a branch of the American Association of University Women in Oxford, and served as Ohio AAUW president in the 1930s. After her retirement in 1945, a women's residence hall built before World War II that would influence all future development in South Quad was renamed in her honor.

As the number of women students increased from 242 in 1906 to more than 1,500 in 1945, Elizabeth Hamilton directed Miami's development into a truly coeducational campus. Women students under her guidance expanded

Dean Elizabeth Hamilton, 1908. Roderick Nimtz Collection.

Senior women camping with Dean Elizabeth Hamilton, ca. 1910. Roderick Nimtz Collection.

their roles well beyond classrooms and "home-like" spaces of the women's dormitories and cottages. Women students, especially those in the Normal College, were encouraged to use their college years to learn how to be "helpful in community life." By 1945 women students participated actively in campus social life, in sororities, in student government, YWCA, Women's League, plays, and concerts, and as reporters for the *Miami Student*.

Hamilton's life after retirement revolved around close family, devoted friendships, world travel, and a beloved house on the Maine coast at Kittery Point where former students and colleagues visited. She died there at age ninety-seven. In Oxford, faculty and administrators remembered "a great woman" with a keen intellect. A memorial presented to University Senate recalled a dean who excelled at "defining, isolating and often resolving points of disagreement," and could "clear the air with tact." Elizabeth Hamilton encouraged and counseled thousands of students, inspired faculty colleagues, and led in shaping a new campus culture that influenced the lives of every succeeding Miami generation.

scene six

Inventing Tradition

MIAMI MEN AND THE COLLEGES

The women of New Miami would become a strong social presence in Oxford during the first half of the twentieth century, yet the traditions of ritualized encounters between Miami men and the women's colleges were not quickly abandoned.

In the late 1880s the annual "Western Walk-Around" by Miami men appears to have been a way of annoying—or attracting—young ladies of the seminary while tormenting their protective principal, Helen Peabody. This involved a serendipitous parade that was "more than a mere walk around Western campus: guns, revolvers, and a variety of other noise-makers were plentiful, and their din indescribable." Pranks were carried out frequently, including painting "M.U." on the Western boathouse, or stealing the horse from Western's carry-all vehicle when it was in town. At one time that horse was painted with stripes and left at the top of Old Main's west tower. Western hired a night watchman, supposedly to keep Miami students at bay.

The principal of Oxford College, Dr. LaFayette Walker, kept a close account of his charges. He designated walking routes for college women and provided them with faculty patrols. "Walker even climbed the college tower and surveyed with a small telescope the road to which his girls had been assigned." In 1914 the *Miami Student* carried a humorous account titled "Big Raid Causes Much Excitement" that detailed an alleged military-style "attack" when Miami fraternity men attempted to occupy Oxford College but were allegedly driven away at gunpoint. On a more harmonious note, in the early days of New Miami, Miami men frequently serenaded the women at Western and at Oxford College in song.

SPIRITS OF THE INSTITUTION

In the first decades of the twentieth century, as enrollment of both women and men increased, courses of study diversified to a degree undreamed of in Old Miami as students chose professional degree programs shaped by social and economic developments beyond the campus. Anticipating these changes, President Benton spoke of the need to cultivate "the spirit of the institution." Students often had their own ideas about how to do that.

Tower Rush, Flag Rush, Tug-of-War

In their first weekend on campus, freshmen participated in the annual "tower rush" that pitted them against sophomore rivals in an elaborate ritual at Miami's main building. Designed for men, it involved physical combat with complex attack strategies. Freshmen placed a flag in one of the towers of Old Main, then late at night or early in the morning rang the Old Main bell, a signal to sophomores to devise plans for taking freshmen by surprise and stealing their flag. Often the game would last for hours as sophomores repeatedly attacked and freshmen defended by wrestling opponents to the ground, sometimes tying their legs together. If the flag remained in place until morning,

Flag Rush, 1906. Photograph by Frank R. Snyder. Miami Archives and Smith Library.

Tug-of-War freshman-sophomore contest, 1921. Photograph by Frank R. Snyder. Miami Archives and Smith Library.

freshmen were declared victors and recognized as a strong, unified class. If sophomores stole the flag, they had bragging rights for a year.

This contest was described as the healthy rivalry of class unity, but some found it excessively violent, even dangerous. In 1902, the first year of Benton's presidency, the tower rush began as usual. At 1:30 a.m. freshmen rang the bell. Sophomores responded valiantly, but at 6:30 a.m. the contest was still a draw. By then President Benton had seen enough. He called a halt, and suggested a timed five-minute contest to decide the winner. Freshmen prevailed, but there would never be another tower rush at Old Main. The following year, Benton and the faculty prohibited it.

In fall 1904 students convinced faculty to revive the tower rush in a new form. Freshmen erected a large flagpole south of the future site of Hepburn Hall. Early in the morning on the first Saturday of the school year they put up their flag, applied lard to the pole, and rang the bell for competition to begin. At 8:00 a.m. sophomores made the first of several attacks, but were beaten back by superior numbers of freshmen. At 9:20 sophomores called a temporary retreat for a "council of war." At 11:30 they reappeared on a wagon. With it they managed to rush to the pole, but the greasy pole prevented a successful climb. When the bell rang at noon to announce the end of battle, the freshman flag still waved triumphantly. Afterward all parties declared the event both a success and an improvement on the tower rush. There was no damage to property and no serious injury. That evening President Benton invited the freshman and sophomore classes for an oyster dinner in the gymnasium to make amends after the hard-fought battle.

In following years the university became more involved in regulating the pole rush. In 1906, it featured President Benton as umpire, enforcing rules against punching and kicking. In 1907, by joint agreement of student council and the faculty, the competition became a three-part contest. The morning flag rush was followed by a tug-of-war, then a game of soccer in the afternoon. The pole was reduced to a height of twelve feet and greasing it was forbidden. The new rules yielded a disappointing contest, as sophomores were able to rush the pole, climb a freshman barrier, and secure the flag in less than two minutes. However, the new tug-of-war made up for that. An immense crowd walked to the banks of the Tallawanda to witness the novel event, for which a long rope was stretched over the stream, thirty men gripping each end. On a signal, both sides pulled with all their might. At first, it looked like sophomores had the upper hand, but freshmen would not concede, and ended up pulling sophomores into the icy water. The *Miami Student* reported it was "without question the best struggle which has ever taken place between the classes in the history of class contests."

The flag rush continued, but the tug-of-war took its place as the most popular event and acquired its own elaborate traditions, including a preliminary parade through the streets of Oxford with participants carrying the rope. By the 1920s the flag rush was phased out completely, but class competitions continued to be a source of campus energy. In later eras Greek Week and intramural sports would inherit the tradition of ritualized competition as a strategy for building college community.

May Day

May Day is known as an international holiday commemorating workers, but it was first observed as a day for honoring women. In the early twentieth century May Day celebrations became popular events at both women's colleges and coeducational institutions. Although women were admitted to Miami in 1887, a Miami May Day celebration did not occur until 1910, when freshman women decided to take matters into their own hands.

On Sunday, May 1, 1910, senior women in Hepburn Hall awoke to find baskets of wildflowers hung on their doors. These were left by freshman women and contained invitations to a May Day celebration and senior dinner the following evening. At 5:00 p.m. on May 2, two processions advanced toward a semicircle of chairs and a Maypole on the lawn east of Hepburn Hall.

Maypole Dance near Hepburn Hall, ca. 1930. Miami Archives.

According to the *Miami Student*, the first group consisted of senior women "in stately cap and gown," and the other was "a long line of girls dressed all in white, bearing on their shoulders twisted garlands of royal purple and gold." Seniors took seats, were joined by other women, and a woman of the freshman class came forward to crown Miami's first May Queen, Florence Van Dyke, chosen by vote of freshman women. After her coronation, freshmen staged a dance around the Maypole. A picnic supper was served to the accompaniment of school songs, and after the meal the May Queen received students of "special rank or position." This ceremony concluded with the women "frolicking" across the campus, singing. According to the *Student*, Miami remained "singularly free of men" while all this took place.

The 1910 May Day celebration began a tradition that would last for nearly fifty years. In 1922 junior women began sponsoring a May Day breakfast for seniors. By the 1930s, new members of women's clubs, honorary societies, and residence hall leaders were appearing before the May Queen. In 1933 women's residence halls began competing for a prize for the most original May Day song, a contest eventually replaced by freshman hall skits. May Day activities were performed outdoors until a run of bad weather prompted a permanent move, first to Herron Gymnasium and then to Benton Hall, today's Hall Auditorium. By the 1950s voting for the May Queen had been expanded to include all university women.

May Day activities would continue at Miami until the 1960s. By that time they were regarded as anachronistic by many students. An article in the April 17, 1965, *Miami Student* cited shrinking attendance at recent celebrations and suggested that many Miami women no longer understood the tradition. For an unrelated reason, the 1965 May Day celebration was Miami's last. In 1966, with introduction of the trimester calendar, spring commencement was held in April. This made the crowning of a senior May Queen a practical impossibility and brought to a close one of New Miami's most colorful spring traditions—one that originated in community-building for women when women were new to Miami student life.

Homecoming

Although November 14, 1914, is recognized as Miami's first Homecoming, alumni reunions were held on campus as early as the 1840s in connection with the annual commencement, and alumni marched proudly with faculty and graduating seniors. The idea of holding a New Miami alumni event in the fall probably originated with President Hughes in 1914. He knew that Homecoming celebrations at other colleges were enjoying great success and was aware of the first Cincinnati alumni banquet held in conjunction with the 1913 Miami-Cincinnati football game. According to the *Alumni News Letter*, that event was "the biggest Miami banquet ever held in Cincinnati." This demonstration of the potential drawing power of a football-related alumni event was not lost on the entrepreneurial Hughes.

At the beginning of the 1914–15 academic year, Hughes assigned planning for a fall reunion to Alumni Association secretary Alfred Upham, also chairman of the English Department. Upham was responsible for preparing a program and coordinating publicity among regional alumni groups. In October 1914 the *Miami Student* announced that "the First Annual Home-coming of the old Miami rooters—the men and the women too" would be held with the Miami-Denison football game November 14. From the outset Upham sought to attract "all ex-members of Miami teams and give them a chance to see and be seen." To ensure the largest possible attendance, Denison alums were encouraged to come to Oxford. The program was to have a distinctly athletic flavor, as all events were on game day, Saturday, November 14. The central event, the Miami-Denison football game, was promoted by the *Miami Student* as a match for the Ohio state football championship. The day would end with a men's smoker featuring "speeches, vaudeville, music, and novelties of all kinds."

Weather was ideal. The influx of alums began Friday and continued until early Saturday afternoon, when a special train arrived from Dayton carrying approximately two hundred Miami and Denison rooters. Many alumni were accommodated by fraternity houses, who made special efforts to attract

The creation in 1911 of the Miami Student Forum and its executive arm, the Student Senate, provided students for the first time with a degree of self-government. Among early issues considered were supervision of the annual Freshman-Sophomore Contest and provision of a new university honor system. In October 1911, they approved a rule requiring all male freshmen in the College of Liberal Arts to wear caps.

The freshman cap, described as gray, with a large green button on top, was to be worn in Oxford and at university athletic events from the day after Flag Rush until April 1. Having served this apprenticeship, freshmen would be permitted to burn their caps, symbolizing full acceptance into the Miami community. Enforcement was left to the freshman class, but violators could be brought before Student Senate if ten sophomores complained. However, no specific penalties were prescribed.

The first freshmen subject to the rule appeared to take pride in their caps. During the 1911–12 school year no violators were brought before the senate, and on April 20, 1912, the first cap-burning ceremony was held at the Athletic Field. According to the *Miami Student*, it commenced as a long line of freshmen marched "in lockstep" toward a bonfire in the center of the field. After circling the fire, freshmen broke ranks; "at a given signal, they all began to run around the fire; when they reached the western side, each man hurled his cap into the fire with a mighty yell." The freshman class then bunched back up and gave a class cheer. The cap-burning ceremony concluded formally, with remarks by freshman class officials and university administrators who gave it their official blessing.

However, subsequent freshmen classes apparently were less enthusiastic about caps, leading the senate and the forum to issue reminders of the rule to the classes of 1912–13 and 1913–14. The *Student* description of the 1915 cap burning said the caps were "much hated" by freshmen. The April 5, 1917, *Student* conceded that leaders of the freshman class "seem to consider the cap a disgrace and use every paltry excuse obtainable to doff it."

While compliance was lax, no effort was spared to enshrine the cap as hallowed tradition. In October 1914, Student Senate and Forum approved extension of the requirement to freshmen men in the School of Education; they also decreed that no freshman class would to be permitted to wear "any class insignia other than the freshman cap." The most eloquent cap justifications appeared in the *M-Book,* the authoritative freshman guide to Miami life. The 1924–25 *M-Book* said incorrectly that the tradition was "as old as Miami" and asserted that it "enables the freshmen to become acquainted with members of their own class and thus develop a strong class spirit."

In October 1916, Student Senate suggested that enforcement should be by the fraternities. That apparently failed: in February 1917, President Hughes told Student Senate that "extreme measures" were required, and the University Senate would support any action Student Senate decided to take. Ultimately four freshmen were brought before Student Senate for not wearing caps, and penalized by having an hour added to their graduation requirements. But subsequent enforcement remained unofficial. The March 19, 1926, *Student* offered this account:

The first step upon catching an offender is to place him on the balcony before the assembled multitude and request that he sing the Alma Mater. The deputies of the court stand by with barrel-stave paddles to insure ease and freedom of delivery on the part of the songster. Pitch, intensity, timbre and other voice qualities are passed upon by these deputies also. Following the singing, a speech of apology is delivered by the erring one. In extreme cases it has been found necessary to submit the offender to the beneficial treatment of a few moments beneath the showers.

A 1915 *Student* article referred to a number of occasions when capless freshmen were thrown into Thobe's Fountain. One incident prompted a direct complaint to Ohio Governor Cox, and construction of "beautiful gold-fish perches" on the fountain to prevent further immersions.

By 1920 many—if not most—freshmen were ignoring the rule, leading the *Student* to call for its enforcement or abolition. In 1921 Senate tried offering a post-cap-burning dance with a paid orchestra as enticement; the dance ultimately served to divert attention from the cap-burning ceremony, which became more rowdy as the decade progressed. In December 1922 Student Senate expressed concern about damage to university property in connection with cap burning. The following year the ceremony was moved from the Athletic Park to the central quad, then in 1925 to a remote location on Cook Field.

In March 1929 the *Student* noted with regret that it was "as unusual these days to see a freshman cap in a crowd as it was to see a lack of the same several years past." The April 1929 cap-burning ceremony was the last one mentioned by the *Student.* The final notice of cap burning was a satirical article in the April 1932 issue of a short-lived fraternity publication, *The Yellow Peril.* By 1934 cap burning was omitted from the *M-Book,* and the 1937 *M-Book* deleted all references to freshman caps, commenting that "not conducive" customs and traditions were being "dropped by the wayside."

a large turnout. Miami alums received red and white ribbons, while Denison supporters were given red and black bows. A 1:30 p.m. freshman versus upperclassman student soccer match ended in a scoreless tie. At 2:00 p.m. a four-mile cross-country race was won by the Phrenocons. The Miami-Denison football game started at 2:30 p.m. According to the *Miami Student,* after "one of the most peculiar games ever played on Miami field" the home team was on the losing end of a 40–33 score, largely because of atrocious defense. For Miami fans the high point may have been half-time entertainment featuring a "snake dance" on the field performed by several hundred students, followed by the launching of hot-air balloons. After the game, sixteen student and thirty-three alumni letter winners attended the first "M" association banquet in the dining hall at Old Main.

Even though Miami's recent women graduates were invited to the festivities, the high point of the first Homecoming may have been regarded by its planners as the evening smoker for men only. Featured speakers included Professor Upham and President Hughes, while alums offered reminiscences of student days. Miami and Denison football coaches spoke, each graciously commending the sportsmanship and play of the opponent. Mathematics professor Archer Young provided a more scientific and less gracious game analysis in the evening's final address—he delivered "rather pungent" remarks on the causes of Miami's defeat. Performances by the Miami Men's Glee Club and band were laced through these speeches. Meanwhile, in addition to ample "eats," alumnus T. C. McDill supplied enough tobacco, cigarettes, and cigars to make even the "most nonchalant . . . light up and bid troubles *avaunt.*"

Although Miami lost the football game, its first Homecoming was rated an unqualified success: an estimated five hundred alumni attended. It established a tradition that, despite interruptions by wars or influenza epidemics, continued with modifications into the twenty-first century. By the 1920s a parade had become a settled feature of Homecoming, and floats appeared in the following decade. In 1934 Margaret Weber was selected Miami's first Homecoming Queen. The first Homecoming King, Allan Oram, was chosen in 1935. As it evolved out of New Miami, Homecoming became a ceremonial occasion for students, athletes, parents, faculty, staff, administrators, alumni, and friends to gather in Oxford annually to reminisce and take part in entertaining ritual events. Although the cozy familiarity of Old Miami at its best was gone, in its place a new spirit of the institution was emerging.

Alma Mater

Just ten days after the first Homecoming, the November 25, 1914, *Miami Student* headline read, "Alma Mater Song Decided Upon." Noting that a new school song had been adopted by unanimous vote of the Student Forum, the

Student offered a history of it. In the early 1890s, it was said, while on a train ride to Cincinnati, a group of students passed the time by coming up with a Miami song. By the end of the trip, one of their party, Alfred Upham, compiled their suggestions into verses sung to the tune of "Oh My Darling, Clementine," a song familiar to them because it was much in favor then at Western College.

The original lyrics of this college song were:

> Up at Oxford in Ohio
> stands a college old and grand;
> Mother she, of mighty statesmen,
> Noblest people in the land.
>
> Chorus
> Old Miami, old Miami,
> Always shows right up in line;
> And where others run against her,
> They get worsted every time.
>
> We are students at Miami,
> Filled with Algebra and Greek;
> We are master hands at Logic,
> And you ought to hear us speak. (Chorus)
>
> Thus we sing at old Miami,
> To the scarlet and the white;
> To the glories of the past,
> And her future now so bright. (Chorus)

Between Upham's graduation in 1897 and his return to Miami in 1908 as professor of English, this song, which he titled "Old Miami," made its way into campus life, even appearing in commencement ceremonies. Feeling that the lyrics were insufficiently serious for events where it was used, and with his own name appearing as author, Upham approached President Benton to ask that the song no longer be sung. According to a *Miami Student* report, Benton was fond of the song and not willing to let it go, but agreed to Upham's request that he be given an opportunity to write more appropriate words.

When Upham rewrote the lyrics to "Old Miami," he removed the competitive and boastful tone of the original chorus and second stanza and recast the entire work in a more nostalgic mode evocative of tradition and past glories. He included explicit references to men in both the first and final stanzas, while acknowledging in stanza three that women were now part of Miami: "Youth and maiden throng thy gates." Upham attempted to give the chorus a dynamic, exciting quality, perhaps fitting for Miami's new energy, by generously adding exclamation points to his words. Thus the revised song "Old Miami, New Miami" came into being, appearing as early as the June 1908 commencement program with its now familiar lyrics:

Old Miami, from thy hillcrest,
Thou hast watched the decades roll
While thy sons have quested from thee,
Sturdy-hearted, pure of soul.

Chorus
Old Miami! New Miami!
Days of old and days to be
Weave the story of thy glory;
Our Miami, here's to thee!

Aging in thy simple splendor—
Thou the calm and they the storm—
Thou didst give them joy in conquest,
Strength from thee sustained their arm. (Chorus)

Now of late, thyself envigored,
Larger usefulness awaits;
Hosts assemble for thy blessing,
Youth and maiden throng thy gates. (Chorus)

Thou shalt stand, a constant beacon,
Crimson towers against the sky;
Men shall ever seek thy guiding,
Power like thine shall never die. (Chorus)

Two years later the musical setting of "Old Miami, New Miami" would also be changed. Raymond Burke, who founded the Men's Glee Club in 1907 and the Madrigal Choir for women in 1908, and who wrote some of Miami's earliest songs (including the "Miami March Song," better known as the "Fight Song"), published a compilation of Miami songs and other popular collegiate numbers in 1910. That collection included three different tunes for Upham's revised lyrics—the original "Oh My Darling, Clementine" melody and two new musical settings written by Burke, one each for men's and women's voices. Burke's setting for men's voices has become today's familiar tune for Miami's "Alma Mater," which in the 1910 publication was titled "'Old Miami' (Alma Mater Song)." It bore the expressive marking "Majestic—*with spirit.*"

The "Alma Mater" as revised by Alfred Upham and Raymond Burke remained intact for more than seventy years, serving as a pietistic community-building hymn for the New Miami, and for much of the National University, eras. Then, more than forty years after World War II, Upham's lyrics pro-

"Old Miami," official alma mater after 1914. Miami University Songs, ca. 1950. Miami Archives.

voked criticism for being insufficiently inclusive of women, a perception probably exacerbated by the custom of singing only the first stanza and the chorus at major university events. In September 1988, one year after the centennial of the admission of women to Miami, at the direction of Miami's board of trustees, President Paul Pearson formed a special "Alma Mater" Committee of students, faculty, staff, and alumni. He asked the committee to consider four alternatives: changing the words to better "reflect the 'new Miami' which admitted women over 100 years ago"; adding a stanza to reflect Miami's

Brothers in Song, Sing On!

adapted from an article by Janelle Gelfand, *Miamian*, Fall 2007

It all started on a cold night in January 1907 as Miami President Guy Potter Benton and a young instructor named Raymond Burke waited for a train. The president informed Burke that the school would retain him as assistant professor of geology. Then, because he had heard Burke was interested, he invited him to form a glee club.

After six months of rehearsals, the twenty-one-member Miami University Men's Glee Club presented its first program on February 28, 1908, in the opening concert for Hall Auditorium (formerly Benton Hall). For the first time, Miami students heard their fight song, as well as new music for the alma mater that Burke had composed for the occasion.

Miami Men's Glee Club, 1910. Photograph by Frank R. Snyder. Miami Archives.

coeducational history while preserving the "Old Miami" context of the lyrics; writing a completely new alma mater; or maintaining the status quo and making no changes.

This committee issued a call for wording recommendations by letters to alumni chapter leaders, an article in *The Miamian* alumni magazine, and requests to campus governance bodies and organizations. They received many. In a report of March 1989, they pointed to a delicate balance between the wishes of those who wanted to preserve "original" words as part of Miami tradition and the concerns of "those who believe a change is needed to avert perceptions of exclusion of any group of people." They felt minor modifications to Upham's "Alma Mater" lyrics would achieve this balance, and suggested that "while thy sons have quested from thee" be changed to "sons and daughters questing from thee." For the third stanza, they proposed that "youth and maiden throng thy gates" be changed to "men and women throng thy gates." Should this be unacceptable, they said, Miami ought to add to the "Alma

Mater" entirely new verse lyrics suggested by those who responded to the call for suggestions, and employ those for official, ceremonial, and other occasions. They read:

> Our Miami, alma mater,
> Ages old yet ever new;
> Sons and daughters from your hillcrest,
> Roam the world, yet ne'er leave you. (Chorus)

> You've embraced the generations,
> Men and women, young and old,
> Of all races, from all nations,
> And your glory will be told. (Chorus)

> Though the years may bring their changes,
> Your bright lamp will ever burn,
> Giving wisdom, truth, and knowledge,
> To each one who comes to learn. (Chorus)

> Our Miami, you were founded
> In our nation's early days;
> Now we join with generations
> In this song of·love and praise. (Chorus)

Percy MacKaye, dramatist and poet, Miami artist in residence, 1920–23. Miami Archives.

Without changing any part of the existing song, in 1989 the trustees adopted the additional verses. Acknowledging Miami's growing diversity, the "Alma Mater" now spoke more inclusively about the gender, race, age, and origins of contemporary students. The final and most generic new verse, however, speaking mostly to the institution's age, would be sung at most official functions. For some events Upham's lyrics celebrating "sons" were retained, perhaps inadvertently underscoring one perception of the New Miami era—that an institution for men had "added" women.

ALFRED UPHAM AND MIAMI TRADITIONS

Alfred Horatio Upham served as president from 1928 to 1945. Only Robert Hamilton Bishop served equally long in this position, and Upham's personal involvement with Miami covered a longer period. He helped shape Miami for more than fifty years, from his 1893 arrival as a student traveling from his home in Eaton by horse and buggy, until his

"Poet's Shack," Lower Campus, used by Percy MacKaye. Miami Archives.

The August 1920 *Alumni News Letter* announced "an arrangement which is probably unique in the history of drama in this country." Nationally known dramatist Percy MacKaye had agreed to become Miami's first artist in residence, and the nation's second at a traditional academic institution.

By inviting MacKaye, President Raymond Hughes was following the lead of the Western College for Women, where composer Edgar Stillman Kelley became the first artist in residence in 1910. Kelley spent twenty-four years at Western with his wife, Jessie, who was Western's director of piano music (and who suggested MacKaye for the Miami residency). Among the first rank of late-nineteenth- and early-twentieth-century composers, Kelley had absorbed diverse musical influences during study in Europe. Writing for orchestral and stage productions, Kelley composed symphonies, oratorios, songs, and symphonic poems, drawing on such literary themes as *The Pilgrim's Progress* (1917), *Alice in Wonderland* (1919), *The Pit and the Pendulum* (1925), and *Gulliver* (1936).

MacKaye's Miami residency, known as the Fellowship in Creative Arts, included a professor's salary, a residence, and a studio built in the wooded Lower Campus at a site not far from today's Upham Hall. In return, MacKaye had no specific duties, although it was understood he would reside in Oxford part of each year and meet occasionally with Miami's most promising students. Miami's goal paralleled the one pioneered at Western—to permit MacKaye to "work on his plays and pageants in the studio on the campus and . . . thus be enabled to create more of his artistic productions for the world," and by his presence, to enhance campus life.

MacKaye arrived in Oxford in September and remained on campus most of the 1920–21 academic year, giving readings to both public audiences and selected students. He composed the narrative poem "Dogwood Common," dealing with witchcraft in New England. In April 1921, MacKaye invited the literary societies to his studio for an evening reading of it. Hewitt Vinnedge, a member of the Erodelphians, recalled the event:

By 9 o'clock . . . we had all arrived, including Mr. Torrence and several members of Alethanai, the women's literary society. Mr. MacKaye was seated by a lamp near the fireplace. . . . Until almost Midnight Mr. MacKaye read to us. All who have heard him know with what emotional play and dramatic effect he reads. We were fascinated, electrified, almost rendered speechless as we heard that tragic tale. . . . It was exceedingly late when we . . . left the shack making our way through the woods. . . . All the girls' dormitory rules had been broken that night, but it mattered not. They felt, as we all did, that they were among the chosen few to hear the first reading of the greatest narrative poem yet written by an American.

MacKaye's appearances sparked talk of an Oxford artists' colony, and the fellowship won national attention and inquiries from institutions hoping to attract artists to their campuses. Notable among them was the University of Michigan, where MacKaye's friend Robert Frost was given a residency in the fall of 1921. The Miami residency, however, did not live up to expectations. When MacKaye came to Miami, he was probably known less for poetry than for civic participatory drama, large-scale pageants, and masques in connection with local celebrations, usually with casts of amateur participants. By 1920 MacKaye was looking for new ideas. He wanted to write about the people and culture of Appalachia, in his words, "to conserve, in forms of imagination, some vestiges of that elusive, vibrant life before its inevitable passing." MacKaye left Oxford at the end of the 1920–21 school year for a stay in the Kentucky mountains.

During the next year MacKaye produced several poems, including one dedicated to Thomas Edison on his eightieth birthday. He began work on a series of plays drawing on his experiences in Kentucky. According to his daughter, MacKaye was largely responsible for Miami's decision to offer Edgar King the position of university librarian in 1922. He gave readings of his work and visited with students. Yet a bout with illness, work in New York to arrange for production of his Appalachian play, and a cross-country lecture tour kept him away from Oxford. Faced with a strained budget caused by growing enrollment, President Hughes was concerned that state officials might question the practicality of Miami funding an artist residency. MacKaye told Hughes he would try to spend "at least two intensive periods of a month each" in Oxford. Hughes discussed this with skeptical trustees who approved a year's extension, but with an addendum expressing "the desirability of securing support or employment of this fellowship from private funds." MacKaye's comedy, *This Fine-Pretty World*, premiered December 23, 1923, at the Neighborhood Playhouse of Henry Street Settlement on Manhattan's Lower East Side. It got excellent reviews, but apparently did not provide justification for continuing the residency. Hughes, citing "the pressure of our increased enrollment together with the fact that it has been impossible for Mr. MacKaye to remain in residence this past year," notified him.

Miami gave MacKaye an honorary degree at its 1924 commencement, and he maintained cordial relations with Hughes. MacKaye's Lower Campus studio, dubbed "The Poet's Shack," was abandoned after his residency. It was razed in 1934.

Edgar Stillman Kelley, composer and first artist in residence, Western College for Women, and Jessie Gregg Kelley. Western Archives.

death in office on Founders' Day, February 17, 1945. Upham warrants particular attention for his impact on popular understandings of the university and its traditions that were learned and transmitted by generations of faculty, staff, students, and alumni.

From 1893 to 1897 Upham was a highly involved Miami student. His artistic talent led him as a freshman to become the artist for the 1894 *Recensio*. His ability to capture ideas on paper allowed him to blossom into a writer, poet, and scholar. As a senior he was editor of the *Miami Student*, class poet, and class valedictorian. He showed an early flair for ritual. His sophomore class revived a student custom from the 1850s called "Cremation of Logic," the ceremonial public burning of the textbook used in the logic class at the end of the school year. Many records exist about that lavish 1856 affair, and about the reenactment of it staged almost four decades later by Upham's class. Upham wrote a poem, "An Ode to the Departed," for this 1895 event, which may have been the beginning of his long quest to uncover and celebrate Miami traditions. As a senior Upham wrote a song that became Miami's alma mater. He also wrote the first Miami University history. When *Old Miami: The Yale of the Early West* was published in 1909 to commemorate the hundredth anniversary of Miami's charter date, a *Student* article credited him with "collecting the most intensely interesting facts and anecdotes concerning Miami's long history—stories that have been handed down through many college generations, and are considered sacred to Oxford and its schools."

Upham left Miami to teach at Bryn Mawr from 1910 to 1913, then President Hughes recruited him to return as chairman of the English Department. He also became director of publications, gathering information for the *Alumni News Letter* and the *Miami Student*. Upham wrote that he "put the *Miami Student* on its feet" first when he was its student editor in 1896 and again as a faculty member when he "personally directed and shaped its development into a weekly newspaper." He also served as advisor to the *Recensio*. Many of Miami's early twentieth-century student newspapers, yearbooks, and alumni publications bear his touch.

Alfred Horatio Upham, president of Miami University, 1928–45. Miami Archives.

When Miami hosted its first Homecoming in 1914, Upham was its organizer. In a speech on behalf of the Society of Alumni he said, "A student body . . . is something more than a group, it is a never-ending procession. The 'old men,' the alumni, are an integral part of the procession . . . they are mighty important factors in what shall come after them and just what those in the rear shall stand for." Upham was interested in what Miamians thought they were standing for. Before the advent of Homecoming, the principal means for engaging alumni was a week of activities around commencement, when students reminisced and celebrated their college years via Class Day and Student Night. In 1915, elaborate performances were introduced as a new entertainment at Student Night, and in 1916 scenes depicted incidents in Miami's past. These inventive pageants of bygone days used nostalgia to foster school spirit. The 1915 production, *A Pageant of Miami History,* showcased memorable moments from the past when Miami was exclusively an institution for men. The *Prologue* included a "war dance" by the Miami tribe, followed by the arrival of white men who forced offending Indians to leave. This may be one of the first recorded times that an Indian reference was specific to the Miami. It focused on their defeat. Other scenes in this pageant, elaborately produced on two separate stages in alternation, depicted Miami's early grammar school, the rivalry between literary societies, the interaction of Miami men with the women's colleges, the wedding of Benjamin Harrison and Caroline Scott, and stories of the Civil War. According to the June 1915 *Miami Student,* the pageant's grand finale included singing the alma mater while the crowd filed out "filled with the spirit of 'Old Miami.'" Upham was one of the faculty members assisting with this production. Many of its details are captured in the 1916 *Recensio.* Inside its cover was a dedication photograph of "Alfred H. Upham, scholar and gentleman."

On June 3, 1916, *A Pageant of Miami History* was presented again, this time on a stage constructed over the front steps of Alumni Library. In the prologue to this 1916 production, a group of freshmen steal and smoke an historic "Miami Peace Pipe," then fall asleep and dream the eight scenes of the show: an Indian campfire of about 1800, ongoing rivalry between the Miami Union and Erodelphian Societies, the Cremation of Logic burning of the textbook, an "Old Time Chemistry Class," the Lottie Moon wedding, the capture of Lottie Moon, the burial of Joel Battle, and a single event from New Miami—the celebrated "Storming of Oxford College" in 1914, when a group of rowdy Miami male students attempted to "capture" the women's building but were repulsed by college authorities. This production also resurrected a Class Day custom of the 1860s, when a student from each of the junior and senior classes presented an insulting speech about the other class, perhaps similar to a "roast" today. It ended, however, on another note of contrived harmony—with the ceremonial smoking of a "Pipe of Peace." In the epilogue, the sleepy freshmen wake when seniors arrive to take back this "Pipe of Peace." The *Student* applauded Miami's second historical pageant as a resounding success, noting a great improvement over the previous year in costumes, scene changes, and, ironically, given the events depicted, electric lighting. They gave credit to the "Shakespeare class of 1915–16 and to Dr. Upham, who are the authors of the entire work."

Upham's Shakespeare class wrote the script for a third pageant amid anxiety that there was no new information to be found and that it would be necessary to repeat scenes from preceding years. Students dug through archives, consulted faculty notes, and interviewed local elders. They found much material about Miami, Oxford, Oxford College and Western College, and created eight scenes: the "Great Spirit of the Miamis" introduces the Spirit of Youth; "Inauguration of President Bishop, 1824"; "Bethania Crocker's School at Tea,

Alfred H. Upham, Old Miami: The Yale of the Early West, *copyright 1909, reprinted 1947.*

PAGEANT

Miami University, Oxford, May 24th

*Announcement of Miami's
125th Anniversary Pageant,
1934. Miami Archives.*

1830"; the "Snow Rebellion, 1848"; "Days of Gid McNutt, 1852"; a "Civil War Camp Fire, 1863"; "Establishment of a Sorority at the Western Female Seminary" (where they were forbidden), 1900; and "Advent of the Miami Girl," about admission difficulties of young women and the positive contributions of coeducation. In recognition of war in Europe, a twenty-five-cent admission was to be charged with proceeds going to the Red Cross Society. Plans changed when the United States entered World War I in April 1917. When Miami men enlisted in the armed services, the pageant was canceled due to a shortage of men to fill male parts, and the production was staged later at 1918 commencement activities. The *Pageant of 1918* was the last large dramatic presentation of Miami history for several years. In three major pageants of Miami history produced over three years, at least twenty-two different scenes from the past were performed for the Miami community. Only three of these were set in the twentieth century, and only the very last took on a prominent feature of New Miami experience. A nostalgic sense of the past was being woven into the spirit of the institution.

Although the first sequence of historical pageants at Miami ended in 1918, the May Day and Founders' Day celebrations at Oxford College yielded historical pageants as well, and those too were elaborate. Perhaps it was predictable that when Oxford College was absorbed by Miami in 1928 another pageant would be produced. In 1930 more than a hundred Miami students and faculty members participated in *Procession,* an elaborate pageant on the Miami varsity field featuring scenes of historical events from Miami, Oxford College, and the Village of Oxford. Alfred Upham had become president of Miami University.

Upham never lost his lifelong affection for historical dramatics. Walter Havighurst's *The Miami Years* mentions a huge pageant presented in Miami Stadium in 1934 to celebrate the 125th anniversary of Miami's charter date. President Upham strongly encouraged the participation of Miami's dramatic, musical, and literary organizations in this ambitious production involving more than five hundred students and two hundred musicians. Its opening parade through the town included bands, floats, performers, and contests, helping to excite the public and encourage attendance. Some familiar names in later Miami dramatics and storytelling were part of this production. Professor Loren L. Gates was chairman of the pageant committee, and Professors Harry Williams and Homer Abegglen were scene supervisors. They assisted in writing it as well, along with Walter Havighurst, Marion Boyd Havighurst, and Professor Joseph Bachelor.

Upham was an important creator of the spirit of the institution emerging with the complexities of the twentieth century, binding together Miami's new diversity in enduring official music, in published stories, and on a grand stage. At his memorial service near the end of World War II, a quotation from Ralph Waldo Emerson was used to describe him: "An institution is the lengthened shadow of one man." Regardless of the accuracy of that nineteenth-century view, much of the lore about Miami's past that we know in the twenty-first century reflects the long shadow of Alfred H. Upham.

Planning and Building an Academic Village

> *In line, scale, decoration, and charm it is classically simple—but so right that it is never a fad or craze of a generation, but always an enormously important architectural style.*
>
> Barbara Trigg Brown, "Restoring Historic Williamsburg, Va., Sets a Standard for Colonial America," *Good Housekeeping* (1934)

A cozy postcard from the early twentieth century shows a west entrance to Miami University on Campus Avenue. Hepburn Hall, atop a gentle rise, is its central focus. The Normal College, today's McGuffey Hall, frames the right margin, and with a decidedly pastoral ambience, curving sidewalks cross a wide expanse of lawn in the foreground. At the entrance to a U-shaped drive connecting Campus Avenue to Hepburn's west porch is a substantial brick gateway. The card bears a New Miami message: "The Gateway of Professional Advancement."

After the turn of the twentieth century and beyond World War II, Miami University presidents and other leaders took systematic steps to build and rebuild the Oxford campus. They began to dismantle what had been a relatively informal campus of vernacular neoclassic architecture as planning schemes intended to systematize the landscape and create stylistic uniformity looked to a different future. The days when Miami students could take part in constructing the physical campus were over, yet it took several administrations, several false starts, and the intervention of an important architect who drew romantic inspiration from the past before a Georgian Revival image of Miami University would emerge from this historical process.

Miami University. *Lithograph by Richard Rummell, 1910. McGuffey Museum.*

The Gateway of Professional Advancement   Miami University   Oxford, Ohio

"Gateway of Professional Advancement." Postcard of west entrance to Miami University, ca. 1910–20. Photograph by Frank R. Snyder. Miami Archives.

FOUR PLANS FOR BUILDING
MIAMI UNIVERSITY, 1904–1928

The layout and architectural style of Miami's Oxford campus is largely the result of four master plans drawn between 1904 and 1928. None was entirely realized. The fourth, conceived by Charles F. Cellarius, was the most influential until the twenty-first century. Although Miami is known for seemingly historic buildings, its dominant architectural image is a New Miami creation.

When Raymond M. Hughes assumed the presidency in 1911, construction of the 1909 centennial campus was not complete. Driven by expanding enroll-

ment, it was focused by a 1904 campus master plan drawn by Chicago archi-
tects Normand S. Patton and Grant C. Miller, but only part of their plan was
attempted. It produced a new wing for Brice Scientific Hall (1904); Hepburn
Hall (1905); the Miami Steam Plant (1907); an Administration and Auditorium
Building (1908); Alumni Library (1909); the Centennial Gate (1909); McGuffey
Hall (1909, 1915, 1916); and Bishop Hall (1912). Although these structures were
subdued in comparison to the neoclassic Beaux Arts flair first envisioned by
Patton and Miller, they were bulky neoclassical structures that more than dou-
bled the size of the campus. The first version of New Miami was in place, but
Miami's rapid growth rate required a plan for expansion, and in 1913 the trust-
ees commissioned George E. Kessler to produce it. A landscape architect from
St. Louis who designed parks, planting layouts, site plans, and vehicular and pedestrian circulation paths, Kessler represented the City Beautiful movement,
an outgrowth of the European Beaux Arts tradition via Daniel Burnham's 1893
World's Columbian Exposition in Chicago, which had influenced Patton and
Miller's vision of Miami as well. Kessler was known for developing a park and
boulevard system in Kansas City and for the Louisiana Purchase Exposition
grounds in St. Louis (1902). One critic said Kessler was "the actual founder of a
new school of landscape architecture, being the first to depart from the formal
plan of civic landscape development followed by European cities."

Patton and Miller's design for the campus gave it a strong front on High
Street, and their building placement created an academic court of honor centered on Old Main, yielding a dignified neoclassical campus in the manner of
Burnham's 1893 exposition. Kessler took a different view. He set buildings in
an irregular grid of pathways intersected by an elaborate version of today's

*Proposed campus plan by
landscape architect George E.
Kessler, St. Louis, 1913. Miami
Archives.*

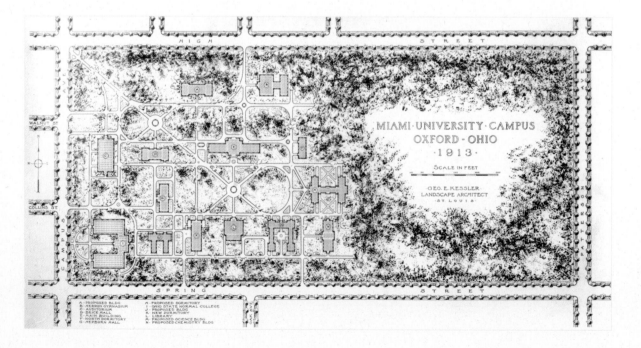

Proposed campus plan by architects Patton & Miller, Chicago, 1904. Miami Physical Facilities.

Slant Walk, and did not show a strong front on High Street. His campus was inward-looking, with the center clearly between Old Main and Alumni Library, and softened by extensive plantings across its layout. What was actually built differed greatly from either plan. Only two structures were located according to Kessler's concept—a science building east of Alumni Library and a chemistry building farther east. The proposed science building became Irvin Hall, although its U-shape was rotated 90 degrees. The chemistry building became Kreger Hall in 1931. Kessler's plan nevertheless cemented the idea of a quadrangle in Miami's imagination, and his inward-looking wooded campus was essentially the landscape that was built. Only in the mid-twentieth century would a strong face on High Street emerge, and campus life would continue to focus inwardly on quadrangles.

Steady enrollment increases between 1904 and 1920 kept the pressure on for new buildings, whose cost exceeded state funding. In 1920 Miami announced the Million Dollar Campaign, and yet a third master plan was drawn to advertise it, only seven years after Kessler's plan had been submitted. The promotional book sent to prospective donors listed university needs and laid out renderings of proposed buildings drawn by Harvey H. Hiestand, professor of architecture. Donors were asked to fund a university hospital, men's and women's gymnasiums, purchase of additional land, development of the athletic field, and an addition to Alumni Library, as well as student loans, university services, and lectures. Once again funds were not forthcoming. The Million Dollar Campaign raised only $222,443, and only a portion of Hiestand's plan was built. Even high-priority structures—new gymnasiums for men and women—did not materialize. A university hospital in the footprint drawn by Hiestand was located south of Spring Street instead of behind Bishop Hall as

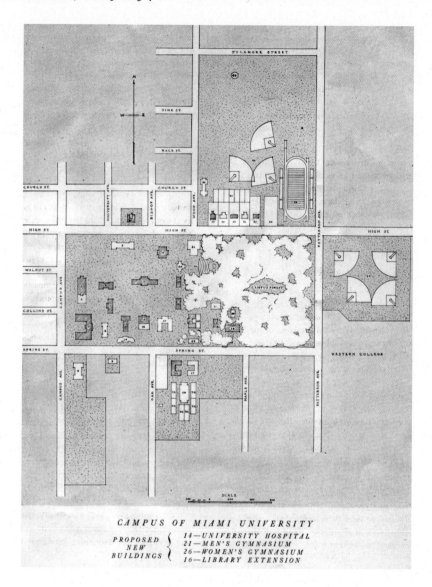

CAMPUS OF MIAMI UNIVERSITY

PROPOSED
NEW
BUILDINGS
{
14—UNIVERSITY HOSPITAL
21—MEN'S GYMNASIUM
26—WOMEN'S GYMNASIUM
16—LIBRARY EXTENSION

*Million Dollar Campaign master
plan by Harvey H. Hiestand, 1920.
Miami Archives.*

he proposed. An addition was made to Alumni Library, but to the east instead
of the south as proposed. And another wing was added to McGuffey Hall.

The long struggle between swelling enrollment and inadequate funding was
eased in 1921 when the Ohio General Assembly appropriated funds for construction at state universities. Miami also received its largest bequest for building a dormitory. With the combination of state aid and private funds, between
1923 and 1925 Wells Hall, University Hospital, Ogden Hall, the south wing of
Swing Hall, the north portion of Gaskill Hall, McFarland Observatory, and
Irvin Hall were constructed. Robert S. Harsh would be responsible for two of
these buildings, Irvin and Swing. In 1924 President Hughes wrote: "As state architect Mr. Harsh had general charge of our architectural work for two years
and his advice and suggestions were excellent. He saved us money, and he looked
after our interests in a most satisfactory way. During this period our build-

ings were being built by other architects, and Mr. Harsh's work was largely advisory." The other architects were Frank L. Packard; H. H. Hiestand; and Dittoe, Fahnestock, and Ferber Fred Wood. They would change Miami's architectural image.

The north and east wings of Irvin Hall opened in 1925. Harsh is credited as architect but apparently was not the original designer. A letter of request for appropriations describes the design process for Irvin Hall: "When the final details of the plans were taken up the state architect made changes in the construction and design of the building which greatly reduced its cost." That the nature of those changes is unknown is unfortunate, for Irvin Hall was the first building at Miami to be fully built from the ground up in neo-Georgian style, and it completed Miami's first quad (Old Main, North Hall, South Hall, Irvin, Alumni Library, Bishop, Hepburn, and Brice Scientific Hall), achieving the loose quadrangle pattern suggested by Patton and Miller, Kessler, and Hiestand.

Million Dollar Campaign brochure, 1920. Miami Archives.

MIAMI'S ARCHITECT

Cincinnati architect Charles Frederick Cellarius began his work for Miami in 1928. A 1913 Yale graduate who earned an architectural degree from Massachusetts Institute of Technology in 1916, his New England years may have stimulated an interest in colonial

Irvin Hall (1925), recitation building and first home of the School of Business Administration in 1928. Miami Archives.

Charles F. Cellarius. Miami
News Bureau.

architecture. Cellarius began a Cincinnati practice in 1921, eventually designing buildings for Berea, Wooster, and Western colleges, Ohio State, and public schools in Cincinnati. He was supervising architect of the model village of Mariemont and an architect of Laurel Homes and Lincoln Court public housing. This list suggests a strong interest in both academic architecture and community planning. His work at Miami over the next forty-two years could be viewed as an extended elaboration on the idea of an academic village.

In 1928 President Upham requested suggestions for future buildings. Cellarius sent two schemes. Although complete drawings of them apparently no longer exist, any full plan he drew would have been the fourth master plan for Miami in only twenty-four years. Perhaps because earlier plans were never fully built, Cellarius could begin his proposals by stating, "Architecturally Miami University suffers at present from the lack of a carefully studied plan of development. Buildings have been erected as necessary and in the absence of a comprehensive plan, it has been impossible to place them to the best advantage." To illustrate, Cellarius proposed one campus plan with scant building in Miami's remaining wooded area to the east, and another plan with more development there. The actual location of future structures, however, received less attention than their stylistic character. "Many of the present buildings are in a style of design that leaves much to be desired," he said. "The University in its expansion has now come to a point where its new buildings will be somewhat separated from the present campus group, and where if desired a change in architectural style would be possible and reasonable." Cellarius had a particular direction in mind, and more than one reason for it. "I would suggest the suitability of the colonial style since it is in harmony with the character of Oxford and with the older University buildings, and since its economy of construction would be an important asset when finances are nearly always a problem."

The year after Cellarius wrote to Upham, the stock market crashed and the United States entered the Great Depression. European governments built socialist-inspired architecture, perhaps partly as a result of the financial and housing crises. In large urban areas modern technology propelled leading design toward sleek buildings in styles influenced by the machine age—Art Deco, Moderne, and Modernist. Yet the neo-Georgian style would also grow in popularity during the turbulent 1930s. The orderly architecture of a distant agrarian past, especially in a style allegedly costing less than other modes, must have appealed to a budget-conscious Miami president who was entranced by historical pageantry. Indeed, in this era much of the country was aware of an elaborate restoration of Colonial Williamsburg in Virginia. That project, undertaken from roughly 1928 to 1934 with funding from John D. Rockefeller Jr., was highly publicized and enormously influential for popular American style and taste.

The reconstruction of Williamsburg was part of a larger interest in preservation during the late 1920s and the 1930s that included creating Henry Ford's Greenfield Village in Michigan and Old Sturbridge Village in Massachusetts; assigning the earliest historic district designations in Charleston, New Orleans, and San Antonio; and establishing the Historic American Buildings Survey. *Architectural Record* devoted its entire December 1935 issue to Williamsburg, and *National Geographic* featured Williamsburg in its April 1937 issue. Cellarius lectured on Williamsburg in Cincinnati in 1946 and again in a speech at Miami's Sesquicentennial summer commencement, at which he received an honorary doctorate of humane letters. By that time he could applaud the return "to traditional values in the arts." "In architecture," he said, "we tried to abandon the past but have learned that we cannot be satisfied with the barrenness of functionalism. The identical glass box[es] along the streets of our large cities have palled. We crave a higher kind of beauty in all art."

Plan for women's residential quadrangle by architect Charles F. Cellarius, Cincinnati, ca. 1950. Miami Archives.

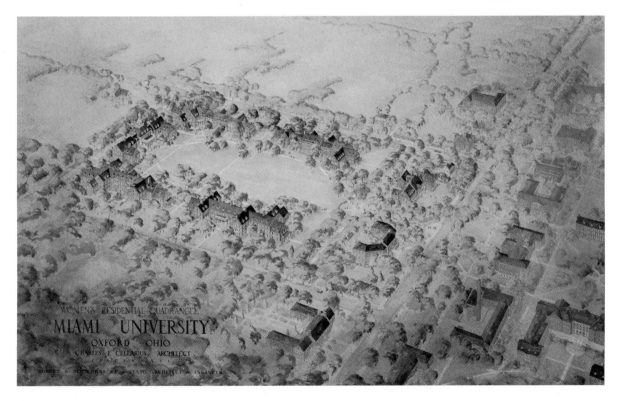

Miami Needs

from *Alumni News Letter, July 1930*

1. RESTORATION OF THE OLD BUILDINGS.
Architects have frequently commented on the way in which the two old dormitories and the Main Building just miss conforming to their period and thus fail to be the real adornments to our campus which they should be. The porches on the Main Building are conspicuous evidences of this situation. On the dormitories the roofs are too low, and a serious mistake was made some years ago in removing all chimneys from above the roof line. Mr. Collarius [sic], a year or two ago kindly prepared a sketch of one of these dormitories as he would conceive of it when restored.

South Hall (1836) in the early twentieth century. *Miami Archives.*

South Hall after remodeling suggested by Charles F. Cellarius in 1928. Renamed Stoddard Hall. Photograph ca. 1937. *Miami Archives.*

In his 1928 letter to President Upham, Cellarius added a footnote. "I again call attention to the possibilities of the north and south dormitories and recommend that these two buildings be restored thru the art of an architect familiar with that style, in the beauty that they deserve and probably once had." The 1828 North Hall, now Elliott, and the 1836 South Hall, now Stoddard, were early-nineteenth-century structures. Reports in Miami Archives from original building committees indicate they were built for a utilitarian purpose in vernacular neoclassic dimensions with little concern for style. Photographs from the late nineteenth century show buildings very different in appearance from the ones visible today, for they were extensively reworked in 1937 along the lines Cellarius suggested. Their interior features, stairs, hallways, and fireplaces, were removed. Floor levels, circulation patterns, and entrances were changed, roof pitches raised, and decorative details, porticoes, and a connecting terrace added. The building footprints, most of the brick walls, and foundations were very likely the only original elements remaining.

The concepts Cellarius shared with President Upham had an immediate effect. Old buildings were redesigned, and after Irvin was completed in 1925, new buildings were freshly designed in the neo-Georgian style. In 1931 the firm of Garber and Woodward conceived the center blocks of Kreger Hall and Withrow Court (both 1931) and the Food Service Building on the western edge of recently acquired Oxford College property (1934) in this style. Restyling of existing buildings to impose an historical image they originally lacked became regular procedure. In 1929 Oxford College was restyled to give it a more colonial appearance. In 1935 center and north wings were added to Swing Hall, and the original wing—which had resembled Ogden, a brick structure with a roof of red tile—was restyled in the neo-Georgian image. University Hospital, now MacMillan Hall, received in 1939 the first of at least three additions that altered its appearance and added allusions to neo-Georgian elements. The Industrial Arts Building, now Gaskill Hall, was restyled to make its functional appearance blend with the more decorative Georgian. These projects cemented the image. Events in the late 1940s and the 1950s would multiply it across the Miami landscape.

" . . . THE BOARD IS VERY WELL SATISFIED . . ."

Symmes Hall, a residence for men, was the first new structure at Miami fully designed by Charles Cellarius. Built in 1939, its original name, "New Freshman Dormitory No. One," suggests that Miami planned to build others—men's buildings placed to the north and women's buildings to the south. In 1940 the neo-Georgian women's residence later named Hamilton Hall, designed by state architect John P. Schooley, opened. South Residence Hall, now Richard Hall, designed by Schooley, was opened in 1941. As state architect, Schooley may have meant his publicly funded structures to establish models for other architects to follow.

After World War II the G.I. Bill produced another housing crisis. By September 1946, 2,000 of 4,100 students were veterans, and temporary buildings were erected to house them. Structures were put up for classrooms, art and architecture studios, laboratories, faculty offices, athletic facilities, a firing range, and the audiovisual service. Cellarius built the temporary Logan Lodge in 1948 as a women's dormitory. A modernistic building in international style unusual for his Miami practice, it earned notice for design novelty and stood south of Wells Hall until 1983.

Herbert F. Hilmer, a 1940 graduate of the Cornell School of Architecture, worked briefly for Cellarius before 1942 and joined his practice after the war. Between 1948 and 1959 Cellarius, and after 1958, Cellarius and Hilmer, designed nineteen buildings at Miami: Logan Lodge; Reid and Upham halls; Miami Steam Plant; McBride and Collins halls; Billings Natatorium; Roudebush and Porter halls; the University Center, now Shriver Center; MacCracken, Scott, and Hiestand halls; Miami Manor; Dennison, Laws, Brandon, and McFarland halls; and to finish the Georgian village, Sesquicentennial Chapel in 1959. Cellarius designed the Beta Campanile in 1940 and Clawson Hall and Boyd Science Hall for Western College in 1946 and 1947. By placing new Miami structures on a symmetrical grid, Cellarius and Hilmer spread the loosely formed quadrangle across the landscape to accommodate the complex and diverse needs emerging in a modern campus, while their buildings maintained a solidly consistent style. Notable among them, Upham Hall (1949, 1950, 1965) provided an iconic centerpiece structure with science labs. Roudebush Hall housed a swelling central administration. Billings Natatorium was a freestanding swimming pool

Symmes Hall (1939), first Miami building designed by Charles F. Cellarius. Miami Archives.

Logan Lodge (1948). Miami Archives.

structure with neo-Georgian decoration that attracted much attention. The University Center was a fully modern student union complete with a bowling alley in the lower level. Hiestand Hall gave art studios their first home. All were neo-Georgian. As counterpoint, Miami Manor for married student housing was one of only two major buildings designed by Cellarius at Miami in modernist style.

Cellarius and Hilmer worked in Oxford through the 1960s as Miami continued to expand, designing eighteen more campus structures: Harrison Hall that replaced Old Main; Bishop Memorial Gates; Culler Hall for physics; Harris Dining Hall; Phillips Hall for physical education; Hanna House for home economics; Murstein Alumni Center and Climer Guest Lodge; the Center for Performing Arts; and Anderson, Dodds, Dorsey, Emerson, Hahne, Minnich, Morris, Stanton, and Tappan residence halls. Every one except Phillips—a modernist facility—was rendered in a neo-Georgian mode. Boyd Science Hall and Edith Clawson Hall at Western College show the ability to work in a spare, modernist version of Collegiate Gothic. Culler blended neo-Georgian scale and balance with a front portal of modernist glass. The Center for Performing Arts is a tribute to the front elevation of the Metropolitan Opera House at Lincoln Center in New York City, a modern take on neoclassicism imitated often across the country, and at Miami, done largely in red brick. Tappan Hall, opened at the beginning of the Public Ivy era in 1970 as Cellarius and Hilmer's last Miami building, added the novelty of Corinthian capitals to its columns but otherwise maintained the restrained neo-Georgian tone of their vast Miami portfolio.

Charles Cellarius and his design partner built at least forty campus buildings for Miami, and thirty-seven still stand in 2008. Cellarius died in 1973, and Hilmer closed the firm in 1974. The volume and consistency of their work sustained Miami's neo-Georgian charm through the terms of four presidents—Alfred H. Upham, Ernest H. Hahne, John D. Millett, and Phillip R. Shriver. When Millett replied to an inquiry from another architect, he explained:

Tappan Hall (1970). Photograph by Robert S. Wicks, 2008. Miami Archives.

A good many years ago, the Board retained Mr. Cellarius as the architect for the University. I have learned in my short time here that the Board is very well satisfied with Mr. Cellarius' services and is determined to retain these services more or less indefinitely. When I suggested a possible modification in architectural style for the new Student Center Building, the Board of Trustees introduced and passed a resolution . . . in which it declared that it was the policy of the Trustees to continue the present architectural style for all future buildings. This resolution, I am sure, was passed to let me know that any suggestions about a modification in architectural style would not be welcomed by the Board.

Cellarius and Hilmer offered an ensemble of harmonious architectural detail in their neo-Georgian vocabulary of symmetrical rooflines, windows, dormers, and colonnaded porches. The Oxford campus they created had pleasant human scale, accented its residential ambitions, and built the sense of the past—all deliberate choices of ambiance. In his 1959 commencement address Cellarius noted that Miami "has preserved the dignity and beauty and restfulness of the only national style America has yet achieved."

Architectural styles take life in particular historic eras, and as Cellarius and Hilmer spread a neo-Georgian village on the Oxford campus landscape, an earlier architectural heritage was erased. Under the pressures of deferred maintenance, constrained budgets, lack of donor support, and changing taste, after 1959 eight historically significant buildings from earlier eras were demolished: Old Main, Hepburn Hall, Brice Scientific Hall, Fisher Hall, Alumnae Hall, President Bishop's House, Tallawanda Apartments, and Herron Gymnasium. The evolving spirit of the institution that reopened in 1885 brought coeducation, professional school curricula, previously unimagined levels of enrollment and financial assistance from the State of Ohio, rituals and ceremonies of student and alumni life, a cultivated intergenerational community, a new sense of the past grounded in romance about glories of earlier eras, and an iconic architecture that vividly captured the charm of cozy residential life. Some of these features would survive the unexpected trauma that Miami would face in 1941. Some would not. The neo-Georgian imprint, however, would endure for at least one more historic era as the postwar university rose to national visibility. Then in the twenty-first century the legacy of Charles Cellarius at Miami would confront its own uncertain future.

Act 3

A National University
1941–1970

Expanding Access

1941–45	December 7, 1941, Pearl Harbor Naval Station attacked; United States enters World War II
	War depletes civilian enrollment, military training schools prepare 10,000 recruits and reserves
1945	President Alfred H. Upham dies in office; A. K. Morris, acting president, 1945–46
1946	Ernest H. Hahne (1946–52) assumes the presidency; "Veterans' Village" ("Vetville") erected
	Graduate School established as a separate academic division
1947	John E. Dolibois named executive secretary of Miami Alumni Association
1949	Reid Hall residence for men, Rowan Hall Naval ROTC building constructed
	Upham Hall center section (humanities) constructed; north wing, 1950, and south wing, 1965 (natural sciences)
1950	WMUB FM Radio founded
1952	President Hahne dies; Clarence W. Kreger, acting president, 1952–53
	Billings Natatorium, Collins and McBride residence halls constructed; Tallawanda Hall (1908) acquired
1953	John D. Millett (1953–64) assumes the presidency
1954	East Dining Hall (later "East End") constructed by Armco Steel with two cafeteria lines to serve 700
1956	Porter residence hall, Administration Building (later Roudebush Hall) constructed
1957	Work begins on Dennison (1958), Center (later MacCracken, 1961), Scott (1957) residence halls
	University Center (later Phillip R. Shriver Center) constructed
1958	Sesquicentennial celebration year, 1958–59; Old Main (old Harrison Hall) demolished
	Walter Havighurst publishes *The Miami Years* (revised 1969 and 1984)
	Hiestand Hall (School of Fine Arts), Miami Manor (married student housing) constructed
1959	School of Applied Science founded; Dean of Educational Services created
	Senator John F. Kennedy speaks at Miami Field; Martin Luther King Jr. speaks in University Center
	McGuffey House (1833) acquired for museum; designated National Historic Landmark, 1961
	Bishop Memorial Gates; Sesquicentennial Chapel; Brandon, Dennison north wing, McFarland residence halls constructed
	February 17, "Sesquicentennial Convocation" marks Miami's first formal Charter Day

	Laws Hall (business administration), Williams Hall (WMUB studios, communication) constructed
1960	Harrison Hall (social sciences) on site of Old Main, John W. Browne Stables constructed
1961	Anderson, Dodds, Stanton, MacCracken (addition) residence halls; Harris, Erickson dining halls constructed
	Culler Hall (natural sciences) constructed
1962	Edwin Fulwider's *Biography of a University* mural created for University Center Heritage Room
	Delta Delta Delta Sundial constructed
	Dorsey, Minnich residence halls; Warfield Hall (Student Affairs) constructed
	Phillips Hall (physical education), MacMillan Hospital center wing constructed
1964	John D. Millett resigns presidency, named first chancellor of Ohio Board of Regents
	Mississippi Summer Project student volunteers train on Western College campus
1965	Phillip R. Shriver (1965–81) assumes the presidency
1966	Miami University Middletown founded
	Flower, Hahne residence halls; King Library phase one constructed
1967	Shideler Hall (geography and geology), Murstein Alumni Center constructed
1968	Miami University Hamilton founded
	Miami European Center (named for John E. Dolibois, 1988), opened
	Benton Hall (psychology), Millett Hall (assembly hall, sports arena) constructed
1969	Institute for Environmental Sciences founded
	McGuffey Laboratory School, Center for Performing Arts (theatre and music) constructed
	Emerson and Morris residence halls constructed
1970	Tappan residence hall, Hughes Laboratories (chemistry) constructed
	April 15, Rowan Hall occupied by war protesters and Black Student Action Association, 176 arrested
	April 16, strike called, Oxford campus; May 4, four students killed by National Guard at Kent State University
	May 7, President Shriver closes Oxford campus; reopens May 17

"National University" Themes, 1941–1970

Miami's third era begins and ends in war. When the United States enters World War II, civilian enrollment drops dramatically as male students and some faculty and staff depart for military duty. The university continues to operate with a reduced civilian enrollment that is primarily female. The war years, however, bring an unprecedented number of people to the Oxford campus when between 1942 and 1945 Miami hosts a U.S. Naval Training School that prepares ten thousand men and women for wartime service.

Allied victory in World War II sparks an era of public investment in state universities, particularly for scientific research. State institutions across the Midwest rise to new national visibility during a quarter century of postwar prosperity fueled by national economic growth, "baby boom" enrollment, Cold War government spending on scientific and technical projects, as well as unprecedented state and federal policy commitments to higher education opportunities for all Americans. New specialized undergraduate and graduate programs serve a rapidly increasing student population that includes both students of traditional college age and adult students funded by the "G.I. Bill." These changes produce dramatic postwar expansion of enrollment, construction, new faculty, curricula, student programs, staff, and managerial bureaucracy.

The Oxford campus grows rapidly and is rebuilt with a "Georgian" architectural motif that was introduced before World War II and is now institutionalized as Miami's official stylistic brand. Off-campus instruction expands at sites across southwestern Ohio, eventually creating new regional campuses at Middletown and Hamilton. The European Center is established at the heart of the continent in Luxembourg, attracting a steady stream of students and faculty. Miami's continuous expansion in postwar years is supported by effective networking with high school counselors that brings to Oxford record numbers of talented students, primarily from suburbs and small towns of the American Midwest.

Intensifying professional specialization and disciplinary research reshape academic life as professional schools continue to grow and Miami creates its first doctoral programs. Scholarship and the successful pursuit of external funding are increasingly important to the professional advancement of faculty, along with a continuing commitment to high-quality teaching and to maintaining personal contact with students in a residential environment. Administrative leaders personalize campus life by promoting a "family" concept said to bind all Miami employees, students, and alumni. Intercollegiate athletics becomes a major investment and a new agenda for cultivating alumni loyalty, along with a steady expansion of thriving student organizations and cocurricular culture.

The era ends when Miami is drawn into a raging national conflict over the Vietnam War. An aggressive police response to ending a student sit-in at the Naval ROTC building results in the arrest of 176 protesters and a night of campus violence involving tear gas and police dogs, and a strike on classes is called. When four student protesters are killed by the Ohio National Guard at Kent State University, the Oxford campus is closed. After Miami reopens ten days later, both governance and academic policies are liberalized.

"...that Miami is gone forever."

I was a sophomore when a cousin from Bellevue, Ohio, Jean Smith, wrote me a note and said, "One of my very good friends, Martha Nye, is at Wellesley College. You might look her up." Well, Yale played Harvard that Fall up in Cambridge, Massachusetts, and I looked her up. And here we are today. Yale won the game with my roommate who was a member of the Yale football team and whose end coach was Gerald Ford, later President of the United States. We met there and had our first date there not knowing that two weeks later an event called Pearl Harbor would take place that completely changed our lives. From that point on we had the war and our probable involvement in it as uppermost in our minds. I went into the naval service at Yale, joining the V-12 unit. I became the regimental commander of the Yale V-12 regiment. I went through a condensed program that took us through the year. Vacations were ruled out. I was commissioned an ensign in the United States Navy and the week following commissioning Martha and I married. Then I went out on a destroyer in the Pacific, saw service at Iwo Jima, Okinawa, and was at Tokyo Bay when the signing of the surrender took place. After the war Martha and I could then live a more normal life, going to Harvard for my master's degree, then to Columbia for my doctorate, and then on to Kent State. At that point, in effect, I was returning home.

Phillip R. Shriver in the U.S. Navy during World War II. Shriver family collection.

Phillip R. Shriver
President, Miami University, 1965–81
Miami Stories Oral History Project
May 19, 2006

OXFORD, DECEMBER 7, 1941

December 7, 1941, began much like many Ohio winter Sundays—cold and cloudy, with a bit of snow. For Miami students it was a day to go to church, have dinner, and relax before another Monday rolled around. Some students had a busy weekend. On Friday night, 750 couples attended the Sophomore Hop at Withrow Court. Saturday night the Association of Miami Independents held its annual winter semiformal dance at McGuffey School Gym. Other students took in a weekend double feature at the Miami-Western Theatre or patronized the Oxford Bowling Center. Many looked forward to returning home for Christmas vacation, less than two weeks away.

Meanwhile, much of the world was at war. Although the United States was officially neutral, the presence of a Civilian Pilot Training Program at Miami already suggested an uncertain future. In recent days there had been radio reports of a Russian counterattack that stopped the German army at the gates of Moscow. U.S. and Japanese representatives were meeting uncomfortably in Washington to discuss Japanese ambitions in Asia. Then late on Sunday a radio report shattered the tranquility of the Miami campus with news that Japanese air forces had attacked the American naval base at Pearl Harbor, Hawaii. Many listeners reacted with disbelief, shock, or anger. The *Miami Student* recorded that Herb Saito, a student of Japanese ancestry whose parents lived in Hawaii, kept repeating "I can't believe it" when he heard of the Japanese attack. Soon he would serve with distinction as a translator for U.S. Military Intelligence.

As the magnitude of the Pearl Harbor attack became known, *Miami Student* staff decided to produce a special edition. Working frantically Sunday night and early Monday, they scooped many of the area's leading dailies. Their front page included the text of Roosevelt's war message to Congress, transcribed from shorthand notes of the radio broadcast. It carried an account of the congressional declaration of war, a brief message from President Upham to students, and results of a poll of eighty-three "representative" Miami men. While more than 85 percent supported the declaration of war with Japan, 10 percent opposed it and nearly 3 percent felt the Japanese attack made a formal declaration unnecessary. A cartoon by *Student* artist Ron Jacobson showed a male student in civilian clothes anxiously peering into a mirror that reflected him in military garb. That cartoon captured an unspoken feeling that life would never be the same after December 7.

The United States enters World War II. Miami Student, December 8, 1941.

Most Miamians faced the immediate future with dour resolution. Said the *Student,* "There was no false crusading spirit this time. No parades, no shouting, just getting down to the grim business of winning a war for survival." Initially many thought this would be war with Japan alone. Although Roosevelt considered Germany an equal threat, public support for war with the Nazis was by no means sure. Four days later Hitler resolved that matter by declaring war on the United States.

WARTIME MIAMI

By December 13 the reality of war came to Oxford in a terse telegram to Mrs. Lawrence Williams. Her son Lawrence had graduated in 1936 with a major in architecture, considered a career in engineering, and in spring 1940 decided to enlist in the Naval Air Corps. He was sent to the Pacific in May 1941 as a scout for the Pacific Fleet. When Mrs. Williams heard of the attack on Pearl Harbor she had a premonition, and the wire confirmed it. Lawrence had been killed in action during the attack, the first Miamian who would die or be listed as missing during World War II.

Some students joined the armed services before the semester ended. Once it was over, two faculty members entered military ranks and another left to work in the industrial sector. Those departures were the first of a vast evacuation that fundamentally changed the university. Of 5,187 members of the Miami community who served in the military, 163 lost their lives. Regular enrollment dropped from 3,303 in December 1941 to about 2,098 before the end of the war. Meanwhile, about 10,000 trainees came to campus for instruction in skills needed for the war effort.

Less than a month after Pearl Harbor, President Upham attended a national conference of educators in Baltimore. He reported to the trustees that participants "emphasized particularly the need for an acceleration of college programs without reducing the standards and requirements for college degrees." They recognized that they had to assess manpower needs and make the most effective adjustments possible to aid the war effort. Many institutions would soon be teaching more women in an accelerated curriculum while offering short-term specialized courses for both men and women in the military. Military officials inspected Miami facilities and spoke about the possibility of using the entire Oxford campus as a physical training center for all men inducted into the navy air forces. In the end they chose to use the campus in ways that would not require complete termination of existing college programs, and Miami contracted to operate a naval training school.

The first class of the U.S. Naval Training School to enter in May 1942 consisted of 151 men from 41 states. They lived on the northeast corner of campus in the former women's college and Oxford Retreat that was now named Fisher Hall. They took meals in a mess hall built beside Fisher Hall, learned how to send and receive telegraph code, then moved on as other recruits took their places. When regular students returned in the fall, they found 600 naval

Women military trainees on review, Cook Field. Photograph by Gilson P. Wright. Miami Archives and Smith Library.

U.S. Naval Training School. Photograph by Gilson P. Wright. Miami Archives and Smith Library.

trainees on campus. In spring 1943 a company of U.S. Navy WAVES—Women Accepted for Volunteer Emergency Service—joined the radio training program. WAVES used their own equipment, set up in Alumni Library, for instruction. A total of 400 WAVES came to Oxford for sixteen weeks of training in a rotation of forty graduates and new trainees every two weeks. In summer 1943, the navy established at Miami a branch of its V-12 college training program to prepare commissioned officers on university and college campuses. Soon women Coast Guard trainees (SPARS), as well as cooks, bakers, medics, and air corps cadets, would arrive. Trainees drilled on campus, performed formal dress reviews weekly at Cook Field, and received "shore leave" to visit the village. An airfield for training air corps cadets was constructed west of Oxford. To many, the scene probably seemed like a navy town, complete with its own newspaper. The *Dispatch,* a Naval Training School newsletter, proclaimed on its masthead: "The Traditions of the Navy Are Great—Remember Them as You Serve."

There were changes to accommodate the demands of war. The 1942–43 report of William E. Alderman, dean of the College of Liberal Arts, noted that a new curriculum for junior and senior women had been approved at the year's first faculty meeting. It included courses in mathematics, physics, chemistry, and industrial education that would substitute for other classes in the interest of better preparing students for the worldwide struggle. Course content was broadened to include international issues, and some faculty members had to teach altogether different subjects. In his 1943–44 report, Dean Alderman observed that faculty members "have prepared themselves in or retooled in a variety of fields foreign to their primary interests." This meant, he went on, that "teachers from English, Foreign Languages, Geology, and Speech have been teaching Code; one teacher of Latin has taught Mathematics; one teacher of Botany has taught Radio Theory; teachers from English and History have taught Navigation; and one teacher of Philosophy has taught Psychology." Liberal arts instructors taught about 80 percent of all academic courses in the V-12 program.

Student life on campus changed sharply. Most essentially, the regular student body became largely female. Women, 41.2 percent of the university population in 1940, made up 84.6 percent in 1943. Women assumed positions of responsibility that had often fallen to men— heading up the editorial and business sides of the *Miami Student,* for example. Women's athletic teams thrived, winning championships in volleyball, field hockey, and lacrosse in wartime years, and participating in archery, horseback riding, tennis, softball, and other sports. Men's athletic teams were hard pressed to make their civilian quotas, and Miami opponents Akron and Cincinnati canceled intercollegiate competition in football. Lieutenant Commander J. F. E. Gray of the Naval Training

Decoding class for WAVES. Photograph by Gilson P. Wright. Miami Archives and Smith Library.

1942–1945
Miami University War Training Program

Civilian Pilot Training	570
War Training Service	1,015
Radio Navy Men	4,314
Coast Guard Men	10
Navy WAVES	1,165
Coast Guard SPARS	50
Women Marines	315
Cooks and Bakers	467
V-12, V-5, NROTC	1,847
Cadet Nurses	42
Total	9,795

Oxford Salutes, *oil painting by Marston Hodgin, 1943. McGuffey Museum.*

School gave formal permission for radio trainees to play on Miami's football squad as early as 1943, a year when the team posted a victorious 7-1-2 season.

Naval Training School activities permeated campus buildings by 1944, and temporary structures were erected, including the first "Redskin Reservation" snack bar, which stood just west of today's Laws Hall. Servicemen and women were housed in Elliott, Stoddard, Ogden, East, and West halls in addition to Fisher. Some women were moved to fraternity houses now emptied of their occupants. Still, the place was crowded. Residence hall rooms that had been doubles became triples, and some students slept in the gymnasium. Dining halls changed to cafeteria-style service in order to feed large numbers of people efficiently.

Professor Marston Hodgin, chair of the Art Department from 1927 to 1963, captured the 1943 wartime scene in a painting still on display at McGuffey Museum. It shows a diverse multicultural crowd of townspeople and children, a student couple, U.S. Navy men and V-12 reserves, WAVES, SPARS and women marines in uniform, enjoying friendly social conversations, eating ice cream cones, or inspecting the Honor Roll sign that the village mounted in West Park to list the name of every Oxford serviceman under the banner "Oxford Salutes Her Boys in Service." Despite the convivial mingling Hodgin depicted and the generally upbeat tone of the work, a serious thread runs through it. The figures move off the canvas in every direction, suggesting the acute transience of this moment in history. A member of the Navy Shore Patrol, keeping watch and bringing authority, moves through the crowd to exit left with baton in hand. In the USO window forming a backdrop to this scene a sign states, "No Beef Today."

Students were keenly affected by the war. They followed news of battles, wrote letters to loved ones overseas, and took wartime jobs during vacations or after graduation that let them feel they were doing their part. Student journals and diaries for courses taught by history professor W. E. Smith offer an intimate perspective on the wartime atmosphere. Barbara Brown, a Miami junior, recorded highlights of two quite different days as Thanksgiving approached in 1944.

November 20, 1944:

At dinner today Dean Hamilton suggested that we have a little party for the girls who will be in the dorm Wednesday night. She suggested a costume party. . . .

November 21, 1944:

When Rit got the telephone call the day after she came back from visiting Bill Pike, she didn't say anything. Bill had been killed in an airplane crash. Rit was a soldier, she never cried until she got a letter that afternoon. She hasn't cried since. Rit went to Bill's funeral and has visited his mother since. She's had nightmares. The shakes, and in spite of it all Rit never complains. She talks about Bill all of the time and has surrounded herself with his pictures and still wears his frat pin and wings. I spend a lot of time with Ritter and listen to her for hours. There are times when I wish that I could bear the brunt of the world's sorrow and let people go about happy and carefree. I know that some day Rit's going to be okay again, but oh if there were no such thing as war.

Some women considered joining the military service. With WAVES on campus and women's branches of other services similarly visible, students could easily see alternatives to women's typical social roles. An ongoing debate in the country and on campus about women serving in the military produced admirers of female trainees among Miami students. Meanwhile, the government attempted to soften negative reactions to the assertive roles women assumed in wartime. "Rosie the Riveter" posters depicted attractive women at work in war plants. Newspaper articles described wartime women workers as "dressed for action in a one-piece coverall that is not only practical but attractively becoming." While Miami coeds were downplaying beauty competitions in favor of an annual "Posture-Perfect Contest" sponsored by the Women's Athletic Association, men of the Naval Training School elected a "Commissioning Day Queen" from candidates representing WAVES and Marine Corps Women's Reserve trainees.

Women who stayed on campus while men went overseas commiserated about their social lives. Most wanted to marry and raise families even though

Commissioning Queen Sue Dearinger. Naval Training School Dispatch, *May 3, 1944.*
Miami Archives.

eligible men were in short supply. But should they plunge into quick marriages with servicemen going to war? Student Jean Gatch wrote in her diary about a friend's brother who married a young woman he had known for only three weeks. Perhaps it was love at first sight, she speculated, "or else they were both desperate." Even before the United States entered the war in 1941, that year's marriage rate was the highest ever recorded, and "impulsive" marriages continued through the war, foreshadowing a high postwar divorce rate.

Like other women around the country, many female students developed a sense of autonomy that sometimes challenged social protocol. In 1943 the campus engaged in a "blue jean debate," as this newly stylish garment for women appeared and "the University asked girls to stop wearing jeans to class, deeming them unladylike and inappropriate." There were fewer dances and sorority parties. Some women chafed under conventional social restrictions and argued that if a person was old enough to vote or fight, such constraints made little sense. Service men and women mingled at a lively USO center operated in uptown Oxford, which recorded 29,825 customers in 1944–45 alone. Archival photographs suggest that Miami coeds and Naval Training School men often socialized. When Navy V-12 men had to be back in their dormitories for a 10:00 p.m. curfew, Miami women whose own curfew was later felt comfortable walking men back to their quarters and then going home alone. Women went out socially with one another and discovered, as the 1943 *Recensio* yearbook noted, that they didn't mind "stagging it." Meanwhile at Western College, jeans-clad Western "Farmerettes" worked alongside navy trainees in wartime gardens on the college farms.

The *Recensio* provides insight into shifting attitudes about the war. The 1942 edition—the first after the attack on Pearl Harbor—noted that "members of this year's senior class faced a world at war. The cockiness they had as underclassmen was gone. . . . The seniors were on the edge of a brink, half eager and half afraid to look ahead." The 1943 edition faced the war even more squarely. One of its first pages featured a drawing of President Roosevelt with his words: "WE WILL GAIN THE INEVITABLE TRIUMPH . . . SO HELP US GOD." Describing Roosevelt's "Four Freedoms" (freedom of speech and worship, freedom from want and fear) and Atlantic Charter pledges for a better world, the yearbook observed with determination, "1942 has shown us that America can and will do all that is expected of her in the winning of the war." By 1944, as the tide of war turned, the *Recensio* described "A CHANGED MIAMI." It asserted that "Miami in wartime is a Miami closer to reality. Many of the superficialities we believed in have been discarded." Through their wartime experiences Miami students may have felt more connected with the rest of the world, by necessity, than had Miami students in previous eras. By 1945 victory was in sight. The *Recensio* said the Class of 1945 hoped "that 1946 will bring the end of the war and a happier graduation year."

In June 1946 the *Miami University Bulletin*, published for alumni, reflected on the changes Miami had experienced. It included a "Roll of Honor" listing war dead, reflective essays by Walter Havighurst and historian Fred B. Joyner, and a piece by W. E. Smith on "What the Student Thought." As Miami and the country grappled with conversion to a postwar economy, integration of former soldiers into the workforce, and ramifications of the G.I. Bill that would bring many former servicemen to campus, Smith observed that "the University of 1945–46 is in many ways unlike the Miami in all its past century and a third of existence." Student editors of the 1944 *Recensio* were even more direct: "Our wartime Miami is a changed place indeed. Although we wistfully recall the Miami of the past, that Miami is gone forever. Now we await another change, another Miami, to meet what the future demands."

scene seven

A Postwar Agenda

EXIT NEW MIAMI

Joseph M. Bachelor graduated from Miami in 1911. As student editor, he modernized the *Miami Student* when he changed it from a monthly to a weekly paper. An honors undergraduate who took graduate work in English at Harvard, from 1917 to 1927 Bachelor was New York editor of the three-volume *Century Dictionary*. Asked by President Hughes to return to Miami, he took up residence in Fisher Hall when it opened as a freshman dormitory in 1927. The next year he was made proctor of Fisher, where for thirteen years he mentored numerous undergraduates as well as his young assistant proctor, Walter Havighurst, who would later write Miami's history.

In 1940 Bachelor moved to a secluded farmhouse on 100 acres of "marginal farmland" he acquired northeast of Oxford. He met with students there, sharing around his fireplace an "inexhaustible world-lore" of life beyond southwest Ohio. He taught English, performing literary characters in a legendary Shakespeare class in Irvin Hall, and offering his persistently over-enrolled specialty, "Words," a course copied but apparently never matched at other colleges. A strict disciplinarian who demanded responsible conduct of his dormitory charges, Bachelor was a New Miami humanist who loved to tell stories. Havighurst described him as highly learned, intellectually engaging, "wise and venerable," as well as "paternal, avuncular, trailing cigar smoke and sentiment, tritely nostalgic and emotional—and unforgettable."

"Joe" Bachelor taught through the end of World War II, then in the spring of 1946 retired to his farmhouse. One morning in 1947 he was found "slumped

Joseph M. Bachelor, proctor of Fisher Hall, 1928–40, and professor of English until 1946 (seated left of fireplace), with Walter E. Havighurst (standing left of fireplace), 1929. Miami Archives.

over a lapboard of books and papers on his rocking chair beside his cold stone fireplace." By that year his land holdings had grown to nearly 400 acres. In his will he gave his entire estate to Miami University. Named the "Joseph M. Bachelor Wildlife and Game Reserve," it was protected from development. Later Miami increased the reserve to 661 acres. In 2007 the land contiguous to the Oxford campus cherished by this lover of students, words, erudition, and Manhattan remained a site for holistic environmental education, ecology research, and woodland walking tours.

On February 17, 1945, the 136th anniversary of its charter, Miami's last alumnus to serve as president died in office. After having dinner with students in a residence hall, taking in a panel discussion, and walking his Scottie dog on Slant Walk, at 1:30 a.m. in Lewis Place Alfred H. Upham suffered a heart attack. By 1947 both Alfred Upham and Joseph Bachelor were gone. As the postwar university emerged out of American military triumph, their world would be replaced.

In the first postwar history of the university, Walter Havighurst quoted a *Miami Student* editorial written by a medically discharged veteran who enrolled in 1944. "The returned student veteran believes in the future of America," the writer asserted. "He has had a part in shaping that future. He knows that his new role of student is not only the greatest of all privileges but is also an obligation born of the blood of the men he has known who have perished in battle." Many returning veterans revealed such seriousness, along with optimism that personal initiative and advanced education would serve both them and the nation. The idea that going to college was an obligation to both self and society would draw unprecedented numbers of

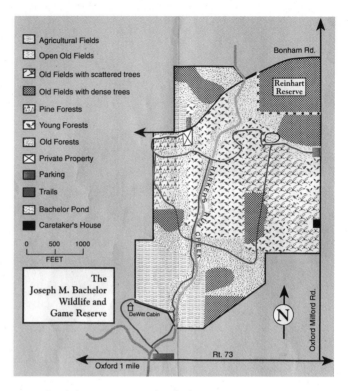

Map of Bachelor property east of Oxford, given to Miami to be maintained as a protected wildlife preserve. *Miami Archives.*

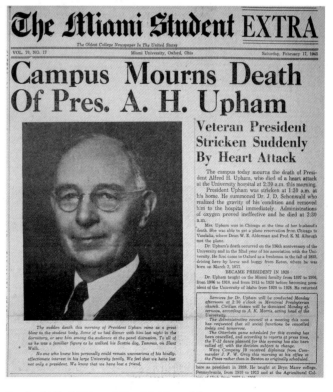

Death of Alfred Upham. *Miami Student, February 17, 1945.*

Miami Wartime and Postwar Civilian Enrollment

	1941–42	1944–45	1941–45 % Decrease	1950–51	1945–51 % Increase
Senior Men	275	23	92%	636	2,665%
Senior Women	230	225	2%	278	24%
Total University	**3350**	**2118**	**37%**	**5037**	**138%**

students, especially men, to public higher education institutions immediately after World War II.

The war ended in Europe in May 1945, and in the Pacific in August. A 1944 act of Congress changed higher education even before hostilities ended. In the Servicemen's Readjustment Act, popularly known as the G.I. Bill, the federal government committed to paying for the college education of returning veterans. In the fall of 1945 Miami's freshman class included four hundred men, and like universities across the nation reacting to the success of the G.I. Bill, Miami lacked sufficient housing. Letters went to townspeople, asking for rental listings. Dormitories were overcrowded. On October 7, 1946, *Life* magazine ran a photograph of men in double-decker beds at Withrow Court. To respond to this crisis, surplus army barracks, named Miami Lodges but nicknamed "Green Mansions," were brought to Oxford from Fort Knox, Kentucky, and set up on the east side of South Oak Street for single men.

Many postwar students were older and more experienced than most students entering Miami today. Another postwar novelty was that some were married, and some had growing families. To respond to these entirely new kinds of housing needs, Miami acquired 196 temporary employee duplex housing units from the Willow Run Aircraft Plant in Detroit, Michigan, moved them to Oxford on trucks, and set them up on eight acres between South Campus Avenue and South Oak Street. On April 1, 1945, the first thirty couples moved into "Veterans' Village." By fall of 1949 an unprecedented total of 5,500 civilian students were on campus.

Temporary housing for married students and their families remained on Oxford's south campus until 1958. In the early years it encouraged a powerful sense of community. Martin Egelston, a 1951 and 1958 graduate who lived there with his wife and baby, documented resident recollections of life in "Vetville." Housing units, each only about 20 x 24 feet, were made of wood sheathed in plywood. They featured flat roofs with ventilators; push-out windows; an oil heating stove with a 150-gallon tank; a stand-up compact bathroom with sink, shower, and toilet; a four-foot galley kitchen with a roaster oven, a two-burner hotplate, and an "ice box"; and many electric fuses. Rent was $37.50 per month, which covered the appliances and "heating oil, electricity, light bulbs, fuses, repairs, and a supportive community." Close quarters and common challenges bred memories. Residents recalled meeting at the centralized laundry facility housed in a Quonset hut that had a grocery in early years and "was a friendly gathering place where frugal students arranged babysitting services, posted meeting notices, and bought and sold used furniture." Automobile traffic was modest and slow, the area had a few shade trees, and residents planted flowers, elected governing officials, and published their own newspaper. Privacy was not the rule, for walls were thin, everyone lived close to others, and pervasive clotheslines strung between units assured mingling. While many Vetville students lived quite frugally by today's standards, apparently they had good humor as well—Vetville wives published a cookbook titled *Fifty Ways to Cook Hamburger*. The success of this temporary community in underwriting Miami's postwar expansion was a step toward the national university that would soon emerge.

HORIZONS

The construction of Vetville was supervised by Wallace P. Roudebush, an alumnus named secretary to the president in 1911 who thirty-five years later was still managing Miami business affairs. President Ernest H. Hahne (1946–52) was in charge. Miami's first postwar president, described by a trustee on meeting him as "sound," looked ahead and initiated a broad postwar agenda. Perceiving the challenge of science and technology facing higher education, Hahne saw Miami as a place where life beyond the classroom could yield the creativity the era needed.

When the trustees chose Hahne to lead Miami they were undoubtedly looking to a future of growth. A professor of economics at Northwestern, Hahne held undergraduate and law degrees from the University of Nebraska, an MA from Harvard and a PhD from the

Students temporarily housed in Withrow Court gymnasium. Photograph by Wallace Kirkland, Life Magazine, October 17, 1946. Copyright Time-Warner, Inc.

Veterans' Village, ca. 1950. Photograph by Gilson P. Wright. Miami Archives and Smith Library.

Veterans' Village family. Recensio, 1949.

*Wallace P. Roudebush, appointed secretary to president, 1911,
and served as business manager until 1956, in a dining hall, 1954.*
Christopher A. Maraschiello, Wallace P. Roudebush, 1993.

Ernest H. Hahne, president of Miami University, 1946–52.
Miami Archives.

University of Chicago. Involved in public administration projects across the
Midwest and East, he was a widely published expert on finance, economics,
and taxation who had served on research projects for the governor of New
York, the City of Chicago, the Bureau of the Budget in Washington, and the
Illinois State Tax Commission. An announcement of his appointment in the
December 1945 *Miami University Bulletin* emphasized his academic qualifications, noted that he held the rank of first lieutenant in the First World War,
and added as a parting observation that among other affiliations and honors,
he was a Methodist and a member of Acacia social fraternity.

The same *Bulletin* reported, "Housing is Miami's number one problem
these days, with every available room on campus occupied" and a waiting list
of hopefuls for second semester. Hahne and Roudebush addressed the challenge. In addition to Veterans' Village and Miami Lodges, they put up a temporary building for art and music, constructed Cellarius's Logan Lodge for
women and Reid Hall for men, built Rowan Hall for the Navy Reserve Officers Training Corps, expanded Upham Hall, and in the early 1950s added a
steam plant to serve the Oxford campus, a west wing to Alumni Library, Cellarius's Billings Natatorium, and Collins and McBride residence halls. They
also acquired in 1952 the neoclassic Tallawanda Apartments, built in 1908 by a
private entrepreneur at High Street and Tallawanda Road.

Faculty hired after the war were welcomed to Oxford during many social
and economic changes. Mobility was rising, automobiles were in vogue, and

Oxford's Fryman Motor Sales deployed military imagery in advertising their "rocket" Oldsmobile. Oxford Lumber Company offered everything needed to build "Your Dream House," a three-bedroom "colonial cottage" with living room, kitchen, a bath, and nine closets. It could be bought with thirty-six-month financing. The wartime gender revolution continued as the number of married women between the ages of forty-five and fifty-four working outside the home more than doubled nationally—from 10.1 percent in 1940 to 22.2 percent in 1950. By the 1950s a new level of consumer-oriented family life in sprawling suburban communities, made possible by federally funded highway networks, fueled an expanding market for disposable goods. The novelty of television brought an entertainment revolution. These volatile

Tallawanda Hall, acquired 1952. Built as Tallawanda Apartments in 1908 on the northwest corner of High Street and Tallawanda Road. Photograph by Gilson P. Wright. Miami Archives and Smith Library.

Inaugural Address of President Ernest H. Hahne, April 19, 1947

from *Widening Horizons in Higher Education*

Today popular opinion limits the widening horizons of education to the physical sciences and appears to be centered in such things as the use of proximity fuses, radar, DDT, penicillin, plastics, television, atomic power, radium, blood plasma, and the unexplored areas of radionics. In the Great Miami Valley at nearby Dayton, a rocket has been invented recently that, it is reported, will fly a distance of 800 miles at a rate of 3,600 miles per hour with an accuracy limitation of half a mile. These same research specialists predict that within a decade greater missiles may be projected with greater speed and with a range of 3,000 miles. Thus it appears that the next age is not the atomic age, but the atomic-rocket age. From these scientific horizons comes the call for youth to enter the fields of pure science, engineering, and technology. Pure scientists called to lead this procession will be numbered by the tens, the engineers by the hundreds, the technicians by the thousands, and those who benefit from scientific progress by the millions. The widening horizons of physical science, now popularly recognized, are but evidences of man's increasing mastery of nature. . . .

A university must give careful attention to the means that would develop in all students the kind of personalities we want our youth to have. Intellectualism is not enough.

Personality is not enough. Both are necessary in the building of sound character. Woodrow Wilson once observed that there was as much education taking place between four in the afternoon and midnight, as there was between eight in the morning and four in the afternoon. Because this is true it is incumbent for university faculty and administration alike to concern themselves with the quality of these associations in which the student lives. . . .

One of the chief virtues of extra-curricular activities is the chance for creativeness. The world has need for creative leadership. Mankind has discovered the greatest weapon of destruction known in history. Nuclear physicists may say the atomic bomb was the result of creative science, but not until atomic energy is put to peaceful uses may that discovery be adjudged creative. Americans long have been proud of their "Yankee ingenuity," but this has been interpreted abroad as the ingenuity befitting a nation of shop-keepers. This individual initiative and ingenuity must be revived in higher education in the form of creative writing, creative art, music, and architecture, and all the departments of university activity. . . . In this direction youth must be encouraged if native abilities are to be discovered. This is probably the most promising antidote against the present state of world bewilderment.

First rising to popularity alongside the movies during the New Miami era, radio had been the nation's novel media since at least the 1920s. Presidents Hughes and Upham regarded it as a public relations tool. On February 17, 1925, Hughes addressed alumni in forty cities on powerful WLW Radio in Cincinnati for "Miami Day," the first in a series of national radio broadcasts between 1925 and 1937 to commemorate the university's chartering. Although these typically originated from Ohio stations, Miami had an early radio presence in the South as well. On January 12, 1934, Miami was featured in a series on leading universities broadcast by WSM Radio, the home of the Grand Ole Opry, a 50,000-watt station in Nashville, Tennessee.

On February 15, 1935, Upham delivered a "Founders' Day" broadcast to alumni and friends via WHAS Radio in Louisville. He offered a capsule history of Miami, celebrated its reorganization into liberal arts, education, business administration and fine arts for "more efficient administration and teaching;" observed that enrollment and faculty had grown steadily since 1902; noted that Oxford College, "rich with the traditions of a century," had been "completely reconstructed" as a "residential center for freshman girls;" praised Miami's new Food Service Building, health service, and intramural sports; and said Miami was "well rounded," "wholesome," "inexpensive," and turning out students that, like its alumni, would be "loyal and worthy children of alma mater."

Radio transmission directly from Miami University in Oxford, however, did not begin until emergence of the postwar national university. It started on electrical wiring, when a student-operated carrier current station began operating from Old Main in 1947. That station, WMUB at 570 KC on the AM dial, run "by the students, for the students," moved to war surplus "Building D" and reached six Miami dormitories with 20 watts of power. It offered disc jockey programming and "popular and classical music, news, sports commentary, and campus announcements" from 7:30 a.m. to 8:00 p.m. These were listed in the October Miami Student as time blocks for Morning Thing, Noon Thing, Evening Thing, Redskin Review, Campus Listening Post, The Real Jazz, New Stuff from the Stacks, Broadway to Benton, Piano Portraits, On the Bench, Carnegie Hall, and the like. Four station managers were each responsible for a full day of programming, and the station put out an appeal for student volunteers "interested in stringing radio frequency lines." Miami administration used this station to release

programs through station WMOH in Hamilton, an affiliate of the Mutual Broadcasting System. WMUB radio was popular, and by December had an impressive staff of twenty students. Its student business manager was John Smale, who later would become chairman of the board and CEO of Procter and Gamble. Within a month, WMUB was carrying live Campus Listening Post interviews from such popular locations as "the Hospital, Mac 'n Joe's, Tuffy's, Thobe's Fountain and the Student office." By 1952 the station, renamed WRMU, also carried newscasts written from items on the United Press International newswire.

In late 1949 a 20-foot antenna was erected on one of the towers of Old Main to serve a new 10-watt FM broadcasting station with the reclaimed call letters WMUB. Directed by theatre professor Hortense Moore, the station was expected to "reach points ten miles away," reported the Alumnus. It planned to carry "educational features," music, and home basketball games. Meanwhile, programming at WRMU continued and faculty members were broadcasting via WMOH radio in Hamilton and WPFB in Middletown. Just five years later WMUB was given a WPFB transmitter that boosted power to 6,600 watts, and a 155-foot tower was put up, said to be capable of carrying the signal to Indiana and Kentucky. In 1958 a 322-foot tower was built by three daring eighteen-year-old workers from Arkansas and North Carolina employed by Ace High Tower Erectors of North Carolina. It was moved to Oxford from station WSAZ in Huntington, West Virginia, and set up near the southwest corner of Spring and Oak streets. That tower was said to be 1,216 feet above sea level and thus "as high as or higher" than towers in Dayton and Cincinnati.

By 1960 the Miami University Broadcasting Service had a Radio-TV Center on South Oak Street behind Bonham House. It boasted three control rooms, seven studios and classrooms, and equipment "to train students for work in communications." The Alumnus noted that the broadcasting tower "is Oxford's newest landmark from a distance." WMUB-TV offered seventeen hours of telecasting weekly on Channel 14, "courses for credit which have been taught for the past several years via closed-circuit television," and programs of the new National Educational Television (NET) Network of forty-five educational stations. In 1964, with a federal grant and local matching funds totaling $176,000, a new transmitter and an antenna extension gave WMUB-TV "an effective radiated power of 151,000 watts." The National University was on the air.

forces produced a "teenage" culture in the white American middle class, as young people of high school and college age had an unprecedented amount of leisure time, access to the proliferating automobile, cheap gasoline and better highways, more products marketed to niche buyers, "fast" food, and television and radio entertainers who fused blues and jazz from African American traditions with country, gospel, and pop legacies to generate rock-and-roll music.

WMUB Radio staff in the studio. Recensio, 1953.

Postwar American society was setting the stage for sweeping developments in higher education. Miami saw early results in the professional cultivation of alumni loyalty, the elaboration of residence life programs, the creation of a new campus climate, and the identification of advanced disciplinary specialization as a bellwether of faculty life.

CULTIVATING COLLEGE CULTURE

As the university expanded after World War II, the student population diversified further by age, gender, and race, while professional studies became more specialized. In this situation the work of blending alumni, students, and faculty into a common college culture required professional attention. It got it.

Alumni Affairs

When President Hahne learned that it would be his responsibility to manage alumni relations at a time when enrollment growth and physical expansion also demanded his attention, he opted for a full-time executive secretary of the Alumni Association. A search culminated early in 1947 with the appointment of John E. Dolibois, Class of 1942, who would later become vice president for development and alumni affairs. Born in Luxembourg in 1918, Dolibois moved to the United States with his father in 1931 when he was a seventh grader who could speak German, French, and Luxembourgish, but not English. He and his father lived with his uncle in Akron, where teachers, responding to the boy's lack of English, began his studies in kindergarten. Soon he excelled in English, and graduated from Akron North High School in 1938 as president of his senior class. He earned a scholarship to Miami, where he became an entrepreneur involved in a host of campus activities as well as in the Boy Scouts of America. Dolibois married in his senior year, and upon graduating worked with Procter and Gamble in Cincinnati before entering

President Hahne and John Dolibois at Oxford College alumnae reunion, 1951. Miami Archives.

Twentieth-Century Milestones of the Miami University Alumni Association

adapted from *Chronicle of Achievement* by Douglas M. Wilson, 1974

1906	Bert S. Bartlow appointed by President Benton as part-time "field and alumni secretary"

—published a comprehensive alumni directory
—raised $40,000 to match a gift from Andrew Carnegie to build Alumni Library
—coordinated centennial celebration of 1909
—published first *Alumni News Letter* in 1911
—established tradition of class presidents as alumni class secretaries
—persuaded Class of 1911 to create first alumni loan fund for students
—organized alumni clubs in eight cities
—initiated class reunions at commencement
—influenced creation of Miami's first Homecoming, 1914
—raised funds to create new athletic field in 1914, and new gates in 1918
—held alumni conferences on business, first in 1915, that led to first business courses

1915	Alfred H. Upham became general secretary of Alumni Association
1918	President Hughes created Alumni Loyalty Fund, first such fund in a state-assisted university
1920	The Million Dollar Campaign launched, seeking pledges to be paid over three years
1922	A. K. Morris, assistant to President Hughes, alumni secretary to 1946, created Alumni Council
1925	February 17, "All Miami Day," alumni in forty cities hear President Hughes on WLW Radio
1947	John E. Dolibois appointed first full-time alumni secretary

the army in November 1942. Although he completed training for service in an armored division, because of his language proficiency he was assigned to military intelligence and involved in the interrogation of top Nazi leaders while an international military tribunal prepared for war crime trials at Nuremberg.

Organized alumni activity at Miami reached back to 1832, but an entirely new era in alumni relations began in 1947 as John Dolibois wove the loyalty of Miami alumni into a program of continuing action. A new office was established. Alumni clubs formed across the country, tripled their number by 1960, and rose to more than forty by 1978. An expanded alumni magazine, today *The Miamian*, was first renamed *The Miami Alumnus*. Donor projects brought results, including creation of the Upham Memorial Room, support of the University Center that became the Phillip R. Shriver Center, and a long-range planning survey that generated many programs and projects. Dolibois and alumni leaders assisted with grants-in-aid for athletes, developed the first Alumni College, created the Artists Guild and Speakers Bureau, organized Miami alumni and friends to support bond issues for public universities, and raised funds for Sesquicentennial Chapel, Murstein Alumni Center, Climer Guest Lodge, the Alumni Merit Scholarship Program, and professorships.

Today Miami's European Center bears the name of John E. Dolibois. After an attempt to create a center in Asia failed with the loss of Japanese sponsors, Dolibois persuaded key leaders on both sides of the Atlantic that a European center would have mutual benefit as well as great value for Miami students. That center would play an important role in making Miami a national leader in students studying abroad. It earned Dolibois a seat on the Fulbright Commission, and when his track record in international education came to the attention of members of President Ronald Reagan's administration, Reagan appointed Dolibois ambassador to Luxembourg in 1981. His successful tenure led Congress to authorize naming the Luxembourg ambassador's residence in his honor.

At the core of Miami's alumni programs was an annual development project that teamed Dolibois with John D. Yeck, Class of 1934, a Dayton direct mail genius. Yeck was born in Akron, and first met Dolibois there at Boy Scout camp. He was Miami's head cheerleader in his senior year. In 1947 Dolibois inherited the job of writing an annual letter to alumni asking for contributions to the Miami Loyalty Fund, and in just three years he more than tripled the return, to over $20,000. Then John Yeck contacted him with suggestions about further improving the effectiveness of annual letters. Beginning in 1953 and continuing until Dolibois became ambassador, Yeck and Dolibois collaborated to craft an impressive series of letters reflecting their "mutual deep affection . . . for Miami." Yeck, named "Chairman of Mail Solicitations," printed the letters at the graphic shop in Dayton where he and his brother Bill ran a thriving printing business. The result was a twenty-year series of informal

Before John Dolibois became alumni secretary in 1947, the Alumni Office had been, in the words of Walter Havighurst, "a desk drawer in the office of A. K. Morris, assistant to the university president." Dolibois's first office was a converted men's lounge in Ogden Hall. In 1956 the office moved to Roudebush Hall and, in 1962, to the new student services building, Warfield Hall. By 1964 it was clear that returning alums did not easily identify with Warfield, and space there was scarce. In the October 1964 *Miami Alumnus* Dolibois cited the need for a suitable office and something more: "An Alumni House is a visitor's headquarters with Miami information and materials, with an archives room where significant mementos are on display and Miami tradition can be studied in an informal and inspiring atmosphere." He closed by announcing a capital gift campaign to establish an Alumni House in either a renovated Oxford home or a new structure.

Dolibois's article appeared when Miami was between presidents. In the December 1964 *Alumnus*, acting president Charles Wilson suggested that Lewis Place would make an ideal Alumni House, and said an added benefit would be removing the president from "such enervating distractions as the all-night pounding of truck traffic on a main commercial highway." Most replies to Wilson's proposal favored maintaining Lewis Place as the president's home, and Miami's next president would agree. In the April 1965 *Alumnus*, Dolibois reported that trustees had appointed a committee to recommend financing and construction of an Alumni Center "to function as a service center for all alumni and development (public relations) activities." In October they approved a site at the southeast corner of Chestnut Street and U.S. 27, contingent upon successful completion of a campaign for $250,000 to pay for it.

Alumni responded enthusiastically by donating cash, equipment, furnishings, and mementos. In February 1966 Dolibois reported that $72,000 had been received, plus pledges for an equal amount. That month the board voted to name the center for William Murstein, prominent Hamilton and Cincinnati business leader and 1960 honorary degree recipient. Although Murstein had not attended Miami, his gift enabled the project to move from planning stages to implementation. Groundbreaking took place on Alumni Weekend in 1966. In October the *Alumnus* reported that trustee Fred Climer and his wife had given $350,000 for construction of a guest lodge adjoining the center. Meanwhile, workers trying to keep on a busy construction schedule laid a cornerstone for the alumni center before a ceremony for that event could be arranged, so a "cornerstone unveiling" was held at the site June 16, 1967.

At completion, the Murstein Alumni Center complex included the Climer Guest Lodge; offices for the Alumni Association director, alumni secretary, and *Alumnus* editor; a library; a lounge; two conference rooms; and the Class of 1917 Room outfitted as a fiftieth-anniversary memorial. Dedication of Murstein Alumni Center and Climer Lodge during Alumni Weekend in June featured guests of honor Max Murstein, nephew of William; Fred Climer; and John Dolibois, now vice president for alumni affairs, whose vision and hard work made the center a reality. In *The Dolibois Years*, Walter Havighurst paid tribute: "This alumni director was a builder whose accomplishment will long outlast the heavenly June day. It stands four-square to all the winds that blow."

The Miami University Alumni Center

Centrum: Alumni Affairs—Development Program/Miami University Foundation/Climer Guest Lodge

Preconstruction drawing, Murstein Alumni Center (constructed 1967). Miami University Alumni Center pamphlet. Miami Archives.

and novel solicitation strategies that yielded "a sense of personal connection with the accomplishments and goals of the University's annual fund-raising, and with John Dolibois, himself." "It gradually developed," said John Yeck, "the most friendly and personal kind of relationship between John and thousands of alumni who had never met him in person."

Like the alumni program, the letters were highly crafted. Some were clever, like one printed backwards with two holes so the reader could hold it up to a mirror and read the message. Others played a sentimental theme, such as a masterpiece that reminded alumni of how beautiful the campus was in the fall with the aroma of burning leaves. The sides of this letter were actually burned with a torch so that nostalgic alumni might sniff something like that aroma when opening the envelope. Often combining humor with sentiment, these letters encouraged alumni to fund a variety of programs. They were crucial to making Miami a consistent national leader during this era among both public and private colleges and universities in percentage of alumni contributors, and the recipient of many national awards for alumni and development efforts. They were also an important personal annual message from Oxford to the growing host of graduates in an extended multigenerational community.

Residence Life

Since at least 1912 Miami expected freshmen to live in dormitories, but because of limited space some male students lived in Oxford rooming houses or with local families. In those arrangements, consistent attention to their college adjustment was unavailable. Some failed to return after their first year. Others joined fraternal organizations offering housing and dining as well as personal and social support. Despite the attempts of organized athletics, clubs, and religious organizations to attract student interest, in the early years of New Miami its officials—like those at other originally male institutions—did not consider the university responsible for student life outside the classroom, except when reacting to obvious problems.

That was not true in Oxford's colleges for women, where a tradition of cultivating student community had long been in place. Following the lead of eastern counterparts, the women's college buildings were designed to support community. They were singular places where faculty both taught and lived in residence, where students lived, and where most academic and cocurricular college functions occurred. In 1925 Miami acquired from the Oxford Retreat the original Oxford Female College building, renamed it Fisher Hall, and two years later opened it as a residence hall for first-year men. In 1928 Miami acquired Oxford College. President Upham was well aware of its communal traditions and the opportunity it offered for undergraduate community. Oxford College would become a residence for Miami women, and both Fisher Hall and Oxford College would be supervised by a live-in faculty member responsible for academic advising and student life.

The decisions to retain Fisher Hall and Oxford College as full-service residence halls with live-in advisors would influence the subsequent character of Miami's residence life programs. Even though a few Old Miami faculty, some with wives, had lived in North and South halls, they had not been responsible for nurturing student life outside the classroom except to enforce college rules. During Elizabeth Hamilton's tenure as dean of women, Miami developed a tradition as an emerging modern university that placed special emphasis on knowing its student residents and assisting them directly—both with academic advice and in their personal lives. Out of that tradition would emerge the practice of placing faculty members, and later young professionals studying college personnel administration, in first-year residence halls, where they lived with students and intentionally helped shape their college experience.

Dean Hamilton retired at the end of World War II, but even during Miami's unprecedented growth thereafter, an emphasis on supporting the success of new students continued. New halls built in East Quad for men and South Quad for women were designed by Cellarius to enshrine the institutional philosophy that all new students, men and women, would be required to live their first year in a relatively small hall supervised by both a full-time staff member and a graduate assistant trained in counseling. Each postwar freshman hall was also staffed with selected upperclass students, later known as resident advisors, who lived with new students in corridors in a ratio of less than 1:15. These trained and paid staff members were charged with knowing students personally and providing community leadership and support. This system contrasted with those of some postwar higher education institutions where incoming students lived in much larger facilities that student residents at times experienced as impersonal. Miami's dual commitments to an architecture of human scale and a legacy of residential community were aimed at avoiding that outcome.

As dormitories came to be considered full social development centers, the term "residence hall" was systematically applied to all housing sites. Well into the 1960s Miami's commitment to community development shared another agenda with the nineteenth-century women's colleges—cultivation of social graces. Seated evening meals, served at 5:30 p.m., were formal affairs, with men in required coats and ties and women in skirts or dresses. Tables were pre-set, and an assigned host formally passed dishes of food brought to the table by properly attired student waiters. At times those waiters were well-known student athletes, working for scholarships. Formal meals proved difficult to sustain, however, as the institution grew ever larger and dining halls moved to cafeteria service. However, to celebrate the sesquicentennial in 1959,

Central Food Stores maintained Miami's personal touch by making individually decorated cakes, with candles, for every dining table on campus.

Three years after acquiring Oxford College, Miami began constructing a food service building on the college's former campus at South Elm Street. This sophisticated facility cost $150,000 by the time it was completed in 1933. It served as a centralized location for managing all of Miami's food acquisition, preparation, and distribution to residence halls. Two to three thousand pounds of ice were made there daily, milk was pasteurized and taken to dining halls in five- and ten-gallon cans, and a central bakery produced large quantities of bread and breakfast rolls. One day a week, bakers made ice cream. This facility featured a management and accounting system devised by business manager Wallace Roudebush, a dietitian's office and test kitchen, a meat department with a large walk-in cooler, and storage areas for packaged and canned goods, staples, and vegetables. It was studied by other institutions, including Purdue, where its system was adopted. At Miami, it laid the groundwork for the cafeteria system.

By the mid-1960s consolidation of small dining halls and construction of larger ones for cafeteria service was under way. Table service was discontinued and classes were scheduled through the noon hour, precluding a common time for group midday meals. In 1965 Martin Dining Hall opened for athletes. Martin was also a site for cook training classes. At the end of the National University era in 1969, an administrative dietitian and six assistant dietitians were employed to expand special events meals, employee training classes, test luncheons, and recipe development and to collect systematized student feedback on satisfaction with dining services. In the Public Ivy era to come, Housing, Dining, and Guest Services would offer specialized snack bars, theme and event dinners, and (for a brief time in Alumnae Hall, then in the basement of Alexander Dining Hall on Western Campus) a rathskeller serving beer.

Students in cafeteria line, ca. 1960s. Miami Archives.

As residence life programs became more professionalized, rules for living in university housing became more precise. After their freshman year, some men were released to live in fraternity houses, and sometimes apartments, if university space was not available. Men could live off-campus in their junior year. Women students, however, were required to live on campus until graduation, in halls staffed by a housemother and selected student staff leaders appointed through a process coordinated by Associated Women Students (AWS), which was assigned primary responsibility for governing all out-of-class activities of women

A casual observer might not have seen anything special about Tuffy's in the fall of 1956. The restaurant had twenty-one booths in three rooms, with a kitchen off one of those rooms and the soda fountain in another, in the basement of a small women's dorm at the corner of High Street and Tallawanda Road. There was also a very small office.

However, Tuffy's was the only place east of Campus Avenue where anyone could buy food, except when the Sangy Man brought his truck around at night. An old Quonset hut, officially the "Redskin Reservation" but usually called "The Res," had been torn down to make way for the construction of Roudebush Hall. The University Center didn't yet exist, and dorms provided food only at meal times.

Tuffy's, essentially the only hangout on campus, was a very busy place, crowded most of the time. The booths were full and people standing and waiting for a booth occupied most of the floor space. For waiters, just getting to the tables was a challenge that required strength and agility. These were the conditions under which my two roommates and I began our careers as waiters. We lived in a spacious corner room in Elliott Hall and had only a short walk to work. Myron T. Potter, who was always called "Tuffy," was interested in getting customers in, getting them something to eat or drink, and getting them out as fast as possible. He was not particularly interested in serving second and third cups of coffee to folks who appeared to be taking too long at a table. Still, I believe Tuffy's was a place where people had a good time.

When we were hired Tuffy told us there were a few rules: "Always show up for work at the scheduled time; never take anything to eat unless I give it to you; wear a clean shirt." We very quickly learned that if we followed the rules, Tuffy was a great guy to work for. He started his restaurant just before the Depression and kept astonishingly detailed records of the flow of business. He knew how many workers to have on duty at any time, so almost never were there too many workers on the job. Tuffy himself was a hard worker who appreciated other hard workers. He had two categories of employees: full-time adults, most of whom worked during the day Monday through Friday; and male students, who usually worked part-time evenings and weekends. No female students were hired to work at Tuffy's. Tuffy worked every morning and every evening from September until May, except when the university was not in session. Later in my tenure at Tuffy's I had valuable opportunities to work with the full-time employees. Some had been with Tuffy for many years and told wonderful stories.

My salary at Tuffy's was 70 cents per hour with 2 percent deducted for Social Security. I worked about twenty hours per week for a take-home pay of $12 to $14 per week. However, that was not trivial. With 10 cents I could buy a Coke or a cup of coffee, 15 cents bought a toasted roll, 30 cents a cheeseburger or hot fudge sundae, and $1.25 might have bought me a steak dinner with French fries, bread, butter, and coffee, but I never did that.

While I worked at Tuffy's the money was important to me. Fifty years later the money has faded, but other things about working there have not. I learned a lot from Tuffy. He worked very hard himself and expected his employees to do the same. He shared jokes, and made you feel welcome after you earned his confidence. Tuffy became a good friend.

I also learned a lot about people while waiting on tables. Occasionally someone would be nice to me, but most customers treated me as if I was a machine, and some were just mean. In my two years of waiting tables I had only one tip. It came from a member of the Cincinnati Symphony Orchestra who came to Tuffy's after a concert at Withrow Court. Today the experience of working at Tuffy's is more important than I could ever have imagined. I learned how important it is for me to be kind to anybody who waits on me. No doubt that person's day has been more difficult than mine.

Karl R. Mattox, Class of 1958

M. T. "Tuffy" Potter at entrance to Tuffy's restaurant, Tallawanda Hall, ca. 1970. *Miami Archives.*

students. New residence halls for upperclass women included sorority meeting rooms, or suites, that served as formal headquarters for sororities and their members. The staffs of the dean of men and the dean of women provided overall supervision and coordination of the student life system. Although continuously evolving in character and significantly adapted to needs and demands of later generations, the framework of residence life forged in the postwar era remained in effect early in the twenty-first century.

Campus Climate

In 1947 a group of distinguished alumni working with Alumni Secretary Dolibois began a comprehensive study of the condition of the university. Employing subcommittees on admissions and scholarships, faculty and curricula, intercollegiate athletics, public relations, and student life, they released a report in 1949.

It recognized the facts of change (there were five thousand students on a once-rustic campus), but it noted that "the size and relative isolation of Oxford, its dignity, charm and lack of distracting interests have helped Miami preserve its character." It placed the greatest value on the quality of instruction in the University and the close personal relationships between faculty and students. Miami, thought the committee, should not grow beyond five thousand and it hoped that with this formidable number the college could retain its past friendliness, simplicity and commonly shared spirit. The report quoted the words of former President Hughes at the inauguration of President Hahne: "I am arguing that Miami's greatest future will grow from high distinction in superior teaching and in care for the individual student."

On Thanksgiving weekend of 1952 President Hahne, struggling with both rapid postwar change and a lingering illness, died. In 1948 he had appointed professor of chemistry Clarence W. Kreger as vice president of the university to succeed A. K. Morris. Kreger assumed the acting presidency for the remainder of the academic year, prior to the appointment of President John D. Millett (1953–64).

John Millett graduated from DePauw University in 1933. He earned an AM from Columbia in 1935 and a PhD in 1938, and taught public administration at Columbia from 1935 to 1953, with an absence for wartime service. Millett came to Miami as a nationally known theorist on higher education finance, having served as executive director of the Commission on Financing Higher Education from 1949 to 1952. Established by the Rockefeller Foundation and Carnegie Corporation, it reconsidered a report of the President's Commission on Higher Education in 1947 that had advocated free tuition in public colleges and universities through the sophomore year. Millett's commission believed that "the economy can sustain higher charges without

John D. Millett, president of Miami University, 1953–64. Posed before post–World War II section of Edwin Fulwider's Biography of a University *mural, commissioned by Millett ca. 1959. Miami Archives.*

serious damage to the ideal of equality of educational opportunity," and concluded that continuing full tuition charges, even increasing them, would "permit sorely needed salary raises and a general improvement of educational excellence." This report, completed the year Millett left Columbia to become Miami's president, signaled the arrival in Oxford of an entrepreneurial leader who would build the postwar university.

Although the expansion brought by the G.I. Bill was beginning to wane when Millett arrived, new challenges of growth loomed as a baby-boom generation moved through the nation's school systems. As growing numbers of young students began to arrive, new programs and strategies were created to serve them. New leadership for a changing campus climate was provided by Robert F. Etheridge.

Born on a farm in Fairfield, Illinois, in 1925, Robert Etheridge grew up with the hard work and hard times of the Depression years. Etheridge became a star football player in high school and was recruited to play for the University of Illinois, where he enrolled in 1943. That plan was altered by military service. Etheridge was a Navy ROTC student, and before his freshman year ended he was in officer flight training school. By the time he completed flight training the war was over. He entered the Naval Reserve, married in 1947, and enrolled at Southern Illinois University to study English and sociology, and to play football. Headed for employment in social work, upon graduation he was recruited to become assistant dean of men at SIU. During a two-year sabbatical he completed an EdD at Michigan State, writing a dissertation on relationships between campus police and regulatory roles of student programs. Encouraged by the dean of men at Miami to apply for the position he was vacating, Etheridge accepted the deanship in 1959 at the age of thirty-three. Over the next thirty years he would transform the character of student affairs programming at Miami University.

A former student of Etheridge's described his approach to building an intentional campus climate: "At a time when many student affairs professionals were relatively passive and mainly responded to student problems, Bob was everywhere on the campus, talking with students, encouraging their involvement in campus affairs, and advocating stronger roles for them in university life. He also established his reputation as a strong administrator who was not hesitant to express his views on topics of student concern and to take students and others to task whom he felt were not performing up to their potential." President Millett appreciated this. On July 1, 1960, he approved a novel administrative change that would set in motion institutional momentum toward treating men and women students equally—creation of a single dean of students to replace Miami's former dean of women and dean of men. Etheridge was named to this position. He joined the president's cabinet in 1966, became Miami's first vice president for student affairs in 1967, and served until 1989. During his tenure Etheridge realigned the gendered services of Student Affairs, bringing offices for both men and women into single entities for residence learning, administrative services, cocurricular programs, housing, social activities, fraternities and sororities, intramural recreation, volunteer programs, and other agencies. Working with the strong support of professional associate deans, he supervised creation of the Women's Resource Center, the Office of Learning Assistance, and the Student Life Research Service intended to assess student attitudes and opinions as a factor in decision making. In 1974 his Division of Student Affairs was an active partner in designing and implementing an academic residential college on newly acquired Western Campus.

As the institution continued to grow, the arrival of more college students meant greater potential for unruly behavior. The dean of students moved to a home behind the president's residence with the expectation that he would respond immediately and personally to problems like "panty raids" and rowdy fraternity parties at any time, day or night. Millett and Etheridge took another notable step by deciding to house new men and women students in adjacent residence halls served by the same dining hall on South Campus, departing from the New Miami social scheme that housed men and women in different areas of campus. They assumed that if men and women had daily contact in living areas, men would have less interest in late-evening disruptive behavior and overall campus civility would improve. That same rationale would be used later to integrate men and women into single residence halls with separated corridors.

In the National University era, student affairs programming was regarded as an integral part of the total educational process. That view led Miami to undertake new research and teaching about student life and its programs. When Etheridge arrived, some older faculty advisors living in residence halls were perceived as routine in their behavior, while students, ever new, were exhibiting a degree of apathy about their advisors. Etheridge convinced the School of Education and the Graduate School "to create a graduate program in college student affairs administration and to assign bright and eager graduate students in this program as academic advisors in the residence halls." Along with its successes in residence life, Miami University would excel in the new academic field of college student personnel administration, and in the twenty-first century would develop a doctorate degree in this area within the Department of Educational Leadership.

Selectivity

In the National University era, enrollment pressure was continuous and new students were accompanied by state funding. Millett, working in a small town and within Miami's tradition of relatively small-scale architecture, determined that instead of expanding as much as possible, Miami would limit growth and become more selective. In the early 1960s the Office of Admission was assigned to the Division of Student Affairs. Millett argued that because living space was at a premium at Miami, and because all new students were required to live in freshman halls to receive the advice, counseling, and supervision essential to student success, access to Miami would be limited to the number of first-year students who could be accommodated in residence halls. Following this restriction, Miami began to accept only certain applicants from Ohio high schools rather than all of them. The decision that admission to Miami required admission to limited residence hall openings would have a long impact on Miami's reputation among potential students and high school counselors. While enrollment in Ohio public universities grew exponentially after World War II, Miami grew more slowly, even though in Etheridge's first fifteen years enrollment doubled to more than ten thousand students.

Controlled growth, a continuing desire that all faculty teach undergraduates, residence halls of manageable scale, and a residence-based advising strategy allowed Miami to provide student support that built a tradition of unusually high retention. Most applicants were admitted on conventional quality measures—grades, estimates of the character of their high school program, and standardized test scores. They succeeded academically, made lifelong friends, graduated in record time, and most found employment or entered advanced study. Over time, many Ohio high school counselors began encouraging qualified students to apply first to Miami, and the Office of Admission networked with them to identify high-performing students.

A presidential commitment to maintaining high quality while expanding access, a residence hall program committed to student success, and an admission strategy committed to selectivity were setting the stage for Miami to be named a "Public Ivy." Academic Affairs would augment these commitments by raising expectations for the professional performance of faculty.

Graduate Studies

Although Miami offered graduate work earlier, the Graduate School was not established as a separate division until 1946. Earlier graduate study was overseen by a committee who wrote in a May 1946 "Report to Trustees" that its procedures were "with slight local variations, standard practice in all universities." With the end of World War II the landscape of higher education would change drastically. In the next thirty years Miami shifted from a university focused on undergraduate education where graduate instruction was taken on as uncompensated overload to a doctoral degree–granting university where graduate education and research would become normal expectations for faculty in most areas.

In his report to the board for 1946–47, President Hahne noted that University Senate had recommended establishing a graduate school. Miami and other universities were anticipating enrollment of returning veterans, and a cadre of graduate students with assistantship responsibilities would help meet a sharp new demand for instruction. "With the abrupt increase in enrollment, graduate assistants could be appointed to aid an overloaded faculty in the handling of courses, laboratories, grading and clerical assistance, provided Miami could offer the same opportunities to work toward a master's degree as were available at other universities." Hahne assured the board there was no intent to offer doctoral degrees.

In 1947 Miami offered five graduate degrees: Master of Arts, Master of Science, Master of Education, Master of Business Administration, and Master of Fine Arts. By expanding graduate education Miami was among many universities reexamining their missions in the light of a changing society. During World War II university research concentrated on supporting the war effort, and when it ended the federal government made commitments to support university scientific research. In 1946 three federal agencies were created to fund it: the National Institute of Health; the Atomic Energy Commission; and the Office of Naval Research. In 1950 the National Science Foundation was created, and in that year the nation went to war again. In the fall of 1950 President Hahne commented: "The Korean War started shortly after commencement last June, setting in motion some fathomless forces that threaten to shape the future of our own lives and of educational institutions." Miami, a newcomer to modern graduate education, needed a strategy. One response was to address a growing need for teachers to instruct the many new students enrolling in colleges and universities. Hahne called attention to a report of the National Conference on the Preparation of College Teachers that asked universities to educate more qualified faculty.

In 1957 the Soviet Union, attempting to demonstrate technological superiority, launched Sputnik, the first orbiting artificial satellite. That act intensified the discussion of whether higher education was meeting the needs of the country in its struggle with the communist world. President Millett said in an August 1958 report to the board: "When Russia successfully launched an earth satellite into orbit on October 4, 1957, American complacency about our educational achievement was rudely jolted." He focused on secondary education by citing a report of President Eisenhower's Committee on Education Beyond the High School: "the most critical bottleneck to the expansion and improvement of education in the United States is the shortage of excellent teachers."

The appeal of becoming a research institution with academic prestige was a powerful postwar stimulus to those who felt that more graduate offerings were both consistent with their mission and a contribution to the nation. W. E. Smith, dean of the Graduate School, wrote in his 1956 Annual Report, "By comparison with numerous graduate schools our facilities, our educational standards, and our trained faculty are quite superior." An early action to address growing demand for college faculty was to offer a second year of graduate work leading to a PhD program at Ohio State. Similar programs were offered by Bowling Green, Kent State, and Ohio University. President Millett seems to have initiated Miami's movement toward doctoral work. Graduate Council minutes of October 10, 1955, report that "the President suggested that we begin making progress toward offering the Ph.D. degree by setting up a co-operative relationship with the Ohio State University." By June 30, 1962, eleven departments had developed formal agreements with counterparts at Ohio State—in bacteriology, chemistry, educational administration, economics, English, geography, geology, government, guidance and counseling, history, and physics. The first graduate of the joint programs was Harry Randles, who received a PhD in education from Ohio State in winter 1964.

Predictions of a shortage of college teachers continued into the 1960s, and six of the departments cooperating with Ohio State eventually developed PhD programs that are still offered today. Graduate Council minutes of

A postwar scientific laboratory. Photograph by John E. Dome. Miami Archives.

October 28, 1963, indicate that Millett approved, requesting "that the Graduate Council undertake necessary preparation for offering eventual full doctoral programs on the Miami campus." John Millett left Miami in 1964 to become chancellor of the Ohio Board of Regents. In a final report he reflected on changes in both society and higher education during his eleven years as president and commented on the role of graduate education and its extra expenses, as well as the prestige accompanying expansion of graduate programs. He noted with pride that thirteen departments had cooperative PhD programs with Ohio State, and concluded, "it seems probable that our role in graduate education should expand in the years ahead."

On October 7, 1965, Graduate Council held a special meeting with newly appointed President Phillip R. Shriver (1965–81). The topic was possible doctoral studies in twenty-four departments that responded to Dean H. Bunker Wright's request for statements of interest in a PhD—art education, botany, business administration, chemistry, classics, curriculum and supervision, economics, educational administration, English, French and Italian, geography, geology and mineralogy, government (political science), guidance and personnel services, history, mathematics, microbiology, music, philosophy, psychology, religion, Spanish and Portuguese, speech, and zoology and phys-iology. Graduate Council imagined a plan to open these new degrees on a staggered basis over the next decade. On November 29, 1965, it reported that Shriver had authorized five departments to go forward: botany, English, geol-ogy, history, and microbiology. In his report to the trustees in 1966, the new president could proudly state that even though the expected program in his-tory was delayed because of potential duplication, and the expected program in microbiology needed to develop a more complete proposal, the "first inde-pendent doctoral programs will begin September 1967 and will be offered in botany, English, and geology." Two decades after World War II, Miami had become a doctoral institution.

By the end of the National University era in 1970 the positive climate for expanding doctoral studies had disappeared. In 1968–69 the Ohio Board of Regents imposed a moratorium on new doctoral programs. In 1972 observ-ers were writing about the oversupply of doctoral degree holders, and ironi-cally John Millett, early champion of graduate education, would as chancellor curtail its statewide growth. In that year Miami had ten doctoral programs, in botany, chemistry, educational administration, English, history, geology, mi-crobiology, political science, psychology, and zoology. It was thirty-two years before another doctoral program—social gerontology—was added in 2004, and three more before approval of a doctoral program in college student personnel.

After 1970 new PhD investment was neither financially feasible nor con-sistent with state and national agendas for higher education. Miami's dra-matic postwar expansion of doctoral education would, however, permanently change the climate for faculty performance. Formerly a collegiate environ-ment devoted almost entirely to undergraduate education, after World War II Miami would evolve as a discipline-focused university expecting specialized instruction and research at the highest level.

Looking Forward,
Looking Back

1949: BUILDING THE FUTURE

"Where there is no growth, there is apt to be death," President Hahne
told the Oxford Kiwanis Club on September 27, 1949. Miami's enrollment, he
said, would grow from 5,200 to 10,000 or even 12,000. He welcomed this, noting that like Ohio State, Miami could continue to give students personal attention "through the professional schools." To support growth he proposed a
"bold plan" for development of Oxford: building homes for faculty, expanding the business district, rerouting truck traffic, designing a railroad underpass
for West High Street, constructing an apartment house, widening Patterson
Avenue, building a hospital to serve both the village and Miami's premedi-
cal training, building a hotel, adding restaurants, and constructing a lighted
billboard welcoming visitors to "the home of Miami University and Western
College for Women." He added that developing Hueston Woods State Park
was important to Oxford.

One week before it reported Dr. Hahne's ideas for Oxford's future, the *Oxford Press* carried a front-page story headlined "Construction Program in Oxford Area Estimated to Cost Over $3,500,000" and subtitled "Huge Building
Plans May Hit Record High for Community." Going up or in active planning stages, it reported, were a modern structure for Holy Trinity Episcopal Church, a major addition to the Methodist Church and one to Stewart
School, a new facility for Oxford Country Club, an earthfill dam at Hueston
Woods State Park, at least ten homes being built for faculty members, and on
Miami's campus, an industrial education building, a library addition, another
wing for Upham Hall, and a new "$1,000,000 student union building." Oxford
was in a postwar building boom, and some were embracing a new aesthetic

McCullough-Hyde Memorial Hospital, Oxford (1957). Photograph by George R. Hoxie, 1957. Smith Library.

Victor Fürth, professor of architecture, 1949–76. Photograph by George R. Hoxie. Miami Archives.

of modernist architecture. Holy Trinity Church, McCullough-Hyde Memorial Hospital, and Talawanda High School would all be completed within a decade in a style that avoided neoclassic proportions and ornamentation in favor of functionalist forms that revealed the character of building materials and employed glass panels, windows, and other visual openings to link interior and exterior spaces. The beauty of this style, it was said, emerged from an organic relationship between form and function.

THE INTERNATIONAL STYLE IN OXFORD

Some new faculty arriving for the expanding National University brought a fervor for modern design. Oxford's residential landscape, built primarily in the New Miami era of domestic homes in colonial or Arts and Crafts styling, was soon dotted with modernist structures. Among them were significant works by Victor Fürth, a Bohemian expatriate from Prague who joined Miami's architecture faculty on an exchange visitor program in 1949. He became a permanent resident in 1954. Fürth had earned an engineering degree in Prague, studied in Florence, and practiced in Austria, Yugoslavia, England, and France until the Nazi invasion of Czechoslovakia in 1939, when he fled to London. He worked there for a decade and after the war was an architectural engineer in Germany and Greece, working with emergency shelter programs. Fürth was to become one of the principal modernists practicing in Oxford. His work was characterized by the diagonal displacement of flowing interior spaces under a flat roof. His houses had built-in furniture of his design, and he would typically include a single circular window as a signature view to a garden.

Fürth's contributions to the residential landscape of Oxford included structures in the village and in a new subdivision to the east of town, Springwood. There Fürth built seven houses between 1960 and 1969. Earlier Fürth had designed a modernist home in Oxford and the Bern Street Apartments on South Campus Avenue. Another faculty member who showcased contemporary styling was C. E. "Mik" Stousland, named chair of the Department of Architecture in 1952. Stousland designed a number of highly modernist residential structures in Oxford, including his own house on Central Avenue supported on stilts. He built at least two homes in Springwood

Billings Natatorium (1952).
Miami Archives.

and modernist additions to existing nineteenth-century homes in use as fraternity houses, the Phi Gamma Delta House on East High Street and the Tau Sigma Delta House on South Campus Avenue. Kep Small and Andy Wertz, together with Hal Barcus, produced many residential and commercial structures in and around Oxford, including notable residences on Fairfield Road and Westgate Drive. They also designed commercial buildings, including a small bank on West High Street at College Avenue, and the modernist Alexander Dining Hall in 1962 and Hoyt Library in 1973 for Western College. Later faculty continued Oxford's modernist catalog. In the 1970s Richard McCommons designed a number of house additions and alterations, and Hayden B. May, chair of architecture and later dean of fine arts, contributed in the 1980s modernist residences reflecting a critical regionalist tendency. Another faculty member working in this direction was Robert Zwirn, who while chair of architecture designed contemporary renovations and new structures in several city and suburban locations.

In contrast with the neoclassic Colonial Revival motif of most Oxford campus buildings after World War II, modernism in the International Style would become a significant counterpoint in the village and its developing subdivisions, and it would appear in campus design as well, at Logan Lodge (1948), Rowan Hall (1949), Billings Natatorium (1952), Cole Service Building (1958), Miami Manor (1958), Phillips Hall (1962), Martin Dining Hall (1965), Millett Hall (1968), and the Miami Art Museum (1978). None of these were designed by Miami's modernist architecture faculty, and, contrary to his tendency at Miami, four were designed by Charles Cellarius. Modernism, however, ran counter to the official image of Miami University. This would be sharply reaffirmed in 1957 as the trustees opened a new center for students.

SPIRITS OF THE INSTITUTION

In 1955 Ohio voters endorsed a constitutional amendment allowing $150 million in bond sales "to meet additional construction needs of the rapidly growing state universities." In the spring of 1956 Wallace P. Roudebush was still on the job. He worked every day through the activist presidencies of Hughes, Upham, and Hahne, and was now managing new construction for John Millett. Roudebush was not responsible for Miami's growth in the twentieth century, but he was responsible for building the campus to accommodate it. When he went to work for Hughes Miami had 700 students. When he went to work for Millett it had 5,000.

Roudebush and his family lived near the emerging center of campus in the McGuffey House. He kept an office across the street in Bonham House. Renowned for mingling with students at dining halls, chapel services, and campus events, he was profoundly committed to the orderly Georgian style and the human scale that came to define Miami architecture during his tenure, and was no doubt a major force in shaping the consistency of Miami's expanding landscape and facilities. When he died in 1956 after forty-five years of service, a classmate who wrote for the *New York Post* described him as the "Spirit of the Institution." In the spring of 1956 Roudebush was preparing to "oversee a $14,000,000 building program involving nine buildings," every one Georgian in style. He had a heart attack in 1954, and in April 1956 went to the hospital with a respiratory ailment. He asked President Millett to promise that no building would be named for him, a promise kept by Millett but not his successor, who named Miami's administration building in his honor. Roudebush, a formidable figure in shaping both New Miami and the National University, was gone. But the "spirit of the institution" was not.

On February 19, 1957, the *Cincinnati Times-Star* carried a front-page story about construction under way at Miami University. A picture of white columns being added to a new brick building with symmetrical wings bore the caption "Typical of controversial pseudo-Georgian style architecture on Miami campus at Oxford is this new Student Union building, in the process of construction." Under the headline "'Extravagance' Is Charged In Miami U Building Row," reporter David Alter revealed details of "a dispute that was quietly carried to former Governor Frank J. Lausche, the General Assembly, the attorney general, the board of trustees and University President John Millett." Alter reported that "graduating students who criticized 'too much' were warned, they said, 'not to carry it too far.'" Controversy had erupted over "the board of trustees' decision to build future buildings in Georgian style to maintain architectural harmony on campus."

Critics focused on plans to build a "proposed $1 million Fine Arts Build-

'Extravagance' Is Charged In Miami U Building Row

★ ★ ★ ★   ★ ★ ★ ★ ★

This Style Stirs Campus Controversy

TYPICAL of controversial psuedo-Georgian style architecture on Miami campus at Oxford is this new   Student Union building, in the process of construction.
—TIMES-STAR Photo.

Dispute Simmers; Architectural Plan Defended

By DAVID ALTER

An architectural dispute that erupted into charges of extravagant spending is simmering on Miami University's Georgian-styled campus at Oxford.

It's a dispute that was quietly carried to former Governor Frank J. Lausche, the General Assembly, the attorney general, the board of trustees and University President John Millett.

IT'S A "HOT POTATO" in more ways than one, so hot that graduating students who criticized "too much" were warned, they said, "not to carry it too far."

The dispute grows from the board of trustees' decision to build future buildings in Georgian style to maintain architectural harmony on campus.

Some students and some faculty members objected violently, charging Georgian style was wasteful . . . poor use of public funds and providing a minimum of education.

Several students who appealed to higher sources said they were warned they might not receive their degrees.

Front-page story. Cincinnati Times-Star, *February 19, 1957.*

ing to be in Georgian style," said to cost an estimated $22.70 per square foot compared to a structure for a similar purpose at the University of Cincinnati said to cost $11.80 per square foot. They charged that the style was "wasteful" because it "has what some call excessive ornamentation," and believed that "future buildings should be along patterns which will get more for the educational dollar and provide adequate space to meet future growth." Unnamed student critics attacked the "false chimneys, slanted roofs, numerous slotted windows, ornamented with outside swinging shutters," as well as "false balconies and special brick exteriors that are costly." Unnamed faculty members apparently joined the dispute. One called the Georgian style "outmoded," and others "figured the cost of heavy roofs on the new Administrative building and Upham Hall was enough to build the new Business Building." Students approvingly cited a passage in President Millett's *Financing Higher Education in the United States,* in which Millett allegedly had written, "In the past much architectural design resulted in considerable wasted space—from full basements and grand staircases to pitched roofs and cupolas." Challenged, President Millett responded flatly that the board of trustees had voted twenty-three to two the previous June "in favor of continuing the Georgian style so that a 'hodgepodge' of buildings wouldn't result," and moreover, he surmised that if there were a vote of Miami alumni and staff, "three-fourths would want to maintain the present architecture." This was not new policy. Two years earlier, in reviewing Miami's growing enrollment and building plans, Millett noted that although a different style would allow Miami "to build cheaper buildings at lower rental costs to students," the board had passed a resolution on January 30, 1954, stating that "the colonial type and style of architecture employed in the last two decades" was to be adhered to in the future. Lausche, now a U.S. senator, told protesting students that "operations of Miami University are vested completely in the hands of the Board of Trustees," and that he would not be involved.

The 1957 challenge to "traditional" architecture emerged well after Miami's neo-Georgian brand was firmly established. The description of the new Miami University Center by the *Times-Star* as costly and "pseudo-Georgian" did not go unanswered. At a meeting on March 30, 1957, the executive committee of the board of trustees passed another "Statement of Architectural Policy."

Miami University for some time has adhered to a unified, traditional type of architectural style. Miami is an old educational institution, founded 148 years ago. It is conservative in educational program and practice. In adhering to traditional architecture, the Board of Trustees has had reason to believe that it spoke the preference of alumni, staff, friends, and even of students. In a recent survey of this year's freshman class, the women gave "a beautiful campus" as the second most important reason for selecting Miami, and the men gave this as their third most important reason. Parents, faculty, alumni, and visitors have spoken emphatically in favor of Miami's traditional architecture. Only a small minority has questioned this practice.

The board added that it had "reason to believe that its buildings were useful, attractive, and economical." They claimed, "Such higher capital costs as have been demonstrated have been off-set by corresponding economies in maintenance. The University cannot afford under any circumstances to be extravagant or wasteful." In defense of the style for Miami's "post-war building program" that erected "structures costing over 12 million dollars, not one cent of which has come from the taxpayers' pocketbook," they reaffirmed neo-Georgian architecture as integral to Miami's character.

1959: REBUILDING THE PAST

Only five more buildings conceived in a modernist mode would be constructed on Miami's Oxford campus in the next half century. Miami was officially "old." The sesquicentennial celebration of 1959 would be designed to underscore this notion as a way of celebrating Miami's progress.

Oxford

Cultivating a sense of the past beyond the New Miami practice of historical pageantry or student traditions would become a theme of Miami's National University leadership. The first effort in this direction targeted the Vil-

DeWitt Log House (ca. 1805), maintained by Oxford Museum Association on property acquired by Miami University east of Oxford campus. Oxford Museum Association.

Doty Pioneer Farmstead (ca. 1836). Maintained by Oxford Museum Association in Hueston Woods State Park. Oxford Museum Association.

lage of Oxford, when on March 16, 1953, the editor of the *Miami Alumnus*, encouraged by Acting President Clarence Kreger, gathered about twenty-five Oxford residents to discuss "reviving or replacing the dormant Oxford Historical Society." Their motives included preparation for Miami's sesquicentennial in 1959, for the arrival of a new president, and for the new Hueston Woods State Park, but "most of all, perhaps, in a community of Oxford's age and tradition," they said, the "lack of any formal historical organization was a conspicuous void."

In tune with the postwar spirit, this group was activist. It "wanted to do something—to create a place which could demonstrate how early settlers lived, and which would invite visitors and participants." The new Oxford Museum Association (OMA) elected an executive board and assumed responsibility for maintaining a farm home and barn on the edge of Hueston Woods

Park as the "Doty Homestead," complete with nineteenth-century furnishings and farm implements. This Pioneer Farm and House Museum public history site opened May 31, 1959. In 1965 an annual Apple Butter Festival showcasing nineteenth-century cooking was initiated, and in 1966 an Arts and Crafts Fair. By the end of the National University period OMA had assumed responsibility for the two-story DeWitt Log House (1805) owned by Miami, said to be the oldest remaining structure in Oxford Township. In 1975 OMA took over control of Oxford's last covered bridge from the Butler County commissioners. Volunteer "Work Days" at OMA sites were popular with community volunteers, often Miami retirees, who joined the association in large numbers. With financial assistance from state agencies, private donors, charitable foundations, and Miami University, restoration of all OMA sites was complete by 2003, the year of the Ohio bicentennial. Then OMA partnered with Oxford Township trustees to restore the 1844 Doty Settlement Burial Ground. Public history had risen in the early National University, taken firm root, and thrived well beyond it.

Phoenix

Vetville was demolished in 1958. Later Martin Egelston, Miami '58 and '61, reminisced about that event.

President John Millett loathed Vetville as a blight and cheapness scarring his vision of tennis courts and beautiful Georgian dorms for students. He fretted aloud that they were firetraps and worried that someday there would be a raging inferno in one of them. His assessments had merit. . . . After the last dwellers moved out, maintenance crews stripped scrap metal from the buildings, and then a bulldozer pushed the wood remnants into several piles for burning. The students would cheer the flare up caused by another unit pushed onto the fire. Surprisingly, they did not produce the raging celebratory bonfire that the university president expected. They did a slow burn.

As Miami prepared for the 1959 celebration of its sesquicentennial, Old Main was again at the center of attention, as it had been for Miami's hundredth anniversary. This time it was honored in a romantic memorial painting by Marston Hodgin, *Harrison Hall, February 1958.* Hodgin chaired the art department at Miami from 1927 to 1958 and supervised Miami's art studios, which were located in this iconic building. Hodgin, who captured Oxford scenes vividly with nuanced watercolors, chose to depict Old Main majestically, nearly filling the canvas with its mass and weight in a suggestive winter scene of stark trees and a partly cloudy, mildly threatening

Demolition of Vetville. Miami: Her 150th Year, 1959. Miami Archives and Smith Library.

Harrison Hall, February 1958. *Watercolor by Marston Hodgin, chair, Department of Art, 1927–63. Miami: Her 150th Year, 1959.* Miami Archives and Smith Library.

sky. Dashed with snow, a bright flag flying atop its north tower, the west wing's stained glass windows lit by an inner glow, Miami's home for 150 years seemed formidable, imposing, old, and charming.

Then it was torn down. In a thirty-six-page sesquicentennial commemorative book bearing on its cover the sesquicentennial seal designed by art professor Robert Butler, the sesquicentennial motto "150 Years of Growth and Service," and the opening words of Alfred Upham's "Alma Mater," "Old Miami from thy hillcrest"/Thou has watched the decades roll," Hodgin's image of Old Main was the full-color centerpiece. The following page depicted a wrecking ball felling the last standing remnants of the building, as an architect's drawing of a new "Harrison Hall" rose like a phoenix from Old Main rubble. Designed by Charles Cellarius to allude in its exterior massing to Old Main by reproducing the impression of a center block with two setback wings and two towers—newly topped with Georgian cupolas—Harrison Hall would become the National University's home for the Department of Political Science.

Opening with a full-page picture of President Millett, the sesquicentennial commemorative book offered a crowded schedule of celebratory events for February through October of 1959, showcased the college and professional schools, the graduate school, library, off-campus learning centers in five Ohio cities, ROTC, sports, Greek life, the Village of Oxford, and "The new

Harrison Hall in transition. Miami: Her 150th Year, 1959. Miami Archives and Smith Library.

August 15, 1957
Dr. John D. Millett
President, Miami University
Oxford, Ohio
Re: Harrison Hall

Dear President Millett:

. . .

I have no reason to change the opinion that I gave you some time ago that an attempt to utilize the present construction would be uneconomical and inadvisable for the needs that now exist. It is true that some twenty years ago we restored Stoddard and Elliott Halls which were older than the major part of Harrison Hall. At that time Mr. Roudebush, I, and the State Architect's Office all recognized that the reconstruction of these buildings would cost as much money as the erection of completely new buildings. The reconstruction which involved the tearing out of everything inside the buildings and even the taking down of the roof construction and the rebuilding with concrete floors, fire stairs, and entirely new heating, plumbing, and electrical work was justified, we believed, on two grounds.

The first ground was the sentimental value of these earliest buildings of the university. The second, was that the exterior walls lent themselves to a practical dormitory plan and the exterior brickwork had a charm that only age can give. . . .

The conditions of Harrison Hall are not at all the same. The building in the first place was built in two or three sections. It does not have the simplicity of design that we would like, nor was it ever a beautiful building from the architectural standpoint. . . .

While I appreciate the fact that a great deal of sentiment exists in connection with Harrison Hall (and I have worked at Miami long enough to be sympathetic) I am sure that a new building will be no more expensive than a remodeling job, that it can result in a far more useful building for meeting the needs that you have outlined, and I am optimistic enough to believe that a building can be designed that will bear enough resemblance to Harrison Hall and have enough artistic merit of its own that future generations will have for it the same feeling that now exists for the present building.

Yours very truly,
CELLARIUS & HILMER
Charles F. Cellarius

Miami" that had been completed since World War II—or was under construction. Millett was emphatic about his intention for the sesquicentennial. He meant to celebrate Miami's future.

A birthday is simply a marker in the endless continuity of time. Miami University has paused to observe an especially important marker, but the life of this institution goes on. Our eyes are lifted to the years ahead, not focused with complacency on the achievements of the past. There can be only one justification for one hundred fifty years of growth and service, and that is as preparation for the next fifty, one hundred, or two hundred years of further growth and service.

It began as a two-story brick dwelling to house the preparatory school some years before the university offered college-level courses. The first stone in the foundation was laid in 1816. A nearby ancient earthwork or mound one hundred feet in circumference and about three feet high was demolished, and the earth from it used in construction.

Franklin Hall, as it was named, had a dozen rooms. Most were used to house students. University trustees decreed a more imposing structure was needed for a proper college and in October 1820 contracted for a sizable three-story structure measuring about fifty-nine by eighty-seven feet. It would have high ceilings, a center stairwell, a pyramidal roof, and a cupola. Heating was provided by twelve fireplaces. Franklin Hall would serve as the west wing. By or before 1838, this appendix acquired a third story that rose no higher than the eaves of center block. An east wing would have to await future funding.

As it was, paying for the new center block was more than the trustees could easily manage. All was to be ready by 1822, but some workers had occupied rooms on the first floor and were enjoying rent-free quarters as construction languished. Once they were turned out work proceeded, but hardly at a rapid pace. The appointment of Robert H. Bishop as president in July 1824 made the completion of classrooms more urgent. Finally, all was ready for a rather late opening of the academic year in November. The cupola was not ready, but Bishop felt that a trumpet would be cheaper than a bell and just as effective for calling students to class. As a clergyman, he knew a chapel in the basement was important to proper education, and there was room on the top floor for literary societies to have private club rooms.

Despite its rather modest cost of $14,000, the center block had attractive features. Doorways and center windows were in the Venetian style with nicely formed arches. An oval-shaped window in the pediment and regular windows were symmetrically located in the façade. The unattractive cupola was removed shortly after the Civil War and replaced with a widow's walk with a low balustrade. The bell stood out in the weather on this open deck, yet seemed to function just as well as when covered.

By 1859 the west wing was decrepit and abandoned. Scarce materials and high construction costs during war years discouraged renovation until peace returned in April 1865. Soon Miami had a new president intent on overhauling the school's decaying physical plant. The old west wing was pulled down and work began on a replacement that was larger, grander in finish, and sturdier, featuring a large chapel on the second floor and a tower that would give the main building the look it needed for a temple of learning. A second tower and east wing were desired but had to wait. As it was, alumni were asked to raise $20,000 toward renovation costs.

The chapel was a success. A local paper described it as a consecrated place bathed in dim and hallowed light. Its lofty ceilings were partitioned into frescoed panels, studded with gilt globes and ornamented in the Corinthian style. Great stained-glass windows made from imported English cathedral glass were named as memorials to past Miami presidents. Seating was available for six hundred, but heating was inadequate for the chapel to be used during coldest months. Visitors, after viewing the splendid chapel, were invited to survey the vista from the widow's walk some eighty feet above campus. Here one could look out over wooded grounds and surrounding countryside with fields, villas, and farmhouses. Four Mile Creek, a limpid stream meandering in nearby fields, was clearly visible. Yet the combined beauty of the new chapel and nature was not enough to save the school. Enrollments remained low due to poor economic times and the emergence of rival colleges. Miami closed between 1873 and 1885, and the campus and its buildings were rented to a preparatory school.

When talk of reopening began in the summer of 1884, the main building was in poor repair. Peeling wallpaper, crumbling plaster, loose floorboards, and rotted windowsills had reduced this noble building to near ruin. Trustees paid off the debt, alumni were again asked to help, carpenters and painters soon had the building in respectable condition, and decorative cast-iron porches were added, but chapel renovations took three years. Trustees announced plans to build a long-projected east wing and second tower in time for Miami's centennial in 1909, authorizing it in 1898. Samuel Hannaford, a distinguished Cincinnati architect who built Music Hall and City Hall, designed a new wing to match the existing structure, but raised the roof by five feet to accommodate a third floor. Space for an enlarged library was in the East Wing, and a boiler for central heating. Thirty feet were added to the West Wing to enlarge the chapel. The building was rededicated May 1899. Long and spacious at 250 feet, it had more than 36,000 square feet of floor space.

(continued)

Yet it was already obsolete, for American taste was in a classical revival mode and the Victorian Gothic details of Old Main were no longer fashionable. When Benton Hall (now Hall Auditorium) was opened in 1912, Old Main chapel was no longer needed. It was converted to a central dining hall called the Commons—a subdued eatery, for stained-glass windows blocked much of the sunlight. When dining halls opened in new dormitories, the Commons became a theatre, and was an art studio in its final decades. Other uses were found for Old Main; the campus radio station was first located in the East Tower. Its prestige was temporarily enhanced in 1934 when the trustees decided to rename it in honor of President Benjamin Harrison.

The 1930s were good for preservation, as there was little money to replace old buildings. World War II dampened new construction because materials and labor were needed by the military. But in the postwar era, Victorian buildings became an endangered species as new construction proliferated. In 1953 Miami's ambitious new president wanted to upgrade and expand the Oxford campus. Old Main projected the wrong image; it was out of date and obsolete. Yet some alumni and faculty loved it for exactly those reasons. Maintenance was cut back as Old Main was scheduled for replacement. In May 1957 state building inspectors declared the building unsafe. When classes ended in the summer of 1958, Old Main was pulled down.

John Dolibois, walking on campus during demolition, saved several stained-glass windows, and three are on exhibit today at McGuffey Museum and at Oxford Lane Public Library. Another is in Lewis Place. The bell was saved and exhibited in the Alumni Center lobby until it was moved to storage in the late 1990s. In 2007 it was retrieved for use at football games. New York preservationist and architectural critic Brendan Gill felt that the loss of historic buildings represents a serious loss to society, for they "nourish us . . . and so become indispensable to our well-being." Many Miami graduates from the 142 years of Old Main would agree.

John Hoxland White, Class of 1958
Honorary Doctor of Humane Letters, 1996

Chapel

However bold John Millett may have seemed in his focus on the future and his willingness to act, his vision was tempered by values he regarded as settled and unchanging. In Miami's first century and a half, he said, "Nothing that has happened thus far has made good education, virtue, religion, and morality any less important today than they were in 1809. These great goals of our endeavor may well serve to guide our future as they have illuminated our past." He would testify to this by building a chapel. The sesquicentennial book showcased projected buildings for business and for physics, mathematics, and aeronautics; a central women's residence hall in South Quad; and a 150th anniversary commemorative structure, the Sesquicentennial Chapel. A donor project that relied on alumni and other benefactors, this chapel was never intended to accommodate large gatherings. It was, however, meant to play an active role in university life.

Raymond Hughes was the first modern scientist to assume Miami's presidency. He was preceded by a Methodist minister, Guy Potter Benton, who conducted chapel services. Hughes seemed intensely concerned about the spiritual life of a campus that had been shaped in the nineteenth century by the Presbyterian Church and in his day was engaging twentieth-century secularism. He advocated what he believed were nonsectarian Christian values for

*Sesquicentennial Chapel
dedication ceremony, 1959.*
Miami Archives.

*Sesquicentennial Chapel
(1959). Miami Archives.*

Miami. In an address to the Faculty Senate in 1919 he stated that every classroom should be "a place where Christian principles of truth, justice, mercy, service, love and unselfishness are taught through, and with, science and the arts and letters."

In *The Liberating Arts*, a reflection on general education published in 1957, John Millett made a characteristically bold claim: "I believe that we who have a profound regard for the importance of knowledge must make clear that there is nothing in our interest which is hostile to the essential claims of religion. The reason is simple. The scholar, like all human beings, has a deep-seated need for religion." Millett would underline that belief in November 1958 by issuing "A Statement of Policy" about the role of religion at Miami.

Miami University recognizes that the intellectual and spiritual needs of the student are complementary, not competing requirements in the process of personal growth. There is nothing incompatible, we believe, between a devotion to learning and a conviction of God's power and love. There is nothing, we believe, in the realm of man's knowledge which is destructive of the essentials of man's faith.

Acknowledging that "the state is prohibited in America from establishing an official church," and that a state-supported university "cannot practice discrimination among religious denominations," Millett said Miami nevertheless had two objectives in this realm: to "emphasize for all its students and staff the importance of religious faith as a vital force in man's life," and "to assist all religious organizations in ministering to the spiritual needs of members of the academic community."

This was to be the precise role of Miami's Sesquicentennial Chapel. In an August 1959 letter to the chair of Miami's religion department, Millett acknowledged "various difficulties which have beset my efforts to realize some kind of organizational pattern for handling the University's interests in the religious and spiritual welfare of the student body." He encouraged presenting speakers and discussion groups "reaching beyond the classroom," and noted that the dean of men and dean of women were doing this. Then he added an enthusiastic footnote.

Incidentally, we already have a very substantial demand upon use of the Chapel. I was very pleased to learn that Mr. Sexton [the University chaplain] had received a request from Hillel to observe the high holy days of the Jewish faith in September in the Sesquicentennial Chapel. I am also pleased that the plans for our Roger Sayles Meditation Room have received the approval of [Catholic] Archbishop Alter. I understand we are experiencing difficulty in scheduling the various [Protestant] groups wishing to hold Sunday services in the Sesquicentennial Chapel.

Here was local evidence of another national postwar agenda—an interfaith ecumenical enthusiasm that would be called "civil religion." Allied commanding general Dwight D. Eisenhower was president of the United States, had been baptized into the Presbyterian Church while president, and in 1954 had signed legislation adding "under God" to the Pledge of Allegiance to the United States flag. Like much of the nation, Miami University would now have civil religion, and President Millett had seen to it that as a fitting memorial to 150 years of progress, it would have a place to practice that faith.

Story

In the late Public Ivy era, Miami's first female provost observed that Miami "knows what it is." Some newly arrived administrators ahead of her had puzzled over the blend of large university and small college traditions they detected, but in the late twentieth century most long-term Miamians could tell a forthright story about the place. That was no accident.

For the 1899 diamond anniversary celebrating the opening of classes in 1824, President Thompson and trustee Walter L. Tobey published a substantial seventy-fifth anniversary volume that presented seventeen essays or addresses on Miami history, major figures, and achievements. For the centennial celebration in 1909, President Benton, A. H. Upham, and B. S. Bartlow, Miami Class of 1893, published an annotated catalog of presidents, faculty, and alumni over the hundred years since Miami's charter date. Miami's lovingly crafted story began in its most public form, however, with Alfred Upham. In 1909 Upham published an adoring review of the university's first era in *Old Miami: The Yale of the Early West*. The experience of Old Miami was also elaborated meticulously by Miami historian James Rodabaugh, whose thorough scholarship—evident in an unpublished 1949 revision of his doctoral dissertation—seemed partly designed to undermine any idea that Miami's progress had been seamless. In the 1950s W. E. Smith, professor and chairman of history, dean of the Graduate School, and director of the McGuffey Museum, was involved in supervising studies by talented graduate students who explored key periods in Miami history, including the important New Miami presidencies of McFarland, Warfield, Thompson, Benton, and Hughes. Smith also wrote on McGuffey, as did Rodabaugh, and their opinion of him differed. Education dean Harvey Minnich, who encouraged the McGuffey Federation of Societies to develop a nationwide network of *Reader* admirers, wrote or edited volumes honoring the famous textbook maker. Yet even with this substantial legacy of writing Miami history at hand, as the sesquicentennial approached no single volume synthesized the heritage of the university in a readily accessible way. Walter Havighurst would rectify that.

Havighurst was born into an academic family in 1901. His father taught at Lawrence University in Appleton, Wisconsin. A younger brother was an historian, and his older brother a professor of chemistry at Miami for a while,

Walter Havighurst, professor of English, 1928–69, regionalist writer. Photograph by George R. Hoxie. Miami Special Collections.

apparently attracting Havighurst to Oxford. He had wandered some, working on freighters on the East Coast and steamers on the Great Lakes, attending Ohio Wesleyan, then completing a degree at the University of Denver. He earned another degree, in theology, at Boston University and was a part-time pastor. He worked on a cattle boat that went to Liverpool, England, where he studied for a time at the University of London, then completed an MA from Columbia in 1928. That year he was hired by Miami as instructor of English and assistant proctor in Fisher Hall, where he was mentored by Professor Bachelor. Two years later he married his Miami office mate, Marion Boyd, a novelist and the daughter of President William W. Boyd of Western College for Women. They would be together, in Oxford, until her death in 1974.

Walter Havighurst became a distinguished writer of midwestern regionalist works. By 1957, two years before Miami's sesquicentennial, he had published five novels, seven historical works, a variety of short stories and magazine items, and three books for teenagers written with his wife. In a 1957 feature for the *Toledo Sunday Blade,* Havighurst discussed his sources of inspiration.

In the past century this region has grown populous, productive, vastly prosperous. Sometimes its life seems thin; it has no lost causes and few deeply cherished traditions. Yet its memories of toil and opportunity have a certain richness, accessible to all, and sometimes its sense of future illuminates the country like sunrise. In the way of literary material it seems to me quite inexhaustible.

Havighurst distinguished his approach as a regionalist writer from that of an historian. His goal was "to make the reader see what life was like in a given region." The regionalist told a moving story: "In choosing his material the regional writer makes only limited use of sources. Instead he skims off what he wants from the work of formal historians." "In Mr. Havighurst's opinion," wrote reporter Harvey Ford, "the regional writer aims at visualization rather than exposition. He writes history as though it were a novel, using the narrative style and focusing attention on persons, scenes and events rather than on movements. He uses the novelist's techniques and has the novelist's interest in the dramatic elements of history." Walter Havighurst spent forty-one of his ninety-two years at Miami, writing at his home in a tree-lined neighborhood bordering Miami's formal gardens. He focused mostly on the region "between the Great Lakes and the Ohio River," producing "nearly forty volumes of fiction and fact" written in longhand, many in student examination bluebooks. One of those volumes was *The Miami Years.*

The Miami Years first appeared in 1958 to prepare for Miami's 1959 sesquicentennial celebration. It was updated in 1969 to comment on subsequent developments, and republished with a third new section in a 175th Anniversary Edition in 1984. Said to have been originally written upon a request from President Millett, *The Miami Years* told a dramatic story of Miami's progress, engaging readers anew in well-crafted accounts of figures, buildings, and events of "Old" and "New" Miami. It drew upon, amplified, and dramatized anecdotes and stories from Miami's past, some told earlier by Upham.

Sequentially across its pages walked all of Miami's presidents and legendary figures: John W. Browne, Robert Hamilton Bishop, Junkin, MacMaster, Anderson, McGuffey, Stanton, McFarland, Hepburn, Warfield, Thompson, Tappan, Benton, Hughes, Percy MacKaye, Upham, Hahne, Millett, Shriver, and Pearson. The literary societies and fraternities, Snow Rebellion, Civil War, Naval Training School, and antiwar protests of 1970 offered punctuation points. Oxford's colleges for women were mentioned intermittently. Events of the sesquicentennial year, and the "Miami mural" rendered by Edwin Fulwider in 1963, had their own chapters, suggesting the import of Miami's past and how it is told.

Years after its publication *The Miami Years* was still given to new faculty members as an introduction to the story of Miami University. In 1988 Douglas Wilson, Miami Class of 1964 and vice president for university relations, edited a collection of stories based on it titled *Our Miami Heritage.* Believing that the "recognition and celebration" of "traditions, a sense of the past, a certain specialness about a place" creates "a sense of belonging among those who populate the institution," Wilson saw his own effort as a tribute to predecessors Upham and Rodabaugh, and especially to Havighurst. *The Miami Years* would be the only text for President Phillip Shriver's popular class in Miami history. "To generations of Miami students," said Shriver, "Walter Havighurst was Mr. Miami, the one who better than any other knew and loved the University, its history, its traditions and folklore." Shriver himself would come to rival that claim, and in 1998, with the aid of Professor William Pratt of Miami's English department, he would publish his own course lectures as *Miami University: A Personal History.* The opening sentence of that work was unequivocal about its inspiration: "In my view, Walter Havighurst's *The Miami Years* is one of the finest college histories that has ever been written."

This ample praise and admiration was often echoed by those who read Havighurst's accessible story of the Miami past. Lacking either cumbersome footnotes or arcane scholarly language, with few illustrations compared to the numerous word pictures it painted, *The Miami Years* would create a memorable and sometimes romantic account of the past. Here Bishop and McGuffey trek into a vaguely threatening forested wilderness, where these hardy frontier educators and their talented students struggle to carve out the nationally prominent and lasting achievements of Old Miami men. New Miami inherits their character, and adds to the story an account of modernizing growth, expansion, and progress. While periodic social disruptions are graphically rendered, the lessons to be learned are the university's continuity of purpose across time and change, and the sustained tradition of individual dedication that alone can yield success. Many admirers of *The Miami Years* may recall, for example, the vivid ending to its 1958 edition, one among many memorable examples of "visualization rather than exposition."

The quest for understanding ticks like an everlasting clock on a college campus. In 1891 when the first section of Brice Hall was built, President Warfield said it would contain the science of Miami for the next hundred years. Now, three times its original size, that hall contains a single department of science—a department that had no separate existence when President Warfield dedicated the building. The course of study changes, but the pursuit of knowledge goes on from generation to generation. And despite all the bread and circuses that have been added to American universities, the meaning of college is still the burning of a study lamp at midnight.

By encouraging the creation of Walter Havighurst's *The Miami Years* as a gift to the university for its 150th birthday, John Millett sanctioned the rebirth of a readily useable past to serve twentieth-century Miami. His successors would rely upon it.

Mounds

Miami's first president and his wife had been interred, since their virtually simultaneous deaths in 1855, on grounds of the Farmers' College in Cincinnati where Bishop had taught after his dismissal from Miami in 1845. Because a new high school was to be built on that site, the *Miami Alumnus* of June 1959 ran the story "The Bishops Come Home to Oxford," reporting in a matter-of-fact fashion that "officials of the University brought the bodies in their original metal coffins to Oxford and reburied them in a grave near the formal gardens of the University on June 20." This event, coinciding with the sesquicentennial and arranged to evoke the continuing presence of the past in an era of rapid progress toward the future, was supervised personally by President Millett and Walter Havighurst. It included ritualistic elements that looked both forward and backward. Bishop's will stipulated that he be buried in an unmarked low mound of earth. This request had been respected in Cincinnati, and would be in Oxford as well, with a supplemental feature: "Men in the maintenance department constructed a new outer box for each, using oak taken from trees cut on the campus to make way for Culler Hall. The trees

Walter and Marion Boyd Havighurst

Walter Havighurst, the son of an Appleton, Wisconsin, college professor who, as Walter said, "couldn't decide if he wanted to teach or preach," fell in love with Miami the first time he visited his faculty member brother, Robert, in 1927. He fell in love again in 1928 with his office mate, Marion Boyd, when Robert left for another teaching position and Walter came to teach English and to be a proctor in old Fisher Hall. These two love affairs lasted his entire life.

Marion, the daughter of the president of Western College for Women, had always said she would never teach, and then taught English. She also said she would never marry a college professor, but Walter and Marion's wedding was the highlight of the 1930 Oxford social season, with more than four hundred invited guests.

At the time of their marriage, the pair made a five-year plan of what they wanted to accomplish. Marion, already a published poet in the 1923 Yale Series of Younger Poets, encouraged Walter to write—and write he did. His first book, *Pier 17*, 1935, was a Book-of-the-Month Club selection and a nominee for the Pulitzer Prize. In the meantime, Marion had begun work on *Murder in the Stacks* (1934), writing in her study carrel in old Alumni Library until she frightened herself so badly that she continued writing at home.

The first modern mystery novel set in a college library, *Murder in the Stacks* is a mystery without a detective, inspired by the loss of a valuable chapbook, *The King and Queen of Hearts*, from the children's book collection of librarian E. W. King. It tells the story of a more accidental than gruesome death of an assistant librarian that occurs in a midwestern college during four days of commencement festivities. Describing the Miami campus of the 1930s as her setting, naming the town "Kingsley" for the librarian, and even including the campus night watchman and President Upham's Scotty dog that wore a Phi Beta Kappa key on his collar, *Murder in the Stacks* offers a fascinating account of social relations during the New Miami era.

For more than fifty years, Walter Havighurst's lyrical writing brought life to stories of the American heartland. While his name is on a scholar-leader room, a special collections library, the Russian studies program endowed with his multimillion-dollar legacy, and, together with that of his wife, on a residence hall designated to honor the intertwined history of Western College and Miami, it is through *The Miami Years* that many students and alumni came to know him. *The Miami Years* was written with the warmth and vitality of a true storyteller fond of his subject. His students became authors, publishers, the poet laureate of West Virginia—and with the many international students he took under his wing, were always his friends, his admirers, his children. One of them wrote that he "set my soul humming with the music of words."

Frances McClure, Assistant to the Curator,
Special Collections, 1985–94

showed marks of age indicating that they were growing on the campus when Dr. and Mrs. Bishop lived here."

The strategy of blending campus change with an active sense of the past— found in the narrative structure of *The Miami Years*, in the visual conception of a new Harrison Hall rising out of the demolition of Old Main, and in reburial of Miami's earliest First Family in new coffins made from trees cut down to build a postwar building for the physics department—would be extended. In 1960 Miami demolished President Bishop's 1834 home on the northeast corner of High and Bishop streets. It had been the site of Old Miami alumni gatherings before the invention of Homecoming, and served as an inaugural celebration site for New Miami in 1888. In the year of its demolition a U-shaped drive was cut through the wooded area known previously as Lower Campus—bounded by Patterson Avenue on the east, High Street on the north, Spring Street on the south, and a cross-campus drive on the west

Reburial of Robert Hamilton Bishop
and Ann Ireland Bishop in Miami
Formal Gardens, 1959. Miami Archives.

that ran parallel to Stoddard and Elliott halls. At access points to this drive
Cellarius and Hilmer erected the Bishop Memorial Gates to honor the great-
grandson of the newly reburied First Family, who was a Miami graduate and
a trustee from 1918 to 1955. The unbuilt area that would be enclosed by the
drive—around which would rise Culler Hall for physics, Shideler Hall for geology and geography, and Hughes Laboratories for chemistry, placed to yield
neo-Georgian symmetry with Upham Hall where botany, microbiology, and
zoology coexisted with history, English, and religion—would now be known
as "Bishop Woods."

Birthday

At its 150th year in 1959, Miami University was now officially old, and had both a popular story about that and campus sites that evoked it. It did not, however, have an official birthday celebration. On February 17, 1809, the Ohio General Assembly approved "An Act to Establish the Miami University," but Miami's birthday had not been observed during the nineteenth century. In 1916, some faculty thought that February 17 might be an appropriate commemoration, and celebrated "Founders' Day" that year with an academic procession, chapel service, and singing of university songs by the choir and student body. Professors Upham, E. E. Brandon, and John Bradford gave talks on Miami history, and an historical exhibit was set up in the west room of Alumni Library.

The 1916 combination of religion, songs, and history lectures set a pattern for later celebrations, but Founders' Day ended in 1922, perhaps overcome by competition with a Mid-Year Play and Greek initiations. In 1925 the birthday celebration was reinstituted as Miami Day for both the campus and alumni across the country. Cincinnati's Crosley Radio Corporation agreed to air a program of speeches and songs from 7:00 to 8:30 p.m. on clear channel WLW. President Hughes, Coach George Rider, and a double quartet from the Miami Sinfonia made the trip to Cincinnati to go on the air. The first Miami Day broadcast was a success, and later shows became focal points for alumni gatherings across the country. Some featured short speeches by faculty. The February 12, 1926, *Miami Student* reported that forty-nine meetings were planned for the upcoming Miami Day. After the 1929 collapse of the stock market the program was shortened to thirty minutes and in 1932 it was integrated into the Armco Band Hour. In 1934 the Miami broadcast moved to WCKY in Covington, Kentucky; then WHAS in Louisville; WHIO in Dayton; and in 1937, WTAM in Cleveland. The last All-Miami Founders' Day broadcast aired in 1937. For the next twenty years Miami's birthday was celebrated neither on campus nor on radio, but at alumni events across the country at various times between February and May.

In preparing for the sesquicentennial, President Millett decided to restore the formal commemoration of Miami's birthday as a major campus event. In a January 1958 letter to university administrators he announced plans to observe Miami's 149th birthday at a university convocation in Withrow Court on February 17, 1958. Its featured event was an historical address titled "Charter Day 1809" by Walter Havighurst. Millett followed with remarks on plans for the sesquicentennial. He intended the 1958 convocation as dress rehearsal for the 150th anniversary celebration, and the Sesquicentennial Convocation held on February 17, 1959, was the first campus event ever labeled "Charter Day." Ohio officials and administrators of other public universities were featured guests, and University of Minnesota president John Morrill spoke on

*Sesquicentennial Charter
Day Convocation, 1959.*
Miami Archives.

"The State University: Its Opportunities and Obligations in American Higher Education." The Sesquicentennial Convocation inaugurated a practice of holding Charter Day convocations at fairly regular intervals over the next thirty years, with prominent speakers who were usually awarded honorary degrees.

The 1976 Charter Day observance added a Bicentennial Ball in Millett Hall hosted by President and Mrs. Shriver. This began a custom of sponsoring a formal dance for students, faculty and staff every two, and then three, years. Soon this dance would supplant convocation as the principal Charter Day event. The last convocation was held March 27, 1985, in conjunction with the Hammond Lecture on the American Tradition featuring former U.S. President Gerald Ford. Thereafter, lectures on the Miami past, imported dignitaries, and prominent honorary degree recipients disappeared. Charter Day Ball nearly fell victim to budget cuts in 1982. It was saved by students when the Shriver Center Program Board held it that year in the Center's Heritage and Towers Rooms. The next year Charter Day Ball returned to the place named for the president who resurrected Miami's birthday in 1959. After 2003 it would draw more than three thousand people, mostly students, to the only repeating triannual event marking Miami's birthday.

"Biography"

President Millett called Professor of Art Edwin Fulwider to his office the day after commencement in June 1962. Millett wanted a mural installed in the new University Center as a gift of the Class of 1962. Fulwider, aware of the president's practice of blending images of the past with images of progress, of-fered to put the now well-known story of Miami on an entire wall. He sug-gested that Walter Havighurst's *The Miami Years* should be his guide. The pro-posed location in a large room on third floor of the University Center to be called the "Heritage Room" was 68 feet long and 13 feet high, but had multiple disruptive openings into a food service area. Convinced of the importance of the project, Millett insisted that the Heritage Room be redesigned to allow for proper placement of the mural.

Again at Millett's insistence, a studio in the new Radio-Television Build-ing was cleared to provide a space large enough for Fulwider to design this public-scale artwork. Fulwider got approval for an overall concept, then com-pleted a half-size drawing of the mural that was projected onto a full-size canvas made from a single piece of primed Belgian linen. Each projected el-ement was carefully aligned, then traced with pastel pencils. His wife, Katy, researched costume designs for the mural's characters, as well as architec-tural styles and other details. She also painted most of the flat areas of the

Making The Biography of a University *mural. Edwin Fulwider, 1959. Miami Archives.*

The completed mural. Miami Archives.

mural. Edwin and Katy Fulwider painted the canvas on weekends and during odd hours beginning early in December 1962. Colors for the mural were mixed in baby food jars, and given names corresponding to their first use in the painting—"McGuffey" for brown, "Harrison" for red, and so on. They finished the mural shortly before commencement in spring 1963, completing the entire project from conception to rendering in less than a year. The canvas was mounted in the Heritage Room in September, just as the University Center neared completion.

Fulwider gave his mural a title: *The Biography of a University*. It offered as backdrop a panorama of Miami buildings showcasing the university's evolution from 1809 to 1959. These were fronted by fifty-four vignettes—each carefully identified in an accompanying explanatory legend—selected to suggest evolving expressions of campus life. The first one represented Ohio's General Assembly passing an act for creation of the university in 1809. The last one depicted the latest Miami trend in 1960s teaching—remote instruction by television. Between these framing images progressive events of Miami's past were depicted. The 1827 publication of Miami's pioneering periodical the *Literary Focus* was here, as was the formation of the Miami chapter of the American Anti-Slavery Society in 1832. The 1836 purchase of Miami's first telescope, later configured on the Miami seal, was shown. The Snow Rebellion of 1848 was rendered to suggest an almost-cheerful event of youthful high spirits, with the participants wearing charming smiles. Miami's first intercollegiate football game in 1888 was depicted, and the Hepburn Hall fire in 1908. Villager Jennie Brooks protesting the 1923 cutting of trees for moving the Gymnasium so Ogden Hall could be constructed was one point of conflict. Another, near the center of this history, was a "brothers' war" image, as Miamians in crisp blue and elegant gray marched in orderly fashion side by side to waiting railroad cars that would take them to battle one another far away. The literary societies, the "Dude Faculty," World War I and the Naval Training School of World War II, as well as bell towers, cupolas, Greeks, and decorous ladies from Oxford's nineteenth-century female seminaries were here, all moving purposefully through time, left to right, a sweeping panorama of the past.

This mural became a source of institutional pride almost immediately, and remained a focus of university events through the 1980s. President Phillip Shriver developed a famous lecture standing before the Heritage Room mural, where he told the vivid stories of its illustrations by heart. Many alumni bought or were presented with framed replicas of *The Biography of a University*. Walter Havighurst's compelling images in words, distantly reenacting Alfred Upham's pageants of the past, had become the literal picture of Miami history. For the next thirty-nine years every Miami student and faculty member would be introduced to it, many at orientation when beginning their first year at the university.

Yet by the time the Corporate University emerged in the middle 1990s, the success of Fulwider's mural—which had become almost a Miami University brand—had been undone by social change. Soon after it was completed in the mid-1960s the turmoil of the civil rights movement came to Oxford and Miami. To that was added antiwar protests questioning the nation's and Miami's involvement in Vietnam. Then came waves of renewed energy in the long movement for equal rights for women, followed by efforts on behalf of rights for gay, lesbian, bisexual, and transgendered individuals, and other agendas of cultural politics involving race, ethnicity, and personal identity. By the early twenty-first century the content of Fulwider's *Biography of a University* was being viewed as an incomplete story of Miami, and therefore, some said, a false one. Critics observed that it showcased, for example, no African Americans and few Miami women among its numerous examples of accomplishment. Some noted that with the exception of one New Miami faculty member playing tennis, virtually all faculty prominently depicted were from Old Miami. The mural's broadbrush style, said by some who disliked it to resemble magazine illustration, had fallen from favor as well, so that even its gentle critics agreed it was artistically dated.

The story of Miami that this vivid mural told was nonetheless deeply ingrained in the hearts of many faculty, staff, alumni, and friends of the university, and Fulwider's mural would not come down casually. In 2003–4, with support of central administrators, the entire Heritage Room was thoroughly renovated with generic neoclassical decoration featuring pilasters and other wall elements that precluded remounting the mural. Since Fulwider had carefully documented its original installation methods in detailed notes and photographs, the mural was removed without damage and stored, with other artifacts of the Miami past that it so faithfully celebrated, in the University Archives.

Guests

President Millett took many steps to generate a living sense of the past at Miami, and he was ambitious for Miami University to achieve wider state and national recognition. He had a U.S. postal stamp struck for Benjamin Harrison, brought distinguished musical organizations including the Philadelphia Orchestra and Metropolitan Opera Company to perform on campus during the sesquicentennial year, hosted a retrospective exhibition of 150 years of American Art in cooperation with twelve major museums and galleries, and sponsored symposia: "The Role of the State University," featuring members of the Ohio General Assembly; "What is a College For?"; "Schools of the Future"; and "New Directions in the Management of Business Enterprise," all with distinguished academics and public figures. He offered The 1809 Lectures "honoring great men born in the year of Miami's chartering: Abraham Lincoln, Edgar Allan Poe, Charles Darwin, Oliver Wendell Holmes."

On April 10, 1959, Robert Frost came to Miami. It was the New England poet's sixth visit. He came first in 1942, again in 1944, when he also read at Western College for Women, and in 1946, 1951, and 1954. He was invited for these earlier visits by Walter Havighurst, a friend of long standing and a regular participant in the Breadloaf Summer Writers Program in Vermont, of which Frost was a founder. Frost once introduced Walter and Marion Boyd Havighurst by saying "these people live in the most beautiful college there is."

Frost made his final visit in 1959, invited this time by President Millett to give a reading during the sesquicentennial celebration and to receive the Doctor of Humanities honorary degree. Frost read—or as he preferred to call it, "said," his poems to a standing-room-only audience in Benton Hall auditorium. When Millett hooded him for his honorary degree, Frost quipped that he always preferred getting a degree to getting an education. Though it was true that Frost had attended classes at Dartmouth and Harvard without earning a degree, he later gained many honorary degrees for his poetry. In 1959 Frost was eighty-five, spry and witty, with snowy hair that matched his name. He had by then won the Pulitzer Prize for Poetry four times, and soon would be acknowledged as the unofficial American Poet Laureate when he was invited by President John F. Kennedy to read a poem, "The Gift Outright," at the 1961 presidential inauguration in Washington.

Frost said his poems from memory, seldom consulting a book, but commenting on them with a twinkle in his eye. Reading his best-known poem, "Stopping by Woods on a Snowy Evening," he remarked that some critics had called it a "death poem," but added that though death hadn't been in his mind when he wrote it, "as long as you go me one better—not one worse—I don't mind what you say." After reading another familiar poem he paused, then went on, "I'll say this one twice, so you can hear the rhymes click. That's what I call fun—making rhymes. Some people ask if I can be so superficial as to write a poem for the fun of the rhymes, and I say, Yes."

Reading his well-known "Mending Wall," with its refrain, "Good fences make good neighbors," he observed, "This is a farming poem, but you've got to watch it—it might be political. 'Might be?' I could write a book on that subject." And when he recited "The Road Not Taken," a poem often thought to be autobiographical because the speaker chooses "the road less traveled by," he explained it was "a tricky poem, because it isn't really for myself, but for a friend of mine, Edward Thomas, an English poet who was always regretting what he had left undone."

A 1959 photograph of Frost reading from a book, taken by Oxford photographer George Hoxie, is on display in the Walter Havighurst Special Collections at King Library. Though Frost read to college audiences all over the

Robert Frost, 1959. Photograph by George R. Hoxie. Miami Special Collections.

country, on his third visit in 1946—the year Miami was reeling from the mounting enrollment pressure of returning veterans—he had been quoted as saying that "Miami University is one of the largest colleges at which I have lectured. I enjoy each additional visit more because I am so cordially received. It gives me great satisfaction to see your 4,500 students so eager for an education that they are unaware of the crowded conditions in which they live." By the time of his final visit in Miami's sesquicentennial year, many of the crowded conditions he witnessed earlier had been addressed, although Miami had grown by at least another thousand students and was moving steadily toward more national recognition—a trend his final visit advanced.

On the morning of September 17, 1959, a chartered Convair landed at Miami's airfield. It carried Massachusetts senator John F. Kennedy, already

John F. Kennedy speaking at Miami Field, 1959. Miami Archives.

a declared candidate for the 1960 Democratic presidential nomination, with a party of seventeen aides and political writers. Kennedy was beginning a tour of Ohio colleges and universities. Less than twenty-four hours earlier he had attended a tea in Washington for Soviet premier Nikita Khrushchev, but now was responding to an invitation from the Miami Young Democrats Club to speak at the opening convocation of the 1959–60 school year. Because of threatening weather the convocation had been planned for Benton Hall auditorium, but Millett, anticipating a turnout exceeding seating capacity, decided to hold the event at Miami Field.

When the Kennedy motorcade arrived at the athletic facility shortly before 10 a.m. the sun was breaking through clouds and approximately six thousand students were waiting. Senator Kennedy had prepared a formal speech on the role of the United States in the conflict between China and India, and his text had been released in advance. Yet when he saw the size and enthusiasm of the audience, typical of his approach to young voters he decided to deviate from his prepared text, and spoke for about twenty minutes on the need for intelligent college graduates to consider a career in politics.

To most Americans no education is considered necessary for a politician, except to learn his way around a smoke-filled room. . . . Politics is one of the most neglected, ignored and abused professions, and we must overcome the disdain shown toward politics by our educational institutions. We stand in great need of the fruits of your education.

Kennedy concluded by urging Miamians to become involved in politics at every level. "It's not essential that you become successful as a candidate," he said, "but it is essential that you participate." Then he spent twenty minutes taking questions—an opportunity to interact with students. But students had competition, as most questions came from news media. They covered topics ranging from President Eisenhower's recent vetoes of housing and foreign aid bills to Jimmy Hoffa to the importance of encouraging prosperity in India. Kennedy took an opportunity to criticize Eisenhower's reliance on nuclear deterrence, noting that "by emphasizing nuclear weapons . . . we also have cut down our ability to fight a war like the Korea action or what's now going on in Laos, and we're going to face this thing for many years." The most telling agenda of the visit surfaced when he was asked if he had a favorite candidate for president. Kennedy grinned and answered emphatically, "Yes, I do!"

With the assistance of Robert Frost, John F. Kennedy would be inaugurated as president of the United States in 1961. Not quite three years later, on November 25, 1963, the Miami community would attend a memorial service honoring the assassinated President. In his eulogy, President Millett mentioned that when he had visited the White House in June, President Kennedy was quick to recall his visit to Miami, telling him, "Yours is a fine institution." Millett underlined this assessment of the university he was building by wryly pointing out, "From an overseer of Harvard University, this was a warm compliment indeed."

BEYOND OXFORD

Even as it confirmed a renewed and visible sense of its past, Miami was expanding beyond the original campus, opening new facilities and experimenting with novel pedagogy. It was alive with the promise of technological change, new student constituencies, and new programs to serve them.

Experiment

Television, a prewar technological development, after World War II moved into consumer culture, where it became a novelty and a craze. Alert to its potential impact, Miami received a grant of $135,600 from the Fund for the Advancement of Education for a "study of instructional techniques . . . designed to evaluate procedures which enable one member of a faculty to teach larger numbers of students." This must have seemed a worthy goal as enrollment

Miami television studio WMUB TV, 1956. Miami Archives.

continued to swell and resources were strained. However, the stated aims of this study went beyond the merely pragmatic: "it is also concerned with the development of the best possible procedures for both small and large groups, and with the improvement of large group instruction," or, "how to make the best possible use of the abilities of the best teachers." The dean of the School of Education stepped down to direct this university project, and teamed with the Student Counseling Service, the Audio-Visual Service, and a psychologist who had just arrived at Miami with a background in testing for the U.S. Army. The project transmitted closed-circuit television from a studio created in the WMUB Radio building to five rooms on the third floor of Upham Hall, where two television receivers served forty students in each room, allowing the project to reach two hundred students per session. Courses initially were offered in physiology, zoology, sociology, and educational sociology. Each had a different instructional component but all used closed-circuit television and all adopted the novelty of meeting twice per week for longer sessions instead of the standard three times per week more briefly. Visual aids, it was said, "would play an important part in the study of educational procedures."

Rather lengthy reports on this venture remain in the Miami Archives, but apparently formal results were inconclusive, and the project was abandoned when the grant expired. Teaching by closed-circuit television was not the only effort to transmit instruction following World War II. As early as 1951 a student in Professor W. E. Smith's history class wrote in his class diary about Smith's initiative to record the class for later broadcasting.

History class has me bluffed this semester. Dr. Smith is recording his lectures for broadcasts and in order to include some class discussion, he calls on a few people each day to stand around the microphone and contribute their two-cents worth. I must admire him for not insisting and trying to force answers when the student doesn't know it (some profs make a specialty of that third-degree cross-examining), but on the other hand, just standing there in front of the class is enough torture in itself. I liked the class much better when there were no recordings and everyone was perfectly natural. Dr. Smith himself was quite a card when there were no broadcasts and going to class then was a real pleasure. I learned because I listened intently to every lecture and I concentrated so because his talks and characterizations were so interesting I didn't want to miss a word. When the "mike" is dispensed with, his free and easy style is always present and I feel that we're really missing something when that recorder is at work. Wish we could do without it permanently!

Applied Science

The late 1950s brought rapid technological innovation. In 1959, two years after the Soviet Union launched the first artificial satellite as a symbolic demonstration of technological superiority and state planning, editorial writers, politicians, and educators were commenting on the failure of the nation's science education and calling for a more "practical" curriculum tailored to business and industry. In this climate, engineering and applied science disciplines received new attention across the nation and Ohio. At a spring meeting in the sesquicentennial year, June 5, 1959, trustees approved a new division that would search for applications of scientific knowledge through professional development in programs leading to bachelor of science degrees. President Millett was a strong supporter.

In both industrial arts and home economics, we are observing greater need for serving those who do not wish to meet the requirements for teaching. Industry tells us that it is has a particular need for persons at the semi-professional level of engineering, and it is this need which prompted us to offer the curriculum in Industrial Technology.

The School of Applied Science was created by relocating existing programs. The Department of Home Economics was moved there from the School of Education. A new Department of Industrial Technology was created in the school from industrial arts education in the School of Education. The new Department of Pulp and Paper Chemistry was moved to the school from the Department of Chemistry in the College of Arts and Science. The

Kreger Hall. Named Hughes Hall when built for the Chemistry Department in 1931 and renamed to honor Clarence Kreger when renovated for the School of Applied Science, 1973. Miami Archives.

new school was meant to promote areas of specialization that would attract students to careers as applied science specialists in industry.

At its inception, Applied Science was administered by the provost working with the deans of Arts and Science and Education. Over 50 percent of initial coursework was taken in Arts and Science, where curriculum clusters formed a program in industrial technology. In 1963 the first full-time faculty members were hired and a director—named a dean in 1967—appointed. The goal of transforming ideas into useful products and services would then be elaborated. In 1963 a Department of Systems Analysis was added. In 1969 the Department of Secretarial Science was transferred from the School of Business, and two-year associate degree programs in nursing, engineering technology, and library technical assistance were begun at regional campuses. In its first fourteen years the new school grew to forty full-time faculty on three campuses—fourteen of them at the Hamilton and Middletown campuses. By 1970 professionally centered technological education was organized into five departments: home economics; industrial technology; paper technology; secretarial science; and systems analysis in Oxford. There were six associate degree programs in industrial technology, library technology, paper technology, secretarial science, systems analysis, and nursing on regional campuses. There had been an increase in student enrollment from approximately 120 in 1962 to about 2,150 by 1973, with about 1,600 students in Oxford and 550 on regional campuses.

In spring 1973 the School's Oxford programs were relocated to the former Hughes Hall, renovated and renamed Kreger Hall. More than 250 guests attended an April 26 celebration, including 18 members of a new Applied Science Advisory Council. At the rededication ceremony President Shriver recognized Clarence Kreger, Miami's former provost, for encouraging development of technical programs leading to creation of the School of Applied Science.

During the Public Ivy era of the 1970s and 1980s, programs in home economics, industrial technology, and secretarial science would be moved, renamed, then eliminated as Miami's national profile was sharpened to emphasize undergraduate liberal arts, advanced research sciences, education and allied professions, and business. Then in the mid-1990s as Miami's corporate culture took hold, Applied Science enjoyed a resurgence of support. In 1999 its name was changed to the School of Engineering and Applied Science, and departments of computer science and systems analysis, electrical and computer engineering, mechanical and manufacturing engineering, and paper and chemical engineering emerged at Oxford, with computer information technology, engineering technology, and nursing located on regional campuses.

In its first fifty years the School of Applied Science, now Engineering and Applied Science, graduated over seven thousand women and men, confirming that Millett's 1959 vision of new needs in business and industry had gained traction across Ohio and the country. In the early twenty-first century extensive new physical facilities were built for the school along High Street (where the original Fraternity Row stood through much of the National University era), with the aim of creating a new academic quadrangle north of High Street and east of Tallawanda Road. University Hall on the Hamilton Campus was created from a former corporate property to house Applied Science programs, including a thriving baccalaureate program in nursing relocated from Oxford.

Academic Centers

Miami offered off-campus education as early as 1914, when the Teachers College established extension centers offering courses for students and teachers who found travel to Oxford inconvenient. The location of the centers varied annually; the main requirement was a minimum enrollment of fifteen students. In 1930–31, the extension program served nearly eight hundred students in fifteen centers in southwest Ohio. By 1947 it had expanded beyond teacher training into an "Off-Campus Center program" financed by legislative appropriation. During 1948–49, Miami off-campus enrollment was more than five hundred undergraduate and graduate students. That year courses were offered in ten extension centers including facilities in Hamilton and Middletown; the campus in Dayton enjoyed the largest enrollment.

On July 18, 1954, the University Senate approved "A Statement of Purpose and Policy for the Extension Program of Miami University." It envisioned a "time when it will be impossible to take care of the entire enrollment on the

[Oxford] campus," and called for consolidation of the extension program into four or five regional centers where course offerings "should begin to include those of the first two years of work . . . applicable toward a baccalaureate degree from Miami University." This provided a foundation for the development of a system of academic centers and regional campuses that would first be presided over by Earl Valentine "Red" Thesken. He graduated from Miami in 1930 and earned a master's degree in 1943, worked briefly in the registrar's office during the postwar growth of 1947, departed and then was rehired in 1955, and in 1959 was named dean of educational services. He served until 1972. His Miami career covered much of the National University era and highlighted one its main objectives—providing access to higher education for new constituencies of Ohio citizens.

Thesken would later be called "father of three campuses." In 1955 he managed summer sessions and off-campus extension teaching, and discovered a growing demand across southwest Ohio. He oversaw offerings of afternoon, evening, and weekend instruction at academic centers in Dayton, Hamilton, Middletown, Norwood, and Piqua, accommodating up to 5,000 students. President Shriver recalled his efforts in a phrase Havighurst would have approved: "In development of regional campuses, Miami became a pioneer; Dean Thesken was the scout, trapper and settler." Two of the centers Thesken supervised would become Miami regional campuses. At first part of a cooperative project with Ohio State, the Dayton center would become Wright State University.

President Phillip R. Shriver with Earl V. Thesken, dean of academic centers and summer session, 1961–65, and dean of educational services, 1965–72. Miami Archives.

Origins of Wright State University

from Wright State University Special Collections and Archives, 2007

In 1961 planners in Dayton began meeting with state officials to secure funding for a new university. Within a year $3 million had been raised in the community, and a site purchased adjacent to Wright-Patterson Air Force Base. In 1964 The Dayton Campus of Miami University and Ohio State University opened with 3,203 students and 55 faculty. It offered a general college, science and engineering, the Dayton academic center of Miami University, and the graduate center of Ohio State University. The following year State Bill #210 authorized creation of Wright State University, named to honor the aviation achievements of Dayton's Wright brothers. It would be an independent entity contingent upon enrollment. In only three years enrollment reached 5,704 and it was granted independent status. Forty years later it would serve 17,000 students on two campuses with 100 undergraduate and 50 graduate degrees.

Dayton Campus, Miami University and Ohio State University (1964), which became Wright State University in 1968. Architect's sketch by Lorenz & Williams. Miami Archives.

A State System

President Millett favored serving a regional community of adult students and extending collegiate instruction to "those with limited financial means." This found a receptive environment in state policy of the 1960s. Republican James A. Rhodes, elected governor in 1962, spoke of "a campus within thirty miles of every man, woman, and child within the state." In 1963 the Ohio General Assembly, responding to Rhodes's request, established a Board of Regents to coordinate that explosive growth. The following year Millett was appointed its first chancellor, charged to develop and supervise a master plan for expanding educational opportunity and access. His successor at Miami, Phillip R. Shriver, summed up Millett's accomplishment in that new office.

Before John Millett assumed the position of Chancellor of the Ohio Board of Regents, there had been six publicly-supported, state-assisted campuses across the state. By

Charles R. Wilson, provost, 1960–64; acting president, 1964–65; provost, 1965–66; vice president for academic affairs and provost, 1966–70. Miami Archives.

Phillip R. and Martha Shriver (seated) and children. Miami Archives.

the time he completed his service, eight years later, there were sixty-five. Guided by master plans developed in 1965 and 1970, the most dramatic growth in higher educational opportunity in Ohio, both in choice and access, was accomplished, all in an orderly and systematic fashion, this notwithstanding the fact that the period was one of the most tumultuous and difficult in higher education as a consequence of continuing protests incident to the Vietnam War.

From 1972 to 1980 John Millett was senior vice president of the Academy for Educational Development in Washington, D.C. Then he retired to Oxford, where he worked and taught for over a decade. This most entrepreneurial of postwar Miami presidents, an aggressive partisan of change, progress, and a sense of the Miami past that would endure into the twenty-first century, a promoter of both liberal education and new professional fields, author or editor of twenty books and numerous studies, a recipient of twenty honorary degrees, and a man for whom buildings were named at Miami and Wright State, had transformed opportunities for educating the public at Miami and across Ohio.

Charles Ray Wilson assumed the acting presidency for 1964–65. A Class of 1926 Miami graduate, Wilson had been active in Democratic Party politics in New York and a professor of history at Colgate University from 1935 to 1961. He was chair of history at Colgate for twenty-one years. In 1961 Millett named him Miami's second provost—the first to be recruited to that office from another university.

Miami's next president would also be recruited from another university, and he would also be an historian. Phillip R. Shriver came to Miami from the deanship of Arts and Sciences at Kent State University, where he had been on the history faculty since 1947. Shriver had developed a teaching field in Ohio history, and at Miami would readily embrace—and over the next forty years greatly amplify—the sense of the Miami past inherited from the sesquicentennial celebration, *The Miami Years, The Biography of a University,* and other sources. In 1965 at the age of forty-two he assumed office as a young and vigorous executive with amiable good humor and an outstanding memory for names that suggested his detailed interest in both his colleagues and his new responsibilities. He was married to Martha Nye Shriver, whom he met at Wellesley. With four of their five children living in the presidential home at Lewis Place, "Phil and Martha" Shriver became personal embodiments of an institutional image that would be cultivated in the later phase of the National University and usher in the Public Ivy—the "Miami Family."

Middletown and Hamilton

Extending the sense of the past into the present and embracing the "nuclear family" concept that came with the rise of postwar suburbia—from which Miami would draw many students in coming years—did not mean adopting a policy of campus isolation. The Millett agenda to provide more campus access had moved to Columbus, and to a new system of state universities in Ohio, and it remained alive in Oxford. In 1961, the same year that visions of an independent Wright State University took hold in Dayton, civic

Miami University Middletown campus (opened 1966) in 1988. Miami Archives.

Miami University Hamilton campus (opened 1968). Miami Archives.

and business leaders of Middletown had visions of a new junior college as a successor to its popular Miami Academic Center. Thesken told them if the institution were sponsored by Miami, "it could lead not only to the benefits they saw in a junior college but also to a continuing education offering for professional advancement." Logan T. Johnson, President of Armco Steel and a member of Miami's board of trustees, then formed a group that met with Millett, who told them to raise half a million dollars. Johnson doubled that goal and signed over the deed to Armco Park as a site for a new campus. The Middletown community raised $1.6 million, a federal grant for education facilities provided $1.2 million, and the State of Ohio provided $1 million more. This model would be adopted widely. Dean Thesken recalled:

But this Middletown Campus—an idea initiated from the community and put across by community-wide effort—this was pioneering. And it created the pattern which was to be adopted later by the Board of Regents and the legislature as the formula for 28 other branch campuses of state universities in Ohio: approximately equal matching shares from the state and the federal government once the community had put its own money on the line.

On September 5, 1966, with President Shriver and Chancellor Millett present, the Middletown Campus of Miami University, a pioneer campus of the regional expansion to be pursued by the Ohio Board of Regents and John Millett, was dedicated and opened for classes.

The "Miami Family" was growing well beyond Oxford, and the story of new access to university instruction would soon be repeated in Hamilton. In

February 1965 Hamilton community leaders obtained a commitment of $1.8 million in state bonds from Chancellor Millett, and a fund drive chaired by Peter E. Rentschler, President of Hamilton Foundry, raised $1.6 million. Part of that pledge came from the Mosler Family Foundation to honor the founder of Mosler Safe Company and his wife. The City of Hamilton and the Hamilton Board of Education owned a tract of land on the Miami River they made available for a token payment of $330, and the City built a boulevard and brought utilities to the site. The goal was to develop a "showcase for the community" near downtown Hamilton and Fairfield. The Miami Hamilton Campus opened in 1968 and was formally dedicated September 26, 1969, with Peter Rentschler, Dean Thesken, Chancellor Millett, and President Shriver among the guests attending. Like Miami Middletown, the campus was to have full-time and part-time faculty and offer a two-year curriculum as well as continuing education. It could accommodate 500 day and 500 evening students, and was projected to grow to 1,500 students by 1975.

Luxembourg

Postwar progress meant expanding access to Miami University within the State of Ohio, and it meant expanding Miami programs to other countries. By the end of the National University era, students would be pursuing many foreign study options, but a special opportunity appeared for them when in 1968 Miami opened the European Center in Luxembourg.

President Shriver speaks to students and faculty at the Miami European Center, Luxembourg, 1973. Miami Archives.

Miami University Luxembourg

adapted from John E. Dolibois European Center Web site, 2007

Two world wars and social upheaval in the 1960s convinced many that global peace and understanding should be advanced through study abroad. Provost Charles Ray Wilson was committed to expanding Miami's global outlook and offering greater international opportunities. The idea for a European Center was conceived by Wilson and a small group of administrators and faculty including Vice President Dolibois, Vice President Etheridge, and professors Warren L. Mason, Jacques Breitenbucher, Howell C. Lloyd, Marcy S. Powell, Dwight L. Smith, and Delbert Snider. Countries initially considered included Japan, Switzerland, France, and Austria. An exploratory group visited potential sites in Europe that would foster an educational center with a high degree of support from the local community. Dolibois first suggested his native Luxembourg and was instrumental in cultivating access on behalf of Miami. In 1968 Miami opened the Miami University European Center (MUEC) in the Grand Duchy of Luxembourg. The ceremony was attended by Grand Duke Jean.

Characterized by international leadership in business and diplomacy, domestic stability, social cohesiveness, and a strong sense of community, Luxemburg would remain very friendly to the United States. Luxembourg families have long been multilingual, easing student immersion into the cultures of Europe, and its location afforded easy access to many countries.

In early days students crossed the Atlantic by ocean liner via Southampton and participated in a three-week study tour of Western Europe prior to their arrival in Luxembourg. The program was open to all majors and designed to be a full-year experience. There was much esprit de corps among students and faculty, and because students remained the entire year, relationships with host families were close.

In 1972 MUEC moved to a building with classrooms, office space, and a student lounge. Beginning in 1975, the center offered Miami faculty unparalleled opportunities for teaching and research in Europe through visiting scholar and visiting professor appointments. In 1979 a student teaching program was created at area international schools and schools of the Department of Defense. In 1980–81 core courses were introduced with field study tours. From its inception, the curriculum was designed to focus on

Warren Mason, director of the Miami European Center, 1968–70, and professor of political science, 1963–2007. Miami Archives.

Europe and to integrate coursework with travel experiences.

In 1988 the trustees voted to rename MUEC as the Miami University John E. Dolibois European Center (MUDEC) to honor Miami Vice President and U.S. Ambassador Dolibois for his service to the university, the center, and the United States. In September 1997 the center moved to a sixteenth-century château and its villa, located in the city of Differdange. In 2007 it served 125 to 130 students each semester as a nexus of international opportunities bridging the Atlantic in arts, science, social science, international business, humanities, research, and engineering.

254

King Urges Definite Stand For All on Race Situation

Betty Maham

With an emphasis on non-violence, Martin Luther King last night presented his views concerning "The Future of Integration", in an overflowing University Center Ballroom.

The history of race relations was divided by the MIA-sponsored speaker into three main periods: The era of slavery, the period of "restricted emancipation" and finally, constructive integration.

During these periods the Negro passed from the state of "a depersonalized cog in the vast plantation machine" to the positive feeling that the basic consideration was not "the texture of the hair or skin, but the texture of the soul."

Legislation Needed

The Rev. King cited several agencies that he felt could do much to further the cause of integration. Foremost among these is the federal government, of which only the judicial has been active. Other branches have remained apathetic and hypocritical, he said, and must take a stand if anything is to be accomplished.

The necessity for legislation was pointed out by noting that legislation seeks to control the outward effects of bad internal attitudes. "Legislation can't make a man love me, but it **can** control his desire to lynch me!"

Churches Important

Also important in the role of integration are religious bodies, the moderates of the white south, and the liberals of the white north. The lecturer remarked that the problem is not a sectional one; merely

Photo by Marty Jones

MARTIN LUTHER KING stressed "non-violence" concerning his views on "The Future of Intregation" in the Center Ballroom last night.

more glaring in the south. These people must cooperate in an effort, leading the way to peaceful integration.

But the problem will never be solved until the Negro himself learns to take the primary responsibility for integration and works for first - class citizenship, he continued.

Three Methods

"There are three ways a Negro can break the bonds of oppression," King said. He can simply resign himself and accept exploitation ("the freedom of exhaustion"), or rise in violent indignation and corroding hatred.

The latter, however, he asserted, will bring only temporary victory and not personal peace. It also brings more social problems than the present one of segregation.

Solution Must Come

The third alternative, the integration leader stated, was that of non-violent resistance. "We will wear you down with our capacity to suffer, and we will win you in spite of yourself," he remarked.

King quoted Tyonbee, who said that every civilization must face a challenge. The survival of the civilization often depends on how they meet that challenge. Americans now face the challenge of integration. Our survival may well depend on the solution. And the solution must come soon.

Martin Luther King Jr. speaks in the Towers Room, Miami University Center. Miami Student, December 11, 1959.

"We Shall Overcome"

Miami would enter the 1960s with a sense of its past refreshed by symbolic campus sites, a newly written history detailing progress over 175 years, and new buildings constructed in an "old" and stately style. It looked forward to new academic programs and centers designed to engage science, industry, and the region's economic needs, and by the late 1960s would establish three new campuses, including one in Europe. Expanding in students, faculty,

Oxford and Miami African Americans

A Timeline of Change, 1941–70

adapted from the Miami University Libraries *African American Timeline*

1945   Myldred Boston and Arie Parks became the first female African American students allowed to live on campus, assigned to a basement room in Oxford College. Boston moved out to room with a family in Oxford. Parks remained for a year.

1945–46   Campus Inter-Racial Club was organized with Franklin Shands, African American senior and fine arts major, as president. It would seek to improve life for African Americans on campus during the next five years and work closely with the Oxford Branch, NAACP.

1946   Campus Inter-Racial Club circulated a petition for full integration of residence halls.

1947   At the urging of Campus Inter-Racial Club, Student-Faculty Council agreed to poll the student body on whether Miami athletic teams should compete against institutions that barred African Americans. Students voted eight to one in favor of barring competition against segregated teams. The university, while reaffirming its commitment to black participation on its own teams, took no action.

Marian Musgrave, director of the Black Studies and Black World Studies programs, 1973–87, and professor of English, 1969–88, with students, 1987. 1993 U.S. Poet Laureate Rita Dove, Class of 1973, is third from left. Miami Archives.

1948   Campus Inter-Racial Club tried to focus student attention on discrimination at McGuffey School. Despite some opposition, Arthur Miller became the first African American student permitted to complete practice teaching at McGuffey School.

1950   Oxford swimming pool opened to African Americans after NAACP lawsuit.

1955   Alpha Phi Alpha became the first national African American fraternity to establish a Miami chapter.

1957   Eta Omicron became the first African American sorority at Miami. It planned to affiliate with Delta Sigma Theta, but disbanded.

1959   The Reverend Dr. Martin Luther King Jr. came to Oxford at the invitation of the Campus Independent Club. At University Center Towers Room he spoke to an "overflow crowd of faculty and students" on the history of civil rights.

Arthur F. Miller, Class of 1949, manager of Central Food Service, 1969–78. Oxford Press.

1960   Board of trustees resolutions on McGuffey School included a statement that admission shall not be restricted by race, creed, or color.

1964   Western College for Women hosted training of civil rights workers preparing to register African American voters in Mississippi during "Freedom Summer." NAACP organized the community support group Friends of the Mississippi Summer Project. African American James Chaney of Mississippi and white students Andrew Goodman and Michael Schwerner of New York were murdered in Mississippi, focusing attention on civil rights and influencing passage of the 1965 Voting Rights Act.

1965   Arthur Miller, an elected member of village council 1959–68, was named first African American vice mayor of Oxford. The first African American students enrolled in McGuffey School, an action sought by the Oxford NAACP since the 1940s.

Heanon Wilkins, director of the Black World Studies Program, 1987–90, and professor of Spanish and Portuguese, 1968–92, with graduate students, 1986. Miami Archives.

1968   Heanon Wilkins, hired in 1964 at the Dayton Academic Center of Miami University and Ohio State University, joined the department of Spanish and Portuguese as the first full-time, tenure-track African American faculty member in Oxford. Charles Churchwell, Miami's first full-time African American academic administrator, was named director of libraries. Alumnus Tirrel Burton, assistant to Coach Bill Mallory, became Miami's first African American football coach. Eighty-six black students enrolled. The Black Student Action Association was formed with Robert Payne as president, with the goal of making Miami "more responsive to the needs of Black Students." BSAA advocated a Black Studies curriculum, recruitment of African American students and faculty, and observance of Black History Month.

1969   Arthur Miller was named food service manager, the first African American staff member to reach managerial rank. Ad Hoc Committee on Human Relations assessed social, academic, and political discrimination against African American students and recommended creating the Office of Black Student Affairs with Kenneth McDowell as its first head. Delta Sigma Theta became the first national historically black sorority on campus. Sherman Jackson joined the history department in response to student demands for a black faculty member to teach African American history. Marian Musgrave joined the English department as Miami's first African American woman faculty member. She served until 1988 and was director of Black Studies from 1973 to 1987.

administrative staff, and programs, Miami was poised to take advantage of postwar prosperity. But the agenda of postwar history was not yet complete.

During World War II President Harry S Truman desegregated the military services of the United States. When many African American veterans returned home, however, they encountered discrimination ranging from overt racial segregation in southern states to covert, and sometimes overt, exclusion elsewhere. A postwar legal movement for equal treatment under the law, led by the National Association for the Advancement of Colored People (NAACP) and supported by many other groups, mounted a revolutionary attack on racial injustice, particularly in southern states. In 1954 the U.S. Supreme Court declared racial segregation in public schooling unconstitutional. Very soon thereafter—visible to all on television—nonviolent protest movements to desegregate public accommodations, schools and higher education institutions met stiff official resistance in southern states. As had been true in the antebellum conflict over slavery, southwestern Ohio again became a border area. In Oxford, returning veterans joined a movement to successfully confront and eliminate public discrimination in community facilities. At Western College for Women a training program for civil rights workers was held in the summer of 1964, and at Miami, activism on human rights issues emerged on all fronts.

Recruiting Black Faculty and Staff

In 1968 Heanon Wilkins joined the Department of Spanish and Portuguese as Miami's first black tenure-track faculty member. Two more African American faculty were hired later that year. Between 1970 and 1976 ten black faculty and twenty-one unclassified staff were hired.

In spite of affirmative action guidelines adopted in 1973, black faculty decreased from twelve in 1972 to five in 1977. A Committee to Review the Status of Racial and Ethnic Minorities concluded in 1977, "The numerical representation of Black faculty, Black students, women faculty, and foreign students, ranges from unacceptably low to embarrassingly inadequate." They recommended sensitizing personnel to negative attitudes through workshops and seminars, and recommended that the affirmative action office and the committee be responsible for monitoring Miami's progress in addressing these issues. Between 1980 and 1985 black faculty and staff increased from seven faculty to fifteen, and from eleven unclassified staff to twenty-five.

Over the next twenty years a continuing increase resulted in part from new and improved recruitment strategies such as attracting a diverse candidate pool by contacting department chairs and directors of graduate study at historically black colleges and universities, and providing a welcoming atmosphere during candidate visits. Between 2000 and 2005 job searches were expanded to utilize media oriented toward minority communities, and *Oxford and Beyond*, a Web site designed to assist spouses of new employees, was implemented. The human resources office developed a network of 135 community contacts including churches, social agencies, and civic groups. As an aid to both recruiting and retention, by the early twenty-first century Miami could point to black role models in important supervisory, administrative, and managerial positions including provost, vice president for student affairs, dean of students, and program directors. The Heanon M. Wilkins Faculty Fellowship attracted exceptionally well-qualified young black professionals to departments across the university. In more than a century between 1885 and 2007, the number of full-time continuing unclassified staff had increased from 1 to 184, and in 2007 there were 39 African American faculty among 814 full-time continuing faculty.

Black World Studies

In 1969 a Committee on Black Studies designed a program to provide students with relevant and challenging educational experiences. Its proposal for an interdisciplinary Black Studies Program in the College of Arts and Science was adopted in 1970. The rationale included understanding humanity through the study of humanity, coupled with the development of self-confidence and personal dignity. The first director of Black Studies, appointed in 1971, resigned after one year. In 1973 Dr. Marian Musgrave, professor of English, was named director. Three years later the program was renamed Black World Studies.

During Dr. Musgrave's service the program was structurally limited because faculty in other academic units taught its courses and the director had little influence in recruiting faculty and staff. Consequently, no new faculty were hired with an academic affiliation in Black World Studies during this time. With no dedicated faculty, minimal control over curriculum, low funding, and little staff support, the program was almost invisible. In 1986 a consultant's report observed, "Since its inauguration at Miami University in 1970, Black Studies has shown very little institutional growth."

Heanon Wilkins, professor of Spanish and Portuguese, was appointed director of Black World Studies in 1987. During a three-year quarter-time appointment, he identified three key goals: publicizing the program, making it visible to the academic community, and encouraging students to minor or major in Black World Studies. In 1988 information about the program was mailed to all incoming minority students and all black alumni, suggestions about future program directions were invited, and a new advising document, "What Can I Do with a Major in Black World Studies?" was created. In addition to existing courses in English, philosophy, and Spanish, new courses in American studies, psychology, educational psychology, French, and interdisciplinary studies were cross-listed with Black World Studies. A minor was approved in 1988. Cocurricular activities were increased with a Martin Luther King Week celebration, Black History Week programs, a film series, and a Black Cultural Festival. In 1990 the series Black World Studies: Retrospect and Prospect brought six distinguished black scholars and artists to campus.

In 1990 Rodney Coates was appointed to a Black World Studies joint faculty position with sociology and anthropology; he became acting director in the 1990–91 school year and was named director after 1991. Coates concentrated on attracting majors and minors. Starting with only one major and two minors in 1990, by 1992 there were twenty and by 2007, fifty. Seven more joint appointments were made between Black World Studies and academic departments, including three at Hamilton and Middletown. By 2007 more than twenty faculty affiliates in Black World Studies were listed. An array of courses was developed, and a popular Penny Lecture Series was begun.

Black World Studies provided students with international study, especially through a Ghana summer program. In 2000 Black World Studies and Latin American Studies sponsored a summer program in Brazil. A Symposium and Lecture Series on Race and Gender, cosponsored with Women's Studies, presented keynote speakers Angela Davis in 1999 and Octavia Butler in 2000. Women's History and Black History Month were cosponsored, and a 100 Hour Marathon Lecture Series celebrated the centennial of W. E. B. Du Bois's *Souls of Black Folk* with twenty-six BWS faculty lecturing around the clock to ninety-six undergraduate and graduate students. Beginning as a response to concern about campus intellectual and social diversity, by the twenty-first century Miami's Black World Studies Program had achieved both visibility and collaborative influence.

interlude

"As We See It"

The early 1960s seemed idyllic. Miami students tackled classroom responsibilities with zest and watched collegiate rivals on the gridiron. They attended lectures by Robert Frost, Linus Pauling, Hubert Humphrey, and Barry Goldwater and musical performances by Ravi Shankar, Louis Armstrong, and the Juilliard String Quartet. They immersed themselves in Freshman Strut, Greek Week, Homecoming, and Little Sis Weekend and established new events such as Air Force Ball. Participation in clubs, organizations, and the arts was high. Fraternities competed for coveted Puddle Pull and Chariot Race trophies. Student government candidates sparred in election debates. The Women's Choral Society, Men's Glee Club, and Campus Owls serenaded, while aspiring thespians assumed roles in *Pajama Game* and *Carousel*. A sense of vibrancy and satisfaction permeated campus. As the 1960s unfolded, that would change.

In 1968 Miami activists sponsored a Black Weekend of African American cultural programs, including an appearance by Theatre West Dayton Players, a student Black Art Exhibit, poetry readings, a black economics lecture, a performance by the Pacemakers, and "rap sessions" on campus racial issues. On April 4, 1968, Martin Luther King Jr. was assassinated. Race riots broke out in cities across the country, and the civil rights movement was somber.

American involvement in Vietnam was heating up. The United States sent military advisors in the 1950s in an effort to contain Soviet influence and communist revolutions in Asia, and between 1961 and 1963 President Kennedy increased troop levels to 16,000. His successor, Lyndon Johnson, added troops and used chemical defoliants to reduce ground cover for North Vietnamese and Viet Cong troops. Beyond conventional battles, this war involved guerrilla engagements and amphibious warfare. After fifteen years and 1.5 million deaths it would end in American withdrawal in 1975. In 1968 it was a power-

As We See It: Vietnam '68.
Forum Brochure, 1968.
Miami Archives.

ful threat to college life, for the United States had a universal draft bringing young men into military service, and deferments for education—or other reasons—were becoming difficult to obtain.

In the late 1960s Students to Educate and Act staged campus protests and sit-ins against Dow Chemical Company, manufacturer of the chemical defoliant napalm, when Dow tried to recruit employees on the Oxford campus. With protest against the war and the draft on the rise, fraternities and sororities struggled to blend social activities with a growing student political agenda questioning "the establishment." In this milieu lecturers visited campus to educate and challenge the university. Some brought viewpoints that were self-consciously "radical," such as Professor Michael Scriven of the University of California, who spoke on "The Right to Revolution." The University of Michigan, Columbia University, and the University of California, Berkeley, were hotbeds of antiwar activism, demanding a role for students in setting campus policies relating to the war. At Miami the majority of students probably remained optimistic, but they coexisted with others expressing disillusionment, anxiety, anger, even despair, as the war and the draft increasingly polarized the campus.

The winter of 1968 was a watershed as unrest became more pronounced. In January a group of Miami students sponsored Voices of Dissent, a program inviting "radicals" to campus to critique American involvement in Vietnam. They challenged the belief that the Vietnam War was either morally just or necessary. Voices of Dissent was a vivid introduction to As We See It: Vietnam '68, a lecture series promoted in superlatives as "the most extensive and comprehensive program ever assembled on this topic in the nation."

As We See It was a project of David L. Spellerberg, vice president of Student Senate. To fulfill a campaign promise to stir up the campus, he invited prominent national experts and commentators on American involvement in Vietnam to come to Oxford for a series of lectures, debates, and discussions. Thirteen prominent speakers—all men—offered ten lectures and a debate during twenty-nine days from February 18 to March 22, 1968. Participants included White House advisors, members of the U.S. House of Representatives and U.S. Senate, journalists, economists, military strategists, news pundits, "hawks," "doves," and academicians. Spellerberg felt Miami students were overly focused on fraternity parties and football games, and seldom discussed national issues beyond government class. He meant to change that. In 2006, thirty-eight years after As We See It, he remembered the program's origin and goals:

Vietnam was going at a fever and I remember talking to some faculty members about it. . . . They said, "If you could get some of these people in here to hear other views, that would be great." So I decided to do a forum with lectures and debates. I wanted it to be the largest Vietnam forum in the United States.

Spellerberg invited numerous national dignitaries to campus before realizing he had sidestepped protocol by failing to consult with President Shriver and Vice President Etheridge. By the time Miami administrators learned about As We See It, prominent national figures had accepted Spellerberg's invitation. This *faux pas* created tension. Spellerberg explained:

They were concerned about problems—mostly protests, and negative publicity. Their concerns were big things to overcome. . . . We were about to spend $25,000 to bring speakers in. We had to bring in pro- and anti-war speakers. . . . We had people flying in from all over. The local newspapers and television covered it—Cincinnati, Middletown, Dayton.

Spellerberg "guaranteed" there would be no protests, claiming he knew his peers. Student Senate solicited advertising from newspapers and television stations to promote the event. National media, including the *National Review*, vigorously endorsed all eleven programs. Spellerberg eventually secured fiscal assistance from Miami to subsidize the program, and to offset costs, Senate charged an admission fee. Organizers distributed more than 20,000 promotional brochures with a note from Spellerberg: "Our goal in sponsoring this program is not only to provide a service to the students and faculty at Miami University, but also to provide a service to you, a citizen of the United States."

As We See It raised awareness, for participation was estimated at 20,000 people. Students, faculty, administrators, alumni, and Oxford community members repeatedly returned to 4,000-seat Withrow Court, where a parade of experts espoused a multitude of views during the month-long series.

President Shriver gave welcoming remarks for the inaugural lecture by Republican Congressman Walter Judd, who said there were no easy solutions to the Southeast Asian quagmire, events taking place in Vietnam had profound influence on lives of all Americans, and in light of suspension of graduate student deferments, "the war has become more immediate than ever." A sixteen-year member of the Foreign Affairs Committee, a delegate to the United Nations General Assembly, and a medical missionary in China, Judd espoused views both provocative and unambiguous. "I can't believe that any government that enslaves men's minds can endure," he said. "Peace in Southeast Asia will come if we can return the Chinese to the free world." This rationale for American involvement in Vietnam pleased the crowd. He went further, arguing that since North Vietnam was already at war with the United States it was imperative that the United States, in self-defense, declare war on the North Vietnamese, and win.

One week later General Maxwell Taylor, former chairman of the Joint Chiefs of Staff, ambassador to Vietnam, and special advisor to both Presidents Kennedy and Johnson, advocated that the United States embrace a more limited war strategy. He endorsed Kennedy's flexible response to aggression, arguing, "It is not the purpose of war to annihilate those who provoke it, but to cause them to mend their ways." Roger Hilsman, professor of government at Columbia University, reviewed the war in the context of Asian developments and American foreign policy. This former soldier, government administrator, intelligence expert, scholar, and diplomat had resigned his post as assistant secretary of state for foreign affairs over conflict with President Johnson. Hilsman advocated ending the war by ending U.S. bombing of North Vietnam. He felt this would de-Americanize the fighting, encourage Vietnamese nationalism, establish a broader-based government in Saigon, and bring peace.

After its first week, As We See It: Vietnam '68 had high community attendance, no student protests, and no agitation by outsiders. Both student government and Miami administrators were pleased. A debate between Harrison Salisbury and Robert Scalapino the following Sunday was the best-attended program of the series. Scalapino, an Asia expert and advisor to the U.S. State Department, supported the war. Salisbury, a Pulitzer Prize–winning correspondent for the *New York Times*, opposed it. Scalapino acknowledged many problems associated with U.S. involvement and contested claims that the war was illegal or immoral, or of little consequence for Americans. Salisbury argued that the government should rely less on power and more on diplomacy. Both agreed that bolstering diplomacy, not military offensives, was the key to long-term regional stability.

Five more speakers visited campus during a five-day period. The Honorable Tran Van Dinh, chief Washington correspondent for the *Saigon Post* and former acting ambassador of Vietnam to the United States, offered the unique perspective of a Vietnamese native. John W. Lewis, coauthor of *The United States in Vietnam*, discussed the cultural revolution in China and China's influence on North Vietnamese policy. Robert Novak and Rowland Evans, leading syndicated columnists, speculated on how the war might influence local, regional, and national U.S. elections. William A. Williams, author of *The Contours of American History* and *The Tragedy of American Diplomacy*, argued that the United States was responsible for the Cold War. As the second week of As We See It closed, conflicting views of the war had been sharply articulated.

In the final week, David Halberstam, Pulitzer Prize–winning Vietnam correspondent for the *New York Times* and writer for *Harper's Magazine*, offered a journalist's view of the war from the vantage point of two years in Vietnam. Thomas Schnelling, professor of economics at Harvard, focused on the economics of war. Senator Strom Thurmond, a member of the Armed Services Committee and former governor of South Carolina, presented an unabashed hawk's plan for winning the war.

Although no organized protests materialized, an ideological scuffle erupted. Some students and faculty accused Miami administrators of unduly influencing speaker selection, charging higher facilities fees than needed, and showing discriminating courtesy to speakers favoring the war. Vice President Etheridge responded. "The administration's relationship with the entire Vietnam forum has been governed strictly by university rules and regulations," he said. Etheridge clarified why President Shriver hosted some speakers and not others. "Any time a person of national prominence or position visits, the University deems it proper that the President be the host." Some faculty members remained skeptical of this rationale. Etheridge also defended the president's decision to lobby Student Senate for an ideologically balanced slate of lecturers. "The program must have the proper political balance, in other words, if they're going to have a pacifist, make sure they have an extreme hawk."

The goal of raising awareness was met. The *Oxford Press* and *Miami Student* published articles on the forum. Numerous editorials appeared, some favoring and others condemning the war. Faculty and students sponsored informal public forums to exchange views, some of them in residence halls. Speakers for and against the war continued to visit campus. Interviewed in 2006, Spellerberg reflected on how As We See It affected him.

One newspaper reporter asked me what I had learned, how I changed. That was a good question. Before we did it I was very conservative, like most students. I came from a conservative family and I was pro-war. I thought, at first, we should be there in Vietnam and we were there for a reason. After all of the debates and seminars, at the end I said in this interview, that it was a mistake and we were in the wrong place at the wrong time. It changed my mind.

As We See It ushered in a new era of intellectual and emotional exchange among Miami students, faculty, and administrators. The generations were now engaged in a struggle that would soon bring the postwar era of uninter-rupted expansion and progressive optimism to a close. Said Spellerberg, "We never know what kind of influence we had, but people were thinking."

act 4

The Public Ivy
1970–1996

Cultivating Image

A "Public Ivy" Timeline, 1970–1996

1970   David G. Brown (1970–82) appointed provost and vice president for academic affairs

1971   Institute for Environmental Sciences, formed 1969, admits first students

1972   King Library completed

1973   Unbeaten Miami football team defeats University of Florida in Tangerine Bowl

McKie Field constructed for baseball

Old Manse (1852) acquired (campus ministry, later comparative religion)

1974   Miami Mission Statement rewritten to emphasize national aspirations

Western College, Oxford's last educational institution for women, closes, merges with Miami and campus acquired

> Langstroth Cottage (1856), Peabody Hall (1860/1871), Tenney Gateway (1890s), Alumnae Hall (1892), Patterson Place (1898), McKee Hall (1904), Sawyer Gymnasium (1914), Kelley Studio (1916), Clark GatGreat. e (c. 1916), Kumler Chapel (1918), Western Bridges (1920s), Ernst Nature Theatre (1922), Western Steam Plant (1924), Mary Lyon Hall (1925), Western Lodge (1926), Presser Hall (1931), Stancote House (1932), Corson House (1930s), Clawson Hall (1946), Boyd Hall (1947), Alexander Dining Hall (1962), Thompson Hall (1963), Hoyt Library (1971)

1975   Goggin Ice Arena constructed for hockey and recreational sports

1977   Multicultural Center opens in Bishop Hall

1978   Women's Studies first available as a certificate-transcript notation

Miami Art Museum constructed

1979   Phillip R. Shriver teaches first course in history of Miami University

Bachelor Hall constructed (English, mathematics and statistics, speech and hearing clinic)

"Greening of the Future" Lilly Grant initiates Miami faculty development programs

1981   Paul G. Pearson (1981–92) assumes the presidency

A new University Honors Program approved by University Senate with Honors Center in Bishop Hall

1982   Summer reading program for all entering students inaugurated

Marcum Conference Center constructed on site of Fisher Hall, former Oxford Female College

1983   Bob Kurz, Class of 1958, publishes *Miami of Ohio: The Cradle of Coaches*

Miami Field Gates relocated to newly constructed Yager Stadium

Walter and Marian Boyd Havighurst Hall constructed on Western Campus

1984   175th Anniversary Convocation, Millett Hall

1985   Richard Moll's *The Public Ivys* ranks Miami a "Best Buy" for quality

1985–90   University Liberal Education Review and Reform Project

     April 6, 1987, "Liberal Education at Miami University: A Statement of Principles" adopted

     February 27, 1989, "The Miami Plan for Liberal Education" adopted by University Senate

     January 1, 1990, University Director of Liberal Education, Liberal Education Council named

1986   Art Building, Biological Sciences Building (named Pearson Hall 1993) constructed

1987   Rita Dove, Class of 1973, awarded Pulitzer Prize for poetry

1989   Myrtis Powell, first African American vice president, named vice president, student affairs

1990   Number of students living off campus in Oxford surpasses number living on campus

Miami Metro bus system established

1993   Paul G. Risser (1993–95) assumes the presidency

1994   Recreational Sports Center constructed

1995   December, Risser resigns to become president, Oregon State University

Provost Anne H. Hopkins becomes first woman to assume acting presidency (1995–96)

"Public Ivy" Themes, 1970–1996

In response to campus conflicts of the 1970s, new attention is given to undergraduate studies, residence life, and faculty involvement in university decision making. After the Vietnam War and national draft end, commitment to professional preparation and personal exploration reemerge as primary concerns of college students, and the era of social protest fades. Miami's "Common Curriculum" for general education of all students is converted to a general education "University Requirement" offering a course menu that expands student choices for general education content and accommodates the increasing professional specialization of academic disciplines. Universities cultivate a more visible public image, and the intensifying competition for talented students becomes a focus of media interest and popular culture. Miami absorbs Western College, the last of Oxford's three independent institutions founded to educate women, and establishes an interdisciplinary residential college on its campus. Miami builds its last residence hall of the twentieth century in 1983. As enrollment continues to grow and campus housing requirements become more permissive, by 1990 the number of students living off campus in Oxford surpasses the number living on campus for the first time since the early 1920s. That trend escalates over the next decade, with Oxford campus enrollment reaching 16,753 by the year 2000.

In the second half of the 1980s faculty restiveness about core academic values and Miami's stature as a university committed to liberal learning motivates the creation of a new University Honors Program and produces a tumultuous review and reform of general education. A new liberal education plan focused on student learning outcomes and contextualizing content is adopted after five years of highly participatory debate and curricular compromise. Faculty governance is decentralized to the departmental level while decision making about overall university direction becomes more centralized. University Senate is converted from an inclusive to a representative body. In this environment a movement for faculty collective bargaining emerges and is defeated. Interdisciplinary and international programs expand, and efforts to achieve multicultural diversity among faculty, staff, and students intensify.

While many universities embrace a multicultural orientation during the 1980s, a neoconservative revolution occurs in national politics. New public policy makers limit taxation, while costs of state and federal services continue to rise, resulting in a decline of government support to higher education relative to both the rising cost of tuition and fees and the level of corporate and alumni underwriting. In this challenging competitive environment, Miami's national stature is enhanced when in 1985 Richard Moll's The Public Ivys names Miami one of the nation's eight "Best Buys" in public education.

prelude

News from 1970

At 2:00 PM Wednesday, April 15, 1970 a rally is scheduled on the north lawn of Roudebush Hall. Between 4:00 and 5:00 the rally disperses. A group of approximately 20 students moves to Rowan Hall. The door of Rowan is locked. It is forced open. The students begin a sit-in to protest the Vietnam War and the University's involvement. The numbers continue to grow. It is estimated that several thousand persons were present at the peak. Black Student Action Association demands are added to the list of war-related demands. The Vice President, Dr. Etheridge, asks the protesters to leave the building at approximately 9:00 PM. He returns at 9:45 and reads a formal statement warning students of suspension. He leaves for five minutes and returns to read a statement which suspends all students in the building, notifies them that they are trespassing and that the State Highway Patrol is coming. At 10:05 Capt. Dwight Carey and forty State Highway Patrolmen arrive and enter the north door. They begin arresting students. Because the bus to transport the students has broken down, the Butler County Sheriff's Department is called. There is a mutual assistance pact among law enforcement agencies in the Oxford area. In addition to the Patrolmen, the Oxford Police and Butler County, thirteen law enforcement agencies show up, with an additional 90 officers in riot gear. The total law enforcement agency presence is more than 150 men. There is no central control. From this point the accounts are often in direct conflict with each other.

Rachel Weidinger, "Space to Dream inside History, Events
of Protest at Miami University, Spring, 1970"

The final class of Naval Radio School trainees graduated in 1944. In July of that year the *Miami Student* reported that the Naval Air Corps Training Program would be discontinued and Miami Airfield released to a civilian pilot program. In May 1945 it reported the U.S. Navy would establish a Reserve

May 17, 1970

MIAMI UNIVERSITY
MEMORANDUM

To: The Faculty and Students of Miami

The following recommendations of our new Coordinating Committee on Campus Concerns have the whole-hearted endorsement of the President:

There are serious problems that face us all.

In view of the curtailment of the quarter, all faculty members are requested to be reasonable in their class requirements. Quality need not be sacrificed to meet demands of quantity.

Faculty members are requested to participate in extra-curricular discussion sections being organized by students and also to announce in their classes that they will be available to meet with students out of class at times mutually agreed upon.

We completed about three and a half days of the advanced registration process for the next academic year. On Wednesday, May 20, this process must begin again . . .

It will be helpful if as many faculty members as possible visit the residence halls during the evening hours of this week to be available for consultation on all matters . . .

Phillip R. Shriver
President

Police removing students from Rowan Hall. Recensio, 1970.

Myra Aronson, arrested at Rowan Hall, April 15, 1970. Aronson was a passenger on American Airlines Flight 11 that crashed into the World Trade Center, September 11, 2001. Miami Archives.

Officers Training Corps (ROTC) unit at Miami. Four years later a modern half-million-dollar facility was completed for it. Located at an emerging center of Oxford campus social life across Spring Street from future sites of the University Center and Sesquicentennial Chapel, Naval ROTC had a sleek red-brick two-story building with a spacious interior featuring the simulated deck and control tower of a naval vessel, complete with artillery and realistic fittings modeled on World War II battleships. Outfitted with windows of modernist colored glass and embellished with naval insignia, this impressive symbol of Miami's commitment to military preparedness was named for another man of Old Miami, Stephen Clegg Rowan.

During the 1969–70 academic year, Oxford was alive with protest. In the village, the Oxford Committee Against Fluoridation ran advertisements in the *Oxford Press* opposing addition of fluoride to the drinking water. "Anyone who desires fluoride," they said, "can readily obtain it in controlled dosage without the entire community being forced to drink it." Folk singers Simon and Garfunkel, known for ironic commentary on society, drew 11,000 people to Millett Hall for the largest musical event that had yet occurred there. Anger about the war mounted, often expressed in tones of a growing "counterculture." The Miami-Western Student Mobilization Committee offered a film festival in Irvin Hall showcasing *Pig Power, Chicago Convention* (after the 1968 Democratic National Convention in Chicago where police attacked antiwar demonstrators), *People's Park in Berkeley* for the "free speech movement" on that University of California campus, and other provocative images of "establishment" power. In October, thirty male students formed a "Flower Brigade" to "march for peace" alongside the Naval ROTC as they drilled near Millett Assembly Hall. "Armed" with sticks, umbrellas, brooms, and a drummer, they drilled for forty-five

Rowan Hall shortly after construction in 1949. Photograph by Gilson P. Wright. Miami Archives.

Stephen Clegg Rowan

After Stephen Rowan studied at Miami in 1825 and 1826, he entered the U.S. Navy. His career included service on the first U.S. Navy ship to sail around the world. In the Mexican War he was at the capture of San Diego—where he helped raise the first U.S. flag—and at Monterey, California. In 1861 he directed the first shot fired from a naval vessel in the Civil War, and later commanded the 4,120-ton ironclad USS *New Ironsides* in the naval blockade of the Confederacy. After that war he commanded the Norfolk Naval Yard, the Navy Asiatic Squadron, the New York Naval Station, and was superintendent of the Naval Observatory. He retired a rear admiral in 1899 with sixty-three years of service. Fifty years later President Hahne named Miami's new Naval ROTC building in his honor.

Rear Admiral Stephen Clegg Rowan, U.S. Navy. Miami Archives.

minutes with the navy, then held a mock battle that no combatant survived. This demonstration was observed by Miami's chief of safety and security, the Oxford chief of police, a lieutenant of state troopers, commanding officers of Naval ROTC and Air Force ROTC, the director of public maintenance, several security officers, and Miami's dean of men. Dean Hollingsworth told the *Miami Student*, "People have a right to protest, and we take precautions to see that all people are protected. If we believe in freedom, we believe in freedom for everybody."

Another student group organized to oppose rules that proscribed all-night "visitation" in residence halls held "The Peoples' Mass Violation Organizational Meeting for 24 Hr Visitation" at East End. Student Larry Clark, president of the Black Student Action Association, kept pressure on for hiring African American faculty. In September black students walked out of a Black History class, complaining that it had "degenerated" into a class on current minority problems. President Shriver met with them and pledged that a new faculty member would be hired to teach Black History. At the Parents' Day football game in November, programs distributed by Student Senate that included football rosters, "six pages of unrelated articles," and "exercises in sensitivity training and political cartoons" were confiscated by security. Student Senate, which had considered and defeated motions such as one "to change the name of the Miami Redskins to the 'Miami Whiteskins' due to the fact that Red offered connotations of 'the international communist conspiracy,'" experienced the resignation of its president, who recommended that Student Senate be dissolved. In January, with more than 50 percent of Oxford students voting in a referendum, they "affirmed Student Senate's right to exist . . . by a vote of 4,710 to 996 dissenters."

Associated Women Students sponsored the lecture series Women—Be Aware, featuring figures of a reemerging national movement for women's rights. A provocative program was held on Charter Day, February 17, 1970. There Sheila Tobias of Cornell noted, "Authority from God to Richard Nixon is male," and observed that "the suddenness of the movement has been a result of the consciousness that the problems of women are not individual, but political in nature." Professor Kate Millett of Barnard College, author of *Sexual Politics*, asserted that "women share the same oppression that Negroes, the young, and minorities are faced with" and added, "The University is rotten ripe for drastic reform in the treatment of women." Program Board and Associated Women Students sponsored a fall "Drug Symposium" that showcased former Harvard professor and "LSD Prophet" Timothy Leary, who allowed that LSD was "the spiritual equivalent of the hydrogen bomb." The symposium held a panel discussion on legalization of marijuana with "a psychiatrist, a former user, a federal narcotics agent, a drug educator and a senator," and sponsored a "psychedelic art show."

Students were not alone in advocating change. Miami's New University Conference chapter issued "a call for radical reform" in a 1969 pamphlet, *The Gentle Revolution.* Signed by sixteen faculty members, it included a commentary on the state of society, observations on educational values, and recommendations. Its tone was direct.

We wish to register our profound outrage over the moral condition of our society as expressed in the values which it honors and serves concretely through its allocation of resources and management of its public affairs; through its inhuman barbarism, colonialism and militarism in Vietnam and elsewhere at home and abroad; through its overt and covert racism; through its ruthless desecration of the face of the earth in metropolis and countryside, and its careless atomic and industrial pollution of the air and water; through the numbing banality of its media of communication; through its systematic crushing of the spark of humanity in millions of those born into the "other America" at the bottom third or fourth of the social system.

The Gentle Revolution called for new kinds of teaching to address these conditions. Favoring "cultivation of the imagination and the development of resourcefulness in the pursuit of inquiry" over "communication of some particular content of knowledge or the development of technical competence," it advocated removing inhibitions against "inter-disciplinary and inter-departmental studies." The "undergraduate years," it said, "should provide a moratorium during which the student is given maximum freedom for the entertainment and exploration of modes of inquiry, and an opportunity to develop a taste for the intrinsic pleasures and reward of inquiry—whether pursued in the modes of idle curiosity and of reflection, or in the modes of rigorous analysis and of experimentation." This would facilitate a student's "search for identity." Other actions, it said, were needed. The university should

Timothy Leary in Withrow Court, November 8, 1969. Recensio, 1970.

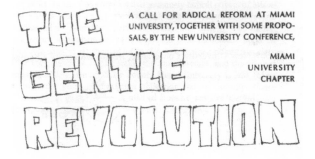

A CALL FOR RADICAL REFORM AT MIAMI UNIVERSITY, TOGETHER WITH SOME PROPOSALS, BY THE NEW UNIVERSITY CONFERENCE,

MIAMI
UNIVERSITY
CHAPTER

"The Gentle Revolution." New University Conference, Miami Chapter, 1970. Miami Archives.

- require three topical seminars for freshmen introducing the nature of inquiry; create writing across the curriculum; eliminate freshman English; reduce the common curriculum; and offer large sections in multiple-section courses;
- create faculty visitation in courses outside the department one week per year;
- create Special Studies to include interdisciplinary studies, independent studies, work studies, honors studies, and graduate "new studies" for frontier research;
- create junior seminars team-taught from two departments or disciplines;
- create a University Bookstore;
- create shared governance via a Faculty Senate and Student Senate mediated by a University Council, all reporting to the Miami University Board of Trustees, with administrators "charged with serving the university by executing the decisions of the various legislative bodies and by providing adequate communication";
- disengage the university "from according any preferential or deferential treatment to fraternities and sororities";
- support BSAA calls for a vice president for black student affairs, a program for high-risk students, recruiting and counseling personnel, black professors, investigation of racial discrimination, 15 percent enrollment of black students in the freshmen class;
- eliminate ROTC;
- "not co-operate with draft boards" or "make available to military and para-military agencies answers to questions about their opinion of any student's loyalty and patriotism";
- "avoid hollow arguments, either about impartial 'town and gown' relationships or about corporate impartiality, to avoid confronting social injustices in the community."

Several of these proposals would be implemented in some fashion by the Division of Academic Affairs over the next two decades. Some of the changes sought in minority affairs would be made. Governance would be reformed two decades later, but not in these directions. The vivid proposal to eliminate ROTC was pointedly rejected.

Throughout the 1969–70 school year, protest actions against the Vietnam War intensified, ranging from political cartoons to demonstrations to physical clashes. In December the *Miami Student* ran a cartoon that depicted President Shriver handing a graduating senior a "draft notice or death warrant" with his diploma.

This image underlined the suggestion of historian Helen L. Horowitz that

the military draft during the Vietnam War unified normally disparate student cultures in opposition to government policy that by extension
included university authority. At Miami, as opponents of the war grew in number, this pattern
became more visible. In October, two thousand
students rallied in South Quad to create the Student Guild, comprising "any student or anybody
who considers himself a student." Speakers at the
rally included Dusty Steytler of Students to Act
and Educate for Peace and representatives of the
Political Action Party and the Ad Hoc Vietnam
Moratorium Committee. They adopted resolutions including "The need for those in power to
realize that the students are responsible adults
capable of controlling their own lives." They
marched to Lewis Place, intending to present
President Shriver with a resolution seeking sus-

Editorial cartoon. Miami
Student, *December 5, 1969.*

pension of classes on October 15 to observe a Vietnam Moratorium, at which
they proposed to discuss instead of "business as usual" the "problems of American involvement in Vietnam." President Shriver was not at home. He later rejected the request, arguing that "the suspension of classes or even a University-
approved ceremony would put 'us in the middle of political overtones.'"

On the day of the moratorium a very large group of students and faculty gathered on Roudebush Hall lawn for a day-long "teach-in." The list of the
dead in Vietnam was recited throughout the day at Harrison Hall. Professors
spoke against the war. A student attempted to lower the flag to half mast, then
another returned it to full height. A confrontation seemed at hand when moratorium organizers announced they had an agreement with the administration
not to lower the flag. At noon 250 students held a one-hour silent vigil under
Oxford's Uptown Water Tower. Back on the lawn in the afternoon, guerrilla
theatre sketches satirized the war, and a representative of Students for a Democratic Society from Harvard addressed the crowd. Mini-classes were led by
Professors Robert Merideth, American studies; Reo Christianson, political science; John Sommer, philosophy; and Roland Duerksen, English. That evening
a thousand people assembled at Western College to hear an Earlham College
student speak about his experience in federal prison as a draft resister. A
double-file torchlight parade from Western to the village square was met by
Ardis Cameron, president of the Western College student body, and the Western College chaplain, who conducted a memorial service. The day concluded
with a speech in Hall Auditorium by Chicago pacifist Charles Matthei.
Throughout the day leaflets and black armbands were distributed, and Alpha

Phi Omega service fraternity sold coffee, with proceeds going to an American Civil Liberties Union student defense fund. About this day President Shriver issued a statement:

Proceedings of the Vietnam Moratorium on this campus were conducted with serious concern and in the spirit of the search for truth and reason which are hallmarks of the academic community. Though I didn't participate personally, I share with all members the prayer which should unite us all: that peace in Viet Nam and throughout the world may be realized soon.

In November the Student Mobilization Committee sent four busloads of students from Oxford to Washington, DC, to march at the national Moratorium Day. A Miami organizer reported that "several people were overcome by tear gas" in Washington, "and one student was hit in the head with a tear gas canister before it exploded. He was hospitalized and then released, but we couldn't find him when we had to leave." In Oxford, thirty-one members of Beta Theta Pi put their names to a flyer that stated, "These Betas support the Moratorium & the March on Washington, November 13, 14, 15." In March an "assembly" of "between 500 and 1,000 people" carrying American flags and a banner reading "Phooey All Over" marched from Slant Walk to the village square to burn draft cards. The *Miami Student* reported that "one huge fake card and 5 or 6 real ones were burned."

War resisters met with resistance. The Voices of Reason, 322 faculty, staff, administrators, and townspeople, signed a published statement titled "The University in a Time of Crisis: Declaration of the Voices of Reason at Miami." They blamed campus disruption on the work of revolutionary organizations.

Separately, the Voices of Reason released a seventeen-page rebuttal of *The Gentle Revolution* in an unsigned pamphlet. The student-led Miami Conservative Club was active throughout this period, handing out leaflets "encouraging

Draft card burning. Photograph by Marwan. Miami Student, March 3, 1970.

The University in a Time of Crisis: Declaration of the Voices of Reason at Miami

from *Miami Student*, September 26, 1969

We categorically condemn the disruptive and often violent activities of communist, anarchist, and other revolutionary groups which have already succeeded in seriously weakening many of our great universities. The so-called Students for a Democratic Society and its faculty counterpart, the New University Conference, as well as certain other militant groups, are the principal sources of revolutionary attacks. They are capable of absurd demands and childishly destructive actions, but one thing is certain: they are not playing at revolution, they are militantly advocating and practicing it. If they are permitted to continue unchallenged, they will disrupt our educational system and with it our society as a whole....

WE ARE FOR peaceful evolution; WE ARE AGAINST militant revolution. WE ARE FOR reasonable discussion; WE ARE AGAINST chaotic confrontation. WE ARE FOR representative democracy; WE ARE AGAINST minority dictatorship. WE ARE FOR order and sanity; WE ARE AGAINST anarchy and emotionalism. WE ARE FOR a university dedicated to the fearless and impartial pursuit of truth; WE ARE AGAINST a university dominated by partisan political activity and intimidated by threats of violence.

people to not seek simplistic solutions to complicated world problems" and to "divorce themselves from the compelling dynamics of popular ideas."

On April 15, 1970, Alan Lee (Dusty) Steytler made what the *Miami Student* reported as "a spontaneous speech against the presence of the war machine on campus" during a Student Mobilization Committee rally on Roudebush Lawn. An aroused group went to Rowan Hall and broke in to hold a sit-in, where at first they ate pizza and listened to a rock band. After a time Vice President Etheridge arrived to read a policy statement on "Disruptive Behavior." Some students departed. He came back later to read a second statement that condemned the actions of those still present as "a flagrant violation of proper conduct and in premeditated defiance of University authority." Invoking a policy of "preemptory suspension," he said they were "no longer students at Miami University." He advised that "if you do not leave the building you shall be arrested for trespassing" by the Ohio Highway Patrol, and charged with "breaking and entering," a "felony punishable by fine and imprisonment." When well over a hundred still did not leave, arrests began. Students were taken, some limp and carried in the manner of civil rights protesters, out Rowan's north door. Mug shots were made on the spot before the protesters were placed on a bus for transport to jail. What happened next galvanized student opinion, fueled a campus

Alan "Dusty" Steytler (wearing flag shirt and sunglasses) at teach-in. Recensio, 1970.

Vice President for Student Affairs Robert Etheridge (with bullhorn) addressing students occupying Rowan Hall, April 15, 1970. Miami Archives.

strike, and triggered a sequence of events that led to the closing of Miami University.

Details of the next hours appear in accounts by a presidential commission and the Associated Student Government Select Committee on the Abuse of Rights (SCAR) that investigated later. A "Diary of Disruption" was kept by the Office of Public Information and used to report to alumni. Elaborate stories were written for campus and community newspapers by witnessing reporters. Pamphlets, handbills, flyers, and other material that was freely distributed remain in archival collections. These documents record another historical turning point at Miami when emotions of unexpected confrontation trumped usual standards of civil order.

For some reason—disputed—the bus broke down. The Butler County sheriff was called to provide transportation to jail and crowd control. Arrested students were moved to other vehicles. A large crowd of onlookers grew in number, anxiety, and—in some reports—anger. Many area law enforcement agencies sent support to the scene, marshaling between 160 and 175 men. They had no good means of communication. Some protesters may have thrown objects, or perhaps not. The Butler County Sheriff's Department brought City of Hamilton police dogs, tear gas, and Mace to confront the crowd. The number of onlookers grew even larger, to perhaps 1,000, filling the south lawn of Rowan Hall and drifting to the east and north where arrest bookings were, or had been, under way. At some point tear gas was released. A lot of tear gas, perhaps. Some students tried to run, escaping across Spring Street or to nearby buildings. There were reports of "indiscriminate" use of Mace. More arrests. Crowds pulled back, regrouped. Tear gas was released across Spring Street and into the University Center, drifting into offices of the *Miami Student* and to Sesquicentennial Chapel, where a headquarters of authority had been temporarily set up. A few faculty members appeared. One said he saw a student Maced while trying to climb a tree. Another reported being arrested after twice requesting the badge number of a police officer.

Students rallied in front of Roudebush Hall. Confrontations moved from Rowan Hall to Uptown. At the intersection of High Street and Campus Avenue a deputy sheriff may have charged into a fraternity house with a police dog on a ten- or fifteen-foot leash—or the dog may have been under better control.

Some students were bitten and treated at the hospital. At the Municipal Building, where a group of arrested students was being processed, another crowd formed. Tear gas was released again. A few angry townspeople may have been there. The night was restless, disorderly, and tense, but the tear gas sent students home. Phase one of Spring 1970 was over, but more than a hundred students would spend the night in Hamilton and Fairfield City jails or in Butler County Jail. Those who had not already paid $50 bail were released the next day, on President Shriver's recommendation for their "honorary cognizance."

The next morning, leaflets appeared early on the Oxford campus proclaiming "Strike!" Now, added to the war in Vietnam, the draft, the presence of ROTC on campus, and Black Student Action Association demands for racial justice were grievances for actions taken by civil authority against student protesters at Rowan Hall, on campus, and Uptown. The *Miami Student* released a special edition headlined "Miami University—STRIKE," with accounts of recent events and listing names of 184 people arrested. Handbills, mimeographed sheets, and a flyer from the Department of Architecture supported strike action. A joint statement of "the Uptown fraternities" Beta Theta Pi, Phi Gamma Delta, and Zeta Beta Tau announced "a coalition in an effort to publicly censure those law enforcement agencies which indiscriminately used dogs, tear gas, and clubs, and *overtly* broke the law on the night and early morning of April 15 and 16."

At 7:00 a.m. on April 16 President Shriver and Governor James A. Rhodes held a press conference in Roudebush Hall. "When a situation gets completely out of hand," said the governor, "we're here to help." He reported that a battalion of seven hundred National Guard troops was "camped at the Nike Base outside Oxford" and "would remain on alert until the crisis situation is over." He added that a "Molotov cocktail" had been hurled through the window of Warfield Hall, causing minimal damage, but that "bomb-throwing is no small fish when it involves a 5 million dollar building."

President Shriver stressed that lengthy efforts had been made to persuade protesters in Rowan Hall to "leave peaceably" before the Ohio State Highway Patrol was called. "I know full well what took place," he said. "I am sickened and saddened by it. I must admit that University authority ends when the state patrol

When forty uniformed members of the Highway Patrol responded shortly after 10 p.m., a group of students came around the west side of the building. They were shouting obscenities, throwing stones, shoes, and other objects. The troopers could have been severely injured. Whenever television cameras would pick up the students in the act of harassment, they would stop and sing "God Bless America."
—Capt. Dwight Carey, Commander, District 8, State Highway Patrol

After we got all the students out of the ROTC building and uptown to the municipal building, a bad situation developed. There's no way I can say all the police officers were one hundred percent right all the time. There's no way of having that many men from so many police agencies and be in contact with every one of them. It came to the point where students carried stuff out of the houses and burned it in the middle of the street, and we felt at that time that they wanted another confrontation with the police and the fire department. At that time I got together with the Butler County prosecutor, all the chiefs of police involved that we could get there, and we made the decision to pull all uniformed personnel and all marked cars out of the area and take them out to the church north of Oxford. We did this and in some forty-five minutes, when the students found out they were not going to get any police action, they went to bed.
—Harold J. Carpenter, Sheriff, Butler County

Three of the uptown fraternities (Beta Theta Pi, Phi Gamma Delta, and Zeta Beta Tau) have formed a coalition in an effort to publically censure those law enforcement agencies which ~~is~~ indiscrimiately used dogs, tear gas, and clubs, and <u>overtly</u> broke the ~~kaw~~ law on the night and early morning of April 15 and 16. We make no claims concerning the ~~legibtim~~ legitimacy of the Strike or the actions of certain students; we are determined only to point out to the administration, faculty, students, and the general public, especially the general public, that certain police groups (not including the ~~S~~ Oxford police, or the State Highway Patrol) were irresponsible, indiscriminate, and incompetent.

These three fraternities in particular have united because many of their members witnessed the happenings uptown between 11:00 P.M. and 2:30 A.M. From this group, we hope to gain the support of the University Senate, the Student Body, and the town of Oxford for a <u>well-publicized</u> censure of those law enforcement agencies involved.

We believe that the Butler County Sheriff's Department was responsible for the magnitude of the violence that occurred. We further contend that Gov. James A. Rhodes allowed these extra forces on campus in a situation that <u>did not</u> justify their use. Finally, we believe ~~tx~~ that the area press clearly misinterpreted and misreported the real events.

Our plan is this:

1. Release a report of the events that actual~~ly~~ events that took place to the students, the University Senate, and the press,
2. Seek a resolution of censure of these law enforcement agencies by the University Senate,
3. Seek a resolution by the student body and by prominent campus organizations to censure these agencies.

Chief Joseph Statum of the Oxford Police Department has informed us ~~atxhixxxffix~~ that his office had <u>no</u> control over the extra law enforcement agencies and did not know how or why some of them came. He also told us that " I cannot condone irresponsible or illegal action by any law enforcement agencies. "

Joint statement of Uptown fraternities on police actions, April 1970. Miami Archives.

takes over." At a packed meeting in Withrow Court that afternoon, the president reportedly said "that standard operating procedure had been followed concerning police action Wednesday night, and that he would follow due process in appealing the preemptory suspensions of 170 students." Commenting on student demands, Shriver said Miami would make an effort to achieve 10 percent black enrollment. He added that he would personally admit students who were "financially able but educationally disadvantaged" and pledged to increase graduate assistantships and to seek "more black faculty members." He added that he did not support establishing a committee to "investigate ROTC" and had no confidence that university governance bodies would either. The *Miami Student* concluded its report of this meeting by noting, "Graduate student Leonard Harris, and BSAA President Larry Clark judged the sentiment of the group to be unsatisfied with Shriver's remarks, and it was decided that the strike should proceed."

On April 21 the *Student* reported that Judge Clem Imfield tried 144 students on trespassing charges in Oxford's Butler County Area One Court at the Oxford Municipal Building, and sentenced 139 to fines of $50 and costs, all suspended. The proceedings were held "amidst the confusion of double bonds, aliases and lost defendants. . . . Snatches of tunes from kazoos and harmonicas filtered their way into the courtroom, while students both in and out read, talked, listened, sewed and strung beads."

Two apparently impromptu three-hour faculty meetings were held in Hall Auditorium. The first, on Saturday morning, April 18, reportedly attracted 170 faculty when it began, and the second, on Sunday, April 19, 21 more. For at least the first meeting, Hall Auditorium was said to be filled to capacity (1,200) with students. On the eighteenth a resolution to "support the present student strike as a proper means of seeking the granting of coalition demands, demands we endorse," passed 62–10 with 15 reported abstentions. A resolution to waive hearings of suspended students passed 70–0 with 1 reported abstention. Perhaps the meeting grew in size as it continued, for a resolution supporting withdrawal of all state police and National Guard troops from Oxford reportedly passed 143–0 with 67 abstentions. Another resolution to establish a committee to investigate cases of student injury at the hands of police and to offer "services of the University" in "instituting formal charges against the officers involved" passed unanimously. Motions passed by overwhelming majorities sought to reinstate suspended students, to support full amnesty for civil charges, to immediately terminate preemptory suspension, to avoid singling out students for legal action, and to make no mention of any of these matters in student records.

Those resolutions were not binding on governance. On April 21 University Senate voted to support a disciplinary review procedure for suspended students. That evening students took a novel mass action. At prearranged hours of 6:00 p.m. and 8:00 p.m., showerheads and faucets were turned on in residence halls and toilets were flushed simultaneously. This "flush-in" was likely intended to demonstrate the collective power of students and call attention to coalition demands. Instead, it generated animosity. Although the flush-in was said by Miami officials to have caused little damage on campus, the *Oxford Press* reported that in the village, "Pressure dropped, sewers overflowed, Oxford's two water [tanks] were drained, a critical fire hazard existed in the town and the campus for at least two hours, and it was necessary to cut off water to campus buildings to permit the village to rebuild pressure." Oxford residents called the action "thoughtless," a "waste of literally millions of gallons of pure water" at a time close to Earth Day,

Larry Clark, president of the Black Student Action Association, issuing statement on student strike. Miami Student, *April 21, 1970.*

Student strike following Rowan Hall arrests. Miami Student, April 17, 1970.

Miami U. Student Revolt Expands To Affect Village

Water Supply Is Latest Threat

A week after the shock of its first experience with nasty violence and classroom boycott, traditionally-placid Miami University continues in turmoil.

It seemed that the issues were agonizingly close to solution—except that of amnesty, on which compromise seemed remote. Yet the student "strike" sponsored by Black Student Action Association and a Support Coalition of Concerned Whites might be kept alive indefinitely—if not in actual defiance, at least in rifts and bitterness and awareness that this could happen here, and could again.

When the blow fell, the night of April 15, it had the whole bit: oratory, seizure, sit-in, drag-out, the crowd-cop clash, teargas, dogs, suspensions, arrests, intimidation real and fancied, mischief, vandalism, rumor. And

building, Governor Rhodes also called members of the National Guard to the Nike Battery site on Todd Road, where they remained until Friday, to be on call should they be needed to quell further student revolt.—Photo by Pete Chappars

Governor James Rhodes, left, joins Dr. Phillip Shriver, Miami University President, in a brief press conference held early last Thursday following the Wednesday night sit-in and disturbance at Rowan Hall, Miami NROTC

President Shriver and Governor Rhodes at April 16, 1970, press conference, Roudebush Hall. Photograph by Pete Chappars. Oxford Press, April 23, 1970.

and a financial cost to the village of about $2,000 in maintenance worker overtime, cleaning, and repairs, plus $2,800 charged to Miami for the excess "use" of 2 million gallons of water. This, said the *Press,* was "going too far." Apparently many students agreed. On April 22 the Student Coalition called a moratorium on the strike and urged students to return to classes. Student Senate apologized for the flush-in.

By April 30 the *Oxford Press* could report that Miami was "Back to Normal" with student hearings over and most students reinstated. Classes were meeting. President Shriver had addressed a special meeting of University Senate on Saturday, April 25, commenting on the past eleven days and repeating public commitments to seek more black faculty and students as well as better services to support them. After the president adjourned and left that meeting, members of the audience remained in discussion for more than an hour.

Then on May 4, 1970, the Ohio National Guard killed four students at Kent State University and wounded fifteen more when firing into a crowd of protesters. President Richard Nixon said "this should remind us all that when dissent turns to violence it invites tragedy." On May 6, "several thousand students" marched nonviolently through the Miami campus in tribute to students killed at Kent. The president and many faculty kept very late hours on campus and Uptown, talking with students, trying to keep Miami functioning, making concessions. According to one report, in a large outdoor meeting on campus at 1:30 in the morning, President Shriver agreed to institute credit/no-credit grading. The next day he closed Miami University indefinitely.

Ten days later students returned to campus and classes resumed. Governance bodies met during the closure, and a special issue of the *Miami Student* on Sunday, May 17, was headlined "12 Students to Sit on University Council." In a front-page editorial, it suggested there would be a new tone in campus relations.

To a considerable degree the University, or more accurately, those faculty, administrators, and students who have been here for the past two weeks, has already proved

May 7, 1970

FROM: William G. Slover
University Secretary
TO: Members of the Faculty and Administrative Staff

On Thursday, May 7, 1970, President Phillip R. Shriver delivered the following statement on the closing of Miami University. This statement is presented in its entirety to you at this time so that the entire campus will be aware of the President's remarks:

"At a scheduled meeting with approximately one thousand of our students this morning, I regretfully announced that school is closed and that we have asked all students to be off campus by eight o'clock this evening. The shutdown applies to all three of our campuses—this central campus at Oxford and our branch campuses at Middletown and Hamilton.

The closing is for an indefinite period. Its length will be determined in part by national developments in the next days and weeks. Certainly, it is our hope that classes can be resumed soon, that our students will be able to earn credit, that this quarter will not be lost in their record. At this time, our primary concern is to clear the campus in as orderly a manner as is possible, yet as quickly as possible. But, I wish to make it clear that as soon as it is feasible, our faculty will begin working out the details of how the academic requirements of the quarter can be completed.

The announcement that we will close was, I am quite aware, a reversal of statements which I made last night indicating that we would cancel classes today and tomorrow and then resume Monday with determination to keep classes going until the end of the spring quarter. Several things have affected the change of policy. There was of course the recommendation made yesterday—by Governor Rhodes—a very strong recommendation—that any state universities in Ohio experiencing disorders should shut down and send their students home and have their faculties make arrangements for students to complete their courses. There were further conversations this morning with state officials about these problems. And, I should make it clear that we were not ordered to close; responsibility for the decision was left with the individual universities, and Miami's decision was made here, by me, as president of Miami University.

There was also the fact that we have been aware of the potential of greater trouble. A non-violent march of several thousand students throughout our campus last night did nevertheless present potential for uncontrolled trouble. Even an indicated willingness to talk out our problems calmly today, on the part of many of our students, did not remove the prospect of violence; indeed, later last night we did experience three minor fires which could have brought great loss.

In my talks with state officials this morning, I found great concern for the safety of our students and for the safety of our buildings. There was desire for this university and others to reach a decision, and, frankly, there was strong suggestion that the decision become the one which we have made. Yet, I repeat that it was a decision made here, by us, and it includes a determination that our students will have opportunity to complete the academic requirements to which they committed themselves when this quarter of the school year began."

University Senate Resolutions

The following is a list of those motions of University Senate which will be in effect for the remainder of this quarter.

1. Course coverage will be curtailed proportionately to time lost from classes through suspension of classes and closure of the University.

2. Full credit will be awarded for any course successfully completed.

3. Classes and laboratories will be conducted as usual in keeping with the published schedule. Departments are encouraged to provide tutorial and review sessions.

4. The use of Incompletes or other inconclusive grades should be minimized so that the students may begin their next academic quarter with as little carry-over work as possible.

5. The deadline for withdrawal from courses or from the University without grade penalties will be extended to the last day of classes (June 5).

6. The present examination schedule will be maintained with the departments having the option of giving one or two hour exams over all or part of the work covered.

7. Each student will be given the option of taking his classes on a credit/no credit basis. Each student will elect within ten (10) days whether the grade shall be on letter basis or on credit-no credit.

8. Regardless of whether or not a student elects to have a letter grade given or credit–no credit, faculty may elect to record a grade of S for any student whose work in his course remains incomplete at the end of the normal grading period.

herself. . . . Wednesday afternoon Faculty Council approved a new University governance proposal which insures that students will have a major influence in the proceedings of the University. By passing the structure of a University Council composed of 16 faculty, 12 students, and 8 administrators, the Faculty Council . . . has at least given students the chance to stay within the channels while still acting for their own interests.

Trustees soon approved more governance changes, including the addition of eighteen students to University Senate and a visitation program for freshman residence halls. When classes resumed there was a sharp relaxation of grading policies and deadlines.

As June graduation approached, Miami's campus turmoil of the 1960s was coming to an end. Although in the fall of 1970 Dusty Steytler would be sentenced to a term in the Mansfield Reformatory for breaking and entering at Rowan Hall, only 5 of 152 students peremptorily suspended at the building occupation were ultimately suspended by Miami. A group of "selected volunteers of faculty and students" created a "University Marshall Program" to watch university buildings at night for any possible danger and to "urge observers in a crowd from becoming involved in confrontation activities." Their services were short-lived. A student-initiated plan to contribute the cost of renting commencement caps and gowns to the Educational Opportunity Program and to parade without them was met with compromise by President Shriver. He eliminated the requirement that a cap and gown be worn, then urged students to both wear them and donate to the EOP. The President's Commission to investigate events at Rowan Hall said there was no evidence that agitators from other campuses were involved in "mass organization" of antiwar protests and suggested, among eleven recommendations, that "'Rap' sessions involving students, faculty, administrators, and trustees should be held at regularly scheduled intervals." The Select Committee on the Abuse of Rights (SCAR) appointed by Student Senate took affidavits from faculty and students and in early June issued an account that ended with five recommendations. Among them: "that police not

It Need Not Have Happened

Events at Rowan Hall, 1970

The police riots that engulfed Miami University on the night of April 15, 1970, and the ensuing disruption for the rest of the semester need not have happened at all. It is only one of the ironies of the spring of 1970 that perhaps the most placid and conservative state university in Ohio was the first of many to explode in violence, boycott, spreading protest, and ultimately closure.

Anti–Vietnam War protests were a staple at virtually all universities by the academic year 1969–70. At Miami, the Student Mobilization Committee (SMC) took the lead in organizing a protest rally on the fifteenth of every month. There was little different about the April 15 protest rally, except that good weather allowed the rally to be held on the north lawn of Roudebush in the midst of soaring Frisbees and sunbathing students. The usual suspects made both reasoned and impassioned demands to end the war and the university's complicity in war promotion through research, ranking students for the Selective Service system, and ROTC programs.

Late in the afternoon, as things were winding down, one hot-headed young man seized the open microphone and demanded real action and not merely rhetoric. He then led about fifty students to the Naval ROTC building, Rowan Hall, broke in, and occupied it. Before long, several hundred students had gathered in Rowan, a band was setting up, and pizzas were being ordered. Demands to end university complicity with the Vietnam War were also issued.

Perhaps nothing could have been done to this point to alter ensuing events. But from this point on, much different could have been done that was not. The students could have made their point and then left, or heeded the threats issued by the university administration and left. This was perhaps the least likely possibility, given youthful passions, the tenor of the times, and how university administrators and police chose to respond to the protest.

The greatest difference would have resulted from a different administrative response to the occupation of Rowan Hall. Instead of sending Vice President Etheridge into Rowan straightaway to peremptorily suspend and threaten with arrest all the students there—thereby stiffening the backs of the approximately 175 who chose to sit down and stay—President Shriver might have heeded the advice of at least one faculty member outside of Rowan Hall: order up several urns of coffee and flats of doughnuts, go in and sit with the students, listen and talk until weariness overtook everyone and the protest ended peaceably.

But attempting to coerce students into submission, and calling police to arrest and remove the occupants of Rowan Hall, led to the next fateful turn. Fifteen uncoordinated police agencies from surrounding locales responded to a call for help from the miniscule Oxford police department. Most numerous, most heavily armed with clubs, tear gas, and dogs, and apparently least disciplined, were deputies of the Butler County Sheriff. Their largely indiscriminate assaults on students outside Rowan Hall who gathered to ogle the goings-on probably did the most to "radicalize" a great number of students and ensure that many more than 175 Miami students would take up subsequent calls to "shut down the University."

The good news is that it could have been much worse. Governor Rhodes ordered the Ohio National Guard to assemble at the Nike Base on the edge of Oxford, preparatory to occupying the campus. They did not come onto campus—presumably President Shriver drew the line here. Had the Ohio National Guard come onto campus, however, what happened at Kent State on May 4 might rather have happened at Miami soon after April 15.

The even better news is that fifteen of the relatively few black students at Miami in 1970, under the leadership of Larry Clark of the Black Student Action Association, chose to make common cause with the SMC and be arrested in Rowan Hall. This alliance doubtlessly led to the first serious attention to demands made by Miami's black students for greater diversity and support. The rest, as we say, is history.

Richard W. Momeyer, Professor of Philosophy

be called onto the campus save in cases where violence has already been initiated or where there is *imminent* danger to lives or property." SCAR also addressed radicals who might plan demonstrations in the future that could in any way be construed as illegal and advised them: "If you want to demonstrate, be absolutely certain what you are doing is legal unless you wish to play with other people's lives." They told area police departments, "You cannot expect students to obey the law and act in a sane, rational manner unless your own men obey the law and act in a sane, rational manner."

As the 1969–70 academic year ended, demonstrations for social and political change ended as well. The chair of the Coordinating Committee for Campus Concerns recommended disbanding it because the campus appeared "very cool and diffuse." At Hueston Woods beach, said the *Student,* there was "wall-to-wall epidermis and sun-tan oil."

Last words, however, were long in coming. Even in the early twenty-first century, participants in oral history sessions could become incensed when recalling the spring of 1970, and some produced written documentation of their experiences saved for three decades. A senior professor of philosophy who was a new faculty member in 1970 could still look back with a sharp critique of university policy choices.

In May, John Dolibois reported that alumni gifts and contributions were running approximately 50 percent behind those of the previous year. Noting that he had "received 419 letters from alumni to date registering displeasure with the developments here, with the great majority indicating that they are withholding their contributions until they see how things work out," he added: "The whole challenge of this development is to be ready to revamp our entire approach to meet the changing times. We can no longer appeal to sentimental pride and nostalgia, so we've got to come up with a new approach to get support for the University."

The search for that new approach would begin vigorously in the fall of 1970. In fifteen years it would earn a name—the "Public Ivy."

Creating the Public Ivy

TEAM

In the fall of 1970 President Shriver introduced a cabinet that would last beyond the end of his presidency in 1981 and create an era of increasing national visibility. Continuing from the Hahne and Millett years were John Dolobois in alumni affairs, Robert Etheridge in student affairs, and the protégé of Wallace Roudebush in financial affairs, Lloyd Goggin. They would now be vice presidents. In the spring of 1970, with a long career behind him at Colgate and five eventful Miami years as Miami's first vice president for academic affairs and provost, Charles Wilson retired. His replacement was David G. Brown.

Dolibois had served Miami since 1947. Etheridge began in 1959. Lloyd A.

Members of President Phillip R. Shriver's cabinet (left to right): John E. Dolibois, Robert F. Etheridge, Lloyd A. Goggin, and David G. Brown.
Miami Archives.

Goggin was a native of Maine who served as a finance officer in the Army Air Corps and after the war earned an economics degree at Bowdoin College. A wartime contact brought him to Oxford in 1947 to be controller under Roudebush. "Once I came here," said Goggin, he "became kind of a father figure to me. He was extremely helpful in seeing that I received an education about Miami University and public universities in Ohio." When Roudebush died in 1956 Goggin assumed control of financial affairs as treasurer. In 1966 he was named vice president for finance and business. In the seven decades between the time Roudebush began work for President Hughes in 1911 and the retirement of Lloyd Goggin in 1982, there would be nine presidents or acting presidents, six provosts or acting provosts (an office not invented at Miami until 1953), and only two chief financial officers.

In the fall of 1970 Dolibois, Goggin, and Etheridge had a total of fifty-seven years of Miami service. President Shriver had been in office for five years. David Brown had begun his career in 1961 as professor of economics at the University of North Carolina, Chapel Hill. An American Council on Education Fellow in Academic Administration at the University of Minnesota, he had served three years as provost and vice president for academic affairs at Drake University before assuming office at Miami in 1970. He was thirty-four years old, and the president to whom he would report was only fourteen years older. "I look at the position," Brown told the *Miami Student* before he arrived in Oxford, "as being responsible for defining a new and distinct academic direction," and added, "I feel Miami will be making some drastic changes within the next five or ten years, and I feel the challenge is such that the changes can be made successfully."

STRATEGY

In *Pattern of Circles*, John Dolibois described the effort to build alumni confidence in the early 1970s.

At Miami we had the wholehearted support of the president, the board of trustees, a vast majority of faculty and students, and, of course, thousands of alumni. I can't recall ever having an Alumni or Development Council proposition turned down. There was never a lack of encouragement or support. It stands to reason such a team effort would lead to success.

John Millett's presidential style had been described as authoritative, progressive, smart, self-disciplined, and decisive. Now, following the campus turmoil of the late 1960s, something else seemed to be in order. President Shriver recognized the need for a shift in tone, and with his colleagues would work out a new decision-making strategy that involved the entire campus in setting new directions.

The post-Vietnam approach to campus change would build on governance. The style of committee work that would preface governance action and administrative embrace of new policies would methodically open decision-making procedures to broad participation. First, the president's cabinet deliberated about directions and set boundary conditions for change. Then temporary committees of well-respected faculty and staff, often with student members, were asked to investigate particular issues in great detail and were given a detailed charge that spelled out limits but encouraged innovation. Committees were expected to actively engage diverse stakeholders in public review of their recommendations prior to governance action. Well-ventilated proposals were then taken to intergenerational governance bodies, where formal debate resolved in governance action. Importantly, decisions made in these ways either led to active administrative implementation or were returned to governance bodies for reconsideration, but were neither circumvented nor ignored. Related to models of bipartisan committee-centered governance found at times in Congress and elsewhere, this strategy would be effective during the Public Ivy era because it was backed by the president and very closely coached by the Vice President for Academic Affairs, because the post-Vietnam mood was to get on with new business, because it promised a new level of inclusiveness in decision making, and because demographic changes in the faculty were bringing new voices to traditional debates.

President Millett employed a management style that expected those reporting to him to bring solutions to problems, or new ideas, fully developed for his approval or rejection. President Shriver modeled a different approach in cabinet meetings. They could last from morning into afternoon and occasionally through the dinner hour. The cabinet met regularly, even if that meant going to homes of those temporarily unable to come to campus. While Shriver made final decisions and took responsibility for outcomes—as he had in dealing with students—he also solicited detailed views from each vice president, who was expected to showcase all of his area's points of view. Employing a legendary ability to listen at length to conflicting perspectives, Shriver sought to draw out of the exchange a consensus or near-consensus on university directions. David G. Brown recalled that "Phil would never step on any one of us and he'd protect each one of us to the ultimate. He respected all of us. Eventually, we had to compromise and figure out a way to move ahead and I think it made the institution very strong and very participant, community-based." Brown remembered this style as a sign of the times.

I think one of the real achievements of the Shriver years . . . was reflected in larger society as well. There was this transition from being an institution where the president pretty much decided what would happen . . . to a kind of consensus that was a controlled consensus. It was controlled by the fact that everybody understood that Miami is to be a rigorous, quality, small, private-like but public-purposed college-university in this wonderful town. . . . There was this bringing into decision making of students; there was the bringing in of faculty. It wasn't a brokenness that happened. It wasn't a case that they weren't there and then they were there. It was a gradual evolution and I think it was partly the senior faculty leadership and partly the stability of the cabinet that made the difference.

Brown also remembered it as partly a strategy for survival in a tempestuous climate.

During this era, I think 92 percent of the presidents of four-year institutions in the United States lost their jobs within a three-year period. They could not deal with the discrepant views of the various stakeholders. Along with those lost jobs of presidents were the lost jobs of chief financial officers, chief development officers, chief student affairs officers, and chief academic officers. . . . In 1980, when I was still here, I was the junior member of this cabinet and I was the eighth-longest-serving provost in the country out of 156 land-grant provosts. And all of my colleagues were in the top five of longest-serving individuals. I think it's that stability—that stability of purpose, that stability of intent—that allowed the institution to move from a top-down decision-making institution to an institution that took full advantage of the best ideas that were bubbling up.

Taking advantage of the "best ideas that were bubbling up" also involved the use of special-purpose committees of senior faculty who had broad mandates to investigate potential changes. The most comprehensive charge of this kind occurred earlier, in 1968, when the president appointed the Committee on Educational Policies. It was to conduct a sweeping review and recommend "changes for the University to consider in shaping its programs, priorities, and operations" over "the next 15 to 20 years." Chaired by Robert E. Berry of economics, this "Blue Ribbon" committee included James Woodworth, political science; E. Gene Santavicca, personnel and guidance; and Walter Havighurst, English. In September 1969 it published an eighty-two-page study with fifty recommendations addressing undergraduate programs, the status of students, faculty and administrative organization, graduate programs, research, public service goals, relations with other educational institutions, mission, and goals, setting an ambitious agenda for the next phase of Miami's evolution.

In the spring of 1970 these ambitious recommendations were awaiting action in committees and administrative units when Miami closed. In the fall of 1970 they got a fresh hearing. The newly appointed provost was to chair a novel governance body, University Council, intended to address student calls during recent years for a clearly defined role within university governance. University Council included students, faculty, and administrators, and served as a working group for the more comprehensive University Senate that was chaired by the president. Legislation moved through an elaborate subcommittee structure guided by the provost to University Council. If passed there by a

David G. Brown, executive vice president for academic affairs and provost, 1970–82. Miami Archives.

sufficient majority, a decision was not reconsidered at University Senate except by request. This streamlined system provided a voice to concerned student leadership, faculty leaders, and major administrators in a single small body that could deliberate extensively and take action. Provost Brown treated University Council as an institution for reaching "controlled consensus" across Miami. During his first three years he took many of the fifty recommendations of the Blue Ribbon Committee to University Council, saw them approved, and implemented them.

RESULTS

Faithful implementation would be important to authenticating any post-1970 process. Provost Brown envisioned lasting changes with effects going well beyond governance, and saw the Office of the Provost as a catalyst for it. He moved that office to the ground floor of Roudebush Hall and kept an open door for faculty and others to drop in. He created a newsletter, *A Campus Report*, that ran a "Blue Ribbon Box Score" tallying implemented changes weekly. A year later that report was expanded to *The Miamian*, consolidating several publications into a "single and official source of university information." He put a map on his office wall with pins showing where new faculty came from, to remind academic deans that he wanted "a broader distribution around the world in terms of faculty." He stimulated a new level of national engagement by encouraging administrators to become involved in leading higher education organizations. He served as president of the American Association for Higher Education and chair of Chief Academic Officers for the American Council on Education. To the new job of assistant to the provost he appointed William S. Hanger, a recent graduate known as a fine negotiator who quickly earned the trust of diverse constituents. For more than a decade Hanger was the provost's right-hand agent in implementing an agenda of change. Among his assignments was working with sixteen committee chairs who were given elaborate charge letters annually, written by the provost as chair of University Council.

Brown established the annual Academic Administrators Seminar—all-day retreats involving vice presidents, deans, heads of major offices, and at times the president—to work through a 150-page notebook compiled by Brown detailing proposed changes and issues that he called "the working agenda for the year." He standardized personnel procedures by requiring departments to either adopt a model governance document offered by a group of activist department chairs or create one of their own. He personally reviewed these for consistency, and one of his faculty administrative interns codified them into Miami's first departmental handbook. He refined a formal promotion and tenure review in which all deans and the provost read and discussed documentation for every candidate before passing recommendations to the president; in some years those reviews occupied full days for an entire week. He monitored codification of promotion and tenure rules, merged the deans of graduate studies and research, instituted ranking in personnel recommendations, implemented a centralized course-review procedure, held regular informal group discussions with faculty and administrators in faculty homes, conducted open hearings on major legislation pending before University Council, invited trustees to meet with faculty and student groups throughout the year, supported creation of community advisory councils at regional campuses, oversaw expansion of the PhD program and creation of associate degree programs at Hamilton and Middletown, supervised revision of the university calendar from the quarter to the early semester, and encouraged widespread curriculum revision. He paid close attention to the Division of Student Affairs and formed a partnership with Vice President Etheridge and his staff to deliberately cultivate community between faculty and students. Among long-lived innovations from that effort was a "popcorn fund" in the Office of the Provost to reimburse expenses when faculty invited student groups into their homes. ROTC was to be a continuing presence at Miami, but the Shriver cabinet moved it from Rowan Hall to the lower level of Millett Assembly Hall, where it was both separated from the center of campus and surrounded by what Brown described as a "moat" of parking lots. Rowan Hall became an example, he said, of "guns into butter"—it was converted to an arts center.

"AFFILIATION AND MERGER"

The post-1970 planning strategy and the milieu of change it was creating would be dramatically tested when Miami acquired Western College. Western had enrolled college students for 119 uninterrupted years, making it Oxford's oldest continuous academic institution. It had formed beneficial partnerships with Miami during every era of its history, provided social and marriage partners for Miami men of all statures including presidents, with Oxford College had helped shape Miami's approach to residence hall life, and in later years had been a strong national voice for civil rights. These facts were known to President Shriver, who had a deep interest in local history. Moreover, Western occupied a large and scenic geographic area immediately on the east side of Miami's Oxford campus. The Shriver cabinet was determined that

Map of Oxford with Miami and Western College land at merger in 1974. Western College is the southeast section. The Western College of Miami University, Oxford, Ohio, 1974–1975. Miami Archives.

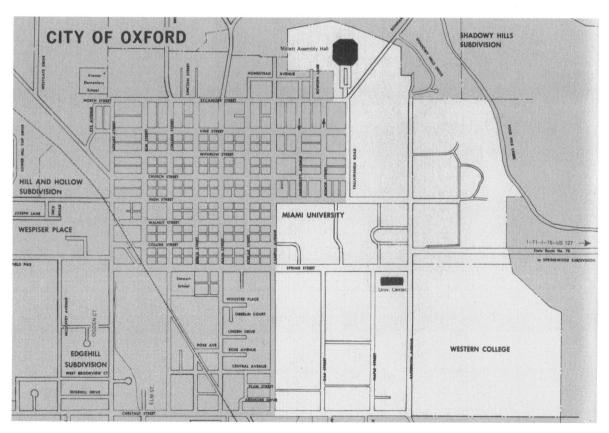

Myron J. Lunine, dean of the Western College of Miami University, 1974–78; dean of the School of Interdisciplinary Studies (Western College Program), 1978–80 (left). Photograph by Cathie Rowand. Miami Archives.

Western Program students and faculty on Kumler Chapel lawn, 1975. Miami Archives.

this property would not fall into the hands of real estate interests when the college closed for financial reasons in 1974.

What would actually be done with it, however, was less certain. The lead idea was to acquire the Chase Law School in Cincinnati and bring it to Oxford. The trustees supported the Shriver cabinet in its plan to acquire the assets of Western College, without firm commitments to its personnel, in return for liquidating a $3.5 million debt. They did not support the proposal to acquire Chase Law School. On a 5–4 vote that may have surprised President Shriver, they rejected the proposal. Now there was more need for planning.

As a first step President Shriver created an eighteen-person special committee to consider the question of "best use" of Western Campus, with Professor Warren Mason of political science as chair. In fall 1973 this committee received more than five hundred proposals from Miami and Western faculty, staff, alumni, and alumnae, and from a former Miami president. Ideas ranged from a "regional zoo" to an environmental center, anthropology museum, facility for business studies, art studios, a humanities college, University College, division for interdisciplinary programs, and other ideas. John Yeck proposed "An Interdisciplinary Approach to Solving Real-World Problems!" in a college setting. Former President John Millett, now chancellor of the Ohio Board of Regents, endorsed employing Western Campus for the "reconstruction of liberal education" advocated by Daniel Bell in *The Reforming of General Education* (1966). "The creation of a new college," said Millett, "affords the only opportunity to undertake a major, comprehensive reconstruction of purpose and process in higher education. And the opportunity only comes once."

It took more than a decade for Miami's residential college to earn the full support of a new alumnae organization—the Western College Alumnae Association, Inc.—that had been established with the support of John Dolibois after Western College closed in 1974. Yet with the emergence of Miami graduates who were enthusiastic about their own collegiate lives "on Western," many alumnae became ardent supporters. They endowed

Western Female Seminary opened in 1855 with a faculty from Mount Holyoke College and a single large building. Its campus would evolve in a manner common to American colleges for women, with multipurpose residential structures clustered on the brow of a hill overlooking a picturesque landscape. "The Western" created an educational community that evolved first into a progressive liberal arts college, then an international theme college, and in the late 1960s, an experimental liberal arts college. Located adjacent to Miami on Oxford's road to Cincinnati, Western featured innovative programs adored by alumnae and praised by educators. Through World War II it operated a growing campus and a variety of farm properties to serve its needs. In the era of postwar prosperity and change, however, it faced daunting challenges, including a national culture favoring coeducation, a low endowment, and, by 1970, almost two decades of accumulating budget deficits.

On August 16, 1973, news media announced that Western and Miami would undertake "affiliation and merger." The initial stated intent was to preserve the heritage of both institutions and add Western to Miami as an experimental program. Ultimately, Miami would liquidate Western's financial obligations and assume its physical assets on October 15, 1973. Western's last class graduated in the spring of 1974. After Miami trustees rejected a proposal to locate a law school on Western's campus, they passed a resolution directing President Shriver "[t]o develop a distinctive educational plan . . . for the best use of a new division of the University to be called 'The Western College of Miami University' on and after July 1, 1974, by taking full advantage of the clustering of all facilities, both academic and residential and including a library, necessary for a college." In ensuing months a few Western faculty and staff were offered employment elsewhere at Miami and others departed Oxford or retired. A Miami committee solicited and reviewed over five hundred proposals and proposed four possible conceptions for a new academic program at Western College. After much public and governance discussion, a degree-granting residential college focused on both liberal education and interdisciplinary studies was approved. It was to develop incrementally and be reviewed for possible permanent status after four years.

Miami planners recruited a full-time faculty for the new college—all but one at entry level and brought from other institutions specifically for the new program—and conceptualized a team-taught curriculum that integrated academic and cocurricular peer learning in residence halls at a new level of academic intensity. That approach was seen as blending Miami and Western legacies to improve coherence in liberal education by a direct focus on student learning. Founding Dean Myron J. Lunine and Associate

Dean Allen Davis came from Hampshire College, an interdisciplinary consortium institution for five colleges in Massachusetts, including Mount Holyoke. An implementation plan drawn up in spring 1974 was influential as new courses were written that summer by newly hired faculty while they were also recruiting the program's initial students at Miami's summer orientation.

Western College of Miami opened with a full class of first-year students in fall 1974, achieving the cherished goal of not allowing any academic year to pass since 1855 without an entering class on Western Campus. In early years both deans, and all faculty except one who joined from another Miami division, lived in Western College houses or residence halls to maximize informal contact with students. Except for science laboratories that met in Boyd Hall, a full schedule of required courses in humanities, arts, and social and natural sciences was offered in classrooms located in Peabody, McKee, and Clawson residence halls. Both deans and all faculty and staff had offices in Peabody, where two floors of students also lived.

The new deans had an intense desire to place residential learning and student development solidly at the center of the effort, and the college unfolded incrementally over four years according to plan. However, the College of Arts and Science did not agree to the initial governance expectation that its degree-granting interdisciplinary programs would move to the new college, so the major for Western students was instead organized by a system of learning contracts that required students to complete three-quarters of their advanced coursework in other Miami divisions and to work with Western faculty in close advising relationships where each student program was tailored to meet individual objectives. Resurrecting the concept of liberal learning favored by Millett in the "Common Curriculum," Western's lower-division general education program became a primary peer-learning mechanism within the residential college. It was a systematic and sequential required curriculum of topical team-taught courses in the main liberal arts fields, plus requirements in fine arts, learning technology, and writing across the curriculum. Required advanced seminars focused on interdisciplinary theory and practice, and development of research skills. The program concluded with a required yearlong senior project completed through a weekly seminar, plus a major public conference at year's end that showcased student achievements to faculty project reviewers from across the university and elsewhere.

Western College of Miami reveled in a buoyant, sometimes raucous atmosphere of democratic critical thinking in both classrooms and an intense peer-learning community. This tested the imagination and stamina of faculty

(continued)

and staff, yet they proved resilient; half of the founders remained for their entire academic careers in a program highly prized by its alumni. Graduates earned the bachelor of philosophy degree from Miami University, the B.Phil., which reform educators considered an older undergraduate degree than the BA and BS degrees and more appropriate to holistic aspirations of the residential college.

By the 1990s Western had won multiple awards from the Fund for the Improvement of Post-Secondary Education, Ohio Board of Regents Selective Excellence Programs, the National Science Foundation, and other agencies, and influenced national reform initiatives such as the Association of American Colleges report *A New Vitality in General Education* (1987) and *Integrity in the College Curriculum* (1984). Its senior project workshop was praised as a model for peer learning by Ernest Boyer in *College: The Undergraduate Experience in America* (1987). During the 1980s and 1990s it influenced creation of the Miami Plan for Liberal Education and redesign of the University Honors Program. In 1995 an award of $1.7 million by the National Science Foundation and National Science Teachers Association allowed four Western faculty to create an online and print journal of science writing for children, *Dragonfly*, that won a Parent's Choice Award and led to a PBS television program. In 1996 natural systems professor William Green won the John Burroughs Medal in Nature Writing from the American Museum of Natural History for a study of his geochemical fieldwork with students at the Antarctic lakes, *Water, Ice and Stone*. Western faculty led Miami initiatives in faculty development, new student orientation, and undergraduate research, hosted an Institute in Integrative Studies where college teachers created interdisciplinary courses for home institutions, and hosted the Association for Integrative Studies, whose executive director, William Newell, published a compendium, *Interdisciplinarity*, for The College Board in 1998.

By the early twenty-first century, led by its full-time faculty and staff, Miami's residential college had sustained notable achievements for three decades, institutionalized a comprehensive set of "alternative college" innovations, had a major impact on the evolution of Miami University, and produced over 1,400 graduates in the arts, sciences, law, media, education, health care, public policy, business, technology, and many other fields. It pioneered at Miami a pedagogy of discovery learning focused on undergraduate research, writing across the curriculum, study of primary texts in general education, and hands-on scientific fieldwork. The surest indication that it was thriving academically came from nationally funded assessment projects in the 1980s and 1990s. They consistently returned results

from alumni and current students showing positive learning outcomes that exceeded national and Miami norms.

~

In 1973 John Millett had a warning for planners of the Western College of Miami University. "I think it is a mistake to speak too loudly about innovation and experimentation in undergraduate education," he wrote. "The words are often misunderstood, especially by the general public." During its entire existence, Miami's residential college faced the challenge of explaining its innovative nature to prospective students who were initially attracted to Miami's professional schools and traditional liberal arts programs. Without vigorous targeted recruiting strategies, Miami's residential college was unlikely to grow. That effort would not be forthcoming, for as early as 1979 a University Senate action cautioned the Admission Office against "special" recruiting for Western. In that year, trustees changed the college's official name to "School of Interdisciplinary Studies (Western College Program)." Responding to an attempt in the early 1980s to merge Western into the College of Arts and Science as one of its departments, the Department of Architecture chose to enroll students majoring in environmental design, and later, interior design, in the Western curriculum to complete Miami's general education requirements. They lived in residence for their first year.

Even with professional school clients added to the residential college, without special recruiting, strategies for cost containment were always necessary. In the 1970s Academic and Student Affairs had shared the costs of the residential college, but in the 1980s major fiscal contributions from Student Affairs were ended. Then Western developed a planning model that controlled for scale by matching available resources to demand. It placed the total number of students living in residential college halls in a fixed number of seminar classes of equal size, and offered a defined number of sections in a required sequential curriculum taught by a set number of faculty who had standardized teaching loads that were higher than typical Miami assignments for liberal arts faculty. For almost two decades from the early 1980s to the late 1990s, Western used this resource model to consistently enroll 250 to 300 students majoring in interdisciplinary studies or architecture and interior design, or completing University Honors or liberal education requirements—without significantly expanding the faculty. The architecture-Western collaboration was positively evaluated by architecture reviewers in the 1980s and the 1990s, but in the spring of 2006 architecture and interior design ended it. Coming in a banner era for professional schools, this action exposed liberal arts Western anew to charges of relatively low enrollment and high cost, with dim prospects for replacing its professional-school clients.

From its earliest days, optimism about the number of Miami students who would take advantage of the residential college had been inflated. Indeed, Western College came to be perceived by some Miami students who did enroll there as an innovative small-college alternative to large pedagogically conservative programs thriving elsewhere on campus. Others viewed it as an alternative student subculture. In the twenty-first century, when many talented mainstream Miami students seemed to blend seamlessly into a milieu of upper-middle-class prosperity and trendy popular culture while migrating to majors in the professional schools, Western continued to appeal to a shrinking number who did not fit those trends. Some Western students were indistinguishable from the majority at Miami, but others were not. Some were offspring of parents working in higher education who had nurtured in them a restless interest in the process of their own schooling. Some were outspoken students on the cultural left, some were fervently interested in political activism, some were offbeat or quirky, or persistent risk takers, and some were both smart and busily questioning authority. Some celebrated Western as a cultural safe house, and others took visible roles in campus reform—protests by women about hazing at the opening-of-the-year campus orientation in the 1970s, demonstrations on behalf of better campus lighting for rape prevention in the 1980s, disruptive symbolic actions supporting Miami workers in a vocal strike for a higher minimum wage in 2003. While Miami's student mainstream moved to the political right in the wake of the Reagan neoconservative revolution, most Western students did not. Not all observers appreciated that. Indeed, there was a thirty-year history of trading negative images back and forth "across the street" in the *Miami Student*, and occasionally, as during an encounter between Miami prowar and Western antiwar factions on the evening of the first Iraq invasion, Western students were physically threatened. In turn, they sometimes attempted to intimidate those in power by noisy public demonstrations of their disaffection with official policies.

By the early twenty-first century the university had embraced the idea of creating "theme learning communities" in most of its residence halls. Miami's initiator and most elaborate practitioner of this residence life strategy was now ironically, perhaps mistakenly, perceived by some as less distinctive than it had been in the past. When a budgetary downturn arrived and central administrators sought candidates for cost savings, the residential college was vulnerable to the argument that even though it claimed only 1 percent of Miami's resources, those ought to be deployed elsewhere.

The last of many political encounters since 1974 over the future of Miami's residential college played out during spring 2006 in a decision-making atmosphere of corporate confidentiality. Despite vocal alumni objections, public records requests seeking to reveal administrative strategies, and patient, articulate, public explanations by current students of the program's value to them, in June the trustees approved a presidential recommendation to eliminate Western as an academic division. In fall 2006 University Senate declined an Academic Affairs proposal to merge it with the University Honors Program into an Honors College. Officials of the College of Arts and Science then declined to accept it as a department. Recruiting of new students for fall 2007 was terminated, and residential college faculty who did not retire or resign were reassigned to other divisions. Some puzzled, astonished, or enraged alumni withheld financial contributions. Current students would be phased out. The final graduates of Western College would make it to the first year of Miami's third century, earning the bachelor of philosophy degree in the class of 2010. Some alumni lobbied for revival of Western's "core values" in a new program, and in fall 2007 a College of Arts and Science committee was discussing possibilities for opening a residential learning community with an individualized learning-contract major, to be headquartered in Peabody Hall.

The saga of the Western College of Miami University was notable among residential colleges in the twentieth century, for it was atypical in several ways. It was created in response to an historical event—the closing of an independent college—on a campus that had evolved for well over a century as a place for successfully integrating undergraduate academic and residential life. Its design may have emerged in part from core conservative desires to recognize inherent value in local tradition and to restore structure to liberal learning. A creation of Miami's Public Ivy era, Western successfully institutionalized the most comprehensive set of pedagogical innovations found at any residential college within a major American university. It earned the loyalty and financial support of separate "old" alumnae and "new" alumni organizations, lasted longer in its original form than any similar college created in the twentieth century, and proved to be, in David G. Brown's observation of 2006, a "fountain of innovation" for Miami University.

Curtis W. Ellison, Dean, School of Interdisciplinary Studies (Western College Program), 1980–96 and 1997–98

The Western College Alumnae Association, Inc.

When Western College closed in 1974, the unique Western College Alumnae Association, Inc., was formed by Western alumnae with the support of Miami Vice President for Alumni Affairs John Dolibois. Governed by a board of fifteen trustees elected from alumnae members, it was headquartered in Patterson Place, the former Western College presidential home, with an executive director reporting to the Miami Alumni Association. In 2007 it boasted as active members 2,900 Western College alumnae, 100 former faculty and friends, and 1,400 graduates of Miami's Western College Program. It had chapters in seventeen states and the District of Columbia. The association's mission was to preserve communication within the Western family and to support education and human values. It published an alumnae *Bulletin* and an e-mail newsletter, held club meetings across the country, and featured an annual all-class reunion on Western Campus. In its first three decades it awarded over $2 million in scholarships and endowed a faculty lecture series, a young artist concert series, a teaching award, three centers for peer learning, and the Western College Memorial Archives in Peabody Hall.

Members of Western College Alumnae Association, Inc., at annual reunion, June 2007. Bulletin, Western College Alumnae Association, Inc., Fall 2007. Western Archives.

peer-learning centers for writing, discovery science, quantitative reasoning, and digital learning across the curriculum in the new Western College Program, and named them for faculty of the former Western College. To sustain the residential academic tradition, one of their members made a commitment to endow a visiting professor-in-residence position, and to honor their Association, they created a memorial archives intended to collect and preserve documents and artifacts from both old and new versions of Western College for use in teaching and undergraduate research.

Western's main building had been home to a degree-granting undergraduate program since 1860 and in the Public Ivy era continued to house 140 students plus staff and faculty, seminar rooms, a theatre that doubled as a lecture hall, a writing center, computer center, networked student rooms, and other academic facilities. With a competitive award from the U.S. Department of Education for a long-term low-interest loan, Peabody Hall received a $7 million award-winning rehabilitation between 1994 and 1996. Working for the first time with an architectural firm specializing in historic preservation, and employing an engaged partnership model between the offices of Physical Facilities, Academic Affairs, and Alumni Affairs, Miami renovated the building to restore its 1871 character while updating it to specifically serve programs of the residential college and Alumnae Association.

Among achievements of the Shriver cabinet during Provost Brown's tenure that nurtured a climate of innovation lasting into the twenty-first century, creation of an educationally successful residential college was among the most visible. After four years of operation Brown gave it a promised review that again involved all elements of Public Ivy decision making—a high-profile committee with a sweeping charge, prominent national consultants offering external assessment, extended hearings, and governance debates leading to a single vote up or down on "permanent status." That was approved by about two-thirds of University Senate in a crowded, tension-filled meeting at Hall Auditorium, where arguments concerning Western's future were frankly spoken as balancing educational quality at small scale against transfer of resources to other programs. After the positive vote on continuation, Brown promptly set up a process for tenuring its faculty.

A CLIMATE OF INNOVATION

When Phillip Shriver announced his retirement from the presidency, David G. Brown was ready to move on. In the early twenty-first century he was still Miami's only chief academic officer to remain in office more than five years. When Paul G. Pearson (1981–92) assumed the presidency, Brown stayed one more year. He left in 1982 to become President of Transylvania University, and later served as chancellor of the University of North Carolina, Asheville, provost of Wake Forest University, and interim president of Georgia College and State University. In the late 1990s he moved to the realm of computer-enhanced learning and continued to publish, speak, and consult. In 2006 he reflected on his twelve years at Miami.

In retrospect it was an exhausting way to lead because you had this character who was sort of consolidating the ideas from higher education nationally and pushing them out there. We were very active during those years, and came up with a lot of innovation, and I know I was accused more than once of pursuing change for its own sake and maybe I was. I'm not sure. I think we did make some very dramatic steps and that's when we started being noticed nationally.

After 1970 Miami would experience three decades of innovation as faculty, students, and administrators responded to a national movement toward active learning.

1971: The Institute for Environmental Sciences

In 1969 faculty from an array of science departments began addressing environmental concerns by advocating an institute to offer a professional Master of Environmental Science degree, engage in interdisciplinary research, and serve communities of southwest Ohio. Vice President Dolibois provided alumni support to develop a full proposal with curriculum, organization, and philosophy. The Institute for Environmental Sciences (IES) was approved and admitted students in fall 1971. Its first facility was at a former Nike missile base; it soon moved to Boyd Hall on Western Campus. It had a half-time director and courses taught by faculty from many departments. With core courses in methodology, measurements, policy making and administration, and statistics; an area of concentration; and a thesis, practicum, or internship research requirement, it led to the MEn degree. There was a student team project, later a public service project. Requirements were rigorous—a comprehensive oral examination after the first year focused on real-world problem solving.

Institute of Environmental Sciences facility at former Nike missile base, Taylor Road northwest of Oxford, early 1970s. Miami Archives.

To maximize work across disciplinary, departmental, and divisional boundaries, IES reported directly to the dean of the Graduate School. It earned a national and international reputation in research, teaching, and service and was selected by the United Nations Environment Program as its U.S. point of contact. External reviewers described IES as being among two or three such programs in the nation. The Universiti Pertanian Malaysia (UPM) chose it as the model for an undergraduate environmental science degree in 1976, and with Fulbright support, Miami faculty worked in Malaysia to develop that program while UPM students came to Miami to earn the MEn. Some Miami interdisciplinary graduate programs were built on the IES model, offering advanced work in theory for an applied field. The Master of Technical and Scientific

Communication (MTSC) program, opened in 1983, was a direct outgrowth of the IES concentration in Public Information and employed most of its programmatic elements.

IES consistently placed students in research projects or internships across the country and abroad, graduating about twenty students annually. They came from the United States, Europe, Asia, Africa, and Latin America and assumed high-ranking environmental positions in their home countries. Public service projects had sponsors in Ohio and Indiana plus two State of Ohio agencies. At times IES was one of the larger external funding units on campus, and after 1989, with a consulting firm, IES operated the U.S. EPA Test and Evaluation Facility in Cincinnati.

1972: The Rise of Women's Studies

Institutionalizing women's studies at Miami required making do with scarce resources in the face of skepticism, and moving ahead as sympathetic faculty joined the university. The evolution of women's studies was profound for women and men who in the early 1970s advocated the importance of a place in the academy where experiences of women could be at the center of inquiry. By 1970 a few faculty were teaching new works on women in their departmental introductory courses. Topical courses specifically devoted to women and gender were taught at Miami after 1972. A curriculum focus in women's studies was not available, however, until 1978. It was twelve more years before a director for an emerging Women's Studies Program was named in 1990, and another decade before the undergraduate major was launched in 2000.

Early women's studies efforts at Miami favored grassroots action by faculty and staff, reinforced by student interest, moving toward a new curriculum. A Women in Politics course was offered in the Department of Political Science by Susan Kay, and another in the School of Business Administration by John Douglass. Mildred Seltzer in sociology organized a continuing education class focused on topics such as aging, politics, workplace discrimination, advertising images, child care, and literature by and about girls and women. Enrollment in that course was overwhelming. Soon courses were available in classics, history, philosophy, psychology, religion and sociology.

Although early coordinators lacked sufficient resources, the commitment of Miami faculty and staff to bring life to women's studies as feminist values emerged at institutions across the country facilitated the dedication of resources from the College of Arts and Science over time. Some advocates were experienced in power politics outside the academy, and some fought resource battles in their departments. Many women's studies faculty were untenured assistant professors, some the first women in their departments, whose

Women's Studies
Women's Studies Web site, March 22, 2007

Women's Studies raises questions about gender as a social construction and the ways in which those constructions affect disciplinary knowledge, the experiences of women and men, our social fabric, the arts, creative writing, institutions, intimate relationships, and the workplace. Women's Studies courses are organized around contemporary feminist research and theory, and focus on women as subjects of inquiry.... With seven core faculty members and over forty affiliates, the Women's Studies program at Miami University integrates expertise in virtually every field of human endeavor.

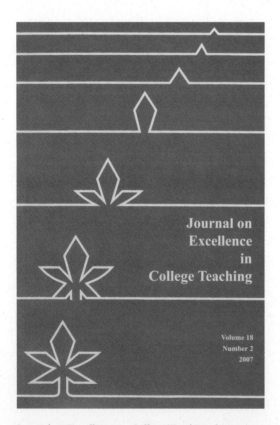

Journal on Excellence in College Teaching, *begun 1990. Cover alludes to "Greening of the Future" Lilly Endowment Grant for faculty development, 1979.* Published by Miami University.

colleagues were skeptical about their interests. For them, the women's studies community was an opportunity to pursue interdisciplinary studies and to take institutional ground. In coming years the formal study of women would become widespread, both within diverse disciplines and in its own major, thanks to the resilience of pioneering advocates.

1979: "The Greening of the Future"

On June 28, 1979, the *Miamian* carried a front-page announcement that the Lilly Endowment, Inc., had provided $50,000 for a postdoctoral teaching awards program under the title "The Greening of the Future." "The program will provide intensive experiences in faculty development activities for eight 'relatively new' Miami faculty who will become Lilly Teaching Fellows, and eight senior faculty members personally selected by each fellow to be their mentors." Lilly Fellows had one-third release time for a year and participated in seminars on teaching and a course auditing project with a senior faculty mentor, as well as retreats and special projects. Twice annually they met with teaching fellows from other institutions—Carnegie Mellon, Indiana University, and the Universities of Tennessee, Rhode Island, and Florida.

When the Lilly grant expired in 1981, Provost Brown took the program to University Council for review via a recommendation of the Committee on the Improvement of Instruction. Council modified it and recommended that it be "picked up" for funding. The next year Milton Cox, an assistant professor of mathematics, was named program director. He would continuously expand the program for the next quarter century.

Later funded by alumni as the Alumni Teaching Scholars, this faculty development initiative proved enormously successful. By the twenty-first century it was one of the nation's premier programs, with a vast menu of professional support options for developing active learning with students. It sponsored annual national teaching conferences in Oxford and in California, hosted the *Journal on Excellence in College Teaching*, and won the Hesburgh Award for its Teaching Scholars Faculty Learning Community model.

1981: The University Honors Program

Concerns about national security and the Soviet space program inspired a national trend to expand honors and gifted education in the late 1950s. In 1958 Miami joined the trend with two programs for high-ability students. The University Study Program offered strong high school students an opportunity to take courses at Miami, and the Undergraduate Fellowship Program, later called Undergraduate Associates, enabled students to work closely with faculty mentors in teaching or research. In 1959 President Millett announced creation of an honors program to "step up the pace for the best students coming here and to make sure they make the best possible use of their time." More than 150 new and 85 advanced students were enrolled by 1961.

At a time when honors education was in its infancy Millett's vision was bold and ambitious. He set a goal of including 5 percent of the student body, opened optional honors residence halls in Stoddard and Elliott, called for discussion-based interdisciplinary seminars, and encouraged honors students to engage in independent readings with faculty. By 1962 almost every department offered honors courses, a student advisory council formed, the honors program published newsletters and held coffee hours, and James Woodworth, social studies, was serving as part-time director. From 1963 to 1970, under the leadership of a half-time director, Wallace I. Edwards of economics, the program burgeoned, reaching one thousand students by 1969.

Campus events of 1970 nonetheless underscored a degree of growing student apathy about honors education. By 1971 the honors report observed that the changing university no longer emphasized academic excellence, and the 1972 report complained about lack of support, resources, course offerings, and physical facilities, as well as difficulties with course registration and retention. University Senate responded by formally eliminating the University Honors Program in favor of a new General Honors Curriculum to be directed by the chair of a faculty committee. It would allow open admissions, offering honors credit for completing additional projects in designated regular courses. Any student who completed twenty-four credits with a "D" grade or better would be awarded "General Honors" at graduation. Those who maintained a 3.25 grade point average would be accorded "General Honors with Distinction."

By 1981 Miami was moving toward active-learning programs that took advantage of the university's residential setting, and the general honors approach came to be regarded as deficient in opportunities for highly motivated and talented students. With support of the Danforth Foundation, an institutional team chaired by the dean of the Western College Program and including the

Richard Nault, director of the University Honors Program (center) with students, 1990. Miami Archives.

Bishop Hall (1912) in 1983. Designated home of the University Honors Center, 1981. Miami Archives.

General Honors Curriculum director, an assistant dean of the College of Arts and Science, and a professor of family studies and consumer sciences attended a summer workshop at Colorado College, where the team worked with national consultants to draft a new honors design for consideration by University Senate. Dean of Arts and Science C. K. Williamson promoted this effort. The new plan, approved by Senate in the fall of 1981, made Bishop Hall an honors center with a director's office and advising facilities in an optional co-educational honors residence hall, and created a required sequence of courses exclusively for honors students across four baccalaureate years. It established an incentive system to compensate departments for honors teaching. Building on this structure, the new program's early directors formed a faculty advisory committee, launched a student board, and developed a first-year colloquium.

Richard Nault came to Miami from Washington University in St. Louis as the result of a national search for honors staff in 1984. When he became the first full-time honors director, he focused strongly on civic engagement and leadership development, invited national leaders to campus, organized service trips, established the Social Concerns Committee, obtained a grant from the Kettering Foundation for an Urban Leadership Internship Program, and created a scholar-leader program emphasizing service learning and community commitment. A senior thesis requirement called for in the program's 1982 redesign, adapted from the Western College Program senior project, was implemented for honors students. The program benefited from new funding. The Joanna Jackson Goldman Prize allowed a senior to pursue a year-long project after graduation, and the Benjamin Harrison Scholarship, a new four-year full-support initiative, aimed to attract outstanding high school graduates to Miami. Slightly over a decade after its redesign the honors program was serving eight hundred students, and its director took the position of associate vice president for student affairs and dean of students.

Under director Susan Barnum, honors offered a biodiversity workshop in Kenya, a series of "high teas" with local dignitaries, a visiting scholars program, a study abroad program at the University of Cambridge, a newly designed first-year colloquium, endowed funds for student research, and an expanded urban internship program. By 1998, facing increasing competition from other institutions for high-ability students, director Mary Cayton undertook with students and colleagues an investigation of exemplary programs across the nation, then implemented a faculty mentoring program, expanded requirements and courses, and created tuition waivers for summer study. Two tiers of honors students were identified, meeting different requirements. Carolyn Haynes became director in 2002. By the early twenty-first century the University Honors Program expanded to over two thousand students, hosted Miami recruitment events, featured holistic admissions using standardized test scores plus other predictors of potential success, and added three honors residence halls.

In twenty-five years honors students earned Marshall, Truman, Goldwater, and Fulbright Scholarships and were named to the *USA Today* All-Academic Team. They contributed research and publications, service projects, and initiatives to recruit students and to engage others in cocurricular programs. More than 120 faculty members offered honors courses annually in a community blending teaching, research, advising, and support for talented students.

University Summer Reading Program Twenty-fifth Anniversary Freshman Convocation, 2006. IT Services.

About the Summer Reading Program

from Office of Liberal Education Web site, 2007

Miami welcomes new students to its community of learning through the Summer Reading Program. In this important tradition, now 25 years old, we underline those activities we value most as a community: critical engagement with ideas; close interaction among faculty, staff, and students; and reading, listening, talking, and learning as characteristics of active, responsible citizenship. We can think of no better way of introducing you to the kind of life you will lead for the next four years than asking you, first, to read a book during the summer and, second, to return to campus in August prepared to discuss it with your fellow students. You will be able to hear the author of this year's text when he or she addresses University Convocation on the eve of your first semester at Miami. University Convocation, a celebratory occasion that includes an academic procession, music, and welcoming remarks from the president of the university and the president of Associated Student Government, marks the formal opening of the academic year.

2007: Eggers, *What Is the What*

2006: Goldfarb, *Ahmad's War, Ahmad's Peace*

2005: Grealy, *Autobiography of a Face*; Patchett, *Truth and Beauty*

2004: Phillips, *Crossing the River*

2003: Ehrenreich, *Nickel and Dimed*

2002: O'Brien, *The Things They Carried*

2001: Prejean, *Dead Man Walking*

2000: Shackleton, *The Endurance: Shackleton's Legendary Antarctic Expedition*

1999: Jones, Newman, Isay, *Our America*

1998: Alexie, *The Lone Ranger and Tonto Fistfight in Heaven*

1997: Verghese, *My Own Country*

1996: Alvarez, *How the Garcia Girls Lost Their Accents*

1995: Terkel, *The Good War*

1994: West, *Race Matters*

1993: Sanders, *Paradise of Bombs*

1992: Rodriguez, *Hunger of Memory*

1991: Phillips, *Machine Dreams*

1990: O'Brien, *Going After Cacciato*

1989: Morrison, *Song of Solomon*

1988: Wiesel, *Night*

1987: Atwood, *The Handmaid's Tale*

1986: Persig, *Zen and the Art of Motorcycle Maintenance*

1985: Thomas, *Late Night Thoughts on Listening to Mahler's 9th*

1984: Vonnegut, *Slaughterhouse Five*

1983: Orwell, *1984*

1982: Toffler, *The Third Wave*

1982: *Modeling Active Learning*

The Miami University Summer Reading Program became one of the nation's most elaborate efforts to systematically introduce students to campus life via the intellectual challenge of reading a provocative book. The Western College Program pioneered this approach at Miami in the mid-1970s, and in 1982 the university adopted it for use with all students.

1983: *"The Cradle of Coaches"*

Bob Kurz, Class of 1958, was sports information director in 1959 when, thinking of the history of Miami football and legendary sports figures who first achieved prominence in Oxford, he coined a phrase that would become synonymous with Miami athletics.

Driving back to Oxford one Saturday night in late October [of 1958], the car radio . . . was tuned to a station picking up a game from Tiger Stadium in Baton Rouge, Louisiana. LSU, coached by Paul Dietzel, a 1948 Miami graduate, was pitted against Mississippi State. . . . It was college football in the South, and I think I was hearing and feeling it for the first time. It gave me an idea. . . . The next morning, after church, I went to the office. . . . Perusing the Sunday papers, I jotted down the records of the Miami

Miami University—Football's "Cradle of Coaches." *Left to right: John Pont, Class of 1952; Weeb Ewbank, Class of 1928; Bo Schembechler, Class of 1951; Earl H. Blaik, Class of 1918; Carmen Cozza, Class of 1952; Paul Brown, Class of 1930; Paul Dietzel, Class of 1940; Ara Parseghian, Class of 1949. Mural by Gary Thomas, 1975.* Miami Archives.

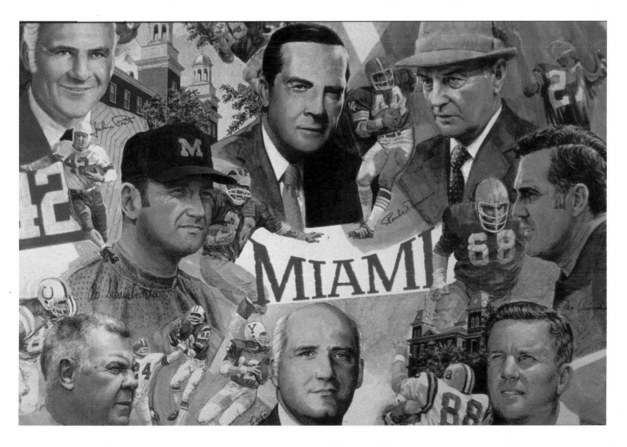

alumni in the college and professional coaching ranks. Red Blaik, Miami '18, the legendary Army coach; Weeb Ewbank, Miami '28, Baltimore Colts; Paul Brown, Miami '30, Cleveland Browns; the aforementioned Dietzel; Ara Parseghian, Dietzel's teammate and classmate, and finally, John Pont, Miami '52 and current Miami coach. . . . Here it was, more than half-way through the season, and these Miami coaches had yet to lose ten games combined. There's a story there, I said to myself, as I put a blank sheet of paper in the typewriter. And on that blank sheet of paper, citing this amazing phenomenon, I called Miami the Cradle of Coaches.

Many college football coaches had an affiliation with Miami. Kurz added Carmen Cozza, Class of 1952, at Yale; Bo Schembechler, Class of 1951, at the University of Michigan; Bill Mallory, Class of 1952, at Indiana University; and Terry Hoeppner at Indiana, Randy Walker at Northwestern, and Ron Zook at Illinois. The "Cradle" grew beyond football to include other sports, and athletic administrators as well. Among others, Bud Middaugh, longtime baseball coach at Miami, went to Michigan and Tracy Smith, former Miami player and baseball coach, moved to Indiana University. Athletic director Eric Hyman went to Texas Christian University and the University of South Carolina, and AD Joel Maturi to the University of Minnesota.

Postwar Miami football had many successes. A legendary 1947 team went undefeated though once tied, and won the Sun Bowl game against Texas Tech, 13–12. It featured players who had served in World War II and future coaches Dietzel at center and Parseghian at halfback. In an atmosphere of emerging tensions over civil rights, Coach Sidney Gilman received prior assurances that he would not encounter discrimination against his African American players.

At the beginning of the Public Ivy, a decade after Kurz coined the phrase "Cradle of Coaches," Miami's Athletic Hall of Fame inducted its inaugural class. It included Walter E. (Smokey) Alston, Class of 1935, who managed the Brooklyn (later Los Angeles) Dodgers to four World Series wins; Weeb Ewbank, Class of 1928, legendary coach of the Baltimore Colts and New York Jets; and Paul Brown, Class of 1930, architect of the Cleveland Browns and Cincinnati Bengals professional football franchises. Between 1969 and 2006, 200 former athletes were named to the Hall of Fame. The first of 18 women was inducted in 1989.

In 1973 Miami clinched the MAC football crown and a trip to the Tangerine Bowl with a victory over Kent on November 10. No one suspected the team was about to

Telegram to Miami football coach Sidney Gilman from Southwestern Sun Carnival Association, December 1, 1947. Miami Archives.

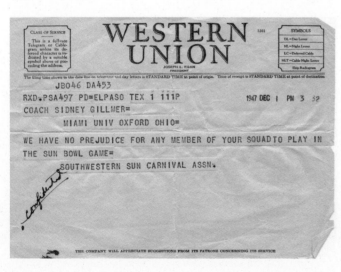

Tangerine Bowl program, December 22, 1973. Miami Archives.

begin its longest run of successful postseason appearances. Miami had a 2-1 record in previous bowl appearances, the most recent being the 1962 Tangerine Bowl, which had ended in a 49–21 defeat by the Houston Cougars. Although the 1973 team ended the season with a Top 20 Associated Press ranking and the top defense in the nation, skeptics wondered whether a MAC team deserved to rank alongside perennial football powers such as Texas and Tennessee.

Miami's opponent in the Tangerine Bowl was Florida, who had a 7-4 record against some of the top teams in the country. Coached by a two-time Southeastern Conference (SEC) coach of the year, Florida ended the season with five victories, the last a 49–0 blowout of archrival Florida State. Many believed Florida to be the clear favorite. Their quarterback was quoted as saying "Man, if we lose this game we'll be the laughing stock of the SEC and maybe even the whole South!"

The game would be played at 61,000-seat Florida Field in Gainesville, making it a home game for the Gators. Before the Miami squad left Oxford, flu shots were administered to the entire team. Florida did not do this, with the result that several Florida players, including the quarterback, had the flu on game day. Kick-off temperature was a brisk 39 degrees and by game's end 37,000 spectators were shivering in temperatures well below freezing. According to one report, press box orange juice froze in its cardboard cartons.

The game was a low-scoring defensive struggle. Miami's top-ranked defense dominated early going, and Florida didn't reach Miami territory in the first half. The Florida quarterback was intercepted once and sacked three times, suffering a back injury that prevented him from returning the second half. Miami offense didn't fare well in the first half—a field goal put Miami up 3–0 at halftime. The second half repeated the first. Miami defense dominated. Two third-quarter Florida fumbles led to a Miami field goal and touchdown, giving Coach Bill Mallory's team a 13-point lead. Florida was unable to score until, with 2:15 left in the game, its star running back crossed the Miami goal on a one-yard run. Miami kicked a field goal with nine seconds left for a 16–7 victory. Florida quarterbacks had been intercepted four times.

The Tangerine Bowl was telecast throughout the eastern United States, giving Miami football the biggest national exposure it had enjoyed to date, and its performance gained well-deserved respect from doubting national pundits. The 1973 season and bowl victory would begin a three-year golden age for Miami football. Over the next three years Miami compiled a 32-1-1 record and won convincing bowl victories over Georgia and South Carolina.

Miami had a band as early as its centennial year of 1909, and a later version, complete with a drum major, appeared at football games as early as 1915. By the 1930s the Miami University Marching Band was under the direction of A. D. Lekvold. Members wore white trousers and red coats and capes. In 1951 Nicholas Poccia joined the music faculty and two years later began voluntarily assisting with marching band. It rehearsed on Cook Field. After World War II it had moved to McGuffey Field on the east side of Campus Avenue south of Spring Street, storing equipment in a temporary building near Benton Hall (later Hall Auditorium). By the 1950s the band had ninety-six members, and in 1955 the now half-century-old tradition of High School Band Day was initiated, with thirty-eight high school bands present. In that decade shakerettes and majorettes were added to the band. By 1936 the Symphonic Band was offering springtime concerts in Benton Hall, a tradition alive in the twenty-first century under the direction of Gary A. Speck.

When Poccia became director in 1960 the band moved to Benton Hall, increased its membership to 144, and got new uniforms of red coats and gray trousers. The band relocated to the new Center for Performing Arts in 1968 and began rehearsing on a field still in use just south of the building. A new uniform jacket was introduced in the late 1960s—deep blue with a large block "M" on the front and an Indian mascot on the back. The Miami Marching Machine, a tanklike plywood structure built over a Volkswagen, was brought onto the field as a marching band feature.

Miami University Marching Band at Macy's Thanksgiving Day Parade, New York City, 2003. Miami University Marching Band.

At the beginning of the Public Ivy era in the early 1970s the football team was earning new national visibility for Miami athletics. Dr. Jack Liles became band director in 1978. In keeping with national trends, he made a major change in marching style by adopting a "drum corps" approach and introducing a color guard. The band acquired new uniforms of red and white, dispensed with the Miami Marching Machine, and introduced the marching block "M" for the pregame show that continued into the twenty-first century.

The marching band grew in popularity during the 1980s, enrolled participants from any Miami major, and expanded from 144 to over 250 members. In addition to performing at all home games, it traveled to bowl games and played concerts and parades on campus. In spring 1998 David Shaffer, principal arranger and assistant director for twenty years, was named director. Under his leadership the band was in high demand for contests, festivals, and parades across the Midwest, and in 2003 was selected as the premier "Santa" band for the Macy's Thanksgiving Day Parade in New York City.

1985: "Public Ivy"

"The message is clear," wrote Richard Moll in 1985; "even the parents with ready cash are wondering if Olde Ivy is worth two to three times the price of a thoroughly respectable public institution." With this query a twenty-seven-year veteran of college admissions embraced the issue of cost versus value in higher education. Contemplating a predicted demographic downturn in traditional college-age students coupled with rapidly rising tuition and fees in the late twentieth century, Moll asked what the public perceived as value in college life. His answer: "exceptional quality," "very selective admissions," "an avowed mission to develop the 'whole person,'" "resources to match ideals with materials and manpower," and "prestige." That most elusive factor, he said, comprised "the mythology, and the visibility that enhance the place and

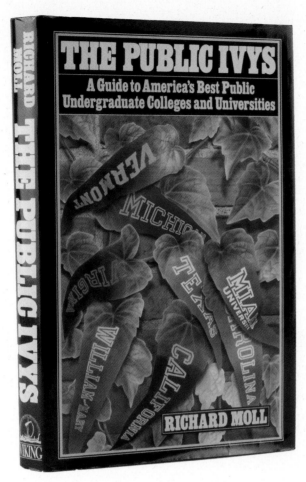

The Public Ivys, *by Richard Moll.* Viking Penguin Inc., 1985.

the name." He designated a few places that he felt had it all as *The Public Ivys.*

Richard Moll developed a method for identifying potential "Public Ivys." He began with data. He considered economic viability as measured by state support in 1983–84, and devised scales of inflation-corrected changes over ten years in higher education appropriations for personnel and operating expenses in all fifty states. He ranked states on appropriations per capita and per $1,000 of personal income. Ohio was eighth in total appropriations but forty-second in the other categories. For each institution under review he mapped scale, freshman class profile, retention rates, most popular majors, and campus budget factors including tuition and fees, sources of revenue, and expenditure areas. Then came qualitative factors, obtained by personal visits to campus. Said Moll,

Each of the following Ivy profiles resulted from a campus visit that lasted several days and included a range of interviews with students, faculty, and staff to learn about academic programs, student life, and resources; a review of the admissions situation; an immersion in local history, lore, and artifacts; and an attempt to become at least tourist-familiar with the college town and area.

There was, in other words, an attempt to "get the feel for the place" as college candidates are urged to do, beyond what the guidebooks list.

Miami demographics fit Moll's criteria. Importantly, he grew up in Indiana and had a high school teacher who was a Miami graduate. Even as a teenager, he knew Miami's regional mystique and prestige. In droll but respectful humor he opened his chapter on "Miami University of Ohio" with a vision.

It's a drab ride to Miami in southwestern Ohio. Corn. Wheat. Endless forgotten fields. Roadhouses. Fifties' tacky houses with immaculate lawns and wrought iron. Small hills to relieve the road ribbons. Tired gas stations, café and motel signs.

But lo, order and a manufactured kind of beauty pop out on the hill-plateau of Oxford (population 8,500), aptly named to house what Midwesterners call "The Yale of the West." (I remember it well from Indiana high school days; the bright and worldly would often apply to the top private colleges *and* Miami.) Trees and shrubs well groomed. A brick main street. Immaculate everything. "Modified Georgian" college buildings, old and new, trying so very hard to look Virginia, not Ohio.

This is surely what Midwestern parents dream of: a replica of *their* college experience of the midfifties. The Williamsburg look. Order. No cars! Academia tilted toward "training for leadership." The minority frat and sorority members holding the majority of influential positions on campus. Pep squads and a new stadium for very serious, rather successful football. And endless monograms on Shetland and cashmere sweaters.

In this setting Richard Moll mingled with students, faculty, and administrators, wandered the campus, and found a "Miami family" culture pervasive. The admissions staff was genuine, warm, earnest, "a family, nodding in agreement with each other, smiling, rarely jarring." "The national collegiate cynicism," noted Moll, "somehow passed this place by." Admissions staff said he was "at the right place for Ivy" for "we're preppy as hell." They praised Miami culture, but added that the "super straight" image might be a drawback. One said, "We are considered the country club of this area's public schools. That has a very prestigious, and surprisingly somber, connotation. On the whole, the Midwest loves the concept." The dean of the College of Arts and Science took up these points. "Our problem is not academic tone," he said. "Our problem is homogeneity. It's everywhere—in the student body, even in the campus buildings. Do we attract it, or do we develop it? Actually, we do the best job we can with the students we get. And the students we get are okay. They don't have sharp edges, though. They expect a 'caring relationship' here, a college family, and they get it."

Moll found the faculty "affable, lacking strong individual idiosyncrasies," and "slightly uneasy." One said, "Quite frankly, it is tiring as hell to keep handing out all the right images." Another claimed, "Eccentric teachers are not tolerated by the students at Miami." President Paul Pearson described Miami students as "conservative, religious, upper middle class. And they want a place now and later that is comfortable. They're good, clean-cut American kids. So let's say we've become selective within a life-style group." He added, "Miami is not on the frontiers of knowledge. But I can't imagine a better place for undergraduate classroom excellence—we're tops in the classroom." Provost David Brown, "whose office was more rumpled than those of the other administrators and his spirit more contagious," lauded Miami's "classroom integrity," its "heavy concentration of textbook authors" in the spirit of William Holmes McGuffey. He praised Miami's commitment to "help *others* teach well," and singled out the "true academic rigor" of the Western program, where even though "enrollments are slipping" its students "have a high profile at concerts and lectures and often lead us in social action: women's rights, the nuclear power issue, the environment, wildlife preservation."

Moll acknowledged that Miami "seems to have become highly selective by an unusual, well-calculated route: placing severe limitations on housing." He emphasized President Pearson's recognition that to maintain its position Miami would need to place high priority on raising private funds. In the mid-1980s its alumni had one of the highest giving ratios in the nation, but "even that must improve." Even so, Moll had no qualms about placing Miami in the company of the University of California, University of Michigan, University of North Carolina, University of Texas, University of Vermont, University of Virginia, and the College of William and Mary. "To the Midwest," he said, "Miami has been for some time and remains not *just* family but a down-home version of royal family."

1987: *Liberal Education at Miami University: A Statement of Principles*

At the beginning of the 1979–80 school year, President Shriver urged attention to a new agenda.

Buffeted by excessive careerism, the disruptions and demands of war, the cry for "relevance," the intrusions of government, the strangulating constraints of budgets, and the fragmentation of the curriculum, liberal education has all but disappeared from many campuses and has been in a beleaguered state of siege on many others. . . . In looking ahead to the decade of the 80s, then, I would stress as our first commitment the reaffirmation of the fundamental validity of liberal learning in the education of our students.

Two years later there would be a new president, and three years later, a new provost. Before that the University Requirement Committee twice failed to achieve governance agreement to modifications of the general education curriculum. In 1985 Provost E. Fred Carlisle, who had been a professor of American literature and assistant to the president at Michigan State, took on this challenge with the aid of several veterans of previous consensus-building projects. What would happen at Miami over the next five years exceeded anyone's expectations for engagement in educational reform.

On May 1, 1989, Miami faculty voted 305 to 292 to ratify The Miami Plan for Liberal Education. A basic change had occurred that would reshape general education at Miami well into the twenty-first century. In fall 1985 University Council had established the Liberal Education Task Force and charged it with studying changes elsewhere in liberal education and proposing a process for reform. The task force was aware that recent attempts to revise university general education had failed at Miami. Yet the national environment favored reform. Preparing for North Central Association accreditation in 1985, a self-study concluded there was pressing need for change. NCA agreed, and Provost Carlisle said the University Requirement

The Miami Plan for Liberal Education, *1989. Miami Archives.*

Miami University

THE MIAMI PLAN FOR LIBERAL EDUCATION

Oxford, Ohio

"appears to be no more than a loosely defined distribution requirement, with little focus or design, that can be satisfied by a very large number of courses."

No one on the task force could have predicted how strong the protective stance about programs and majors would be. Yet to counteract it, they called for the broadest possible participation in a university-wide review process, and proposed to proceed in two distinct stages: first, establish a statement of principles for liberal learning for which there was broad support, then develop a coherent plan for implementing those principles via curricular or other means. In fall 1986 the Fund for the Improvement of Post-Secondary Education granted support for external consultants, and the twenty-eight-person University Liberal Education Forum representing multiple constituencies began operating. Its first step was literature review and education about the assignment with the aid of consultants Jackson Newell, Dean of Liberal Education at the University of Utah, and Joseph Katz, a prominent theorist of general education and professor at Princeton University. Its second step was engaging all Miami campuses in debate about liberal education. The very first success, one that forum members would recall with pride, was that Miami faculty started talking quite openly about liberal education.

A formal period of discussion was keynoted by Ernest Boyer, a national spokesman for education reform. President Pearson shortened his State of the University address to allow Boyer to address University Senate. This was an important display of presidential support. Forum sponsored a practitioners' seminar with directors or deans of liberal education from other institutions, and a symposium on values underlying liberal learning at which six Miami faculty presented their views. Printed in the *Miami Report*, their statements provoked debate across campus. At one extreme, Henry Giroux of educational leadership argued for radical reform to empower marginalized student voices; at another, William Pratt of English argued for a return to a classical curriculum that prized canonical works of literature.

The forum's first attempt to pursue consensus was a discussion paper, "The Purpose of Liberal Education at Miami University." Faculty response was impressive. The organizing principle of "Nurturing Intellectual Maturity" was the overwhelming first choice and "Achieving Personal Perspective" was the clear second choice of numerous faculty who shared their views. Working with these ideas, the forum was able to draft a statement of principles for debate in University Council. This new statement represented a key shift in thinking about general education at Miami, for it moved away from an emphasis on categories of content knowledge to be taught, toward a pedagogical process of nurturing intellectual and social development. On April 6, 1987, University Council approved the *Statement of Principles* with virtual unanimity.

Forum was on schedule, had guiding principles that seemed sound, and had a mandate for reform. However, it would soon become clear that not all

LIBERAL EDUCATION AT MIAMI UNIVERSITY:
A STATEMENT OF PRINCIPLES

PURPOSE

The diverse educational communities of a comprehensive university have a common interest in liberal learning: it nurtures capabilities for creatively transforming human culture and complements specialized work by enlarging one's personal and vocational pathways. Liberal education involves thinking critically, understanding contexts, engaging with other learners, reflecting and acting, habits that extend liberal learning through a lifetime to benefit both the individual and society.

THINKING CRITICALLY

Thinking critically promotes imagination and intuition along with reasoning and evaluation. These diverse abilities contribute to achieving perspective, constructing and discerning relationships, and gaining understanding. Confidence in working with data and materials, skepticism in analyzing arguments or presentations, persistence in engaging complex problems and facility in communicating about technical matters are central to thinking critically. A skillful use of written and spoken languages, an informed use of mathematics and an ability to employ contemporary information sources are integral to thinking critically.

UNDERSTANDING CONTEXTS

Liberal learning cultivates the perspective that present cultural circumstances are an historical and a changing situation. Decisions about what is to be studied, the forms in which knowledge appears and the ways reasoning develops are to be continually examined. Ways of knowing need active attention: gender, class, racial identity, ethnicity, economic status and regional identity condition our understanding; temporal and spatial relationships, institutional traditions, religious commitments, philosophic perspectives, and political objectives shape our assumptions; influences originating beyond geographic and social boundaries affect what we know. Crucial to our future is knowledge of the conceptual frameworks and achievements of the arts, sciences, and technology, as well as understanding of the earth's ecosystem and the character of global society.

ENGAGING WITH OTHER LEARNERS

A healthy exchange of conflicting ideas and differing viewpoints encourages rethinking of accepted perspectives; it requires making choices and taking risks. Diversity among learners, a supportive atmosphere of group work, active listening, opportunities for presenting and criticizing the results of inquiry and creative effort encourage learning, aid growth and stimulate imagination. Thoughtful and systematic inquiry about the learning process supports shared efforts, and positive advising situations and experiences outside the classroom reinforce them.

REFLECTING AND ACTING

Thinking critically and understanding contexts for knowledge in an engaging learning situation lead to reflection and informed action. Making thoughtful decisions and examining their consequences enhance personal moral commitment, enrich ethical understanding, and strengthen civic participation.

Adopted by University Council, April 6, 1987

10

Liberal Education Statement of Principles, 1987. Miami Archives.

faculty agreed. After wide review of discussion papers on alternative designs and implementation strategies, it was obvious that departing significantly from a disciplinary distribution requirement was too much change for Miami. A few isolated voices praised the idea of a core curriculum, but all extended discussion centered on revising the University Requirement. The question was how to do that.

Members of the forum conducted seventy-two meetings during spring 1988 with every department and program. A small avalanche of written responses was mailed in. Four features had obvious support: a freshman seminar; a set of intellectual foundation courses; a vertical element of some sort creating liberal education through a student's four years; and a capstone course or experience. In early summer the forum met with consultant Joseph Katz to assess the situation. This was a crucial point in the project, for some members doubted there was a way forward. Katz argued persuasively that the large response to the forum's efforts, even the most critical commentaries, represented a collective investment in the idea that basic change was about to occur, and a desire to influence it. His enthusiasm for the presence of pro *and* con voices in the debate stimulated the forum to work over the summer to prepare a comprehensive proposal that Katz suggested be named "The Miami Plan for Liberal Education," emphasizing a structure for *evolutionary* reform of liberal learning over time.

In January and February 1989 a newly constituted representative University Senate took ownership of the plan, made substantial changes, and voted forty-five to eight in favor, four members abstaining. After a Faculty Assembly reconsideration by mail referendum, the new plan was adopted May 1, 1989.

Two years later Eulalia Benejam Cobb of the Fund for the Improvement of Post-Secondary Education reviewed Miami's project. Her evaluation captured the Public Ivy affection for seeking authentic change via participatory and consensual decision making.

To me, the single most impressive aspect of the project is the deep understanding it demonstrates of the pace and rhythms of the academy. For example, before beginning to plan the new curriculum you allowed one year of public comment on the purposes of the liberal arts. Although that kind of time frame might strike some as a lux-

Governance Reform, 1987

In 1986 an ad hoc committee of eleven faculty members from three academic divisions, plus a student government representative, conferred with external consultants, held hearings, then recommended a new form of governance to President Pearson. It was adopted in fall 1987.

The system in place since 1970 featured an inclusive University Senate comprising all faculty plus many administrators and Student Affairs staff, chaired by the president; and a University Council, a relatively small body consisting of nineteen faculty, six students, and three presidential appointees, chaired by the provost. Council acted first on university business and Senate convened occasionally to reconsider actions or review other matters with the president.

After 1987, faculty governance would be mostly in the hands of a University Senate of sixty-six members comprising ten faculty elected at large; thirty-four faculty apportioned to the college, schools, regional campuses, and the library; seven administrators or unclassified staff appointed by the president; twelve students selected by student government; and two graduate students selected

by their association. A Faculty Assembly comprising all tenured or tenure-track faculty, chaired by the president, could reconsider senate actions via a petition process.

This basic change to a representative system was rationalized as moving Miami to a more efficient and workable governance process. Also at issue, apparently, was the inherent authority of a small strategically positioned governance body chaired by an activist provost; the new system would ensure, it was believed, "vital communication" with many diverse constituents. While it increased the representation of groups for legislative debate, the new senate may have also curtailed the activist role of committees in shaping formal floor deliberation. The new enabling act may have limited the scope of senate authority as well. The board of trustees delegated to senate "primary responsibility for curriculum, programs, and course offerings and advisory responsibility on all matters related to Miami University." It could legislate, however, only on "educational programs, requirements, and standards; faculty welfare; and student conduct." The post-Vietnam era of governance designed for Public Ivy activism was ending.

ury, it was in fact essential to obtaining the faculty support for a curricular reform of the Plan's magnitude. . . .

Surely the 72 meetings and 169 pages of commentary by 56 individuals achieved in one four-month period in 1988 must stand in the annals of higher education as a monument to management by consensus. Now that the Plan is in place, I am certain that the five years of argument, exposition and dialogue will prove a solid base on which the new curriculum will prosper.

Implementation of Miami's liberal education plan would not unfold without stress, but by the twenty-first century its language, procedures, and expectations seemed to be internalized across all Miami campuses. The most ambitious innovation of the Public Ivy had been achieved.

1995: PROJECT DRAGONFLY

At the end of the Public Ivy era an inspired collaboration yielded another innovation. Project *Dragonfly* would reach millions of people worldwide through participatory science programs, learning media (print, radio, Web, television), public exhibits, and university courses. It began in 1995 with the launch of *Dragonfly* magazine. Funded by the National Science Foundation

Dragonfly *magazine, May/June 2000.*

(NSF), edited at Miami, and published by the National Science Teachers Association, *Dragonfly* was the first national magazine to feature investigations and discoveries by children. It gained a sterling reputation for demonstrating the power of children's voices and altered widespread assumptions about the role of children in science. The magazine won national notice, including the Parent's Choice Gold Award, but the best evidence for *Dragonfly's* success came from such studies as Saunders (1999) on pair-bonding in dolphins, Schamel (1997) on nest predation by arctic foxes, and Taylor (1998) on the relationship between music and memory—all investigators younger than twelve years of age, whose work was published in *Dragonfly* magazine.

Dragonfly's "real kids doing real science" mission led to exciting programs in formal and informal settings, such as *Dragonfly* QUEST science clubs for the Boys & Girls Clubs of America. Project *Dragonfly* also teamed with Miami's *Project Discovery* to create *iDiscovery*—a graduate program for inquiry-driven reform that enrolled more than two thousand Ohio educators annually. In 2000 *Dragonfly* completed a transition from a print magazine to a national PBS television series. Developed in partnership with Emmy-Award winning producers of *Newton's Apple* at TPT television, the NSF-funded *DragonflyTV* gave young investigators a national audience of more than 25 million viewers annually. It continued a tradition of science programs for kids from *Mr. Wizard* to Bill Nye. In its sixth season *DragonflyTV* aired on 292 PBS stations covering 90 percent of the United States, and won the World Silver Award of the New York Festival and the CINE Golden Eagle Award. The *New York Times* said of *DragonflyTV,* "For the young and the curious, the world of science and math is cracking wide open. "

Project *Dragonfly* initiated a global science and conservation program in 2002, *Earth Expeditions,* bringing educators and scientists together every year at conservation hotspots in Africa, Asia, and the Americas to promote inquiry-driven, community-based learning to benefit ecological communities, student achievement, and global understanding. Another twenty-first-century initiative was a public engagement project called *Wild Research.* Funded by a $2.5 million NSF grant and created with the Cincinnati Zoo and Botanical Gardens and a national consortium of partner institutions including the Brookfield Zoo, Santa Barbara Zoo, John G. Shedd Aquarium, and Zoo Atlanta, *Wild Research* developed a new class of inquiry-driven exhibits. Equipped with observation tools, recording devices, and themed investigations, *Wild Research* stations enabled direct research by families on zoo grounds, with real-time access to results on site or at home on the Internet. *Wild Research* media included the voices of conservation scientists such as Jane Goodall alongside voices of young investigators.

Project *Dragonfly* was initiated in 1995 by Chris Myers and Lynne Born Myers, who worked with Hays Cummins, Carolyn Haynes, and Christopher Wolfe to write the first proposal to NSF that launched *Dragonfly* magazine from the Western College Program, where team teaching and team projects in discovery science formed a culture of innovation that helped inspire it. Two of these faculty members were brought to the Western Program by competitive Ohio Board of Regents Academic Challenge Grants. By the twenty-first century, with contributions from students and faculty in every Miami division, Project *Dragonfly* had become a broadly collaborative effort that NSF called "a true innovation . . . a model of what active learning should be."

scene ten

Turbulence

TAKING STOCK

Negotiating the Miami Plan for Liberal Education required the energy of many people during the last half of the 1980s. It was the most elaborate project to use the proactive "controlled consensus" strategy, in which a broadly representative committee named by the president or provost studied an issue at length, listened to external consultants, held public hearings, then issued a public report with recommendations for governance debate and decision—all prior to administrative action. Liberal education reform took a year to achieve agreement with broad principles. After that, its every step produced partisans for or against change, in particular directions. This process tried the patience of some, and in the Corporate University that emerged not long after, executive leadership favored more efficient decision making.

Near the end of the Shriver administration Provost Brown had an idea about thinking ahead. He invited any member of the faculty to submit a "position paper idea" about Miami's future. He got thirty-three proposals. These were "refereed" by faculty members of University Council, with contributors chosen for a two-week workshop to exchange views and write their papers. As a shrinking demographic of traditional college students threatened admissions levels and budget difficulties loomed, in June 1980 nine faculty and staff, and the provost, issued *Miami Faculty Perspectives*. Topics foreshadowed areas of turbulence to come: governance; university planning; how "heritage" should affect policy; improving liberal education; student learning outcomes; achieving "excellence by specialization;" residential programs; enhancing teaching; affirmative action. Several of these, such as the paper on governance, were early calls for change that would be enacted. The affirmative action paper measured Miami policy against federal laws, court decisions, and the university's track record of diversifying faculty and students. It found shortcomings.

Paul G. Pearson assumed the presidency in the fall of 1981. He had a doctorate in zoology from the University of Florida and a record as a distinguished faculty member and ecologist. With his wife, Winifred, he came to Oxford from the office of provost at Rutgers University. Pearson's first address to the university set forth plainspoken goals. He favored reviewing programs at all levels, improving continuing education, reducing the number of committees, adding named professorships, raising salaries, recruiting for diversity, and raising new funds. He was particularly keen on fiscal planning. He proposed writing a five-year master plan coordinated in the president's office. He would solicit opinions broadly, draft a plan for review and criticism, revise the plan and give it presidential approval before "decisions are communicated to the appropriate people for implementation." He underlined the "broad-based and participatory" element of planning, but made clear where responsibility would be located.

Paul G. Pearson, president of Miami University, 1981–92. Painting by Charles Meng, 2007. Miami University.

I will invite and use the views of the faculty, staff, and students in the development of general policy. I will also make every effort to communicate the nature of the decisions reached, how I reached them, the financial resources or other constraints which influenced the decisions, and the degree of consensus about the decisions. But I must also state that sometimes an overwhelming consensus will not or cannot be reached; and for the good of the University, I will nevertheless have to make a decision.

President Pearson brought a decisive frame of mind, a willingness to lead by personal involvement, and a posture that called on faculty and staff to share responsibility for building Miami's public image.

The message that each of us must carry to our families, our friends, our associates, and the public is that institutions of quality such as Miami University are of significant public value. Further, we need to emphasize that the work of the University results in an educated citizenry, the people we need to run the modern machinery of our high-technology society, and the business and community leaders of tomorrow. We need to emphasize how much the arts and humanities add to the quality of life in a region. Each of us in his or her own way must take the responsibility to speak positively of the benefits of higher education to the citizens of the state. In this way, Ohio's citizens will be prepared to appreciate the significance of their investment for the long-range economic and cultural well-being of the state. Certainly the President has a leading role in conveying the institutional image to decision-makers and to the citizens of Ohio. But I want each of you to understand that you have a responsibility, too.

TAKING EXCEPTION

In five years Richard Moll would give Miami's image unprecedented national visibility, but on the Oxford campus there were clear signs of underlying conflict. Faculty and staff workload indicators were rising as enrollment continued to grow. Between 1965 and 1980 the number of baccalaureate degrees granted annually increased by 48 percent, from 1,603 to 3,077. The numbers of new degrees granted in business and in natural sciences, in particular, were well above national averages. In the same period the university operating budget rose from less than $20 million to more than $80 million, and expenditures of the Educational and General fund more than doubled, while state subsidy, which had risen sharply to 1970, leveled off. Student-faculty ratios fluctuated slightly during this period, from a low of 21:1 to a high of 25:1. There was one plainly negative trend. When expressed in constant 1967 dollars, faculty salaries had increased sharply and steadily in every professorial rank between 1965 and 1970, then declined steadily in every rank to 1980.

Some faculty perceived this as a mismatch of public image and faculty welfare, at least as measured by income. During the 1980s, while reform of the honors and liberal education programs and a basic change in governance were playing out, there would also be new scrutiny in program review across Miami's campuses, plus departmental realignments, selective cuts, and highly visible program eliminations such as the closing of McGuffey Laboratory School. In this milieu a three-year campaign was conducted by a faculty group to affiliate the Miami University Faculty Association (MUFA) with the American Association of University Professors. A positive vote in a state-governed representation election would place all continuing Miami faculty in a collective bargaining unit.

Advocates in favor saw "a growing and increasingly centralized administration which has become corporate management," and cited, among other concerns, a "unilateral decision" to reduce health insurance benefits, "the persistent creation of ad hoc committees and commissions without University Council, now University Senate, involvement," and the transfer of funds into "reserves created out of unrestricted public money" without consulting faculty committees, or in opposition to their advice. The bargaining initiative was contested. Twenty-five faculty announced formation of "Faculty for Collegial Governance," a group opposing collective bargaining as "further deterioration of the collegial tradition." To demonstrate the impact of faculty opinion on

THINK ABOUT IT...
VOTE "NO"
ON APRIL 11 or 12

FOR CERTAIN EMPLOYEES OF

MIAMI UNIVERSITY

INSTRUCTIONS: 1. MARK AN "X" IN THE SQUARE OF YOUR CHOICE.
2. MAKE NO OTHER MARKS ON THIS BALLOT.
3. DO NOT SIGN THIS BALLOT.

DO YOU WISH TO BE REPRESENTED FOR PURPOSES OF COLLECTIVE BARGAINING BY:

MIAMI UNIVERSITY FACULTY ASSOCIATION/
AMERICAN ASSOCIATION OF UNIVERSITY
PROFESSORS

*COMPULSORY union dues or "fair share" assessments
*MORE administrators and higher expenses
*RISK of strikes
*INTERVENTION by national AAUP headquarters
*ADVERSARIAL environment
*ONE union group speaks for all

NO REPRESENTATIVE

*PROTECTS your equal voice in governance
*RETAINS the right to criticize administrative decisions
*PROMOTES collegial action to change policies
*AVOIDS expenses associated with collective bargaining
*PRESERVES the collegial character of the faculty

Miami Faculty for Collegial Governance

Flyer, Miami Faculty for Collegial Governance, 1989. Miami Archives.

administrators through existing structures, a Faculty Assembly referendum was used to create "Collegial Evaluation of Administrators." Miami administrators displayed favorable comparisons of average salary increases by percent with increases in the consumer price index for 1981 to 1988, as well as data on "total compensation"—salaries plus fringe benefits valued at an additional 24.5% of salary.

On April 11 and 12, 1989, more than 85 percent of eligible faculty voted in the first election conducted by the State Employee Relations Board under Ohio's collective bargaining law adopted in 1984. The outcome was 243 in favor of MUFA/AAUP representation and 416 opposed. President Pearson said the vote "establishes a strong faculty consensus in opposition to collective bargaining," but added, "the reservoir of good will in the university has suffered." He called for "a time of healing, a time of listening and planning together to strengthen the university." MUFA leaders told the *Miami Student* they would "work through existing university governance structures to affect change." The director of the news bureau credited "alternative methods of governance reform such as annual evaluation of administrators" with a "significant impact on the vote."

PURSUING AFRICAN AMERICAN DIVERSITY

President Pearson was committed to vigorous affirmative action and took advantage of favorable court rulings and a supportive national legal environment to implement a "voluntary affirmative action" program that facilitated new minority hires. This meant that if an academic hiring unit had never had an African American faculty member on continuing appointment, and a pool of applicants for a position included minority candidates qualified for appointment, the search committee legally could, and by policy should, interview the highest-ranked minority candidate along with other highly ranked candidates. That strategy provided a level of candidate consideration that had not previously existed, and although it was controversial in some departments and programs, more minority faculty were hired.

PURSUING MULTICULTURAL DIVERSITY

The history of Asians in the United States over the last two hundred years has been in large part determined by immigration policies and laws. In the late nineteenth and early twentieth centuries the U.S. Congress passed laws and adopted policies severely restricting immigration from China and Japan, including the Chinese Exclusion Act of 1882, renewed in 1892 and 1902 and extended indefinitely in 1904, and the Gentlemen's Agreement with Japan of 1908. The 1917 Immigration Act created the "Asiatic Barred Zone" that extended restrictions on immigration to other Asian nations, and the 1924 Immigration Act made Asian immigrants ineligible for naturalization as U.S. citizens. After World War II these strict policies began to ease, and in 1965 comprehensive immigration policy reform removed restrictions on Asian immigration. Asians then became one of the fastest-growing minority groups in the United States.

Myrtis H. Powell, executive assistant to the president, 1981–89, vice president for student affairs, 1989–2002. Miami Archives.

The arrival of Asians and Asian Americans at Miami paralleled the larger national history of immigration. There were fewer than thirty Asian students at Miami before 1940. The first Asian students at Miami appear to have been two Chinese, both from Canton. Ha Lew attended Miami's preparatory school in 1904–5, while Yim Shew was the first Asian student to attend the University, in 1907–8. The first Asian student who graduated from Miami was Kiyoshi Tomizawa from Japan, who began at the preparatory school in 1907 and received a BA in liberal arts in 1912. Tomizawa received the Bishop Medal in 1937, awarded to alumni for meritorious service to humanity. Asian students came earlier to the Western College for Women, and during the 1950s the college developed a curriculum based on international and

Oxford and Miami African Americans

A Timeline of Change, 1970–1995

adapted from Miami University Libraries *African-American Timeline*

1970   In April, African American students joined a Vietnam War protest in Rowan Hall, headquarters of Naval ROTC, to draw attention to black student grievances, particularly the lack of African American faculty, students, and curricula. In October, the Association for Black Faculty and Staff was formed, with mathematics professor Robert Smith as president. Total number of black faculty at Miami was twelve.

1971   The Office of Black Student Affairs became the Office of Minority Student Affairs under Student Affairs. William Hargraves II was named the university's first African American Air Force ROTC officer.

1973   Miami adopted affirmative action guidelines. William Slover, university secretary, was assigned as first affirmative action officer. Professor Marian Musgrave was named director of the Black Studies Program. The Miami Gospel Singers, directed by graduate student Eddie Jones, performed its first Christmas concert.

1975   A survey of African American students suggested there was much to be done to improve campus racial climate. Miami enrolled 299 African American students in a total student population of 14,200. During the previous five years, the number of black faculty dropped to 6 among 566 continuing faculty.

1976   A U.S. Department of Health, Education, and Welfare study ranked Miami last among Ohio schools in minority student enrollment, at 2.8 percent of the total student body.

1976–77   A committee on the status of women and racial or ethnic minorities concluded "there are deep and disturbing divisions between males and females, blacks and nonblacks, as to the most basic issues of equality" and asked for a Black Cultural Center. In September the Multicultural Center opened in Bishop Hall.

1979   The board of trustees approved steps intended to improve minority recruitment efforts. The Miami Gospel Singers began its annual Gospel Fest.

1981   Despite attempts to recruit minority students, Miami ranked lowest of Ohio colleges in percentage of minority students on campus, at 2.5 percent. The Minority Student Affairs Office reported black freshman enrollment at a three-year low of 62 African Americans among 3,500 entering students. There were 7 African American faculty, 7 professional staff, and 4 administrative staff. Black civil service workers comprised approximately 5 percent of classified staff. The Pearson administration implemented a vigorous affirmative action program to increase the number of black and women faculty, administrators, and professional staff.

1981   Myrtis Powell, PhD, was appointed executive assistant to President Paul G. Pearson. Under the oversight of Director of Minority Student Affairs Lawrence Young, the Bridges program invited black high school seniors to weekends on campus.

1982–86   African American basketball player Ron Harper set numerous university records, including most games started, most points scored, best scoring average, and most field goals. Harper would later help win three NBA championships with the Chicago Bulls and two with the Los Angeles Lakers.

1980–85   African American undergraduate student enrollment increased from 250 (1.9 percent) to 297 (2.2 percent). Black civil service employment remained steady at 5 percent to 6 percent. There were 15 black faculty, 16 professional staff, and 9 administrative staff. Ohio Governor Richard Celeste named alumnus and business executive Wayne Embry, Class of 1958, as Miami's first African American trustee.

1985   John Cager was elected Miami's first African American student body president.

1986   Affirmative action report, *Status of Black Faculty, Staff, and Students*, indicated modest success in the administration's affirmative action efforts.

(continued)

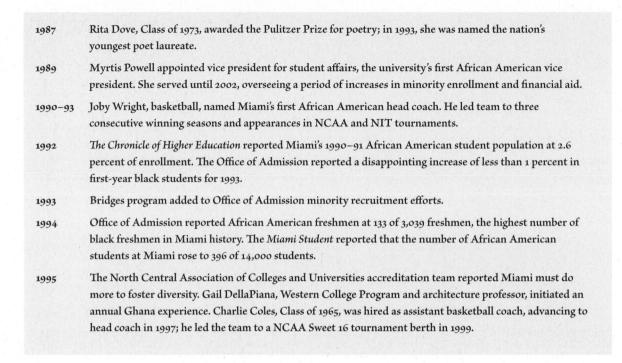

1987   Rita Dove, Class of 1973, awarded the Pulitzer Prize for poetry; in 1993, she was named the nation's youngest poet laureate.

1989   Myrtis Powell appointed vice president for student affairs, the university's first African American vice president. She served until 2002, overseeing a period of increases in minority enrollment and financial aid.

1990–93   Joby Wright, basketball, named Miami's first African American head coach. He led team to three consecutive winning seasons and appearances in NCAA and NIT tournaments.

1992   *The Chronicle of Higher Education* reported Miami's 1990–91 African American student population at 2.6 percent of enrollment. The Office of Admission reported a disappointing increase of less than 1 percent in first-year black students for 1993.

1993   Bridges program added to Office of Admission minority recruitment efforts.

1994   Office of Admission reported African American freshmen at 133 of 3,039 freshmen, the highest number of black freshmen in Miami history. The *Miami Student* reported that the number of African American students at Miami rose to 396 of 14,000 students.

1995   The North Central Association of Colleges and Universities accreditation team reported Miami must do more to foster diversity. Gail DellaPiana, Western College Program and architecture professor, initiated an annual Ghana experience. Charlie Coles, Class of 1965, was hired as assistant basketball coach, advancing to head coach in 1997; he led the team to a NCAA Sweet 16 tournament berth in 1999.

intercultural studies, including a focus on the "Far East." Many students from abroad studied, with financial support, at Western. Summer seminars held abroad often connected with Western's international alumnae, while visiting faculty from China, the Philippines, and Japan taught at Western during the academic year.

After World War II Miami experienced an increase in Asian students, especially from China, Japan, Korea, the Philippines, and Thailand. In 1955 there were around 40 students from various Asian nations, while in 1995 there were around 140. The population of Asian American students at Miami grew throughout the twentieth century, rising from about 40 in 1980 to 220 in 1990 to 450 in 2005. By 1991 there were 33 Asian American faculty members, and by 2005 there were 48.

The first course to focus on Asian or Asian American subject matter was Far Eastern Politics, offered in the government department by Professor Harold Vinacke in 1919–20. The Department of East Asian Languages and Literatures, offering courses in Chinese and Japanese, was begun in 1965–66 but was merged into a new department of German, Russian, and East Asian Languages (GREAL) in 1972. In 2007, Miami began offering courses in Hindi, and offered Korean more regularly. Topical courses on Asian American literature and drama were offered in the late 1990s, and Asian American Literature became a Miami Plan foundation course in the Department of English in 2003—the first course in Miami's curriculum focused exclusively on Asian

American culture. Introduction to Asian American Studies was offered in 2005 through the American Studies Program. By 2006 the Farmer School of Business was creating new programs in Korea and China.

Cocurricular opportunities for exploring Asian and Asian American culture have a longer history. In the 1920s the Cosmopolitan Club sought to create an option for international and American students to learn about different cultures and traditions. In the twenty-first century student groups such as the Japanese Culture and Language Club, Asian American Association, Chinese Students and Scholars Friendship Association, and Indian Students Association have sponsored a variety of events to celebrate and share cultural traditions while also making a place for themselves at Miami.

Ron Harper, Miami basketball all-time points record holder, 1982–86. *Miami Archives.*

DEMOGRAPHICS OF CHANGE

The last three decades of the twentieth century were marked by dramatic social changes spurred by movements for civil rights for African Americans, women, gays and lesbians, and people with disabilities, as well as by a nationwide sexual revolution, the emergence of new media, and the increasing consumer power of the baby boom generation. These changes brought white women and people of color into higher education, accompanied by an influx of white women into the larger labor market, rising numbers of dual-income families, Title IX legislation, gradual acceptance of newly visible gender and sexual identities, and rising ages for marriage and first childbirth. These trends stimulated new curricular offerings and affected daily life on Miami's campuses.

The dramatic increase in employment of women over the past fifty years transformed work and family arrangements. In 1970 about 40 percent of married women with children were employed, compared to 75 percent in 2002. Such changes generated childcare needs. Childcare centers were created after the mid-1970s at Hamilton and Middletown campuses, where nontraditional students created a demand for them. Both were originally parent coops, funded in part by Student Affairs as a student organization and in part by parent-students who volunteered at the centers. Both campuses had childcare centers with hired staff by 1997, and in 2005 both received accreditation. In May 1997 a university survey confirmed pressing need for affordable childcare in Oxford, and five years later the Miami University Child Development Center opened on Miami's Western Campus. A need-based parent grant

Tuesday, June 6, 1989, started as another routine morning for me until 7:00 a.m. when I turned on the television news as I always did before I left for my office. I could not believe my ears and eyes. Headlines on every channel were reporting a "military crackdown in Tiananmen Square," Beijing, People's Republic of China, in response to a prodemocracy march organized by university students. Even more striking was a camera shot showing a column of armored tanks which almost came to a halt when a lone prodemocracy protester wearing a white shirt raised his right hand and walked right in front of the muzzled cannon of the lead tank. This image was a unique one compared to the prodemocracy marches by large groups of students that had been occurring for weeks in Chinese cities under the watchful eyes of government agents.

I knew from my many years of service on the Graduate Council and English Language Proficiency Committee that Miami University had a large contingent of graduate students from China. As soon as I arrived in my office, I contacted Jianguo Wu, president of the Chinese Student Association, regarding the conditions of Chinese students on campus and their family members and friends in China. Although our Chinese students were generally reluctant to speak openly about sensitive political issues back home, it became clear to me that they were emotionally distressed, extremely worried about relatives and friends, and apprehensive about their own future because of the serious incident in Tiananmen Square that morning. I felt they needed strong moral support from the university during this time of confusion. I assured Jianguo that I would convey Chinese students' concerns to the appropriate university authorities.

I called President Paul Pearson directly that morning and related my conversation with Jianguo. President Pearson was aware of the Tiananmen situation and agreed immediately to offer his moral support to the Chinese students and their family members. However, President Pearson added that "we need to provide more than just moral support." I was thrilled by his comments and assured him that I would convey his concerns immediately to Dr. Joseph Urell, associate provost; Dr. Gary Knock, associate dean of the Graduate School; and Mr. Donald Nelson, director of international education services. The same afternoon, Dr. Urell informed me that, at the president's direction, he was working with the graduate dean on several academic and other support programs for the Chinese students. He asked me to organize a meeting of all Chinese students and their spouses with President Pearson in a day or two.

That afternoon, I met with Jianguo and several other Chinese students. I relayed the message from Dr. Urell and requested that all members of Miami's Chinese community attend this very important meeting with President Pearson. When concerns were expressed about possible political reprisals against the families of meeting participants, I assured the students that President Pearson was determined not to do anything that might harm them in any way. Mr. Nelson's office subsequently invited all thirty-nine Chinese students enrolled at Miami to attend. The meeting was held Friday afternoon June 9, 1989, at the Shriver Center Towers Room. President Pearson, Dr. Urell, Dr. Knock, Vice President for Student Affairs Myrtis Powell and Associate Vice President Gilbert Siegel, Donald Nelson, News Bureau Assistant Director Donna Boen, Communications Department Chair Gerald Sanders, and I were present. Several other faculty members and department chairs also attended, as well as a large number of Chinese students and their spouses. It was an extraordinary gathering, so many high administrators assembled to address the concerns of one group of our international students. What followed was even more extraordinary.

President Pearson opened by thanking everyone for their attendance, and specifically, the Chinese students for choosing Miami as their institution of higher learning. He expressed his personal concern, support, and sympathy, and that of all Americans, for the Chinese students and their families in light of the recent events at Tiananmen Square. The president went on to assure the students that the university would provide all necessary educational and emotional support to reduce their anxiety and to enable them to complete their Miami education successfully. Dr. Urell, on behalf of the president, announced several specific support initiatives for the Chinese students. These included a request that department chairs and faculty allow students up to an extra semester to complete academic assignments, theses, or dissertations. Other initiatives included a general extension of student assistantships and other financial support, and a year's extension of admission and assistantships for Chinese students admitted for next fall but currently lacking passports to leave China. Dr. Powell announced that the university counseling service would provide individual counseling to Chinese students and their spouses. Also, each student would be permitted two free long-distance telephone calls anywhere in the U.S.A. or China. This offer was very significant in that pre-cell phone and pre-e-mail era. Don Nelson closed, expressing his personal concern and full support for Chinese students and for their families, many of whom were seeking to maintain the visa status required for completion of academic degrees.

In the wake of this extraordinary meeting, on June 13, 1989, Provost E. Fred Carlisle sent the following memorandum to all deans, department chairs, and summer session faculty.

The events of recent weeks in the People's Republic of China have been especially disturbing to Miami's community of Chinese students. Many are concerned about the well being of family and friends and apprehensive about their own futures. In some cases, the emotional strain of unfolding events has been sufficiently distracting to affect students' ability to concentrate and to keep abreast of their work. During this particularly trying time, I urge you to be sensitive to the deep concerns of our Chinese students and considerate of their special academic needs.

On Monday morning, June 12, 1989, I contacted Jianguo about the reactions of Chinese students to President Pearson's comments and special support initiatives. In an excited voice, he told me that everyone was very happy and grateful for the kind words and support of President Pearson and other university officials. I asked him if he had written a letter of thanks to President Pearson. When he told me he had not, I encouraged him to do so. The next

day, he and his co-officers sent the following message to President Pearson.

On behalf of all Chinese students and their spouses at Miami University, we wish to express our appreciation to you and university authority for your sympathy, concerns and understanding of our situation at this very special moment. Especially, we would like to thank all university officials and professors who attended the meeting with us on last Friday (June 9, 1989).

We, all Chinese students, feel honorable and joyful to study at Miami University. We would like to think that it is also our responsibility to try our best to keep the academic excellence and to bring about an even better image of Miami University.

President Pearson's compassionate leadership and support initiatives in the wake of the Tiananmen military crackdown did not compromise university academic standards nor cause a serious budget deficit. In contrast to the scene of inhumanity displayed in Tiananmen Square, Paul Pearson and his colleagues set a gold standard for how an American university should care for its international students, living far from home, in a strange and foreign land.

J. K. Bhattacharjee, Professor Emeritus, Microbiology

program provided financial assistance for eligible faculty, staff, and students to help defer costs of sending their children to the center.

The Oxford campus experienced changes in student gender composition that matched national trends. In the late 1940s male students outnumbered females. That proportion shifted in the late 1970s. At Miami, the proportion of women students rose to 53 percent of the undergraduate population by 1980, and women continued to outnumber men after that time. The percentage of women graduate students increased even more. In 1970, one-third of Miami's graduate students were women, and by 1990 women comprised over 50 percent.

There were also clear trends in residential preferences. By 1935–36 Miami's enrollment surpassed 2,500 and more than half, about 57 percent, lived in university-provided housing. In 1955–56 the percentage of students living on campus—72 percent of a total enrollment of 5,219—was at its highest point in the twentieth century. By 1974–75 enrollment was booming at 12,442, yet because of postwar building programs Miami could still accommodate more than 60 percent on campus. However, in the decade between 1980 and 1990 enrollment continued to rise and the percentage of students living on campus declined to about 46 percent. A decade later in 2001–2, enrollment was 16,757 with about 42 percent on campus in Oxford. In 2006, with about 39 percent living on campus, some 68 percent of sophomores elected to do so, about 35 percent of juniors and approximately 10 to 15 percent of seniors. Perhaps in an effort to attract more students to campus living when facing competition from off-campus rentals, room assignment policies were altered to reduce occupancy per room. This resulted in the number of beds decreasing from a high of almost 8,000 in 1983–84 to about 7,000 in 2004–5. By 2007 only first-year students and new transfer students were expected to live in residence halls, although a proposal to reinstate the requirement that all sophomores live on campus was approved that year, to be implemented fall 2009, with the objective of creating a more intellectually engaged living experience.

These trends appeared because Miami enrollment continued to expand throughout the Public Ivy era without a corresponding expansion of housing. Tappan Hall, the last Cellarius structure, was completed in 1970. No other new residence hall was built until 1983, when Havighurst Hall was completed on Western Campus, although Miami did acquire Thompson, Clawson, Mary Lyon, McKee, and Peabody residence halls during that interval. After 1983, however, Miami was neither building halls nor acquiring them. At the same time, off-campus options became more attractive to students—new apartment complexes designed with appealing amenities, as well as more rental properties available near Uptown as faculty and staff moved out of the Mile Square. Private enterprise stepped vigorously into the market for off-campus housing after the mid-1980s. Miami attempted to influence student residential choices by increasing the number of coeducational and themed residence halls and by offering more comfortable accommodations along with flexible meal plans and dining options. It built no new housing, however, until construction of luxury apartments, Heritage Commons, on Chestnut Street in the early twenty-first century. They were designed to compete with off-campus apartments that offered students a higher degree of autonomy, instead of following Miami's older practice of requiring students to live together in residence halls where peer community could more readily be cultivated. The beginning point of these housing trends coincided approximately, perhaps ironically, with publication of *The Public Ivys* in 1985.

Changes in student residential patterns affected transportation. The Miami Metro bus system began running in August 1990 to accommodate increasing numbers of Oxford students living off campus. Throughout the 1980s students had been officially prohibited from bringing cars. Some could receive permission to have a car, and an increasing number brought cars to Oxford with or without permission. The popular drive-through fast food chain McDonald's opened in Oxford during the 1983–84 school year, new student condominiums were showcased on the west side of town near a new Kroger grocery, and the *Recensio* ran a "House Photo Contest" where the most popular pose showed partying students happily gathered around beer kegs.

By 1989, in a continuing quest for more student autonomy, the "No-Car Rule" was under serious assault. A student survey returned results saying there were 5,351 "unregistered" student cars in Oxford. It also said that 60 percent of all students wished to bring a car to Miami and claimed that their main reasons were "to run errands" and "travel to home." In that year a color-coded parking permit system was implemented. In August 2004 the no-car rule was lifted for all except first-year students, who were still required to petition for permission to keep a car. By the end of the Public Ivy era in the middle 1990s there was steady pressure for more parking, and in the late 1990s Miami began to construct parking facilities.

The increasing number of students living off campus transformed the Oxford community by displacing faculty, staff, and the local population from Oxford's Mile Square. Through at least the 1970s most faculty probably had an informal expectation that they would live in Oxford or its immediate area. By the 1980s, however, faculty in increasing numbers began to live in Cincinnati, Dayton, and their growing suburbs. Perhaps in an effort to entice new faculty to stay closer, or at least to ease their transition to southwest Ohio, Miami maintained two dozen residential rental properties, and from 2003 to 2008 offered a forgivable loan program to assist faculty and staff in purchasing homes in the City of Oxford.

NO CARS

Miami's no-car rule came into existence in 1919 when it replaced the university's no-horse rule. In 1970, the no-car policy read, "A student while enrolled at Miami University shall not have or drive a motor powered vehicle (including two-wheeled motor vehicles) without prior University permission." The *Catalogue* bluntly elaborated on this decree: "Students who feel it is desirable to bring a motor vehicle to college, but have no need for one, should select another institution." This reiterated the institution's long-standing position regarding student automobiles and reaffirmed the university's *in loco parentis* philosophy.

Proponents of the no-car policy were plentiful, and their resistance to change was fierce. In 1970, Vice President Etheridge predicted "a near disaster if the University were to liberalize the automobile regulation. . . . The introduction of cars would have an immediate impact on the community. . . . It would definitely make it more of a suitcase college." Mayor Calvin Conrad forecast, "A liberalization or change of the present University car policies would only create many problems in Oxford and increase tax costs for

Miami car impound lot, 1965.
Miami Archives.

citizens." Roy Young, president of the Oxford Retail Merchants Association, said the village "could just not handle the volume of traffic which would flood the downtown areas." In a 1972 letter to alumni, President Shriver gave an educational rationale: "The no car regulation makes sense academically in that the presence of automobiles does, indeed, tend to detract from the student's application of his time and energy to his studies."

Student leaders rejected arguments that automobiles would compromise academic achievements, safety, or campus and village aesthetics. Their fervor to rescind the no-car policy symbolized something more than gaining mobility—it represented a growing desire to redefine their relationship with the university. For two years they surveyed peers about the no-car policy, held awareness campaigns, and introduced student government resolutions. As conventional efforts to initiate change failed, students came to realize that if change on this issue was to occur within usual channels, it would be incremental, deliberate, and slow.

Their bold reaction—an unprecedented step—was to take Miami to court. On matters of personal autonomy, gone were the days when administrators and students resolved "family" disputes by private negotiation. In 1972 Robert Destro filed a lawsuit against Miami in Butler County Common Pleas Court for withholding his final grades, transcript, and diploma because of an unpaid Uptown parking violation for his unregistered car. Destro argued that the university's authority over a student did not extend beyond the campus to include the town. The courts concluded that "withholding grades and diploma for a student's failure to pay a penalty imposed by the university for a motor vehicle violation is too severe except in the case of repeat offenders." Judge Fred Cramer ordered Miami to certify Destro's grades and award him a diploma, and ordered Destro to pay his $15.00 parking fine. Although a clear victory for Destro, the decision was anything but a triumph for the campaign against the no-car rule, as an excerpt of Judge Cramer's ruling reveals: "A university may adopt standards of conduct to be complied with by the students off the geographical campus when such standards are reasonable and necessary and bear a reasonable relationship to the University's carrying out its educational functions and mission."

However, students were not laying this issue aside. After five more years a 1977 *Miami Student* editorial captured both the dismay of students at the pace of change and their unswerving determination to continue the fight. "It's almost an annual event now; the administration killing of student resolutions and actions of the past year dealing with the no-car rule just before the year ends. But this spring, things may be different. Senior Political Science major John Magera has filed a class action suit against Miami in protest of the no-car rule."

Like Destro, Magera argued in Butler County Common Pleas Court that Miami trustees lacked jurisdiction over Oxford. He explained. "I am really involved with civil rights and liberties and I'd like to see this inequity end." Unlike Destro, Magera pursued the constitutionality of the no-car rule, but after a prolonged and expensive legal battle the court dismissed his lawsuit on a technicality. By the time it was prepared to hear his complaint Magera had graduated. The court refused to act. Student body president-elect John Coble reacted: "The University is treating us essentially as nonadults. . . . We're offended and insulted. . . . They're depriving individuals of their due process. It's a classic example of the University dictating students' lifestyles." In 1978, students David Starr, Stuart Bassin, and Edwin Dean Townsend filed a third lawsuit against the no-car policy. Miami requested dismissal but the battle continued. Months later, Starr, Bassin, and Townsend abruptly withdrew. Peers speculated that the plaintiffs lacked funds for the legal battle.

President Shriver attempted to create a solution to the controversy acceptable to both the university and the city by creating a joint Oxford-Miami committee to again study the issue of cars in Oxford. By February 1979 the committee submitted recommendations. Student body president Steve Ricchetti endorsed their proposals, a result of three years of coordination between student government and Miami administration. Proposed changes would allow upperclassmen to have cars in the Oxford area but not on Miami property. The proposed policy also restricted first-year students from having cars unless they commuted or had a physical disability. The university submitted the committee's report to Oxford Council, which tabled action due to a perception that the committee had "exceeded its charge."

In February 1980 the joint committee presented a final report to the trustees that included modest recommendations for change: designation of streets with no parking between 3:00 a.m. and 5:00 a.m. and certain streets with 24- and 72-hour parking limits in return for curbside parking permits for residents with no off-street parking options. Trustees did not act on these recommendations, arguing that they needed time to study proposed changes. Frustrated student government leaders then solicited the assistance of the American Civil Liberties Union in Columbus. The ACLU prepared a memorandum in August 1980 concluding that the university did not have legal authority to control student use of cars by either contract or state statute. Associated Student Government, in conjunction with the ACLU, held public meetings to determine if students would support another class-action suit against Miami University. ASG and the ACLU's months of planning resulted in a class action suit against the no-car rule in April of 1981. Federal District Court Judge Carl B. Rubin upheld the no-car rule. He argued that "University officials have inherent authority to make all necessary and proper rules and regulations for the orderly management of their institution."

Despite persistent activism and public engagement with policy formation, becoming a force in implementing institutional change on automobile regulations was no easy task for students during the Public Ivy era. As that era passed into history, however, the no-car rule was eroded by a new administration's increasingly permissive review of permit eligibility. In 1997 a joint City of Oxford and Miami task force recommended abolition of the "No-Car Rule" for undergraduates, and this time the university took a significant step in that direction by permitting all seniors to bring cars to campus. The following year, that permission was extended to juniors, and in 2004 to sophomores. Freshmen would now be the only class still required to justify bringing automobiles to campus.

"TAKE RISKS"

In 1993 President Pearson retired and Paul G. Risser (1993–95) assumed the Miami presidency. Risser grew up on a wheat and cattle farm near Blackwell, Oklahoma, attended Grinnell College, and earned a doctorate at the University of Wisconsin. An expert in grassland and forested ecosystems and landscape ecology, Risser was a fellow of the American Academy of Arts and Sciences and of the American Association for the Advancement of Science. Just before coming to Miami he was vice president for research and provost at the University of New Mexico.

President Risser brought a sense of humor, a national perspective on the importance of strengthening the intellectual climate, and a devotion to achieving multicultural diversity in order to create a contemporary learning

Inaugural Address of Paul G. Risser, April 16, 1993

We must profit from our history, not be a prisoner of it. As one of the nation's premier institutions, Miami University will also change, albeit slowly, with adequate discussion (perhaps even more than adequate discussion) but with an unwavering eye on the essence of quality.

With the burgeoning number of facts spewing forth into our world today, and the multitude of ways in which we are bombarded with this firehose stream of information, it becomes increasingly important to be able to sift through information, to find what is significant and decide how information is significant.

This sifting and winnowing is only possible if one has a broad basis from which to evaluate, if one recognizes that information can be used in different ways, and if one is adept at critically evaluating the quality of information. These evaluative characteristics are the ingredients of success in any scholarly endeavor, in any profession, in solving problems of society, and they are the basis for life-long learning. It is just these characteristics that make the Miami Plan such a powerful focal point for the education of Miami graduates.

But the Miami Plan is not just a change in the curriculum. It is an invitation to the faculty and staff to be innovative, to experiment, to try entirely new approaches, to take risks. It is a new context in which to re-evaluate the entire curriculum, to question whether the current structure of each major program meets the intellectual rigor expected by the discipline and meets the needs of its graduates, both today and tomorrow.

The Miami Plan and the surrounding curricular changes demand that we increase the intensity of the intellectual climate on campus. We will expect more.

We know that different people learn in different ways. These different styles are partly innate, but they also depend upon our cultural origins, on our history, on our economic status, and on a host of other formative experiences. This diversity has two major implications. First, because students learn in different ways, and because we come to understand ideas in different ways, the best colleges will of necessity provide a variety of learning experiences and approaches. Today may be the most exciting time ever for building a rich academic experience because we now know more about the processes of peer education and learning in groups as well as learning by individuals.

If we are to maximize this situation, there must be a variety of different kinds of peers if we are to provide the richest learning environment. This is why the ethnic and

Paul G. Risser, president of Miami University, 1993–95. Miami Archives.

cultural representation on this campus must become more diverse. Providing this intellectual and cultural diversity remains one of our most vexing, yet important imperatives. We must succeed.

In that future, this university will become intellectually more intense. It should become a cauldron of intellectual ferment, where issues of all kinds are discussed and considered. We need to become more proficient in this discourse.

We will all demand more of ourselves, we will challenge ourselves not just in productivity but in our approach to life, generosity, compassion, integrity, responsibility, participation, tolerance, curiosity, courage. . . . There will be invigorated peer leaning styles; greater integration of undergraduate and graduate learning; an expanded and more integrated concept of scholarship, with a broader array of activities that contribute to the solution of society's greatest challenges; a culturally and intellectually more diverse campus; and an increased intensity and sophistication of dialog and discourse.

environment. He had a nuanced view of student learning and scholarship, and a predilection for innovation. His time in Oxford would be marked by challenges, including a controversy over the Miami mascot. After three years he departed to assume the presidency of Oregon State University. Eight years later he became chancellor of the Oklahoma State System of Higher Education, then in 2007 was named acting director of the National Museum of Natural History at the Smithsonian Institution.

Mascot

During Miami's Public Ivy era a national controversy emerged over the use of Native American mascots by athletic teams. Miami would be among many schools to change their nicknames, but it would require an arduous 25-year process that engaged the Miami Tribe with Miami University for the first time in 163 years.

"INDIANS"

The use of Indian images by Miami students can be traced to Old Miami. "Smoking the Pipe of Peace" was a popular tradition in the late 1860s on Class Day of commencement week. Senior and junior classes selected Sachems (sometimes dressed as Indian chiefs) who verbally "roasted" members of the other class before they shared a Pipe of Peace together. The juniors kept the Pipe of Peace to be passed to the next year's junior class. The Pipe of Peace tradition was revived by the class of 1897.

When New Miami revived the *Miami Student* in 1888, its masthead included a peace pipe graphic for a year. The peace pipe then appeared on the editorial page until 1891. In April 1910, the *Student* masthead depicted an Indian in a beaded sash, facing a tower of Old Main. That graphic appeared on page one throughout the 1910–11 school year and then on the editorial page until July 1914. The cover of Alfred Upham's *A Pageant of Miami History* in 1916 used a pipe image.

Peace pipe graphic, Miami Student, November 1888.

Indian depiction, Miami Student, April 21, 1910.

339

"REDSKINS"

Until the 1920s few nicknames were commonly used for Miami athletes. In 1889 a joint faculty-student committee chose scarlet and white as official colors, though by 1909 the student handbook listed varsity colors as red and white. By the mid-teens the "Red and White" was a popular designation for teams. Scrapbook clippings of the football squad captain have phrases like "the Red and White team," "Red and White Beat Cincy," "dual meet won by Red and White." In 1916, 1917, and 1918, as Miami enjoyed undefeated seasons, a new team designation emerged: the "Big Red."

Ralph J. McGinnis, Class of 1921, was class president, associate editor of the *Recensio,* and athletic editor and editor of the *Miami Student.* With Professor Upham as advisor, McGinnis was responsible for stories in 1919–20 that used phrases he associated with Indians—the football banquet of 1919 was the "pow wow on the commons," and a basketball headline in 1920 declared "Big Red Warriors Go on Warpath." An often-quoted line anticipating later use of "Redskins" was a January 1928 headline: "Bearcats Come to Oxford Saturday Seeking Hides of Big Red-Skinned Warriors." When Upham became president in 1928 he hired McGinnis as publicity director. The October 1936 *Alumni Newsletter,* likely written by McGinnis, said "Miami reveled in the name 'Big Reds' until 1928 when R. J. McGinnis, Miami publicity director, coined the name Redskins."

The popularity of varsity sports in the 1920s led Miami and rivals like Ohio University and Ohio Wesleyan to build new football stadiums. Miami's program was doing well under the direction of George Rider and football coach Chester Pittser. Pittser came to Miami from the University of Illinois, considered one of the finest programs in the country, where the greatest college player, Red Grange, had starred. This connection may have influenced Miami's choices, for in 1926 the "Fighting Illini" began a tradition of halftime performances by an Indian mascot, Chief Illinewek.

McGinnis was ready. The *Alumni Newsletter* of March 1, 1930, carried a column titled "TRIBE MIAMI" with a silhouette of an Indian head captioned "The Big Red." With a modified headline, the *Miami Student* of March 25, 1930, ran the same article. Spurred by its football competition, Miami would now have an official mascot, with a rationale.

Henceforth and hereafter the term "Big Red" is to have a meaning. Since the state is over-run with Bearcats, Wildcats, Bobcats, Musketeers, and other such-like small deer, members of the Athletic Department went into a huddle not long ago and decided that Miami teams ought to have a monaker [sic] and a symbol. As the very name of Miami is taken from an Indian tribe and the term "Big Red" smacks of Redskins and the warpath, an Indian brave in war lock and feathers was thought a suitable insignia. This will be found displayed at appropriate places and on appropriate occasions. It is hoped that with the injection of the Big Reds into the Buckeye forests some of the other cats will be exterminated or at least tamed.

According to Indian custom, the brave on the warpath symbolizes his prowess by means of feathers in his head-dress. Every feather means something. In this brave's scalplock are two feathers indicating that two enemies have been slain. A feather worn at a slant in the back would indicate an enemy had been wounded or that the wearer had been in combat and had drawn blood. The tuft of hair just behind the forehead indicates the brave has been officially made a warrior.

"The Big Red." Alumni News Letter, *March 1, 1930.*

Descriptions of this sort aligned with stereotypes perpetuated in this period by fictional literature, history writing, Wild West shows, and Boy Scout activities. Miami was creating another version of the noble savage for use against athletic opponents. President Upham's Miami Day speech on February 19, 1930, contained the claim that "Miami University was named from the valley of the two Miami rivers in which she was located, and these in turn took their name from the Indian tribe that fished and hunted on their shaded banks." About two weeks later the silhouette mascot and rationale appeared.

Publicity that announced the *M Book* guide for new students in 1931–32 set a tone for how "Redskins" would be woven into campus lore. In May the *Student* reported, "Next year's frosh bible will carry an Indian head in white on the red leather cover instead of the traditional M. The change is thought advisable because of the popularity of the Redskin symbol." For fifteen of the next seventeen years an Indian image would be the only graphic on the *M Book* cover. The 1932 *Recensio* had the Indian silhouette in the corner of every page. Cheerleaders and coaches showed it on their garb, and the band "introduced a Redskin war chant."

The 1935 *Recensio,* in addition to the silhouette on the cover, imagined that early nineteenth-century college men coming to this university had found "one building, the one evidence of civilization in the midst of forests, dense and black, with the stillness of their solitudes seldom broken save for the war-whoop of savages." The January 1937 *Alumni Newsletter* carried a new sketch of an Indian and a rationale that considerably extended racial stereotypes of the noble savage.

The Miami Indian was the best type of noble savage. It is true that he almost always was rather high in odor, what with rancid bear grease and an aversion to water for bathing purposes, and he never missed an opportunity to lift a scalp, but he had courage and natural dignity, fought for what he thought was right, and didn't say 'Uncle!' to anybody.

None of this affirmed any actual association between the university and the Miami Tribe. Perhaps few image-makers in the 1920s and 1930s were aware that members of that Tribe were forcibly removed from Ohio and Indiana in 1846 and that their descendants were living in Oklahoma.

THE BAND INDIAN

In 1936 director A. D. Lekvold brought energy to band performances with crowd-pleasing drum majors and majorettes. The next year he petitioned the Student-Faculty Council for $75 to purchase two Indian costumes so dancers with tom-toms could "revive lost Indian traditions." Lekvold and intramural director Tom Van Voorhis created a program for the weekly assembly: Van-Voorhis presented a talk, "Indian Traditions of Miami," and the band played musical selections that featured a quartet singing a swingy arrangement of "The Scalp Song." The songwriters—President Upham for lyrics and Mayor R. H. Burke of Hamilton for music—were presented, and while the song was performed, juniors James Cerny and John Sarles performed a costumed war dance.

A photograph of the Indian performer appeared in the 1942 *Recensio.* During the 1943 and 1944 football seasons the band comprised military men instead of college students and the appearance of a woman as the Indian was one of many instances when women filled in for Miami men serving in the armed forces.

Miami University Band with Indian performer. Recensio, 1939.

"HIAWABOP"

By September 1946 veterans made up almost half of Miami's student population. Some created a magazine called the *Miami Tomahawk.* It relied on Indian images, sexual content and innuendo, and drinking references. Among its regular columns, *Off the Reservation* captured "those fantastic rumors which are always in the air." *Smoke Signals* printed letters to the editor. *Scalping Knife* allowed anonymous authors to disclose latest romantic news such as pinnings, engagements, surprising date combinations, and other juicy gossip. The *Tomahawk* was advertised in the *M Book:* "UGH! Heap smart squaws and braves savem wampum to getum THE MIAMI TOMAHAWK. . . . Get your subscription."

More caricatures appeared in 1947. By October 1948 the *Tomahawk* depicted a little pot-bellied, hook-nosed, loincloth-clad character wearing horn-rimmed glasses and sporting a "Sun Bowl Champs" award on his bare chest. He was crying, he said, because "I ain't got no name. . . . So here I am. I don't know who I am, or what I am, except that I'm an Indian." The person suggesting the best name would win ten dollars, for the character was to be a regular feature. He became eye-popping happy in the December 1948 issue: "I GOT A NAME. Just call the TOMAHAWK office and ask for 'HIAWABOP'—that's me." John MacDowell, a senior Sigma Chi, won the naming contest.

In the Homecoming 1954 issue, Hiawabop was on the inside logo page holding a stick of dynamite behind his back, with the byline "Blessed Are The Censors For They Shall Inhibit The Earth." The magazine's sexual and suggestive content had become problematic for the University Publication Committee, who declared it in "bad taste." They made no mention of caricatures, stories, and references to Indians. The last issue appeared in October 1956. Hiawabop, however, did not die, but moved to the cover of the *M Book* to point out things new students should learn about the campus. Perhaps to protest the death of *Tomahawk* magazine, the name "Hiawabop" shifted to the marching band Indian, and by the early 1950s Hiawabop's head image replaced the Indian silhouette on the bass drum. In the 1958 *Recensio*, the marching band page referred to "Hiawabop, the dancing Miami redskin."

By the 1960s any decorum that had existed in the performance of the Indian mascot was gone. If there were early attempts to dress in authentic ways, those efforts were no longer visible. The original outfit purchased by the band director had given way to a loincloth, feather headdress, and any other accessories that were useful, such as athletic socks.

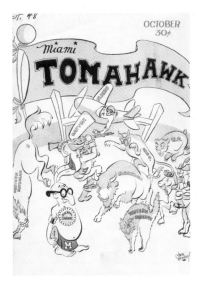

Miami Tomahawk *with Indian caricature, October 1948.* Miami Archives.

Miami Tomahawk *with "Hiawabop," October 1954.* Miami Archives.

Miami mascot performing at Homecoming pep rally. Recensio, 1967.

The "Redskin Reservation" campus snack bar. Recensio, 1949.

"THE REDSKIN RESERVATION"

In 1948 Miami converted one of the barracks brought to campus after World War II into a student eating and gathering place named the "Redskin Reservation." News articles about its opening used phrases like "Brave Meets Squaw," "New Tepee Attracts 24,000 Redskins," "Big Chief is the big wig in the wig-wam." When a new university center opened in 1957 the name "Redskin Reservation" was transferred to a short-order grill area on the lower level nicknamed "The Res." Many alumni who graduated before the early 1980s used this nickname for the entire building. By this time Indian images and references were everywhere on campus. Dining halls used Indian terms for food choices: "Big Chief—a double-decker cheeseburger; and Little Squaw—a ham-and-swiss on a twisted roll."

The cover of the May 1969 *Miami Alumnus* carried a photograph of "a life-size Indian sculpture in war-dance attitude atop a boulder." The Miami Redskin sculpture, commissioned by Pi Beta Phi sorority in recognition of their 1967 centennial and Miami's 160th year, was created by Miami Art Department chair Robert B. Butler for display in Millett Hall, Miami's basketball arena. A silhouette of this image became the new athletic representation of "Redskin" in the early 1970s. The statue would be stored in the Miami University Archives in 2007.

CONTROVERSY, 1971–72

Sports Illustrated for March 4, 2002, reported that since 1969 more than six hundred schools and minor league clubs had dropped nicknames deemed offensive by Native Americans. In December 1971, Dr. George Fathauer, professor of sociology and anthropology, met with President Shriver to share articles by Native Americans about the racist nature of Indian-related mascots. Fathauer suggested that Miami abandon "Redskins" and all related symbolism. Shriver responded that derogatory stereotyping was unintentional, and he was willing to consider arguments made in the articles. He consulted the Athletic Advisory Board, who believed the use of Indian symbols, "if produced and used as authentically and as proudly as possible, can be truly honorific and not in any sense derogatory." They said a nickname change would require a vote by the student body.

Dr. Fathauer discussed the matter with his Indians of North America class, generating student reactions both favorable and unfavorable. The class "concluded that information should be given to the student body by an article in *The Miami Student*." Fathauer asked for a student to write a letter, but the class preferred that a faculty member be the first to present this controversy to the student body. One student offered his help. In the April 4, 1972, *Miami Student*, Fathauer's letter, "Redskins and Hiawabop: Racism at Miami," appealed for elimination of the term "Redskins" and the Indian dancing character Hiawabop. Fathauer agreed that Miami never intended to derogate Indians, but pointed out that "this is one of the most pervasive aspects of racism; the dominant group is not even aware that its stereotyping is objectionable to a minority."

The motivated student from Fathauer's class roomed with the student body president, who took the idea of abolition to Student Senate. Three days later, on April 7, 1972, Student Senate voted unanimously to abolish the use of "Redskins" and remove all Indian caricatures. Student Affairs Council considered the issue May 31 and after "spirited debate" passed a motion to abolish the use of "Redskins" because it was derogatory, and to no longer use caricatures or other images with "Redskins" or any Indian mascot. The vote was 19 to 2 with four abstentions. That recommendation was sent to President Shriver. Ten days after Fathauer's letter appeared, a *Student* editorial, "A Matter of Conscience," endorsed the action of Student Senate and suggested that "Miami students, who years ago created the 'Redskin' nickname, are in 1972 in the position to correct this slur on the Indian heritage."

President Shriver had difficulty balancing the opinions of Athletics and Alumni Affairs with the position taken by Student Affairs Council, a standing committee of university governance. On June 22, 1972, he appointed an "Ad Hoc Committee to Investigate the University's Identification with the Miami Indians and with the Use of the Term 'Redskins,'" and asked for their report by September 1. That committee consisted of Fathauer and one other faculty member, one administrator, the director of alumni affairs, the director of sports information, and a former student who had performed as the Indian dancer. The committee was given two questions:

1. In what ways are the current University practices demeaning to the culture and heritage of the Miami Indian Tribe and to the American Indian in general;

2. In what ways can the University retain an appropriate identification with the Miami Indian Tribe while simultaneously pursuing a course of national leadership in providing educational opportunities for deserving American Indian students and generally enhancing our community's understanding and appreciation of this people's heritage and present needs?

Their report included two separate minority reports plus nineteen appendices. The major issues yielded split opinions: retention of "Redskins" was favored 5–2; elimination of Hiawabop was favored 6–1. Several suggestions were unanimous: eliminate all derogatory caricatures; encourage elimination of derogatory items sold in local stores; change the student eating area name from "Redskin Reservation" to just "RES;" insist that all Indian dress and activities must be authentic, dignified, and in good taste. The committee recommended placing emphasis on Indian heritage, displays of Indian art, and Native American scholarships, and devising a system for continuous evaluation of issues.

Indian leaders had been solicited for personal opinions about the mascot issue. In a letter of July 21, 1972, Forest D. Olds, chief of the Miami Tribe of Oklahoma, stated, "I find no objection to the use of 'Redskins' if it is not used in a derogatory manner. Of course I don't see where 'Redskins' pertains to Miamis only, to me it covers all Tribes." Another letter arrived too late to be included in the report, but was sent by Fathauer to President Shriver and committee members in March 1973. LaDonna Harris, president of Americans for Indian Opportunity, wrote, "The naming of sports teams in 'honor' of Indians is racist. . . . Scholarships designated for Indian students—perhaps a Miami— seem more appropriate if honoring Indian people is the intent." The report had commented on this division. "The committee came to realize that the Indian community is badly divided on the subject. It can be argued that since the leaders of the Miami Indians do not oppose our use of the word Redskins, then there is no problem. However, the appellation Redskins does not refer only to Miamis, but has reference to Indians in general."

OFFICIAL STATEMENT OF THE MIAMI TRIBE OF OKLAHOMA

Raymond Standafer, a Miami alumnus whose thesis was on the Miami-Erie Canal, was principal of Rosedale Elementary School in Middletown. He was struck by the controversy over the use of "Redskins" and resolved to become better acquainted with Miami Indians. Standafer traveled to Oklahoma, located the Miami Tribe, and introduced himself to Chief Forest Olds. The two continued a connection via letters and phone calls, and Standafer offered to host Chief Olds during a trip he was planning to southwestern Ohio in 1972. Olds was a director of the Northeast Oklahoma Rural Electric Cooperative. The September 3, 1972, issue of the *Middletown Journal* reported that he came to Cincinnati the previous week for "a convention on rural electrification." Standafer met Olds in Cincinnati and hosted him at his Middletown home for "three days and nights." They toured several locations in Ohio together, including "Piqua, the seat of his ancestors, and then . . . Miami University, named in honor and respect of his tribe." Several Miami Indians of Olds's generation knew of a university "back east" that was named for their people, but no official or member of the Tribe had ever visited Miami University before this occasion.

In Oxford, Olds and Standafer stopped by the president's office, where Olds introduced himself as the chief of the Miami Tribe. President Shriver was not there. The dilemma of how to handle this unexpected visitor was resolved by taking him to meet Vice President Etheridge. A campus tour was quickly organized. They were "taken to the football field as the Chief wanted to see the team named the REDSKINS. The team was in practice and one of the coaches talked to him. Olds later expressed pride in the use of the term, and told the Alumni Director and Standafer to keep the term REDSKINS as the nickname was not derogatory."

Following Chief Olds's visit an idea emerged to ask the Tribe to officially sanction the use of "Redskins." President Shriver recalled that Robert Wilkin, editor of the *Alumni Bulletin*, drafted a resolution that was sent to Oklahoma for the Tribe to consider. Floyd Leonard, who was second chief, remembered that before it passed this request provoked controversial discussion among the general membership at their annual meeting on September 9, 1972. In Oxford, the approved resolution was displayed in the president's conference room at Roudebush Hall.

As the 1972 football season opened, the decision to continue using "Redskins" while eliminating Hiawabop was implemented. The fraternity that had proudly portrayed Hiawabop for the past several years attempted to continue that tradition at the first home game, but President Shriver asked to have those two students removed from the stadium. Indian caricatures, however, continued to appear in print. A new decal was developed depicting the Indian statue in Millett Hall. Other efforts were made to develop credible, dignified images. The offices of Development and Alumni Affairs commissioned John R. Ruthven, internationally known wildlife artist and conservationist, to create "the most authentic portrayal of a Miami Indian ever to be painted."

After extensive research, including consultation

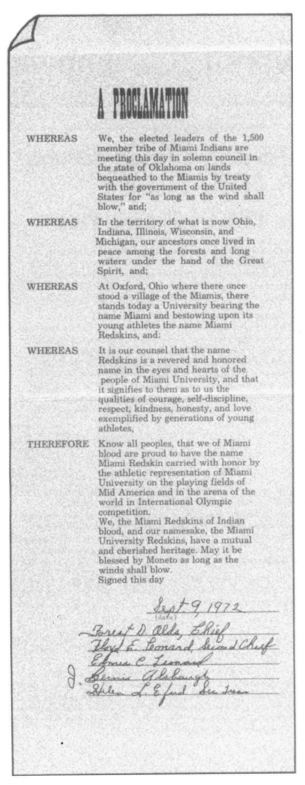

Miami Tribe proclamation, 1972. *Miami Archives.*

Unveiling of Miami Indian I *painting, 1974. Left to right: artist John Ruthven and Miami Chief Forest Olds.* Miami Archives.

with Miami Tribe representatives, Ruthven produced the first in a series of Indian paintings, *Miami Indian I.* Chief and Mrs. Olds were invited to Alumni Reunion activities in June 1974, and together Chief Olds and Ruthven unveiled it. Chief Olds proclaimed, "Now, that's a Miami," and Ruthven gave the painting to the university. During that trip, Chief Olds met President Shriver and was awarded lifetime membership in the Alumni Association. The Offices of Development and Alumni Affairs produced a limited edition of one thousand numbered and signed lithographs of *Miami Indian I.* An approved Miami University Indian head logo evolved from the Ruthven image, and in the twenty-first century was still in use for athletics, apparel, decals, and other merchandise.

Floyd Leonard was elected chief of the Miami Tribe at its annual meeting in September 1974. In 1975 Miami's director of development, David Lawrence, requested the Tribe's opinion concerning another Indian mascot. The Tribe's Business Committee motion was passed June 17, 1975, to support the mascot effort and provide assistance through an appointed Oklahoma liaison, Sharon Burkybile. Later that summer both Chief Leonard and Burkybile visited the university. Following the trip, Mrs. Burkybile sent films of performing dancers to show varying styles of dancing and outfits to consider.

An October 1975 article in the *Miami Student* reported that the "Athletic Promotion Committee was searching for someone versed in the art of Indian dancing to serve as mascot for the athletic department at Miami sports events." Those efforts were tempered over the next several months by memos from President Shriver reminding both the vice president for student affairs and athletic director about the strong hesitation of the 1972 ad hoc committee to engage students in the role of an Indian mascot. He suggested shifting the emphasis from human impersonation to a symbolic representation of importance to the Indian community, like a drum or an arrow. However, by late fall a student had been identified as a potential Indian performer and arrangements were being made to acquire an outfit from Oklahoma.

The first student chosen, Wayne Breakfield, roomed with a basketball player at Miami, and the cheerleaders began promoting a new idea, "Redskin Spirit." They hoped to include a performing Indian to personify this spirit at basketball games. Breakfield, a student in the Navy ROTC program, had some Blackfoot Indian ancestry, increasing hopes that the criticism would be reduced. Arrangements were made for Breakfield to obtain "a beginner's grasp of Indian dance." Breakfield traveled to Oklahoma for orientation and, in an extraordinary gesture of hospitality, Chief and Mrs. Pat Leonard hosted him at their home. Chief Leonard patiently explained the significance of the regalia and helped Breakfield understand how to wear it.

Chief Miami made his debut at a basketball game on February 2, 1977. He entered a darkened Millett Hall under a spotlight and was greeted by a standing ovation. The assistant director of development said "his presence adds an exciting dimension to the games, instilling new spirit among the spectators." This mascot would continue performing at basketball and football games for the next fifteen years. The fancy dancer outfit was purchased for about $600. The red shirt, made by Sharon Burkybile, was adorned with white ribbons to complete the Miami University school colors and was typical of traditional Indian ribbon shirts worn by Miami Tribe men. The drum, which had a "rawhide head across a shell made from a section of a hollow log," was a gift from Chief Leonard, and allowed Chief Miami to provide some drumming on his own when the marching or pep bands were not available for accompaniment.

Wayne Breakfield, the first "Chief Miami," 1977. Miami Archives.

In the year of Chief Miami's debut, 1977, a new student organization appeared on campus. The American Indian Awareness-Action Group aimed to support Native Americans' drive for self-determination and control over their own lives. Professor Fathauer's concern about appropriateness of the mascot reappeared. He again wrote to the *Miami Student*, complaining that the winner in the Homecoming float contest was an insensitive and offensive display. He contended that as long as "Redskins" was the symbol for athletics, inappropriate results would appear.

The last football game at Miami Field was November 6, 1982. Arrangements were made to symbolically pass the game ball from "old stadium" players to future teams that would play in Yager Stadium beginning in 1983. At Yager opening ceremonies, a new mascot, Tom-O-Hawk, a plump red bird with a trademark plaid tie, would make a debut by breaking out of a giant egg. Unlike the more reserved and stoic Chief Miami, Tom-O-Hawk engaged in humorous antics and interactions with local fans and the opposing team's mascot. As part of the final Miami Field game, a student who was Hiawabop in the early 1960s led the team onto the field by riding on horseback. Why not have Chief Miami lead the team onto the field at Yager Stadium on horseback? Brief conversations with Floyd Leonard and Sharon Burkybile in Oklahoma resulted in no objection. They indicated that a "paint" horse would be appropriate. Exotic plans were made to obtain a spear that could be lit like a torch for Chief Miami to throw as a signal to begin the game. A lance was purchased through Sharon Burkybile, but Physical Facilities staff nixed the flaming spear. Horseback riding, however, did become part of the standard opening for home games.

Chief Leonard's assistance and support was recognized at Reunion Weekend 1982 when he was awarded lifetime membership in the Alumni Association. The 1988 Miami-UC game was the hundredth anniversary of Miami's first intercollegiate football game. Floyd Leonard was invited to be grand marshal of the pregame parade, and he represented the Tribe at halftime ceremonies, presenting a new resolution to President Pearson, reaffirming the Tribe's agreement to the use of "Miami Redskins" as an honorific name for Miami athletes.

CONSENSUS ENDS, 1990s

At the 1991 World Series between the Atlanta Braves and Minnesota Twins, ABC News reporter Dick Schapp presented a segment about American Indians protesting games in Minneapolis, home to a large population of Indian activists and birthplace of the American Indian Movement. The report showed Ted Turner, Jane Fonda, and other Atlanta fans engaging in the "tomahawk chop." That coverage had an effect. Indian protests at the 1991–92 Super Bowl between the Washington Redskins and Buffalo Bills were covered in newspapers across the country. Sports and news columnists offered a rash of anti-mascot columns. When the National Coalition on Racism in Sports demonstrated in Cleveland during the 1995 World Series between the Atlanta Braves and Cleveland Indians, many journalists called openly for elimination of Indian mascots.

Miami Chief Floyd Leonard presents tribal resolution to President Pearson at 1988 Miami-Cincinnati football game. Miami Archives.

During the controversy of the 1990s Miami University and the Miami Tribe had developed a new relationship based on honoring the Miami Tribe through education. Educational programs offered on the Oxford campus presented information about the contemporary Miami Tribe—people who are not warriors, do not appear in regalia and feathers, and do not ride horses in daily life. Financial assistance was provided for accepted Miami Tribe students, and one Tribal graduate student and two undergraduates enrolled in August 1991. Between 1991 and 2007 more than fifty Tribal students attended Miami University, and in fall 2007, twenty undergraduate students were on campus. During the 1993–94 school year a committee developed recommendations for strengthening the university's relationship with the Miami Tribe, including appointment of a staff member to work with the Tribe on a regular basis, and to address negativity associated with the Native American mascot.

This issue greeted Miami president Paul Risser on his arrival from New Mexico in 1993. Risser organized a public forum to discuss the mascot controversy. Writing later about that experience, he said that his motivation was to demonstrate the educational value of informed discourse and debate. In hindsight he felt the assumption "that somehow a group of diverse people would ever arrive at a consensus on such an emotionally charged issue is simply unrealistic." In the end, the decision was to maintain the term "Miami Redskins" for current teams and publications, "as long as it was used with respect. All other university-sponsored publications and organizations could adopt the term 'Miami Tribe' as a symbol of the university's long-standing connection with the tribe."

WHEREAS: We realize that society changes, and that what was intended to be a tribute to both Miami University, and to the Miami Tribe of Oklahoma, is no longer perceived as positive by some members of the Miami Tribe of Oklahoma, Miami University, and society at large; and

THEREFORE BE IT RESOLVED that the Miami Tribe of Oklahoma can no longer support the use of the nickname Redskins and suggest that the Board of Trustees of Miami University discontinue the use of Redskins or other Indian related names, in connection with its athletic teams, effective with the end of the 1996–97 academic school year.

Miami Tribe Resolution, July 1996

"Old Miami, New Miami" illustration depicting evolution of mascot from "Redskins" to "RedHawks." Miami University.

This was an ambiguous response to an increasingly volatile issue. Moving Miami to a more definitive posture would result once again from action by the Miami Tribe. In July 1996, after Risser departed Miami, the general membership of the Miami Tribe passed a resolution at their annual meeting asking for a change in Miami's mascot. In September, at a volatile public meeting marked by pronounced differences of opinion, Miami's board of trustees passed a resolution offered by new president James Garland (1996–2006) to discontinue use of "Redskins" out of respect for the Miami Tribe. The vote was seven in favor, one opposed, and one abstaining.

A committee was then established to recommend options for a new mascot. Chaired by President Emeritus Shriver, it solicited ideas and received more than six hundred suggestions. Those were narrowed to five, and an extensive marketing study was done on each before a final recommendation was made. Miami University athletic teams, known as "Redskins" since the beginning of Alfred Upham's presidency in 1928, would now become "RedHawks." An era favoring executive decision making from a national perspective was beginning.

Act 5

The Corporate University
1996–2009

Encountering the Education Marketplace

A "Corporate University" Timeline, 1996–2009

1996   James C. Garland assumes the presidency

Health Services Center constructed

Global Rhythms World Music Ensemble founded

1997   Responding to the Miami Tribe, trustees change mascot from "Redskins" to "RedHawks"

Institute for Learning in Retirement established

No-car rule ends: seniors allowed to purchase automobile permits; juniors 1998; sophomores 2004

1998   Oxford water tower demolished

Campus-wide Institutional Diversity Plan released

Ditmer Field Parking Lot completed

1999   Wally Szerbiak scores 43 points defeating Washington in NCAA Basketball Tournament

Responding to Title IX and President Garland's recommendation, Division I men's soccer, tennis, and wrestling are eliminated

School of Engineering and Applied Science created from former School of Applied Science

2000   Responding to Oxford NAACP, President Garland creates Freedom Summer Memorial on Western Campus

Michael J. Colligan History Project created at Hamilton campus

Women's Studies becomes a major

Provost Ronald Crutcher creates First in 2009 Coordinating Council

2001   Integrated Strategic Plan for the Arts at Miami presented to board of trustees

Campus Master Plan for 2009 initiated, projecting $500 million of construction

Verlin Pulley Bell Tower constructed

MacMillan Hall renovated to create Center for American and World Cultures; opened 2003

2002   Child Development Center constructed on Western Campus

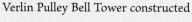

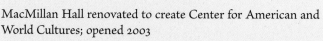

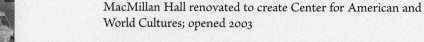

2003   PhD Program in Gerontological Studies established

Vice President for Information Technology position created

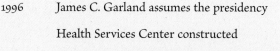

Division I night football first televised on ESPN from Yager Stadium

Ben Roethlisberger quarterbacks Miami to MAC championship and GMAC Bowl win

2004 President Garland releases strategic vision statement, First in 2009: The Spirit of a Remarkable University

Women's precision skating team wins national championship

2005 *For Love and Honor* capital campaign launched, with $300 million goal

Richard T. Farmer designates Miami's largest gift to Farmer School of Business

Heritage Commons Apartments for students (six buildings) constructed

2006 Information Technology Strategic Plan creates an entirely wireless campus

Campus Avenue Garage constructed

Goggin Ice Arena (1975) demolished, larger Goggin Ice Center constructed near Recreational Sports Center

Psychology Building constructed, to begin a new academic quad north of High Street

Trustees terminate the School of Interdisciplinary Studies (Western College Program)

David C. Hodge assumes the presidency

For Love and Honor campaign goal increased to $500 million to fund professorships and a Bicentennial Student Center

2007 Women's Softball Stadium constructed

School of Engineering and Applied Science facilities constructed in new academic quad

2008 North Parking Garage completed

2009 Farmer School of Business facilities completion target

Voice of America Learning Center for workforce transition completion target, near Interstate 75

"Corporate University" Themes

Pursuit of an image of excellence is central to recruiting the talented students desired to fulfill aspirations of a nationally competitive university. Under increasing scrutiny by the board of trustees as well as by government policy makers, accrediting agencies, media, and customers, university decision making shifts toward a corporate model favoring executive authority. Major investments are made in faculty salaries, facilities, and leadership for professional schools, and fundraising becomes a high priority. Part-time and temporary instructional staff increase relative to full-time, tenure-eligible faculty, and more uniform productivity standards for teaching are implemented. All Miami campuses witness a revolution in uses of the Internet, digital electronic communication, data storage, and new applications of educational technology.

Business studies grow in popularity, and specialized offerings in science, technology, and engineering expand as students recruited from affluent middle-class families prioritize attractive employment options in a global marketplace. Neoconservative policy makers in government oppose new taxation, and state support declines compared to rising tuition. Development campaigns of unprecedented ambition are initiated to raise funds from private sources and alumni, and Miami attempts a single tuition plan in the style of private universities. Higher national visibility via intercollegiate athletics is cultivated, new auxiliary enterprise facilities are built, and plans are laid for a half billion dollars in new construction and renovations to be completed by the bicentennial year, 2009.

Student popular culture defines consumerism in new ways, including an escalating demand for upscale housing and personal mobility. Departing from a long tradition of required peer-group living in residence halls for undergraduates, Miami constructs rental apartments for students in the style of luxury condominiums. In an expanding housing market, most residential areas of Oxford's "Mile Square" are transformed into student rentals and the "Miami Metro" bus system accommodates them. More faculty live on the outskirts of Oxford, in booming suburbs of southwest Ohio, or in settled neighborhoods of Cincinnati and Dayton. As suburbanizing trends erode older campus housing traditions and professionalism increasingly guides undergraduates' educational choices, Miami leaders abandon a three-decade commitment to the university's residential college division on Western Campus.

As the Miami Bicentennial approaches, a new president announces his desire to create the "engaged university"—a public university that prizes engaged student learning, multicultural diversity, endowed professorships, access for students from all economic backgrounds, and new levels of alumni support. The For Love and Honor campaign goal is increased to $500 million for 2010, and plans are announced to extend Miami's building boom by constructing a new donor-supported student center. Ground is broken on property just off Interstate 75 between Cincinnati and Dayton for the Voice of America Learning Center catering to adult learners.

Oxford, 1998

On November 4, 1997, a majority of Oxford voters sanctioned the removal of Oxford's most prominent landmark. The Uptown water tower in the East Park, the highest structure visible when approaching Miami on any of the area's distinctive network of two-lane roads, epitomized small-town Oxford for its citizens and virtually all living alumni. During the 1990s a raucous debate over the future of this iconic tower—no longer in use by the city's water system—divided citizens, students, faculty, and alumni, and became perhaps the bitterest local civic controversy in recent memory.

The idea of creating a water tower was first proposed in a report by the municipal board of public affairs to the Oxford village council in 1920. The new tower was key to improving Oxford's water system. In August 1921 a majority of Oxford voters approved a $56,000 bond issue to erect it. This action was challenged in court, necessitating a second confirming vote, yet the council proceeded with construction as an "emergency" measure, using cash from the city light fund. To reduce cost in this contentious climate, the tower was placed in a public park in the center of the Village of Oxford.

The water tower was completed before the end of 1922, and for seventy-one years served as Oxford's main reservoir. By the 1940s it had become an integral part of community rituals. In one popular activity, Miami students would climb the structure to paint their class years on it. "Under the water tower" was used locally as a phrase synonymous with informal community socializing and youthful rendezvous.

Oxford Water Tower (1922–98). Photograph by George R. Hoxie, 1948. Smith Library.

Molyneaux-Western Bell Tower (1978). Miami Archives.

By the early 1990s the age of the tower and its maintenance costs prompted calls from some city leaders for demolition. In March 1993 a faulty instrument system caused the tower to overflow, and in October 1993 it was retired from service. By this time other water sources had made the tower outmoded, and city leaders were left to determine the fate of a highly visible structure regarded by some as an historic landmark and by others as an obsolete, and potentially dangerous, eyesore.

At the outset a resolution to this matter seemed to be coming in a leisurely way. Oxford City Council voted in March 1995 to authorize demolition of the tower, but reversed its decision the next month. In 1997 a new mayor, who was also a professor in Miami's business school, assumed office with an activist agenda for city development. In that same year a majority of Oxford voters, in a referendum said to be advisory to the city, rejected spending public money to preserve the water tower. Oxford's Historic and Architectural Preservation Commission approved tower demolition in March 1998, but reversed course at a heated public meeting the following month. Then the Board of Zoning Appeals ruled in favor of the city's petition to demolish. Subsequently a group of preservation supporters who had raised a large amount of private money to restore the tower sued the city, but lost in Butler County Court in a judge's ruling that some observers believed was based on erroneous information.

Demolition began July 22, 1998, and was essentially complete before classes began in August. Meanwhile, entrepreneurs collected pieces of the tower and framed them for sale as relics, and photographs and tower paintings quickly

Pulley Bell Tower (2001).
IT Services.

Beta Campanile (1941).
IT Services.

proliferated in local shops as nostalgic symbols of Oxford's disappearing small-town past. Recalling Oliver Wendell Holmes's "Old Ironsides," a partisan penned these lines on the landmark's fate:

> Her tank was once the village pride,
> Way back in '22
> When progress came in many shapes,
> And brick-paved streets were new,
> For years she stood a guardian's watch,
> O'er parades and protests, too;—
> But now the city has decreed
> "Her job is done; she's through."

Most twenty-first-century students have no memory of Oxford's tower, or of the controversy over its demolition. Yet many Miami alumni, and those who lived or grew up in Oxford during the New Miami, National University, and Public Ivy eras, fondly recall seeing this symbol of home and college life come into view as they drove into town, or remember meetings there of friends or family in the heart of the village.

Today Oxford's East Park—renamed "Oxford Memorial Park" in 1996—is a manicured space with festival seating on a lawn sloping toward a donated performance pavilion on the east side, where musical groups entertain on summer evenings. This civic center of the town's central square, surrounded by an array of fast-food restaurants, upscale boutiques, and apartments that cater to students, clearly proclaims the desire of city leaders to support contemporary student culture while also offering outdoor events for the broader community. Music festivals, town-gown celebrations, and theme activities have used this space in the twenty-first century, as the city has catered to its new suburban style on the site of departed structures from earlier eras.

To opponents, every significant demolition may appear to be a unique disaster. Yet on the campuses of Oxford's educational institutions, several other towers had been destroyed as Miami rumbled through time. Old Main, with a tower bell that pealed to Old Miami, New Miami, and National University students, came down just before the Miami Sesquicentennial in 1959. The tower of Fisher Hall that once graced Dr. Scott's elegant Oxford Female College was demolished in 1978. James Renwick and J. W. Yost's Alumnae Hall bell tower at Western College had been razed a year earlier, in 1977. Like the Oxford water tower, both Fisher Hall and the Alumnae Hall tower were focal points of preservation controversy. Nothing was saved from Fisher Hall, but a new donated conference center, alluding in style to the Wren Building at the College of William and Mary, rose on its site. Most of the Alumnae Hall bells were rescued and later hung in a new tower, a modernist iron structure 53 feet high, located directly across Western Drive from Peabody Hall.

The Molyneaux-Western Tower was dedicated June 18, 1978, to formally commemorate the union of Western College with Miami University. It featured fourteen bells—eleven from the original Heath Chimes, in the Alumnae Hall tower since 1924, and three new in 1978. The chimes, a gift of Elizabeth McCullough Heath, Western Class of 1884, summoned Western students to morning chapel, Sunday service, or academic ceremonies for more than five decades. Controlled from a console in Kumler Chapel, their tower honors John Molyneaux, who attended Miami and served on the Western College Board of Trustees from 1914 to 1953. Plagued with tuning problems possibly related to their relocation, these bells were renovated in 1977 and again in 1989 with support from the Molyneaux Foundation and William W. Pulley.

The Beta Theta Pi Campanile, Miami's tallest tower at 128 feet, has stood east of Ogden and north of Elliott halls since early in World War II. Architect Charles Cellarius claimed that this tower was the world's only campanile in Georgian style. The Miami Triad fraternity erected it to commemorate the centenary of Beta Theta Pi's founding in 1839. The bells arrived in July

1939 and were first hung in the east tower of Old Main. Construction of their new tower was complete for dedication nine months before Pearl Harbor, on May 17, 1941. The Campanile features four bells named "Beta," "Theta," "Pi," and "1839–1939." They play progressive segments of the Westminster chime on the quarter-hour, with "Beta" striking the hour. All World War II and postwar generations of Miami students, faculty, and staff have timed their days and nights to the sound of Beta's sonorous toll.

At the beginning of the twenty-first century the legacy of Oxford's nineteenth- and twentieth-century towers was extended in a significant way. The Verlin L. Pulley Carillon and Clock Tower, 98 feet high, was dedicated on November 11, 2001. This most complex and technologically sophisticated of all Oxford towers again showcased neo-Georgian styling and ornamentation. Located at the southwest corner of Cook Field, it greets visitors arriving on either Ohio Highway 73 or U.S. Highway 27 at a motorist gateway to the Oxford campus. The full carillon was the gift of William W. Pulley, who earned a Miami MBA in 1958 and became the successful entrepreneur of an Oxford-based international dry-cleaning business. The Pulley Carillon honors his father, who founded the family business and served on Miami's board of trustees from 1959 to 1965. Its fifty bells, built by Cincinnati's venerable Verdin Company, span more than four complete octaves. An official university carillonneur plays them from two electronic keyboards offering melody and synthesized string sound to create harmony and bass. The Carillon is showcased in live concerts on occasional Sunday afternoons, and selections from its recorded repertoire of over 150 songs, ranging from Bach to the Beatles, are played daily.

The fates and glories of Oxford's iconic towers—water tower, Alumnae Hall tower, Beta Campanile, Pulley Carillon—suggest that the past is hardly a story of social progress untouched by conflict and executive decisions. On a quiet morning an attentive observer tuned to the Oxford soundscape can detect several different melodies at once, each with a distinctive beauty, source, and history, blending in a song of time and change. The experience of Miami University in the eventful decade 1996 to 2006 bears similar testimony.

Pursuing "First in 2009" Prestige

CUSTOMERS

Like other universities, Miami at the end of the twentieth century was an institution engaged in far more than traditional academic activities. It sought to enhance a public image that it could provide young people with unparalleled opportunities for reflection on ideas in a cozy learning environment, and it treasured its nonprofit status as a state-supported institution. It functioned, however, more and more like a complex business. As the nation's neoconservative political revolution took deep hold on public policy in Ohio, traditional sources of state support declined relative to increasing operating costs. Some doubted that the tuition strategies in place could continue to offset the cost of maintaining Miami's Public Ivy advantage in an increasingly competitive education marketplace.

Nowhere was the new customer orientation more evident than in the university's efforts to satisfy intensifying expectations of students—and parents—that Miami and Oxford provide a living environment to support lifestyles of young people coming from prosperous middle-class communities. Making the case that Miami could meet that challenge would become a major effort in the Corporate University era.

NATIONAL RANKINGS

Miami administrators told the university's constituents and prospective students a story of first-rate facilities, strong student organizations, high academic expectations, noteworthy alumni success, and sterling financial value, via press releases, Web sites, and media. In support of these claims,

U.S. News and World Report *and* Newsweek *issues promoting college rankings, 2005 editions*

national rankings of prestigious universities scored Miami highly. In 2006 the most popular evaluator of American higher education, *U.S. News & World Report,* continued Miami's long record of high standings by ranking it twenty-first among the nation's public national universities, describing it as offering "outstanding examples of academic programs that are believed to lead to student success." *Kiplinger's* ranked Miami thirty-eighth nationally and the top bargain in Ohio, and the *Fiske Guide to Colleges* described it as "one of the rising stars among state universities." Similar praise came from *The Insider's Guide to Colleges,* the American Association for Higher Education's *Student Success in College,* the *Kaplan-Newsweek College Catalog,* and *BusinessWeek.* The National Association of College and University Food Services gave Miami five awards as a top campus food program.

Such rankings were believed to have a significant impact on admissions. They were typically based on empirical information about such items as expenditure per student combined with subjective information such as peer reputation surveys. While most thoughtful educators could readily critique the methods of the ranking agencies and explain their perceived deficiencies, when their university's score was high it was promoted to seek advantage in the admissions market.

This was not a new phenomenon at Miami, for it had appeared in the *U.S. News & World Report* college rankings since they began in 1985. Aspiring to rise in a hierarchy of "America's Best Colleges and Universities," in the late 1980s and early 1990s Miami did tantalizingly well, yet did not reach the top. Soon Miami's president would announce a goal to become "First in 2009."

STUDENT LIFE IN OXFORD

Successfully meeting such an objective meant continuing to recruit talented students, and that meant responding to their evolving expectations, sometimes in locally controversial ways. By 2004 most students could officially register the cars that many had earlier brought to campus anyway, granting them greater freedom of movement. This change encouraged students to live in a growing number of rental properties well removed from campus, and required expansion of the Miami Metro bus system along with construction of more parking areas. A lot was built at Ditmer Field east of Oxford in a former greenbelt, and previously disallowed parking garages, open to faculty, staff, and students for a fee, were built on the Oxford campus. A visible price of more automobile autonomy was congested traffic in Oxford's clogged streets, which retained the scale and configuration they had when first laid out for the village in 1810.

Relaxing restrictions on cars sent a clear signal of accommodation to student desire for autonomy over their personal lives. Students living in off-campus apartments enjoyed new levels of personal freedom even as they dealt with landlords, fell victim to petty and sometimes serious crimes, ran the risk of injury or death by fire in old homes refitted for rental, and had to deal with the consequences of sometimes abusing the property where they lived. Just as in college towns of Athens, Kent, and Bowling Green, Ohio, many permanent residents of the City of Oxford welcomed students for the money they spent while deploring raucous and sometimes destructive behavior at all hours of night.

Conflicts between students and university officials tended to center on excessive consumption of alcohol, especially at parties in rental properties and in Uptown bars. On occasion, big weekend celebrations led to serious confrontations between police and intoxicated students. In the first decade of the twenty-first century, robbery and sexual crimes, at times perpetrated by individuals not affiliated with the university, were not infrequent occurrences. In the spring of 2005 three students died in an off-campus house fire. In spring 2007 another student died after being hit by a train in early morning hours, and Oxford Police charged four of her acquaintances with permitting underage alcohol consumption at a private place, and a fifth for furnishing alcohol to an underage person at a bar. In coverage of this story, the *Cincinnati*

Campus Avenue Garage (2006), Miami's first automobile parking structure, South Campus Avenue, Oxford. Photograph by Robert S. Wicks, 2008. Miami Archives.

"Green Beer Day," celebrated in Oxford since the 1980s. Recensio, 2005.

Enquirer reported, "In Oxford, police cited 243 people as underage drinkers during the 2006–07 school year." The report noted that Miami "took disciplinary action against 747 students during the last school year for alcohol-related violations" and "23 students were suspended."

An "After Dark" social program was begun earlier to attract students to alcohol-free functions on campus, and in 2006 Miami began taking more active steps to address excessive alcohol consumption. Forty-one recommendations of a presidential Alcohol Task Force were quickly adopted. These included ending delivery of alcohol to residence halls, increasing education fees for students with alcohol violations, requiring those who used fake identification in bars to take a class on ethics and honesty, and creating a group intervention program. The Office of Off-Campus Affairs was established as a Miami-Oxford partnership to foster academic success via education for personal and social responsibility, including appropriate use of alcohol. In 2007 a proposal to build a new student center on campus envisioned it in part as a social alternative to Uptown bars, without alcohol.

An annual Uptown ritual named "Green Beer Day" epitomized these issues. Some Oxford businesses encouraged a tradition of devoting the Thursday before spring break to drinking, by opening at early morning hours to serve green beer all day, allegedly in honor of St. Patrick's Day. Complaints about disruptive and potentially dangerous consequences failed to check the popularity of what many regarded as fundamental rights to sell, to consume, and to party. Named in 1982, as Green Beer Day evolved in subsequent years some alumni began to return to Oxford for annual alcohol-consumption festivities, even as university officials reminded faculty that classes were to be held without interruption. In a related alcohol issue, during 2007 an effort by Oxford City Council to place limits on outdoor drinking games was contested at length and resulted in minor restrictions.

While student culture was tightening its grip on Oxford's inner city, Miami employees were joining a national trend toward commuting. Oxford's "Mile Square" had provided homes for most Miami faculty and many staff through the National University era, and that tradition, augmented by expansion of Oxford subdivisions, lingered well into Miami's Public Ivy phase. A tally of full-time continuing faculty who provided their home addresses for the Miami *Directory* suggested a clear trend. In the three decades marked by academic years beginning in 1974, 1984, and 1994, the percentage of faculty living in the Oxford ZIP Code area dropped from 92 to 88 to 80 percent. In 2002 it was 74 percent, and in 2007, 65 percent.

Oxford's League of Women Voters reported in 2007 that over several decades the City of Oxford changed from 70 percent owner-occupied housing to 33 percent. Remaining permanent residents of the "Mile Square" often complained about the social strain of living in close quarters with students who viewed partying late and loud as a basic part of the college experience. Meanwhile, the city installed more traffic lights at intersections and joined Miami in an effort to create new regional transportation routes by supporting plans for a federally and state-funded bypass as well as a locally funded thoroughfare system.

By the early twenty-first century a visible segment of the Oxford student body, with its strong academic qualifications and professional aspirations, was also known among college-going peers for a lifestyle showcasing very trendy clothing, constant networking via cell phone, expensive automobiles, and night-time party life. Many students also marked their four-year passage through Oxford by a vigorous competition to bestow memorable names on the houses where they lived.

In the 1970s residents christened a student rental "The Ivy League," and by the 1980s a house-naming contest sponsored by a local merchant had turned a fad into a naming tradition. A study by an anthropology class in 2004 claimed that most house signs employed witty slogans referring either to sex, drugs, or alcohol, or to the Christian faith of house occupants. They documented distinct signage groups. The largest reveled "in the ability of their signs' sexually charged double entendres to give onlookers pause," even though sign-makers went "to great lengths to decry their responsibility" for this effect. The smaller group offered "an invitation to onlookers to share Christian 'fellowship.'" By the time city council acted to limit the scale of all such forms of public expression in 2006, letters of complaint had appeared in the local newspaper about the potential negative effect of risqué signage on young children.

Student on cell phone at Tuffy's in Shriver Center, 2008. Photograph by Robert S. Wicks. Miami Archives.

Student rental property house sign. Recensio, 2005.

STUDENT LIFE ON CAMPUS

As Miami approached its 200th year, the collegiate ranking culture had produced many indicators of strong academic quality, and in 2007 the Miami "Recognition" Web page noted these achievements. Miami's Farmer School of Business was highly ranked at a time when, in 2007, the largest undergraduate major in the United States was business—with 22 percent of degrees nationwide awarded in this field.

As the twenty-first century moved forward, national and state climates for outcomes assessment—efforts to determine what and how well students were learning—intensified. To augment regional accreditation, in 2007 the Board of Regents asked each Ohio college and university to create a Student Success Plan that acknowledged unique institutional strengths while showing commonalities with other Ohio institutions. This plan was to focus on assessing learning outcomes from general education and undergraduate majors, setting higher expectations for content, competencies, abilities, and successful completion, and engaging faculty and staff in continuous improvement.

High Academic Standards

adapted from *Recognition*, Miami University Web site, 2007

In *Business Week* magazine's 2007 ranking of undergraduate business programs, Miami's Farmer School of Business ranked fourteenth among the nation's public universities, the best showing of any in Ohio. Describing Miami as a "tight-knit community," *Business Week* also ranked our business school twentieth among both public and private universities for "Return on Investment."

Because our academic reputation is a magnet for employers, Miami sponsors one of the largest collegiate career fairs in the country. Compared with on-campus recruitment programs at other universities our size, nearly twice as many employers recruit at Miami, and four times as many on-campus interviews are conducted.

According to the NCAA, Miami's graduation rates for student-athletes are among the highest nationally, ninth among NCAA Division I public universities (80 percent), and first in Ohio.

Of all qualified students applying to medical school, 67 percent of Miami students are accepted, compared to 50 percent nationally. The figure rises to more than 93 percent for Miami students who earn at least a 3.2 grade-point average and score at least average on the MCATs.

In 2005—and for the second year in a row—three Miami students received the Barry M. Goldwater Scholarship, the most prestigious award of its type for undergraduates in mathematics, engineering, or the natural sciences. Nationally, Miami was one of 33 schools—and one of only twenty public schools—to have three or more recipients. In 2004, Miami joined a select group of universities in the nation that has produced a Rhodes Scholar, a Truman Scholar, and a Goldwater Scholar in the same academic year.

A *U.S. News & World Report* online ranking for 2005 listed Miami's graduate program in speech pathology and audiology in the top ten among universities nationwide that offer a master's degree in this field. Miami's undergraduate and master's degree programs in accountancy were ranked twelfth and fifteenth in the nation, respectively, by *Public Accounting Report*.

For ten years in a row, Miami placed among the top twenty universities in the nation for the number of students studying abroad; in 2005, Miami ranked tenth among research or doctoral institutions. Nearly 30 percent of Miami students study abroad before they graduate.

Premier Student Organizations, 2007

adapted from *Recognition*, Miami University Web site, 2007

2004:   At the North American Interfraternity Conference in April, Miami's Alpha chapter of Beta Theta Pi was named the best undergraduate fraternity chapter in the nation.

        For the sixth time in seven years, Miami's Gamma Gamma chapter of Pi Sigma Epsilon, a national marketing fraternity, was named top chapter.

        First-place honors went to Miami's team of paper science and engineering students, who designed and built a paper snowboard for the national Energy Challenge competition, sponsored by the U.S. Department of Energy and other organizations.

2005:   For the second year in a row, Miami students won the RecycleMania competition, a ten-week contest held among forty-eight colleges nationwide.

2007:   Miami's speech team won the state title at the Ohio Forensics Association tournament in February. Results from the American Forensics Association and National Forensics Association show that since 1999, Miami's speech team has won twenty-one national championship titles—more than any other university in the country.

One feature of a Miami education for most students, from Old Miami through all subsequent eras, was participation in organizations. In spring 2007 Miami Associated Student Government recognized 273 organized groups on the Oxford campus alone. The enormous diversity reflected the interests of students who organized to promote political, religious, and professional agendas, as well as social fraternities, musical groups, intramural and club sports, support for racial and ethnic minorities and women, honoraries, hobbies, and community and social service. The University Office of Community Engagement and Service assisted any student who desired to earn added academic credit through extended study or service learning in a liberal education course, and offered an array of resources and opportunities for community-based experiences aimed at liberal education goals of thinking critically, understanding contexts, reflecting and acting.

For most students, however, noncontroversial aspects of college life apparently attracted the greatest attention beyond the classroom. That included personal attention. On February 13, 2006, Miami's News and Information Office released a story on a "Miami Mergers" initiative of the Division of University Advancement

RecycleMania competition scorecard, Recreational Sports Center, 2008. Photograph by Robert S. Wicks. Miami Archives.

Safe Zone display card, 2008. Miami GLBT Services.

"Miami Merger" valentines. Private Collection. Photograph by Scott Kissel, IT Services, 2008. Miami Archives.

that reached across Miami's two most-recent eras. Since 1973 it had mailed annual valentines to alumni who married other alumni. Among 151,000 living alumni, it was believed that in 2006, 25,570 were married to other alumni—almost 15 percent, compared to an alleged national average of 3 percent.

EXPECTATIONS FOR RESIDENTIAL LIVING

Student expectations for quality and amenities in on-campus life rose markedly in this era. Miami students wanted greater degrees of convenience and comfort than in the days when their predecessors arrived at college with a couple of suitcases full of clothes, a manual typewriter, a pocket full of change for the pay phone and a few personal items, then headed for the bookstore. Residence hall rooms had to be ready to handle many innovations in electronic communication—computers, television, fax, CD and DVD players and recorders, as well as digital technology devices of various kinds.

In the Public Ivy era Miami had begun an ambitious effort to hardwire all facilities for digital communication, but now the demand was for instantaneous wireless communication everywhere on campus. A new division and vice president for Information Technology were created by President Garland and charged to move the university into the twenty-first century with intensive enhancements in digital technology support. The new division formulated an Information Technology Strategic Plan that met the demand for campus-wide wireless connectivity by 2006.

Dining halls were no longer cafeterias alone. They offered a variety of

President David C. Hodge
and University Ambassa-
dor Valerie Hodge sampling
Miami dining hall food,
2006. *IT Services.*

options including salad bars and themed food bars with Chinese, Italian, American Grill, vegetarian, and other choices. On special nights and before holidays, dining halls served elaborate themed meals. Specialized food facilities were created, including deli emporiums that kept longer hours, and convenience stores. An elaborate food court opened at Ogden Hall near the center of Oxford campus, and a popular coffee shop opened at King Library. Students living on and off campus could use diverse meal plans in any dining hall or university facility, and special offers were made to faculty and staff to encourage their use of dining services. While these innovations responded to students' rising expectations for personal autonomy, they also catered to healthful dining, and diversified sources of revenue.

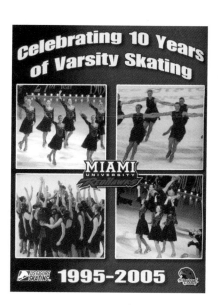

Synchronized skating team, 2005.
Synchronized Skating Media
Guide, 2005–6. *Miami Archives.*

The university built a new health center in 1996. Miami's Recreational Sports Center, opened in 1994, offered students swimming pools, basketball and handball courts, an indoor track, exercise equipment of many varieties, a climbing wall, and dozens of classes in everything from aerobic exercise to yoga, archery, and ballroom dancing. The Recreational Sports program offered an aquatic center, club sports, fitness center, group fitness programs, intramural sports, an outdoor pursuit center, and Rec Kids Camp. The center regularly hosted high school, college, and university swim tournaments, and it served as a site for Olympic training. Center amenities were open to faculty, staff, and members of the community on

Miami University Recreational Sports Center *Recorded Participations November 2006 to November 2007*

Students—444,244

Faculty and Staff—51,308

Community—34,205

Tour Guests Signed In—35,000

Faculty and Staff Memberships—1,106

Community Memberships—1,065

Food service, Recreational Sports Center, 2008. Photograph by Robert S. Wicks. Miami Archives.

Swimming facilities, Recreational Sports Center, 2008. Photograph by Robert S. Wicks. Miami Archives.

Housing and Dining Receives National Food Service Awards

Miami *News Briefs,* July 21, 2006

Miami captured two awards in 2006 contests sponsored by the National Association of College and University Food Services (NACUFS). Miami was one of five schools nationwide named "best in the business" for convenience stores ("c-stores"), winning in the food applications category with Scoreboard Market. The Scoreboard Market is located in Martin Hall's lower level. As a "best in the business" winner, it was featured in a presentation at the "Neighborhood Marketing: The Campus C-Store" workshop at the NACUFS convention in Toronto. Miami's housing and dining services regularly received high marks in student evaluations. The Scoreboard Market received a 97 percent approval rating for quality of food and 95 percent for speed of service in a 2005 survey.

Miami also took first place for "best vegan recipe," an award the university also received in 2004. Miami's 2006 winner was cinnamon applesauce waffles with vanilla tofu pudding, blueberries, raspberries and homemade granola. Beverly Rambo, Miami culinary specialist, said recipes were judged on taste, flavor, texture and appearance. Other criteria also had to be met; for example, each entry had to contain at least eight grams of protein per serving. The Miami waffle entry more than doubled this, with 19 grams per serving.

Rambo said Miami's housing and dining services constantly works to improve vegan offerings. "We try to respond to student requests and concerns," she added. Recent comments from an online "Miami Expressions" comment box included: "I love the tofu potpie. When will you serve it again?" "I can't say enough about Vine Dining. It makes my day." "The vegan pumpkin bread was awesome." About 3 percent of Miami's student population is vegan.

Broomball. Recensio, 2007.

a fee basis. Miami's embrace of the "Rec Center" was impressive—its management estimated in November 2007 that since opening in September 1994 it had recorded between 6,500,00 and 7,000,000 participations.

Completion of the new state-of-the-art Goggin Ice Center in 2006 adjacent to the Recreational Sports Center on South Quad showcased nationally successful ice hockey and synchronized skating teams. At 174,000 square feet, this new $32 million arena also made it possible for students to indulge their passion for broomball. Begun in 1981 as an effort to maximize participation in ice sports, in 2006 Miami's 107 intramural broomball teams made its broomball program the nation's largest. In his first year on campus, President Hodge joined a team.

A major symbol of Miami's response to student consumers emerged in 2005 with the construction of Heritage Commons Apartments. The modernist Miami Manor designed by Cellarius as married student housing and celebrated at the Sesquicentennial was taken down to make room for these new attractions for undergraduates. They offered six buildings of luxury rental apartments with a common living room and kitchen, two bathrooms, and four private bedrooms. In a nod to the past, the new structures were named for demolished residence facilities: Logan Lodge, Fisher Hall, Pines Lodge, Tallawanda Hall, Blanchard House, and Reid Hall.

Goggin Ice Center (2006). IT Services.

Synchronized Skating Earns Silver Medal at World Championships

Miami *e-Report*, April 1, 2007

Posting the highest finish ever for a United States skating team, the Miami University senior synchronized skating team turned in a silver-medal finish at the 2007 International Skating Union World Synchronized Skating Championships. Standing third after the completion of Friday's short program, the RedHawks registered the second-highest score in Saturday's free skate to become the first U.S. team to medal in the ISU World Championships. Miami trailed only Sweden's Team Surprise in the team standings, and followed up on last season's fourth-place finish, which equaled the highest finish ever by an American skating team. Miami and Team Surprise were the only two teams to finish among the top three in both the free skate and the short program. The RedHawks bested Canada's Nexxice for silver-medal honors. They have earned a spot in the World Championships in five of the past seven seasons, and finished no lower than ninth in the competition.

Heritage Commons Apartments (2005). Photograph by Robert S. Wicks, 2008. Miami Archives.

ATHLETICS TURNS A CENTURY

Constructing apartment housing for students was partly an effort to remain competitive in admissions, but that step was only one of a variety of new attractions Miami could promote by 2007. While athletic, musical, cultural, and arts events had attracted attention in the past, as this era opened steps were taken to make university campuses centers of entertainment for the public as well students, faculty, and staff. Nowhere was this more apparent than in intercollegiate athletics, which produced national stars in basketball and football and took other actions to increase Miami's public visibility. Two special players brought national attention to Miami sports.

Wally Szerbiak, Class of 1999, became the second men's basketball star nearing the close of the century to draw wide attention before entering a professional playing career. In 105 games over four seasons, he became the second Miami player to score over 1,500 points and make 500 rebounds and 200 assists, like Ron Harper ahead of him. He became Miami's all-time leader in three-point field goal percentage, and second in career scoring. Mid-American Conference Player of the Year as a senior, in 1999 he scored 43 points in Miami's victory over the University of Washington in the NCAA Tournament, leading all tournament players. Szerbiak's professional career included playing with the Minnesota Timberwolves, Boston Celtics, Seattle SuperSonics, and Cleveland Cavaliers. Miami retired his number, 32, in 2001.

Ben Roethlisberger, who became a football quarterback in his senior year at Findlay High School, passed for over 4,000 yards and 54 touchdowns in 1999. He played three years at Miami, and in 38 games passed for nearly 11,000 yards and 84 touchdowns, setting Miami's all-time record for total offense. Named during his senior year to the All-American First Team for the National Football League Draft, he joined the Pittsburgh Steelers, where he compiled a 13–0 regular season win record and broke NFL rookie quarterback records for completion percentage (66.4) and passer-rating (98.1). At age twenty-three he then became the youngest starting quarterback ever to win a Super Bowl.

In 2003, Roethlisberger's senior year at Miami, nighttime football was televised by ESPN cable sports network from Miami's Yager Stadium. The following year permanent lighting was installed at Yager and the Cradle of Coaches Plaza was constructed, honoring a long line of prominent coaches and athletic administrators who were Miami undergraduates.

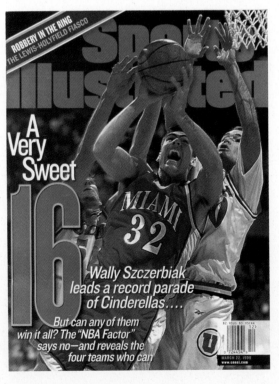

Wally Szerbiak on the cover of Sports Illustrated, *March 22, 1999.*

Ben Roethlisberger, record-setting quarterback, 2004.
IT Services.

Title IX of the 1972 Education Amendments to the U.S. Civil Rights Act of 1964 states: "No person in the United States shall, on the basis of sex, be excluded from participation in, be denied the benefits of, or be subjected to discrimination under any education program or activity receiving Federal financial assistance." No institution receiving federal funds was immune from this legislation; however, there was more than one path to compliance.

In 1999 President Garland recommended elimination of four men's sports—golf, tennis, soccer, and wrestling—as a way to comply with Title IX and

Concept drawing, Yager Stadium lighted for night games,
2004. Miami Physical Facilities.

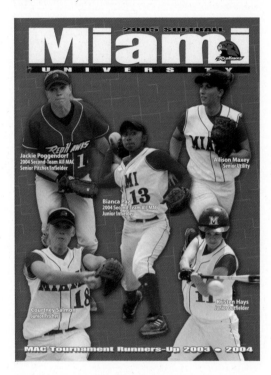

Women's softball Media Guide, 2005. Miami Archives.

remain fiscally viable. Cuts of $441,000 annually combined with anticipated additional revenue of $500,000 via fund-raising and ticket sales would, the president said, address a projected $1 million athletic budget deficit while taking a major step toward creating gender equity in Miami intercollegiate athletics. After 1999 Miami reduced the number of part-time coaches and hired additional assistant coaches for women's sports, built and upgraded their playing and locker facilities, and increased budgets and salaries to create closer comparability with men's sports.

TWENTY-FIRST-CENTURY ARTS AND CULTURE

The Miami Art Museum, a modernist structure designed by Walter Netsch and completed in 1978, was accredited in 1984 by the American Association of Museums. In the early twenty-first century it featured five galleries of changing exhibitions, a permanent collection of sixteen thousand artworks, a lecture hall, library study room, and three acres of sculpture park grounds. Museum exhibitions featured historical and contemporary art, decorative arts, and world cultures, on display to twenty thousand visitors annually. An emerging theme in exhibitions was cultural diversity and social justice—art from many ethnic groups and regions spanning Papua New Guinea to contemporary Outsider Art, as

Elimination of three team sports.
Miami Student, April 20, 1999.

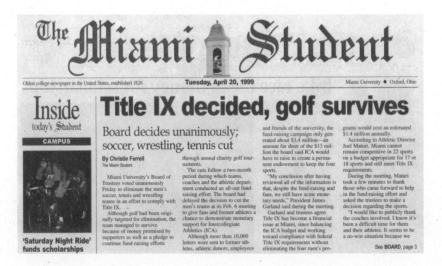

Art Museum Sculpture Park, ca. 2000. Miami School of Fine Arts Collection.

well as ancient through postmodern Western art. Exhibits included Ceremonial Art of the Coral Sea, The Post-War Russian Avant-Garde, Pueblo Pottery, Buck Rogers in the 25th Century, The Heritage of the Miami Tribe, and many others.

At William Holmes McGuffey's 1833 Federal vernacular home on Miami's Oxford campus, an historically appropriate rehabilitation was completed in 2001 to create a contemporary public history museum interpreting the significance of the *McGuffey Readers,* historic preservation of vernacular architecture, nineteenth-century domestic life, arts and design, and the history of Miami University. The William Holmes McGuffey Museum formed partnerships with academic programs, museums, archives, and community agencies to support teaching, research, and public programs. Its collection featured an octagonal desk said to have been designed by McGuffey, many rare editions, early nineteenth-century furniture and decorative arts, and items pertinent to Miami history. McGuffey's home acquired National Historic Landmark status in 1961, and the Ohio Historical Society recognized its rehabilitation with a 2003 Award of Merit.

William Holmes McGuffey Museum, a National Historic Landmark, ca. 2000. IT Services.

Other museums had renovations or major enhancements in this period, including the Robert A. Hefner

Miami University Art Museum (1978). Photograph, 2007. IT Services.

Zoology Museum, in its fiftieth year of educating K–12 students and members of the Miami community in 2007; the Willard Sherman Turrell Herbarium, with a vascular plant type collection of 539 sheets of primarily North American specimens and a collection of over 2,000 lichens and 3,000 fungi; the Anthropology Museum, which received a major donation of circus artifacts in 2007; and the Karl E. Limper Geology Museum, which featured lecturers, on-campus or online tours of fossils, minerals, rocks, and meteorites, and visits to a local park of geological interest.

The Miami University Hamilton Artist Series had for nearly thirty years showcased a blend of rising stars and established performers in bluegrass, Latin, jazz, folk, and R&B entertainment for a devoted audience from southwest Ohio. Initiated in 1979 and supported partly by the Bever family, this popular series brought nationally prominent musicians to Parrish Auditorium on Hamilton campus.

In August 2007 Miami University Hamilton opened a downtown center focused on civic engagement in the arts, offering live music, art displays, theatrical performances, classes and lectures, and a venue for scholarship activities and community meetings. After 1966 Miami University Middletown presented artists from around the world at Dave Finkelman Auditorium, also the performance home of the Middletown Symphony Orchestra. Middletown's Lyric Theatre began there as the Campus/Community Players, and the Southwestern Ohio Symphonic Band was founded there. In 2001, Fantastic Free Fridays provided opportunities for schoolchildren to experience free live performances, and by 2007 more than 30,000 young people had enjoyed opera, ballet, jazz, international music, and theatre through a unique program also made possible in part through generous support of the Bever family.

The Miami University Performing Arts Series traces its origins to 1935. Described in its mission statement as "a window through which to view ideas, cultures, and art forms, as well as to provide a mirror in order to reflect upon our selves, our history, our own culture," it became a highly visible attraction bringing diversity in the arts to the Oxford campus. In 2007 it announced a series including the U.S. Army Chorus with the Miami University Men's Glee Club, concerts of violin and organ music, the African Children's Choir, a courtroom drama on the battle for access to the Pentagon Papers, *Charlotte's Web,* a Latin Dance

Miami University Hamilton Harry T. Wilks Lecture Series poster, 2007. Miami University Hamilton.

Night, a satirical puppet show from Broadway, a family of five classical pianists, *Cirque Le Masque* circus dance theatre, the comedy group Chicago City Limits, The Watts Prophets with the Oxford Area Hip Hop Choir, and a multimedia dance production performed in Russian about the transition between Imperial and Soviet Russia in Turkistan. Artists spent time on campus with students, gave master classes, and engaged in community outreach projects

Miami University Middletown Artist Series performance, 2000. Left to right: Julius "Juice" Davis, Class of 1978, piano; Skip Edwards, bass; Bill Albin, drums; Rod Nimtz, Class of 1979, piano. Roderick Nimtz Collection.

Miami University Perform-
ing Arts Series advertisement,
2007–8. *Miami Archives.*

Global Rhythms performance, 2007. IT Services.

such as meeting with cancer survivors at McCullough-Hyde Hospital, with students and community members at Miami's Center for Community Engagement in Cincinnati's Over-the-Rhine, and with teachers in Talawanda Schools. Students and community members at times took part in major performances.

Miami had an active Symphony Orchestra beginning in 1915, that by the twenty-first century was offering opera productions. Global Rhythms began on Miami's Oxford campus in 1996 as a combination of traditional and nontraditional world music sponsored by the School of Fine Arts, Office of the Provost, and Center for American and World Cultures. It employed an eclectic blend of Middle Eastern, Caribbean, Indian, African, Brazilian, Latin, Australian, and Western instruments to produce a unique sound. Conceived by Miami alumnus Srinivas Krishnan, a master percussionist from India who performed on the tabla, ghatam, Middle Eastern dumbek, Irish Bodhran, and mridangam in over a thousand concerts with world musicians and composers, Global Rhythms engaged Miami musicians in a fusion of Indian and Western cultural musical styles. It relied on the concept that "music is a living demonstration that different people can sit down on a stage and play together" because "underneath our differences we are really similar and share certain values." By 2001 Global Rhythms had eighty-two members, mostly Miami students, and worked closely with Miami Collegiate Chorale. Its popular concerts included the Miami Gamelan Ensemble, a Klezmer Fiesta, Drumline, dancers, and prominent guest artists.

Miami Hamilton Downtown, Robinson-Schwenn Building, 221 High Street, brochure, 2007. Miami University Hamilton.

HISTORY FOR THE PUBLIC

The Michael J. Colligan History Project was an undertaking of the Colligan Fund Committee of The Hamilton Community Foundation and Hamilton campus. The brainchild of a prominent educator working with a longtime Miami Hamilton faculty member, it was made possible by the bequest of Michael J. Colligan, a businessman and amateur historian. The Project began in August 2000. Its main goal was making the appreciation and study of history accessible and enriching for members of the university and the community. By January 2007 it had sponsored more than fifty lectures, including talks by five Pulitzer Prize winners, six Organization of American Historians Distinguished Lecturers, the Librarian of Congress, the granddaughters of Winston Churchill and Dwight D. Eisenhower, and the editor of the Lewis and Clark papers. In addition to featuring important chroniclers of history, it created the John E. Dolibois History Prize for a nationally recognized historian and the Jim Blount History Educator Award for public school teachers who changed lives through innovative pedagogy. The Colligan Project received an Honors for Excellence Medallion from the Hamilton City School District and a Vision 20/20 Prize from the City of Hamilton.

Miami University Hamilton Michael J. Colligan History Project flyer, 2007. Miami Archives.

The work of the Colligan Project with school districts brought three U.S. Department of Education Teaching American History (TAH) Grants by 2007, and a Congressional Academy in History and Civics Grant, in excess of $3.4 million. Each TAH grant provided a three-year history immersion experience for social studies teachers featuring instruction by Miami faculty and other distinguished scholars. The Congressional Academy grant program "Journey to Freedom" took three groups of forty high school students to sites of slavery and emancipation. These programs epitomized engagement by people of all ages and walks of life in examination of our collective past and shared national experiences.

PLANNING FOR GLOBAL DIVERSITY

The Center for American and World Cultures, established in MacMillan Hall in 2003, became Miami's "primary locus for intercultural and international education, advising, outreach, and advocacy." Cultural diversity had taken root in Miami's cultural and arts programming. This interest in diversity had counterparts in campus diversity planning that began earlier and came to center stage during the Corporate University period. Finding Freedom Summer was a project developed by the Center and the Department of Theatre. It involved expanded curricula, a guided walking tour of Freedom Summer sites on Western Campus, and an original performance exploring 1964

Concept drawing, 1999, for Freedom Summer Memorial, constructed on Western Campus in 2000, Miami Physical Facilities. Miami Archives.

University Statement Asserting Respect for Human Diversity

from Miami *General Bulletin*, 2000–2002

Miami University is a multicultural community of diverse racial, ethnic, and class backgrounds, national origins, religious and political beliefs, physical abilities, ages, genders, and sexual orientations. Our educational activities and everyday interactions are enriched by our acceptance of one another; and, as members of the university community, we strive to learn from each other in an atmosphere of positive engagement and mutual respect.

Because of the necessity to maintain this atmosphere, bigotry will not go unchallenged within this community. We will strive to educate each other on the existence and effects of racism, sexism, ageism, homophobia, religious intolerance, and other forms of invidious prejudice. When such prejudice results in physical or psychological abuse,

harassment, intimidation, or violence against persons or property, we will not tolerate such behavior nor will we accept jest, ignorance, or substance abuse as an excuse, reason, or rationale for it.

All who work, live, study, and teach in the Miami community should be committed to these principles that are an integral part of Miami's focus, goals, and mission.

(Note: This statement was adapted from a statement written and published by the University of Southern California, Student Affairs Division. Miami University is grateful to the University of Southern California for allowing us to use their statement as a model.)

Miami's Journey with Diversity

No text can fully capture the struggle to bring Miami to a place where, in 2007, diversity became one of three central themes in President David Hodge's agenda. The most significant accomplishment to date was adoption of the Statement on Respect for Human Diversity in 2005. That statement signaled formal embrace of the notion that diversity is at the core of true excellence by contributing intercultural sensitivity, intellectual challenge, social development, and interpersonal growth for both students and the entire learning community.

Much occurred in the aftermath of the civil rights era to lay a foundation for diversity at Miami. A small cohort of African American faculty in the 1960s and 1970s would grow into a critical mass over the next four decades. Heanon Wilkins, Joseph Cox, Ray Fleming, Marian Musgrave, Larry Young, and many others broke new ground in faculty and staff ranks, rose to leadership positions, and proved that scholars of color could enhance the university. Miami also embraced cultural centers, a result of growing multicultural student populations calling for a visible presence on campus and a place of their own.

President Paul Pearson, who launched an aggressive agenda to recruit minority faculty in the 1980s, promoted Miami's diversity agenda in a major way. Academic divisions began to examine their roles in recruiting, retaining, and advancing diverse employees. The 1980s ended with signs of diversity taking hold, yet an agenda for the next decade was creating an appropriate diversity climate. It wasn't enough to bring diverse people to campus, for the

experience they had after arriving was at issue as well. Leaders were charged with educating faculty and staff about these matters, and diversity institutes brought scholars like Ronald Takaki and Marsha McIntosh who challenged core beliefs.

After a North Central Association accreditation review commented pointedly on Miami's relative lack of diversity and asked for future reports, in 1998 an institutional diversity plan was written with widespread campus involvement, and the Multicultural Advisory Council created. The diversity plan laid a foundation for addressing climate, community composition, and curriculum. The council gave advice to President Garland. An admissions campaign, "I Am Miami," signaled publicly that multicultural students belonged here, and by 2005 the formal diversity statement was adopted.

The twenty-first century brought a new lens for viewing diversity, revealing it to be more complex and inclusive than perhaps had been understood. A revision of Miami's diversity statement, for example, clearly articulated that diversity is essential to intellectual excellence, as well as to qualities of community such as avoiding complacency, and ensuring that everyone has a role in deepening Miami's engagement with diversity as an educational, civic, moral, and economic imperative.

Gerri Susan Mosley-Howard, Associate Vice President for Student Affairs and Dean of Students summer training of civil rights workers at Western College. Supported in part by a President's Academic Enrichment Award, Finding Freedom Summer included classes on civil rights history and race relations, lectures by scholars, presentations by Freedom Summer participants and families, oral histories, and workshops with theatre artists to explore memories and creative representations of events.

THE HAVIGHURST CENTER AND
THE SILK ROAD

The Havighurst Center for Russian and Post-Soviet Studies was established with a multimillion-dollar bequest from English professor Walter Havighurst, who died in 1994. The Center was designed to rely on faculty associates from many departments drawn together by mutual interests in exploring issues related to Russia and the post-Soviet world. It fostered joint research by Miami faculty and scholars from Russia, eastern Europe, and Eurasia, and from other American universities; created service and learning activities for Miami students in order to provide greater understanding of this region; and offered programs fostering interdisciplinary research. Lectures by scholars and authors, musical programs, visits of political figures, symposia, brown bag lectures, a cinema series, an international young researchers conference, publications, and study abroad were featured. Its Silk

Temporary gold domes on Harrison Hall for Havighurst Center inauguration, 2001. Havighurst Center for Russian and Post-Soviet Studies.

Russian Domes on Harrison Hall, Home of the Havighurst Center

from Havighurst Center Web site, 2002

The domes on the top of Harrison Hall are from a design based on those of a Russian Orthodox church. The project was a team effort overseen by Miami University's Department of Physical Facilities. The domes, first installed in spring 2001 for the Imagining Russia festival and inauguration of the Havighurst Center, are reusable and were designed by Graham Obermeyer and Partners Limited Structural Engineers of Cincinnati. They measure 15 feet in diameter and stand 19½ feet tall, including the crosses. Structural considerations included wind load, as the domes are 65 feet in the air. Built of plywood with ribs bonded together and crafted in two pieces that are joined on site, they weigh 2,000 pounds each. Building was done by Rick Buck Construction and other local contractors.

Road project took faculty from several departments on a trip along the trade route that connected China and the Mediterranean for many centuries. In some years the Center temporarily transformed the Georgian cupolas of Harrison Hall into Russian Orthodox domes.

SCIENTIFIC RESEARCH

Changing expectations for faculty and staff accompanied other campus shifts by the twenty-first century. A severe contraction of the academic job market in the late 1990s allowed Miami to recruit faculty with extensive research interests as well as a commitment to teaching. As new faculty with a national professional orientation in their disciplines arrived from premier research universities, administrators encouraged research and publication with an eye to improving faculty stature, Miami's scholarly image, and entrepreneurship for securing grants, contracts, and external funding. President Garland quickly signaled an intention to measure every faculty member who sought promotion and tenure against rigorous external standards of achievement in a national context. In this environment, scientific research, which had received unprecedented funding after World War II, and the doctoral science departments of the College of Arts and Science became a particular focus of attention.

F. Alton Wade (left), professor of geology, 1936–54, participant in Byrd Antarctic expeditions. Miami Archives.

In 1922 E. W. Scripps created at Miami the Scripps Foundation for Research in Population Problems, the world's first research center of its kind. In the early twentieth century Miami physical scientists made fundamental, even exotic, scientific contributions. F. Alton Wade studied the geology of Antarctica during early years of polar exploration, participating in the second (1933–1935) and third (1939–1941) Byrd Antarctic expeditions. He was the first geologist selected for the third expedition, where he was in charge of the Snowcruiser, a 75,000-pound vehicle designed for travel in Antarctica.

In 1990 William K. Hart was one of three geologists on a multidisciplinary international research team responsible for discovery and naming of one new genus and numerous new species of human primates, and for establishing the most complete, nearly continuous record of human evolution to date, based on geological deposits and paleontological and archaeological remains preserved in the Middle Awash Valley, Afar Rift, Ethiopia. Numerous publications resulted in both scientific and popular outlets. In 2006 John M. Hughes unraveled the first atomic arrangement of lunar merrillite, a mineral collected by the crew of Apollo 14.

The Department of Chemistry and Biochemistry was a consistent leader in research and extramural funding. Its Molecular Microspectroscopy Laboratory was said to be one of the first and finest laboratories in the world for molecular research. Miami scientists proved that a supposed twelfth century "Archaic Gospel of Mark" acquired by the University of Chicago was not authentic, by demonstrating that pigments used in the text were unavailable until the eighteenth century.

In 2006 the Department of Botany celebrated its one hundredth birthday. Kenneth Stewart and Karl Mattox were pioneers in understanding the evolution of green algae, the precursor group of land plants. Hardy Eshbaugh was an international leader in systematics, ethnobotany, and science education. His research on the evolution and domestication of chili peppers in the Andes was a landmark study. Martha Powell was a leader in research on the structure of aquatic fungi called chytrids. John Kiss undertook extraterrestrial research on plants in microgravity environments via the space shuttle and the International Space Station.

At the beginning of the twenty-first century, zoology was Miami's largest science department. The mechanisms by which insects survive multiple freeze-thaw cycles were not well understood, and Richard Lee's 1987 article in *Science* reporting the discovery of a rapid cold-hardening response was fundamental to understanding this phenomenon. Largely for this work, Lee was named a Fellow of the American Association for the Advancement of Science. Neuroscientist Robert Sherman published fundamental work elucidating an elementary basis for the acquisition of learning in simple neural circuits.

Microbiologist John Stevenson and his students pursued the effects of protein malnutrition on the developmental function of the immune system, demonstrating that one symptom of malnutrition is inhibition of key components of the immune system, helping explain why protein-malnourished individuals are more likely to develop serious infections.

In Miami University's early days, the cost of classroom scientific demonstrations was modest and mostly covered by tuition. In the twenty-first century, costs soared to the point where federal government programs offered highly competitive funds for scientific research—$40 billion in 2006. In that year Miami faculty received a record $24.9 million in grants, contracts, and technology transfer fees, an 8.7 percent increase over the previous year. It was the fourth consecutive year for record external funding. Sixty-five percent of these funds were for research, and the National Science Foundation was the single largest source, at $5 million.

John M. Hughes, Associate Provost and Dean of the Graduate School, 2003–6

Richard Lee (center) with research team, Palmer Station, Antarctica, 2005–6. The Antarctic Connection website, 2008.

STRIKE!

While the university sought better visibility in a national culture of college rankings, worked on balancing high academic standards with changing expectations about student life off and on campus, brought global cultures into the arts, addressed challenges of campus diversity, and vigorously pursued national and international agendas in faculty research, some of its classified employees were said to draw salaries near the federally determined poverty level. In October 2003, Local 209 of the American Federation of State, County and Municipal Employees, AFL-CIO, conducted a thirteen-day strike. A group of student sympathizers calling themselves "Students for Staff" organized to support this action by participating in public demonstrations, conducting research on the "living wage" at Miami, circulating petitions, encouraging staff testimonials for Miami's Classified Personnel Advisory Committee, hosting a Web site, and sponsoring an open forum. A parallel Faculty for Staff group signed petitions and departmental resolutions, joined demonstrations and contributed funds to striking workers.

AFSCME Local 209 strike action. Oxford Press, October 3, 2003.

In a seven-page letter to Miami faculty on October 7, 2003, President Garland, Provost Crutcher, and Richard Norman, Senior Vice President for Finance and Business Services, acknowledged that members of Local 209 were "responsible, caring people who work hard for a living" and "bring enormous credit to the university," but the three declined to support "some of the policies and practices" advocated by the union. Regarding wages, the administrators wrote, "While it is obviously important that their concerns about wages be taken seriously, a desire for higher pay, however fervently expressed, is to some degree a separate issue from whether or not Miami's pay structure fairly values the labor of its work force." They added, "based on a comprehensive analysis of our wages, vis-à-vis those paid by other employers, we believe that our bargaining unit compensation (which averages $23,670, exclusive of benefits) compares quite favorably with that of other organizations."

COSTS AND OPPORTUNITIES

Another factor in Miami's approach to labor relations at the beginning of the twenty-first century may have been the continuously rising cost of operating a competitive university that had become, in effect, a large business enterprise. While the response of Miami administrators to an employee strike action embraced a free market economic rationale, on other issues management would take different directions.

One was a decision to invest in employee health. The stated mission was "to positively influence the health and well-being of university employees by promoting purposeful and healthy living within a caring culture and community." The strategy was offering "a variety of Health & Well-Being activities, events, and experiences that not only prevent and reduce risk for lifestyle-related diseases and conditions but also enhance quality of life." Through a well-advertised curriculum of publications, topical discussions, and access to fitness facilities and classes, this popular program sought for Miami's investment a return in long-term employee productivity.

DOMESTIC PARTNER BENEFITS

The Gay and Lesbian Employees at Miami University (GLEAM), a counterpart to the student group Gay, Lesbian and Bisexual Alliance (GLBA), posted a "Timeline Towards Equality" on its Web site, detailing a tradition of activism that crossed the Public Ivy and Corporate University eras. In 2003 *Princeton Review* had ranked Miami the fifth-worst school in the nation for gay, lesbian, bisexual, and transgendered individuals, and that year Miami opened the Office of GLBT Services. In 2004 President Garland publicly opposed a bill adopted by the Ohio Assembly denying civil rights to GLBT people.

A June 25, 2004, decision by the board of trustees to offer benefits to same-sex domestic partners of faculty and staff culminated a process that had begun more than a decade earlier. A Domestic Partners Task Force was organized in October 1991 in response to a recommendation from the Faculty Welfare Committee of University Senate. In November 1992 the task force recommended that Miami provide the same benefits to employees with domestic partners that it provided to married employees. Within three months, the University Human Relations Commission also recommended adoption of this provision. However, another year would pass before University Senate, in April 1994, adopted a resolution supporting domestic partner benefits. By September the Faculty Assembly was also on record in support of that resolution, but in October 1994 President Risser told the board of trustees that he declined to recommend a change in university policy governing benefits.

Nearly a decade later the board of trustees supported President Garland's recommendation to change that policy. His decision came four months after University Senate, in a second resolution of support for same-sex domestic partner benefits, voted forty-five to one to extend medical, dental, and other benefits to domestic partners. Garland based the decision to revise university policy on three points. He noted that both University Senate and Faculty Assembly had called for change and that their resolutions had been formally supported by as many as seventeen academic departments and Student Senate. He called attention to the university's "ability to recruit and retain talented employees" and argued that the cost would be modest. He estimated that in 2004 Miami's cost for domestic partner coverage would be $50,000 to $100,000 when Miami's total health insurance cost was $22 million.

Eighteen months after this change was adopted, State Representative Tom Brinkman (R-Cincinnati) filed suit against Miami, claiming that same-sex domestic partner benefits violated Ohio's constitutional ban on same-sex marriages approved by voters in 2004. Lambda Legal, a national organization that had supported lesbians and gay men since 1973, represented two lesbian professors who argued that Representative Brinkman had no standing to sue. On November 20, 2006, the Butler County Court of Common Pleas dismissed Brinkman's lawsuit.

THE OHIO SCHOLARSHIP PROGRAM AND MIAMI ACCESS INITIATIVE

In his sixth State of the University Address on August 16, 2001, President Garland reviewed the financial circumstances of the university. Miami's endowment had doubled in size during the previous five years, $100 million in new gifts had been raised, and funded research had risen by a third. While these achievements were encouraging, and "careful fiscal management" was moving Miami forward compared to other institutions, the State of Ohio, Garland reported, had again cut annual subsidy funding by 1 percent. He offered his perspective.

This cut, which will remain in effect for at least two years, continues a 50-year Ohio pattern of under-funding higher education. As many of you know, Ohio today ranks near the bottom of the states in per-capita support of its public colleges and universities. As a percentage of our total revenues, the state's investment in Miami University is now only about half what it was 50 years ago. Today, less than 25 percent of our budget comes from the State of Ohio, and each biennium that percentage continues to decline.

Garland drew this lesson:

Miami University cannot depend on the State of Ohio to meet future financial needs. Declining support of higher education is a chronic condition in Ohio, and I see little on the horizon to suggest a turnaround. While we can hope that there will be state initiatives in the coming years aimed at rejuvenating Ohio's colleges, unless they are accompanied by a new way of thinking, Miami is unlikely to benefit significantly from those initiatives. If we are to meet our long-term goals, we must learn to rely on ourselves.

The centerpiece of Garland's move toward self-sufficiency was a bold restructuring of the university's scholarship and tuition policy. Recognizing that seven of Miami's ten principal competitors were private or highly selective public institutions, and that more than half of Oxford campus students—

59 percent of incoming Oxford first-years in 2007—were reporting family incomes over $100,000, Miami adopted a single-tuition strategy in 2004. The Ohio Scholarship Program asked all students—in state and out of state—to pay the same tuition, but in turn awarded scholarships to Ohio residents. It left open the future possibility of adjusting scholarship awards in response to family income, need, or merit, as independent institutions may do. This approach precipitated discussion in a national environment where entrepreneurial public higher education leaders were contemplating alternative funding schemes when faced with similar financial challenges. Some regarded it as a bold move that might allow the university to shape its undergraduate student body with awards of financial assistance. Others read it as a system of discounting in-state tuition without clear advantages for student consumers and their families, and perhaps with hidden risks.

By 2007 a drawback of the plan was appearing: the nation's media, including college rankings publications, were sometimes listing Miami's tuition at its highest figure without noting its built-in financial assistance to Ohio residents. Additionally, it was reported that Miami had, by far, the highest tuition among state institutions, and a national study showed Ohio with the second-highest state tuition levels in the country—close behind sparsely populated Vermont. This did not, however, deter students from applying, and Miami's application pool continued to grow.

Governor Ted Strickland, who entered office in 2007, began scrutinizing Ohio subsidies and university tuition levels. He proposed that all state-assisted institutions limit tuition increases severely in return for more state subsidy. It appeared that this might disable the option for long-term tuition flexibility that had seemed an implicit rationale for Miami's single-tuition strategy. And to counter the perception that Miami was a costly place for all students, in a variation of an approach pioneered in Kalamazoo, Michigan, a new dean of Miami Middletown began exploring possibilities for a community partnership that could offer free tuition.

Soon after taking office in 2006, President Hodge directly addressed the perception of Miami's high cost by announcing the Miami Access Initiative. That program, for Ohio residents entering the university via the Oxford campus as first-time, full-time freshmen, was designed to help make Miami accessible to more academically qualified students from families with annual incomes below $35,000. By combining existing scholarship funds, income from a new gift, matching funds, and other financial aid resources, the Miami Access Initiative was a guarantee that eligible full-time students would receive funds that met or exceeded the cost of tuition and fees. In February 2008, Miami trustees responded to a state-mandated zero percent increase by again differentiating in-state and out-of-state tuition charges. They raised costs to non-Ohio residents by 6 percent for the bicentennial year.

Roger and Joyce Howe Center for Writing Excellence, King Library, 2008. IT Services.

CAMPAIGNING FOR CAPITAL

In 2005 Miami launched *For Love and Honor,* a $350 million capital campaign. It focused initially on student financial aid, faculty support, student learning opportunities, facilities, and grounds. Among early successes was a $30 million gift from Richard T. and Joyce B. Farmer. In 1992 the Farmers provided a cornerstone gift to the School of Business. In 2005, they announced a $30 million leadership gift through the Farmer Family Foundation, of which $25 million helped underwrite the construction of a new facility for the School. The remaining $5 million was earmarked for faculty support.

A major gift from Roger and Joyce Howe funded the Howe Center for Writing Excellence, an initiative for "encouraging and aiding academic departments to incorporate writing assignments into courses and seminars, assisting faculty members in the preparation of and evaluation of writing assignments," and "providing individualized writing assistance to all undergraduates."

In fall 2007, President Hodge increased the campaign goal to $500 million, linked the campaign with the university's bicentennial, and added a new academic project. The Professorship Initiative offered matching funds to alumni and friends to invite them to create an endowed professorship, with a goal of one hundred endowed professorships and endowed chairs. "Miami's faculty is the University's greatest resource," said Hodge. "We are committed to exploring all opportunities available in order to remain competitive among colleges and universities nationwide. The quality associated with a Miami education rests fundamentally on our ability to recruit, retain and support highly qualified faculty."

James C. Garland, president of
Miami University, 1996–2006.
Miami Archives.

A DECADE OF NEW DIRECTIONS, 1996–2006

On March 6, 2007, the *Miami Stories* Oral History Project interviewed a group of station managers and other employees significant in the history of Miami's public radio station, WMUB. A suggestive story emerged. In the National University era, it was said, President Shriver justified support of the station as a training laboratory for students. When President Garland took charge, he shifted the mission focus to promoting the image of Miami University.

In an era when Miami was encountering a new education marketplace, President Garland articulated a vision. "To become the leader in the nation," he said, "Miami University must be a vibrant, energetic, forward-looking institution which seeks continuously to enhance its academic and intellectual vitality." He set specific goals.

First in 2009

Strengthening the academic profile of entering students

Strengthening the academic profile of new faculty and the academic support for existing faculty

Developing a curriculum for the twenty-first century at both the undergraduate and graduate level

Strengthening academic standards and enriching campus intellectual and cultural life

Increasing diversity of the faculty, staff, and student body

Enhancing the campus facilities, buildings, and systems

Strengthening the university revenue base

Developing improved benchmarking with peer institutions

President James C. Garland, February 2000

Such goals, he said, "must be refined by benchmarks and specific outcomes." Although all Miami employees would be involved in the effort, selecting benchmarks was ultimately an executive responsibility. "Therefore, the divisional vice presidents and other senior officers, with appropriate consultation, are being asked to set divisional goals and embark on a planning process for their own areas. . . . If plans and objectives entail significant policy changes, the University Senate and other appropriate governance bodies will be consulted for comments and recommendations."

REBUILDING MIAMI

As may have been the case in earlier eras as well, the executive goal-setting process was quite clear in the area of facilities planning. Recognizing that state subsidy was unlikely to increase and that Miami had significant concerns about facilities maintenance over the next two decades, the Garland administration set out to secure funding from many sources—including the State of Ohio—to rebuild and expand Miami's physical plant as a "First in 2009" objective.

In 1999 a "total landscape master plan for the Oxford campus as related to outdoor spaces, pedestrian/vehicular circulation, site furnishings, vegetation" was completed. In 2000 the Facilities Condition Report to Trustees pointed out that a significant percentage of the campus had been built shortly after World War II and that a plan was needed to address "block obsolescence" through rehabilitation or replacement. Master planning meetings began in 2001 with a steering committee that comprised all vice presidents; the directors of Institutional Relations and Intercollegiate Athletics; the associate vice presidents for Auxiliary Services, Facilities, and Finance and Business Services; the University Engineer; the Facility Planner; and the University Architect & Campus Planner. The steering committee was encouraged to respect Miami's heritage, think in terms of thirty to forty years, make best possible use of the environment, maintain and enhance campus beauty and charm, make decisions in the context of institutional history, and emphasize the importance of operational and maintenance cost.

The Exterior Campus Master Plan was completed in 2001. In addition, a long-range facilities plan considered capacity and overcrowding in academic and recreational buildings, vehicular and pedestrian traffic, and residence hall condition and functionality over the next twenty years. The new Vice President for Information Technology addressed applications of technology in facilities for administration, teaching, research, and residence life. Rehabilitation of existing sites was undertaken—Yager Stadium, MacMillan Hall, McGuffey Hall, Phillips Hall, and the Shriver Center Heritage Room, among others.

The steering committee determined that a new site was needed for the School of Engineering and Applied Science, that the School of Business could no longer function in Laws and Upham halls, that instructional and research laboratories needed to be relocated and consolidated, and that additional laboratory space was needed. Increased vehicular traffic and parking required attention. Overcrowding in Bachelor Hall needed relief. Demands on Goggin Ice Arena dramatically exceeded capacity. Programs that encouraged all students to experience the arts called for a performance hall in a new center for the arts. Potential building sites for the future should be identified. A timetable for action was established and approved.

A Campus Planning Timetable

2002–2006

- Rehabilitate McGuffey Hall for the School of Education and Allied Professions
- Create an academic quadrangle between Tallawanda, High and Patterson Avenue with a new engineering building between Pearson and Benton Halls; a new psychology building north of Pearson Hall; consolidated laboratory support facilities; a drive running east and west to align with the center of Withrow Court; deconstruct Goggin Ice Arena and build under-ground parking in its place with a landscaped quadrangle above
- Build a new ice arena on Oak Street between Recreational Sports Center and Phillips Hall for varsity sport hockey, senior division and collegiate synchronized skating teams, intramural hockey, intramural broomball, and community functions
- Build a new parking structure on Campus Avenue between the Recreational Sports Center and Health Center for parking demand as a result of recent and anticipated construction
- Deconstruct Miami Manor and build student apartment housing on the site for four hundred students
- Rehabilitate King Library
- Build an indoor practice facility at Yager Stadium for varsity sport teams
- Rehabilitate Presser Hall for departments of music and theatre
- Rehabilitate Warfield Hall for Division of Student Affairs
- Rehabilitate Yager Stadium: install synthetic turf, replace east stands, add field lighting
- Build new infrastructure: Steam loop connections as alternate routes for reliability of central system; expand McGuffey Electric Substation for increased electric demand; upgrade high-voltage electric distribution for new buildings; build electrical cogeneration unit gas engine generator to meet two-thirds of electric demand

2006–2009

- Rehabilitate Benton Hall for School of Engineering and Applied Science
- Deconstruct Robertson Hall and Reid Hall
- Construct new School of Business on East Quadrangle site of Reid Hall
- Continue rehabilitation of Yager Stadium: create Hall of Fame Plaza; upgrade concourse
- Build new park for women's softball
- Build two new parking structures for new Center for the Arts and Shriver Center north of Morris Hall and between Art Building and Shriver Center
- Begin renewal of residence halls with rehabilitation of two buildings to be identified
- Relocate Williams Radio and Television Tower away from Oxford campus
- Rehabilitate Martin Dining Hall

MIAMI UNIVERSITY
...BUILDING TO BE

first
in 2009

Concept drawing, School of Engineering and Applied Science, High Street, 2007.
IT Services.

By 2007 most of Miami's renovation or new construction plans were completed or well under way. Controversy erupted in 2004 over the possibility that the new home for the School of Business would be built in the wooded area of Bishop Circle, and after public hearings, a decision was made to place the new facility elsewhere. By 2007 an elaborate new 210,000-square-foot Georgian Revival building by Robert A. M. Stern, Architects, was emerging on the site where Cellarius's 51,000-square-foot Reid Hall had stood. Soon after assuming office, President Hodge announced an additional goal of building a bicentennial student center funded by alumni contributions. In fall 2007 Miami received a Getty Foundation Campus Heritage Grant to survey historically significant structures on Oxford campus, with the goal of influencing future long-term planning to enhance sites and spaces important to Miami's heritage.

CHANGES, ANXIETIES, ASSESSMENTS

Witnessing the directions and rapid pace of change, more than a few friends may have felt Miami was losing some of its distinctive character. If the supposedly timeless neo-Georgian charm of the Oxford campus, Miami's strong sense of community, and its commitment to undergraduate teaching were in danger, it might become almost unrecognizable to those who had known it well at midcentury. Others welcomed the directions and pace of change as necessary, healthy, and in some cases overdue. These conflicting perceptions fueled conversation throughout the Garland presidency about how to respond to change, and at times, about what constituted the basic character of Miami University.

A question about university governance was part of this conversation. The Garland administration employed a corporate management style; many faculty, students, and alumni—even those who agreed with executive decisions and policies—would have preferred more consultation and deliberation with a broad spectrum of the community than they saw as Miami entered the new century. Much of that feeling centered on the role of University Senate, a body that had acquired great presence in postwar years as a deliberating and decision-making institution. Some believed that President Garland regarded the Senate as a bureaucratic barrier to progress and that university officials in the new era too often or too quickly found ways to bypass it in their haste for change. Administrators denied this and cited long lists of Senate recommendations that had been accepted, most without controversy.

Tension about faculty participation in decision making, often politely buried, changed to open conflict during spring 2006 over an administrative intention, backed by the board of trustees, to terminate the School of Interdisciplinary Studies (Western College Program). Public review of this presidential recommendation in several Senate meetings yielded near unanimous votes asking first that a Senate committee be allowed to explore other possibilities for the school's future before its divisional standing was eliminated, and when this was denied, recommending that the remaining program be established as a department. Then College of Arts and Science authorities rejected departmental status. The outcomes of this conflict between faculty governance and executive authority sent a clear message that the degree of power sharing on setting academic priorities that had characterized the Public Ivy era no longer prevailed.

Another adjustment for faculty and staff was adoption of corporate-style benchmarking as a strategy for continuous program assessment. This strategy aimed for improvement by asking that specific practices be measured against parallel or related ones in peer and aspirational institutions. Academic programs were expected to make periodic reports on their benchmarked enhancements. Miami's well-established academic program review process, inherited from the Public Ivy era, was also given more teeth when the provost began providing cash rewards to programs that scored well in the review process—and indicating that significant consequences would follow poor reviews.

Strategic planning emerged in many areas during the early twenty-first century, including those with venerable traditions such as intercollegiate athletics. On August 27, 2006, an event was held in Hall Auditorium for all Miami student athletes, the entire athletic department, and university officials,

A New Facility for the Farmer School of Business

Concept drawing, Farmer School of Business, Patterson Avenue and High Street, 2007. Miami Physical Facilities.

The mission of the Farmer School of Business is to be a premier business program providing students with a lifelong ability to acquire knowledge and translate it into responsible action in a competitive global environment. A strategy consistent with this mission means housing all aspects of the school in one building to improve programs, student services, and effective communication. To prepare students for leadership in twenty-first century business organizations, this building will:

- Foster an environment embracing continuous improvement and valuing creativity and innovative problem-solving;

- Model the team orientation prevalent in today's workplace;

- Eliminate artificial barriers that exist among business departments and disciplines and present an integrated curriculum, developed and taught only when faculty members understand the broader context of business beyond narrow confines of their doctoral training;

- Promote daily interaction among faculty members within a shared space that will result in expanded frames of reference, collaboration, and greater receptivity to new ideas.

The school has been located in buildings, offices, and lecture rooms best suited for solo endeavor. By contrast:

- Instructional spaces will reflect a shift toward small group work, seminar instruction, and experiential learning;

- Office design, while providing privacy, will encourage interaction among faculty members;

- Meeting and conference spaces will support the school's interdisciplinary centers, student development programs, and more than twenty student organizations providing valuable cocurricular experience for students; the school will continue to distinguish itself through the excellence and accessibility of such resources;

- Space allocated for career services reflects a strengthening partnership with the Office of Career Services and offers accessibility to both graduate and undergraduate students;

- Sophisticated technology will be used in instruction and research, including electronic communication (podcasting, distance learning, videoconferencing, RSS feeds), interactive media, and Web technology.

Raymond F. Gorman, Senior Associate Dean, Farmer School of Business to unveil a new planning process. Athletic Director Brad Bates summarized the goals: "A *'Culture of Champions'* is a concept that calls us all to live lives of excellence and integrity on a daily basis—in everything we do." The mission statement articulated in June 2007 aimed to make the department "the model by which intercollegiate athletics operates" and emphasized that "excellence is a lifestyle."

The spirit of Public Ivy inclusiveness, however, remained in the process devised for completing a decennial Accreditation Self-Study Report in spring 2005 for the North Central Association of Colleges and Universities (NCA). This complex project, chaired by English professor Paul Anderson, focused most critically on how Miami measured its effectiveness by assessing learning outcomes. A comprehensive review was devised along content lines suggested by NCA. An array of committees explored Miami's organization, mission, and integrity; preparation for the future; student learning and effective teaching; the acquisition, discovery, and application of knowledge; engagement and service; and diversity progress since the last review in 1995, then sent forward reports incorporated into a final document. This comprehensive and participatory review earned both full reaccreditation for the maximum period and praise from NCA reviewers as a model process.

scene twelve

A "Culture of Innovation"

OVERTURES TO THE FUTURE

Two major events marked Miami's movement into the twenty-first century—one an elaborate 2005 celebration formally initiating the Miami University Campaign *For Love and Honor*, which would become by 2007 a $500 million bicentennial capital campaign, and the other a community inaugural ceremony for Miami's twenty-first president, David C. Hodge.

On the evening of April 9, 2005, Millett Assembly Hall was transformed into a lavish setting for a gourmet dinner and black-tie gala dubbed "For Love and Honor and All That Jazz," an "historic celebration" catered to 725 invited donors, potential donors, faculty, staff, trustees, officials, and important friends. Following ornate *hors d'oeuvres* with cocktails mixed and chilled through elaborate ice sculptures banked by floral settings, the formal program opened. The Men's Glee Club offered three numbers followed by Alfred Upham's "Miami Fight Song" and "Alma Mater." The evening's theme music came from two notable performers—jazz pianist and Dean of Fine Arts Jose Bowen accompanying vocalist Greta Pope Wimp, president of the Western College Alumnae Association, Inc. Music performances continued with a full jazz orchestra playing throughout an elaborate dinner served with precision by student workers and featuring beef tournedo à la perigourdine and Chilean sea bass, plus truffles au chocolat with a brunoise of infused quince, mango, and pineapple. After-dinner speakers included a member of the Class of 2006, distinguished faculty, and alumni members of the campaign steering committee. They lauded Miami's plan to raise millions of dollars for student financial aid, faculty support, student learning opportunities, facilities, and grounds. A video of special Miami places and themes was

For Love and Honor *development campaign kickoff gala invitation, 2005.* Miami Archives.

unveiled, and the surprise finale was an appearance by country music artist Wynona Judd, introduced as a favorite singer of President Garland. It was an evening of which even the finest corporation might have been proud, and one all those present would likely remember.

On the afternoon of October 20, 2006, Millett Assembly Hall hosted another event, the inauguration for President David C. Hodge. Described as a "community ceremony" for his formal installation, it began with an informal gathering near the campus hub east of Elliott and Stoddard halls, where students, faculty, staff, officials, trustees, and the new president formed a loose and lively procession led by bagpipers and Miami's University Marshall carrying the Western College mace. It made its way toward Millett Hall, in a leisurely walk between Miami's oldest residence halls, past the Beta Bell Tower, down Tallawanda Road to the cheers of fraternity men and onlookers. International students carried flags of their countries, student organizations marched gaily behind their banners, and any and all were welcomed to join. Platform dignitaries at Millett included former presidents and the Chief of the Miami Tribe of Oklahoma.

Billed as a "colorful, inclusive celebration for the entire university community," the afternoon's highlight was the new president's inaugural address, focused on "the special opportunity Miami has to blend our missions of teaching, research, and service to create a dynamic, energetic learning environment—a 'fusion of learning.'" Elaborating on themes he called "Adopting the Mind of a Scholar," "Embracing Difference and Diversity," and "Extending Learning Through Technology," President Hodge said he looked toward "an amazing and exhilarating time to be in higher education . . . a moment of

President David C. Hodge and University Marshall Emily Murphree in inaugural parade, October 20, 2006. Miamian, Spring 2007.

David Hodge, Miami University's 21st president, leads students, faculty, staff, alumni, and other friends from the Hub down Tallawanda to Millett for his inauguration ceremony Oct. 20, 2006. Joining President Hodge at the head of the procession is University Marshal Emily Murphree carrying the Western College Alumnae Association mace. The festive occasion embraces one of Miami's earliest traditions as her first president, Robert Hamilton Bishop, was formally installed in office March 30, 1825, after a march from the Methodist Church down High Street to the college's front door.

Adopting the Mind of a Scholar

from *Inaugural Address of President David C. Hodge, October 20, 2006*

It is a prime quality of universities that they attract people who are by their nature consumed by curiosity. We hunger to understand the unknown, to make sense of a messy world, to imagine new thoughts or artistic expression that challenge what or how we know. Of course, curiosity is only the beginning. Curiosity provides the spark, but disciplined reasoning and methodological rigor (both quantitatively and qualitatively), the essence of scholarship, provide the means to answer the questions posed by curiosity. That is why it is so important that we have a research-active faculty who continue to develop and use their research capabilities to answer questions that challenge us. Historically in higher education, graduate programs have been at the forefront in the approach to an education that encourages disciplined curiosity while contributing directly to the scholarly output of our faculty. In so doing, graduate programs at Miami University not only provide advanced education, but can, at their best, also contribute substantially to the construction of an exciting learning environment that benefits everyone, including undergraduates.

Unfortunately, throughout most of higher education, the common approach to undergraduate education does not engage students as active research agents. In my experience, we spend too much time telling students what we think they need to know, and not enough time using their curiosity to drive their learning. Miami is fortunate to have the potential to lead the charge toward a new form of active, engaged education for our undergraduates through the fusion of scholarship and teaching—in essence, lighting the fire of learning. The key is our conceptualization of learning itself. Marcia Baxter-Magolda, professor of educational leadership, has outlined an approach to an effective learning environment that she terms the "Learning Partnership Model." The model supports students as inquirers through three focal points: (1) validating their capacity to construct knowledge, (2) situating learning in their experience, and (3) emphasizing that knowledge is mutually constructed with knowledgeable peers. One of the best examples of the application of this concept on campus is Project *Dragonfly*. Created by faculty, staff, and students at Miami and led by Professor Chris Myers, *Dragonfly* is guided by the core principle that "the most powerful way to engage people in science is to invite them into the community of science, to allow people to see themselves as investigators." In the project, participatory science asks students to share questions, test ideas, author knowledge, and communicate with peers and experts.

I want to be clear here, that adopting the "student as scholar" model is not just about actual research experiences, although it bears noting that such experiences are important and that Miami has some absolutely terrific research opportunities for students. Rather, I am emphasizing that "student as scholar" is a frame of mind that should motivate all of our teaching and learning, from large introductory classes to the special opportunities to work on a scholarly project with a faculty member. In fact, I would argue that it is particularly important to adopt this approach to introductory-level courses because it is in those classes that we have the unique opportunity to introduce students to the expectations of the university and to the habits of mind of a scholar.

remarkable transformation, a moment when a student-centered approach to education, the hallmark of Miami University over most of its 200 years of existence, can be fully realized."

If the *For Love and Honor* capital campaign gala reveled in Miami's ability to marshal one important strength for the future—the loyalty of important alumni and major donors—the inaugural celebration called on another—the innovating power of inclusive educational community. Following the inaugural address all attending were invited to a casual outdoor dinner of picnic food and ice cream under large tents, where the affable new president greeted well-wishers.

Ahead of President Hodge would be contemporary versions of long-standing challenges, among them, coping with inadequate state support while finding ways to meet the public obligations of a state university, meeting the increasing challenges of private fundraising by cultivating both special donors and a broader base of alumni, providing facilities that would attract talented students and retain distinguished faculty and staff while maintaining the character of Miami's distinctive campuses, nurturing an educational community that would continue to be genuinely intrigued by the power of both accumulated and new knowledge, and situating Miami in the suburbanizing region of southwest Ohio while also addressing national, global, and multicultural knowledge markets. In his first State of the University Address on August 18, 2006, President Hodge said, "Our excellence depends on our ability to create a culture of innovation that will challenge everything we do." As Miami looked toward the unclear future of higher education, it could draw on important strengths that had been built across its historic eras.

ACTIVE LEARNING

Since early in the Public Ivy era Miami had consciously cultivated student involvement in learning, both in conventional classroom settings and beyond them. The "Statement of Principles" of the Miami Plan for Liberal Education in 1987 had come out of intense public discussion that yielded a formal commitment to goals of liberal education focused on active learning: *thinking critically, understanding contexts, engaging with other learners, reflecting and acting.* Beginning in 2000, George Kuh of Indiana University directed the National Survey of Student Engagement (NSSE) in affiliation with the American Association for Higher Education (AAHE), "to identify and describe policies, practices, and other properties of colleges and universities that are unusually effective in promoting student success." His work involved site visits and case studies of "about twenty colleges and universities that have higher-than-predicted scores on five clusters or 'benchmarks' of effective educational practice and higher-than-expected graduation rates." After two formal Oxford campus visits, Kuh's team reported highly positive observations about student engagement at Miami. In 2006 Miami's new president encouraged an extension of active learning to large classrooms. The Top 25 Project provided incentives for faculty teaching the twenty-five classes with the highest enrollments to design student-centered learning via innovative pedagogy that encouraged critical thinking. Assessment-centered, this phased initiative began with six projects in diverse fields. "We need to begin the process on the first day," said President Hodge, "creating an active learning environment in which students 'adopt the mind of a scholar' as soon as possible." He added, "This means turning many of our courses upside down."

November 4, 2003

Miami students described their peers to us as "eager learners," "highly motivated," and "incredibly involved."

So, what are Miami students involved in? In addition to their "informal" activities and social lives, about 25% are employed on campus. Many participate in one or more of the hundreds of student organizations and . . . volunteering on and off campus. Recreation and physical activity are particularly important; one brochure indicated than more than 10,000 students are part of 1,800 intramural teams in 45 sports.

More than 80% of first-year students reported that they "often" or "very often" worked on a paper or project that required integrating ideas or information from various sources. This percentage is significantly higher than other doctoral intensive institutions and other NSSE schools.

Many academic departments offer students the opportunity to enroll in departmental honors courses. Independent thinking seems to be especially valued. As one faculty member explained, many programs have been developed to offer students a chance to "learn what independent research is like."

Average class size is 24 students; 70% of first-year classes have 30 or fewer students; 88% of first-year classes have 50 or fewer students; and only 5% of first-year classes have more than 100 students. The University Honors and Scholars Program, the Oxford Scholars Program, and other special programs provide students additional benefits of small seminar classes and close interaction with faculty.

Working with others on projects and assignments is a common experience for Miami faculty and students. Collaboration takes several forms, including students collaborating with one another, students collaborating with faculty members, and students participating as active members of various campus administrative and governance groups. NSSE results for items related to working with peers in groups during class and outside-of-class to complete assignments were particularly high. In fact, first-year students' and seniors' scores were significantly higher than students at other doctoral intensive institutions and other NSSE schools.

More than 83% of first-year students expect to be involved in community service . . . and about 75% of seniors participated in service (the percentage for seniors at other doctoral intensive institutions was only 57%).

Miami's enriching educational experiences benchmark scores for first-year students and seniors were both above the 98th percentile compared with other institutions. First-year students at Miami have very high expectations for participation in internships, field experiences, com-

munity or volunteer service, study abroad, and capstone or similar culminating senior experiences. . . . An astounding 97 percent of seniors reported participation in a culminating senior experience such as a thesis, capstone course, or senior project.

Another excellent example of connecting academic study with out-of-class experiences is the "Over-the-Rhine Design/Build Studio," a project that began in 1996. Over-the-Rhine is a Cincinnati community that is a socioeconomically and racially different place than Oxford, consisting primarily of low-income residents. . . . This collaborative effort between the Department of Architecture and Interior Design and community organizations . . . has been so successful that it has led to the Miami University Center for Community Engagement in Over-the-Rhine.

All residence halls at Miami are considered living-learning communities. Fourteen of the 15 living-learning community options offer specific themes focused on a particular area of interest: Celebrate the Arts; Environmental Awareness Program; French Language Floor; German Language Floor; Health Enhancement and Lifestyle Management; Honors and Scholars; International Living and Learning; Leadership, Excellence and Community; Mosaic: Individuality and Diversity; Residential Service Learning; Scholastic Enhancement Program; Technology and Society; Women in Math, Science and Engineering; Western College Program.

Western College . . . is striking. Interdisciplinary and intense, this specially designed program includes team-teaching, broad thematic core courses, a rich co-curriculum, intensive writing assignments across the curriculum during students' four years in the program, a rigorous year-long senior thesis or project, and classes that emphasize independent thinking and participation in serious discussions, both in- and out-of-class.

Leadership development opportunities at Miami are plentiful. Some . . . are in the form of service on the myriad university task forces, committees, and other forms of governance and decision-making. Although they are non-voting members, two students serve as members of the Board of Trustees. . . . Many other leadership opportunities are offered in "a comprehensive leadership development program" . . . administered by the Office of Student Affairs. . . . Miami's Leadership Commitment is stated explicitly: "Non-hierarchical leadership development is one of the cutting-edge concepts in college and university environments today."

LIFETIME LEARNING

Entering the twenty-first century, Miami's educational activities were expanding to encompass the full life cycle. In 2002 Miami in Oxford joined with Mini University, Inc., to open a child development center in a new facility built on Western Campus. It offered programs for children six weeks to thirty-six months of age, a preschool program for ages three to five years, kindergarten and before- and after-school programs, and summer options for school-age children. Center literature stated, "Children and teachers are actively involved in discovering their environment" through a program that encouraged individuality and emphasized the acquisition of social skills, community awareness, and other abilities. Miami established the Partnership Office in 2005, developed initially from a formal agreement signed in 2001 by the university and Talawanda Schools. By 2007 it was seeking ways to facilitate university engagements with other community agencies and projects. In 2006 Miami announced "an affiliation to foster cooperation and interaction" between Miami and The Knolls of Oxford, a continuing-care retirement community operated by LifeSphere, a nonprofit service provider. This strategy mirrored practice at about one hundred colleges and universities and created "intergenerational exposure and activities and research and internship opportunities for Miami students" as well as "educational experiences for Knolls residents." All these efforts to expand the scope of educational initiatives had an important predecessor in Oxford's Institute for Learning in Retirement, which celebrated its tenth anniversary in 2007.

Faculty Learning Communities: What Are They?

from Miami Faculty Learning Communities Web site, 2007

The work of Alexander Meiklejohn (1932) and John Dewey (1933) in the 1920s and '30s gave rise to the concept of a student learning community. Increasing specialization and fragmentation in higher education caused Meiklejohn to call for a community of study and a unity and coherence of curriculum across disciplines. Dewey advocated learning that was active, student centered, and involved shared inquiry. A combination of these approaches in the late 1970s and '80s produced a pedagogy and structure that has led, among other things, to students' increased grade point averages, retention, and intellectual development. . . .

A faculty learning community (FLC) is a group of trans-disciplinary faculty, graduate students and professional staff of size 6–15 or more . . . engaging in an active, collaborative, yearlong program with a curriculum about enhancing teaching and learning and with frequent seminars and activities that provide learning, development, transdisciplinarity, the scholarship of teaching and learning, and community building. A participant in an FLC may select a focus course or project to try out innovations, assess resulting student learning, and prepare a course or project mini-portfolio to show the results; engage in biweekly seminars and some retreats; work with student associates; and present project results to the campus and at national conferences.

Forty percent of the current full time faculty have participated in an FLC. Grants from the Ohio Board of Regents, the U.S. Department of Education Fund for the Improvement of Post-Secondary Education (FIPSE), and the Ohio Learning Network have supported Miami mentoring of other institutions in the FLC approach.

Stumbling into History

How Luck and Student Research Made an Historian

Working as student staff in Murstein Alumni Center our senior year at Miami University, a friend and I wandered into the building's library one summer day in 2003. A simple room with the same décor it had when built in the late 1960s, the library housed various artifacts in glass cases and bookshelves donated by alumni and friends of the university. As undergraduate history majors, these objects were fascinating to us, but on a whim we decided to open the ivory-colored cabinets lining the floor to see what lay beneath the books, paintings, and memorabilia. Within the cabinets, much to our surprise, were white boxes containing scores of dust-covered letters, scrapbooks, newspapers, photographs, autograph books, and clothing—all related in some manner to the past. We had stumbled upon a treasure trove of voices, many of which reached back to very near the opening of Miami's doors in 1824. Why not catalog this stuff, we thought, and try to make sense of what we had found?

Fortunately, undergraduate education at Miami is structured in a way that allowed us to pursue our interests. Miami students have the remarkable opportunity to be partners in their own learning. The university believes that it is not enough for young people to attend classes and listen to professors report on the latest research, but that they must be actively engaged in the process of inquiry as well. My friend and I contacted Dr. Curt Ellison, who teaches Miami history. Together, we devised a plan to catalog the objects, write about our experiences, and create pathways for additional projects of historical interpretation based on our discoveries. Over the course of the following year, like many of our classmates in a variety of disciplines across campus, we became student scholars.

That experience changed my life. Much of my deci-

sion to pursue graduate study at Miami in U.S. history was based on my work in that project. Indeed, what began as the "Amos Library Archival Project"—intended to catalog library holdings, assess them in a written report, and mount an exhibit of special items in the McGuffey Museum—led me well beyond original expectations to a professional conference paper, two public presentations, a major research paper, and two contributions that appear earlier in this book. Beyond that, letters within those boxes written in the 1860s by David Stanton Tappan, a nephew of Abraham Lincoln's secretary of war, Edwin M. Stanton, helped us piece together a picture of Miami and Oxford during the Civil War. Tappan's words provided a starting point from which we have begun to construct a portrait of a community plagued by division, fear, and harsh realities of war.

Miami's commitment to providing avenues for students to explore their passions made it possible for my friend and me to tell real stories of the past, helping to add complexity to the history of Miami University and southwest Ohio. Luck often has something to do with storytelling, as does skill with research, grammar, and verse. For historians, a windfall comes with the discovery of original documentary sources in unexpected places. Letters, diaries, photographs, newspapers, and a host of other items comprise the smorgasbord of material from which they attempt to reconstruct a person's life or a particular moment in the past. Such sources are the lifeblood of any historical project, but they are often spread across great distances, occasionally written in different languages, and always singular pieces of a much larger puzzle. But sometimes, as I discovered a few summers ago, the genesis of important untold stories waits quietly in unassuming white boxes.

James Patrick Ambuske, Class of 2004

Oxford was cultivated as a retirement location for at least the last quarter of the twentieth century, and many retired faculty and staff chose to remain near the university. As the 2009 bicentennial approached, celebration planners recognized an opportunity to obtain firsthand testimony from participants in university affairs going back to World War II and initiated a focused oral history project. Beginning in 2005 and coordinated by the University Libraries, the *Miami Stories* Oral History Project invited groups with common experiences— alumni, emeriti, retirees, faculty, staff, students, and others—to recall their

Campus Owls dance band rehearsing for Reunion Weekend, 2007. James Olcott, professor of music, conducting. Photograph by Cathy Greene. Miami Alumni Association.

Miami Stories Oral History Project story circle interview, July 2006. McGuffey Laboratory School Faculty, 1960s–80s (left to right): Kay Trusty Walla, Johnny Hill, Mary Melvin, Richard Simmons, Phyllis DeMass. Miami Archives.

Miami years and hear reminiscences of others in a moderated story circle format that created themed small-group discussions in which peer exchange by participants could amplify accounts of the past. Its premier event was a story circle with President Emeritus Phillip R. Shriver and his cabinet filmed at WMUB Studios by a communications class and aired on WMUB Channel 15 cable television. All sessions were recorded on digital video and preserved in University Archives for use by scholars and the public. Under way by Reunion Weekend in June 2006, by July 2008 more than fifty sessions could be viewed on the *Miami Stories* Web site.

DIGITAL COMMUNICATION

Anyone visiting Miami's early twenty-first-century campuses could be struck by the proliferation of cell phones, iPods, and other personal digital devices, as well as laptop computers in use for e-mail, writing, and research at every formal and casual place in a fully wireless environment. WMUB FM had gone online, offered daily podcasting, and was promoting its three HD radio channels. In fall 2007 a presidentially appointed review committee proposed that WMUB "develop dynamic partnerships with both commercial and noncommercial media and appropriate university academic programs" to broaden its base of support and underwriting. The technological, educational, and financial agendas of mass media were changing as a digital revolution reshaped personal and public communications and higher education pedagogies.

Many faculty and staff had been activists in the application of digital technologies to teaching and research since the Public Ivy era, and as more students entered college with advanced technology skills, new initiatives emerged. In 1995 Project *Dragonfly* launched a Web site central to its award-winning multimedia work with scientific discovery by young investigators. Faculty in the Department of Teacher Education were awarded a partnership with Apple, Inc., in 1998 to pilot digital communication among advisors and teacher interns working at sites distant from the Oxford campus.

Since March 1997 an important resource has become remarkably popular with retirees and strongly influenced the decision of some to make Oxford their choice for retirement living—the Institute for Learning in Retirement (ILR). Pat Baugher, then an administrator with Miami's Scripps Gerontology Center, returned to campus from a professional meeting in 1996 full of enthusiasm for a steadily growing national trend to create institutes oriented to lifelong learning. Baugher, Luan Luce, Becky Lukens, and others became founders of Miami's ILR. Although its founders were Miami faculty and staff or retirees, and ILR has a strong connection to Miami, since 1996 it has become a joint effort of town and gown and is governed by a board of directors chosen by its membership. Miami's Office of Lifelong Learning provides the professional staff and office that manages day-to-day details of the organization. The Scripps Gerontology Center and the Western College Program were ILR supporters from the beginning, and the institute uses university classrooms and auditoriums when available. Courses and special events also make use of facilities at the Knolls of Oxford, at bank meeting rooms and churches, and at Hamilton's Berkeley Square and Westover Retirement communities.

Institute for Learning in Retirement participants, ca. 2006. Miami Archives.

Originally the exclusive focus of ILR was offering courses during five-week terms in the autumn and spring. Classes typically offered topics such as current events, history, science, hiking, religion, music appreciation, geography, gardening, literature, tai chi, bridge, among many others. Some are lecture oriented while others depend heavily on discussion and participation. Others focus on crafts, or physical fitness. Instructors come from the community and the university and have the enviable task of teaching mature, experienced students with a lively interest in the topic. And there are no exams or papers to mark! Social gatherings have been held at the beginning and end of each term. During the first term in 1997, nine classes were offered in Oxford, attracting seventy-six participants, many of whom took more than one. Interest grew rapidly, and only nine years later an average of thirty classes were offered with over two hundred participants taking an average of three and a half courses. By 2007 the membership of ILR (informally defined as anyone who participated in any of its programs during the most recent eighteen months) was about six hundred. Members were originally from the immediate Oxford area. In 2007 members came from across Butler County as well as neighboring counties in Ohio and Indiana.

Even in early years it became apparent that members wanted activities beyond autumn and spring classes. One-day outings were created and quickly became a popular option. Four or five of these are now offered annually, such as trips to Connor Prairie (a history village near Indianapolis), to museums in Cincinnati and Dayton such as the U.S. Air Force Museum, to plays and concerts in Cincinnati and Richmond, and to tour modern architecture in Columbus, Indiana. International travel began in May 2001 with an extended study tour of England and Scotland. ILR study tours have visited Great Britain; Ireland; Luxembourg, Brugge, Normandy, and Paris; Eastern Europe; Russia; Spain; Italy; Greece; the Peruvian Amazon and Andes; China; the Canadian Maritimes; Costa Rica; and other destinations. Shorter trips have been taken as well, the first to the Stratford Shakespeare Festival in Ontario. All study tours are preceded by a course on the area to be visited, and an ILR member with special knowledge or experience in the area accompanies each travel group.

Miami's Institute for Learning in Retirement is one of about three hundred ILR programs across the nation. Its tenth anniversary year in 2007 featured community concerts, luncheons and receptions to recognize those involved, special event outings, and a two-day seminar on aging and learning. ILR released an illustrated calendar of people and activities during its first decade that included a written history of achievements. The years 1997–2007 saw the Institute for Learning in Retirement become a major attraction to Oxford retirees, a vital producer of lifelong learning, and a resource of great promise for the twenty-first century.

Richard V. Smith, Professor Emeritus, Geography

Students with laptops and cell phones, Shriver Center food court, 2008. Photograph by Robert S. Wicks. Miami Archives.

The Miami Libraries pioneered digital applications during the Public Ivy era through statewide leadership in Ohio-Link, an electronic consortium of Ohio colleges, universities, and state libraries. Now the Libraries embraced a mission to become a digital information portal for Miami University and the public. The Inez Kamm Electronic Instruction Room in King Library, dedicated in 1998, began offering a multitude of digital media workshops for faculty and staff as well as classes for students. In 2001 the Libraries created the Center for Information Management (CIM), "an electronic facility designed to provide the computer hardware and the software necessary for students to make effective use of information." This popular facility offered specialized digital hardware and software, individualized training and help sessions, classes, workshops, and other support strategies for classroom and individual digital applications. By 2006 all manner of databases, electronic journals, technology and information management workshops, reference materials, digital reserves, and other resources were online.

The BannerWeb administrative computing system was implemented before the appointment of a vice president for Information Technology in 2003. After that time comprehensive university-wide strategic planning for technology enhancement was completed, and Miami took major steps to improve classroom facilities and equipment, real-time assistance to instruction, workshops on implementation of Blackboard to support instruction, and creation of entirely wireless campuses. The context for digital learning was swirling by 2007 with new initiatives, including Miami's role as an *iTunesU* school and the expansion of distance-based learning. Among its drivers was the Center for Interactive Media Studies. On February 26, 2008, Michael Armstrong, former chief executive officer of AT&T, and his wife Ann Armstrong, both of the Class of 1961, announced gifts of $14.7 million to benefit Interactive Media Studies, which in that year involved about eight hundred students and was projected to grow dramatically.

FRONTIERS

In 2005 Thomas Friedman published a book he titled *The World Is Flat*. It described the twenty-first-century global economy for many readers, who saw in the worldwide digital technology revolution a corresponding reduction in economic as well as communication barriers. This concept intrigued managers of higher education, and in 2006 Miami planners were focusing on new markets in Asia.

China, with more than a billion people and an economy growing by 2006 at 11 percent annually, received much of this new attention. A major was created in Asian languages and culture, and 125 students enrolled in the challenging language course Mandarin 101. A themed learning community in Chinese culture was established in Oxford for undergraduates, and China study options were actively pursued by the office of international education. China exchange agreements were signed with Peking University for business and Liaoning Normal University for education. In 2007 HanBen in Beijing awarded Miami funds, administrative support, and books to create a Confucius Institute, promoting study of Chinese language and culture, international economic change, and opportunities for business growth in China. The Miami Men's Glee Club performed at ceremonies associated with the 2008 Summer Olympic Games in Beijing. "In a perfect world," said Provost Jeffrey I. Herbst, "all faculty and students would have a semester in China."

Another favored destination was Korea, where exchange agreements existed with Yonsei University, the University of Seoul, Korean National University of Arts, and Kansai Gaidai University. The CEO of Byucksan Engineering and Construction, Seoul, also president of Miami's Korean alumni association, established the Higgin Kim Asian Business Program to support exchange opportunities with Asian universities. Beyond China and Korea, programs were being developed or plans being laid for global education destinations in Chile, Ghana, India, Russia, and Vietnam. In addition to Chinese, Miami language departments were teaching Arabic, modern Hebrew, Japanese, and Korean to increasing demand.

Back home, plans for education of the Ohio workforce also revealed global incentives. In 2007 the Ohio Board of Regents announced that a

Interactive Media Studies

Interactive Media Studies (IMS) is an interdisciplinary faculty-student collaborative that explores how frontiers of traditional disciplines are changed by digital users. IMS finds opportunities for students, entrepreneurs, scientists, teachers, artists, and others to redefine collaboration, community, commerce, visualization, education, and aesthetics, and to improve understanding of broadband-networked society in ways not previously possible due to distance, language, time, or differential access to technology. As a digital incubator for collaboration, IMS conducts teaching and research beyond the capability of single disciplines. It offers nearly thirty courses; three thematic sequences; two minors, including a game design minor with computer science; and a co-major. It has jointly appointed or affiliated faculty in every academic division, teaching in state-of-the-art laboratories, and an immersive virtual environment. IMS students consult with businesses and nonprofits to create digital solutions such as Web applications for Procter & Gamble, financial dashboards for Convergys, PDA applications for Cintas, and online training for Hewlett-Packard. IMS capstones have taken students to Shanghai and Dublin.

In 2008 Miami received a gift of $14.7 million from Michael Armstrong, Class of 1961, to enhance the role of IMS as an international leader for digital technology. It will support professorships and collaboration in every academic division. Armstrong is former CEO of AT&T and of Hughes Electronics.

Miamian *alumni magazine, Fall 2006.*

Voice of America Learning Center

from Voice of America Learning Center Web site, 2007

In the twenty-first century Miami's regional campuses are actively diversifying programming to meet citizen needs by offering alternative scheduling options and delivery methods. Miami's Center for Online Learning is headquartered in Middletown. Engineering Technology delivers a baccalaureate program to ten satellite locations across the state. Regional campuses support business and industry with specialized corporate training for workforce development.

Further addressing its role to serve the region and state, Miami is building a learning center at the former Voice of America site in West Chester, halfway between Cincinnati and Dayton and adjacent to both Interstate 75 and Warren County. Groundbreaking for the Voice of America Learning Center took place September 5, 2007, and classes are scheduled to begin January 2009.

This multipurpose instructional facility will offer graduate and undergraduate courses and programs, as well as customized training opportunities for business, industry, school districts, and government agencies. Miami programming is intended to serve persons who are:

- entering the workforce for the first time;

- beginning college or working to complete a degree;

- seeking opportunities for career and professional advancement by gaining new knowledge and skills;

- meeting continuing education requirements to maintain professional certification or licensure.

At just over 23,000 square feet, the center can support more than seventy-five classes per week offered during daytime, evenings, and weekends. Center facilities also will be available to community groups for meetings, seminars, community forums, and other events, and Miami's Alumni Career Services will extend its outreach to the center.

The center is located on land once part of the Voice of America (VOA) Bethany Relay Station. Working in consultation with West Chester Township and Butler County officials, Miami in 1996 applied to the U.S. Department of Education for twenty acres of the former VOA site and received title to the land in 2000. Through capital appropriations the State of Ohio provided $1.5 million of the project's estimated $7.5 million cost. Miami trustees approved issuing bonds to complete center financing, in order to fulfill Miami's commitment to the people of West Chester and surrounding areas.

Concept drawing, Voice of America Learning Center, West Chester Township, 2007. Miami Physical Facilities.

Chinese Academy would be offered at Miami University Hamilton, in parallel with similar opportunities at Ohio State and Cleveland State. This language and culture program was aimed at high school juniors and seniors, who could attend with tuition, books, an iPod provided at no charge, plus a stipend. And to serve southwestern Ohio more visibly while also reaching to global partnerships, the new Voice of America Learning Center would open in Miami's bicentennial year.

postlude

Education for the
Twenty-First Century
A Twenty-Year Retrospective

MARCIA B. BAXTER MAGOLDA

"Before, it was getting a lot of the facts down. And now, it's truly trying to analyze, trying to really think. Looking back, I can see that steady progression from freshman year." As a Miami senior captured his college experience, he described his progression of courses as first getting the facts, followed by opportunities to explore opinions, and finally working with facts and opinions to form his own conclusions. His reflection resonates with Miami University's mission to educate responsible, informed citizens—those who can think critically to extend the frontiers of knowledge and serve society in doing so. What kind of education would support this mission in the twenty-first century?

I began interviewing 101 students who entered Miami University in 1986 to trace their intellectual and social development throughout college. I intended to learn how students moved from learning facts to thinking critically for themselves. The 80 students who returned to interview annually throughout their four years at Miami graciously shared their successes and struggles with learning in college. Because most were still in the midst of this transition upon graduation, we continued our annual conversations. Now, as participants near age forty, they continue to offer their life stories to help educators understand what it takes to succeed in life. They report that the key to success is self-authorship, or the internal capacity to define their beliefs, identity, and relations with others. Twenty years of interviews reveal the characteris-

412

tics of teaching and learning built on partnerships that support young adults as they define their beliefs, identities, and roles in today's complex society.

JOURNEYS TOWARD SELF-AUTHORSHIP

Participants entered college having been molded by their parents and teachers to be dedicated students. In mastering the demands of adolescence and pre-college schooling they became dependent on external authorities for what to believe, how to define themselves and how to relate to others. In college, at first they perceived faculty as the primary source of answers on questions of knowledge, peers as the source of guidance for social success, and to varying degrees, parents and other adults as the source for questions of purpose. Eileen explained this approach to learning: "The information is there—all you have to do is soak it into your brain." However, soon their Miami professors asked them to learn in more complex ways. As Gwen explained, "before . . . they would tell you what to think, as opposed to now, when they say, 'What do you think?' and you [say to yourself], 'Oh, I'd better think of something.'" They found themselves working in groups to negotiate diverse perspectives and decide what to believe for themselves. In the face of uncertainty, they also watched authorities carefully to discern the best way to learn. Gwen captured the lesson many took from college with this perspective: "We're taught to make [our] plan. 'Plan your work and work your plan and you're going to get where you want to go.'"

Although following plans acquired from others worked reasonably well for most participants during college, plans fell short as they struggled to understand diverse perspectives and complex issues, and to make choices about their roles in the world. Their Miami education challenged them to reevaluate what they had been molded into, to make it their own. Mark articulated this challenge:

Making yourself into something, not what other people say or not just kind of floating along in life, but you're in some sense a piece of clay. You've been formed into different things, but that doesn't mean you can't go back on the potter's wheel, and instead of somebody else's hands building and molding you, you use your own, and in a fundamental sense change your values and beliefs.

Although this challenge arose during their Miami years, its magnitude demanded time for them to respond. One of the most difficult aspects of this was reframing their perspectives about what others thought of them. Realizing the need to do so is much easier than achieving it, as Kurt described a struggle that occupied most of his twenties. His peers concurred.

I'm coming from a position where I get my worth and my value from other people, which is, I think, wrong for me to do. But that's where I am right now. . . . The power of choice is mine, I have a choice of how I want to perceive each and every situation in my life. . . . Obviously I'm not to that point yet because I choose to make myself happy and make myself sad on what other people are thinking.

Upon graduation the participants became professional employees, spouses, domestic partners, and parents. Their professions spanned business, education, human services, law, and government. They faced incredible complexity, substantial responsibility, and broad autonomy in their work roles. Their decisions affected other lives and carried financial implications for their workplaces. At home, they often faced the complexity of relationships with partners when both were struggling with what others thought of them. Those who had children found multiple perspectives about how to raise, educate, and advocate for them. Some had to cope with their own or family members' major health problems, many of which necessitated alterations in their life course. Military families had to cope with serving in Iraq and the uncertainty of that conflict. Everywhere participants turned, the demand for self-authorship persisted.

Participants coped with these demands by working to develop a clear understanding of themselves—how they felt, what they believed, what they judged "right" and "true." They moved external influence from foreground to background so they benefited from, but were not controlled by, perspectives of others. Evan described this emerging internal sense of self:

As my personality and sense of self have really begun to develop and become more refined, my ability to direct my life accordingly has become increasingly confident. As I realize who I am, and what is important to me, it becomes easier for me to establish my priorities. Identifying and arranging my priorities has helped me to develop a "road map" for reaching short- and long-term goals. Don't get me wrong, I am not trying to predict the future and I by no means know exactly what I want, but I have developed a general idea and use my knowledge as a guide.

Evan's confidence in his ability to author his own life enabled him to sort out what he could and could not control and to become comfortable with change. This openness to change coupled with the confidence to manage one's own response led to what Dawn called inner wisdom. Dealing with multiple sclerosis in her mid-30s, she said:

I feel like I'm in this situation where I'm learning a whole new side of me that I suspected might have existed before, but never had opportunity to get to know it or put it into practice. Starting to feel—more like wisdom than knowledge. To me knowledge is an awareness of when you know things. You know them as facts; they are there in front of you. When you possess the wisdom, you've lived those facts, that information so fully that it takes on a whole different aspect than just knowing. It is like you absorbed that information into your entire being. A point where knowing you are going to do something—the knowledge has a deeper level—internal, intuitive, centered in entire being, the essential part of you that just—makes the basic knowledge pale by comparison. I called it inner wisdom.

These stories illustrate that the transition from "soaking information into your brain" to "inner wisdom" is a complex journey. And although their Miami education started them on this path, it was at times too supportive. Phillip reported that during college he simply asked his professors and they told him how to do something. In the work world he found that, "you have to use your own wits as opposed to asking somebody . . . you're just on your own."

LEARNING PARTNERSHIPS—GOOD COMPANY FOR A COMPLEX JOURNEY

The most important insight I gained from twenty years of conversation with participants is that collegians are capable of complex thinking and self-authorship early in adulthood, as long as the context demands it and others support it. Some argue that only time and experience yield wisdom. In today's world, young adults do not have the luxury of making personal and professional decisions without an internal sense of self and beliefs. The participants were capable of self-authorship when good company was available to help them achieve it. Their descriptions of that company illustrate how higher education should function to promote self-authorship during college.

Participants met the challenge to create themselves—to achieve self-authorship—by participating in learning partnerships. Partnerships offered autonomy, acknowledged their capability, and yet provided guidance by actively involving participants in working through complex situations. Rich described one such partnership in a course he took his senior year:

The whole focus of most of my classes in college have [sic] been just regurgitating the facts, with the exception of a few like Winter Biology where the base facts were given to you on the ground level and where the actual learning was coming in above and beyond that. The learning was coming in where he would ask, "What do you think about this?" and you couldn't just look on your notes, you couldn't just remember what he said. It is not just blatant memorization; learning comes into it when you are utilizing the ideas toward something new that hasn't been done. . . . This class gave more interest into the applications, what is going on right now, ideas of it, theories on what they don't know. The other classes it was "here is what we know and you have to know it too." There wasn't any fairly mutual exchange between the instructor and the class, no formulations of ideas beyond.

Rich's biology instructor portrayed the key dynamics of an ideal learning partnership. Good learning partnerships emphasize the complexity of knowledge and value learners' capacity to think in complex terms. Rich's instructor portrayed complexity and students' capacity to address it by involving students in applying ideas beyond what is currently known. Effective learning partnerships situate learning in learners' experiences and invite them to bring their sense of self to learning. The Winter Biology instructor provided data in class for students to analyze and asked them to bring their perspectives to the task.

Good learning partnerships, however, do not leave learners without guidance. They involve them in sharing authority and expertise to mutually construct the best decisions. Erica, another student in the Winter Biology course, said this of the instructor: "He takes the approach that he wants you to do it on your own. He will help you plot through your ideas and he will help you sort out what you are thinking and help direct you and he still encourages you to work independently." Good learning partnerships place the responsibility for learning on the learner, offer the appropriate challenge to help learners develop and come to trust their own abilities, and provide the support learners need, depending on their progress in the journey toward self-authorship.

As Rich noted, learning partnerships were the exception rather than the rule in participants' undergraduate experiences. Encountering learning partnerships in employment and graduate or professional education helped the participants become informed, responsible citizens who can think critically, respect diverse others, and negotiate meaning in the face of complexity. Learning partnerships have succeeded in promoting self-authorship in under-graduate science, mathematics, multicultural, experiential, and residential education. Given the demands of twenty-first-century society, it is imperative that colleges do more to help graduates achieve self-authorship.

Participants in my study are already concerned about whether their children will be ready for twenty-first-century adulthood. Anne, an accountant whose spouse has a disability, wonders whether preventing her first-grader from joining a cheerleading squad that travels to multiple schools will harm her daughter's social development. Genesse works to assuage her first-grader's stress over missing a point on an assignment. Al, a family doctor with insights into child development, believes in giving his young children autonomy but finds himself restricting their adventures out of concern for their safety. Mark, an attorney by training, calculates the degrees of freedom he affords his son on the playground in hopes of teaching him to handle his interactions with others. In a society where even elementary school is highly competitive and violence can make parents extra vigilant about protecting their children, opportunities for sowing the seeds of self-authorship may not be plentiful. All the more reason that higher education must serve the transition from authority-dependence to self-authorship. The next generation of Miamians deserves nothing less.

coda

A People With a Past, Not From the Past

Miami University and the Miami Tribe of Oklahoma

Bobbe Burke and Daryl W. Baldwin II

Long before forced Indian removals of the 1830s and 1840s, the Constitution laid the groundwork for a unique legal relationship between the United States and Indian Tribes. Article I, Section 8, delegated power to Congress to regulate commerce with Indian Tribes, as well as with states and foreign nations, recognizing their inherent rights as self-governing entities. Over the last two hundred years those have been continually tested by the losses of ancestral homelands and treaty lands, treaty violations, forced relocations, community fragmentation, and a long struggle over sovereignty and self-determination. In a modern context, that meant the Miami Tribe found itself with a great deal of social, economic, governmental, language, and cultural repair to do.

Under Franklin D. Roosevelt the federal government enacted the 1934 Indian Reorganization Act forcing tribes to create written constitutions, a concept entirely foreign to their traditional way of government and decision making. The Miami Tribe wrote its first constitution in 1937 through a separate but related act specifically for Oklahoma tribes called the Oklahoma Indian Welfare Act. This document, with subsequent revisions, remains the basis for tribal operations.

Throughout the twentieth century the Tribe had committed leaders who provided community stability and political perseverance in the face of many challenges. Harley Palmer was Chief for over fifty years. Working alongside Palmer were Forest Olds and Floyd Leonard, whose collective service to the Tribe spanned more than forty-five years. These men and others overcame many hardships in order to meet challenges of their times, including government attempts in the 1950s to terminate their status as a sovereign-dependent Indian nation. They made efforts to rectify violations of compensation and title for treaty lands, and to gain greater control over tribal operational funds through a self-governance compact with the Bureau of Indian Affairs.

Linked by kinship ties, shared history, and continuing traditions, in the early twenty-first century the Miami Tribe had a growing population of citizens nearing 3,500 and a tribal land base of approximately 2,000 acres. These resources were critical to the Miami Tribe in the twenty-first century, as they continued to rebound from years of loss, separation, and displacement from the landscape that continues to bear the prints of their human history in Indiana and Ohio.

In 2007 a variety of programs and projects provided direct services to their citizens.

- A Title VI grant is administered in a consortium with Ottawa and Peoria Tribes to provide lunchtime meals in two locations five days a week for Native Americans fifty-five years and older. In 2006–7, 85,000 meals were provided, with 24,600 delivered to homebound elders.

- The Miami Tribe Library is a full-service facility at Miami Nation headquarters. It has a large patronage of persons over the age of fifty-five and emphasizes tribal history, culture, and genealogy. Free books and bibliographies are provided to young tribal members as they enroll.
- A wide range of social service programs is available to tribal citizens dealing with child welfare, foster and adoptive families and care, substance abuse, domestic violence, on-the-job training, GED, and parenting classes.
- The Tribe earmarks funds for several educational initiatives including the Leonard Learning Center, a licensed childcare facility for ninety children six weeks to twelve years of age. Two-thirds of children enrolled are Native Americans.
- A senior complex is being developed to include the Miami Nation Community Center, assisted and unassisted senior living facilities, and a health and wellness center.

During the late 1990s the Miami Tribe, in partnership with the Modoc Tribe of Oklahoma, opened the Stables Casino. This economic venture brought much-needed resources into the tribal community and funded cultural, language, and other educational efforts. Its revenues facilitated creation of Miami Nation Enterprises, the business arm of the Tribe that manages fifteen diversified businesses dedicated to making the Tribe financially independent and self-sufficient, with or without gaming.

Much tribal development and growth corresponds with increasing interaction with Miami University. Educational programs offered on the Oxford campus showcase a contemporary people who are not simple depictions of their past, but instead an evolving and growing community with a rich history and culture. This relationship emphasizes the Miami as a people with a past, rather than a people from the past. An early goal was achieved when three Miami Tribe students, one graduate student and two undergraduates, entered Miami University in August 1991. Fifty-five Tribal students have attended Miami since 1991, all receiving the Miami Heritage Award. In fall 2007, the number of Miami Tribal students on campus rose to 20.

In July 2001 Tribal member Daryl Baldwin became director of the Myaamia Project at Miami University, whose mission is to preserve, promote and research Miami Nation history, culture and language. The first major publication of the Myaamia Project was *A Miami Peoria Dictionary*, in 2005. Miami University students and faculty are involved in other initiatives relating to language and culture. A doctoral dissertation catalogued the cultural uses of plants of the Miami and created a comprehensive database that aided the Tribe in protecting important cultural resources on tribal lands. A Geography Department project, "The Historical Landscapes of the Miami," mapped

Partners in Learning logo.
Miami Tribe of Oklahoma.

physical and cultural landscapes and land uses from around 1650 to 1850. The *Miami Children's Language Curriculum* booklet and CDs were created by a student and distributed to Miami Tribe households. Baldwin also served as a resource for cultural enrichment programming for students, faculty, and staff, and taught or appeared in many classes. Since 2003, Tribal students have gathered weekly to strengthen and reinforce cultural ties through seminars on Miami ecological perspectives and history, Miami language and culture, and contemporary Tribal issues. Because members of the Tribe reside throughout the United States, this was a first opportunity for some students.

When possible, academic projects have been designed to help meet current needs of the Miami Tribe, and classes have visited Oklahoma to complete projects. Long-term environmental projects, architectural projects that incorporate culture into design, and other projects in mass communications, anthropology, journalism, linguistics, history, and English have developed. Reciprocal benefits and educational outcomes have been enhanced by a uniquely vibrant contemporary American Indian culture. Miami students, presidents, vice presidents, deans, faculty, and administrative staff have traveled to Oklahoma to participate in annual Tribal events, including a January stomp dance, June powwow, and other community gatherings.

At commencement ceremonies in May 2005, Chief Floyd Leonard received an Honorary Doctorate of Humane Letters from Miami University for his career as an educator, having retired as a school district assistant superintendent, and for supporting ties between the Miami Tribe and Miami University. In March 2006, Chief Leonard of the Miami Tribe of Oklahoma and President Garland of Miami University signed a "Memorandum of Understanding." This document agreed to expand a strong and trusting relationship, to support each other's educational and developmental needs, and to develop projects of mutual interest.

Miami University and the Miami Tribe of Oklahoma may have created the only partnership of its kind in the United States. The Tribe created a logo to represent that relationship. An eagle feather represented the Miami Nation, and a redtail hawk feather represented the university. A red string binding the two symbolized the trust and respect at the foundation of this partnership in learning.

chorus

For two centuries the glory of Miami University has been the complex but enduring engagement of its students, faculty, staff, trustees, emeriti, retirees, and alumni with one another, and their loyalty to alma mater. This unusual learning community has evolved to distinction in Oxford, Hamilton, and Middletown, in Luxembourg, in the diverse communities Miami serves across Ohio, and in national and global settings. While Miami's first two hundred years revealed many pathways of change and innovation as old ways were left behind and new ones emerged, this university continued to thrive because it was still doing what it was doing in the early nineteenth century—asking questions, testing theories, thinking aloud, analyzing data, debating answers, arguing, insisting on satisfaction, changing minds, shaping and reshaping ideas and values, taking action, and reforming society. This is a legacy worth knowing and a bicentennial treasure for Miami's multitude of energetic creators.

A journey through five historic eras ends with a new work emerging from the most recent one. In 2005 Randy Runyon, Professor of French and Italian and University Carillonneur, created a melody that one day may mingle with other songs of loyalty to Miami University.

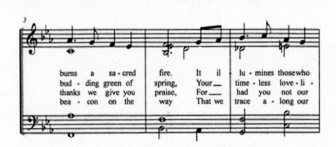

"A New Alma Mater" by Randy Runyon, 2008. Copyright by composer. Courtesy of Randy Runyon.

(Song continues on next page)

Appendices
Source Notes
Selected Bibliography
Index

Undergraduate Student Enrollment, All Institutions, Oxford, Ohio, 1824–2007

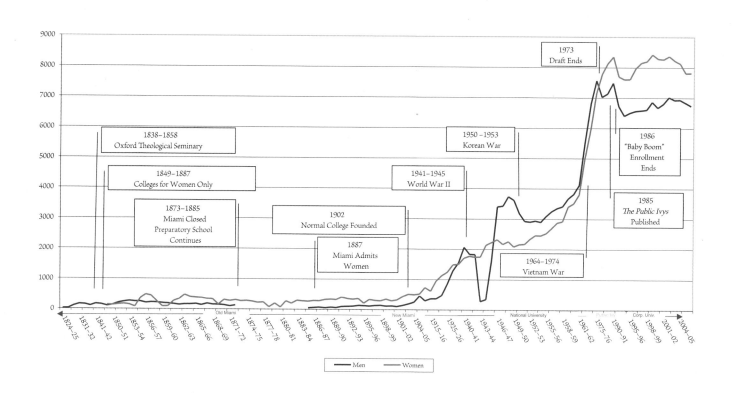

Presidents of Miami University, 1824–2008

Robert Hamilton Bishop, 1824–41

George Junkin, 1841–44

John McArthur, President Pro Tem, 1844–45

Erasmus MacMaster, 1845–49

William C. Anderson, 1849–54

Orange Nash Stoddard, President Pro Tem, 1854

John W. Hall, 1854–66

Robert Livingston Stanton, 1866–71

Andrew Dousa Hepburn, President Pro Tem, 1871–73

Robert W. McFarland, President Pro Tem, 1885–88

Ethelbert Dudley Warfield, 1888–91

William Oxley Thompson, 1891–99

William Jasper McSurely, President Pro Tem, 1899

David Stanton Tappan, 1899–1902

Guy Potter Benton, 1902–11

Raymond Mollyneaux Hughes, 1911–27

Edgar Ewing Brandon, President Pro Tem, 1927–28

Alfred Horatio Upham, 1928–45

A. K. Morris, President Pro Tem, 1945–46

Ernest H. Hahne, 1946–52

Clarence W. Kreger, Acting President, 1952–53

John D. Millett, 1953–64

Charles Ray Wilson, Acting President, 1964–1965

Phillip R. Shriver, 1965–81

Paul G. Pearson, 1981–92

Paul G. Risser, 1992–95

Anne Hopkins, Acting President, 1995–96

James C. Garland, 1996–2006

David C. Hodge, 2006–

Officers of Miami University

Vice President of the University	Andrew D. Hepburn	1902–8
	Edgar E. Brandon	1908–31
	Adelphus K. Morris	1937–46
	Clarence Kreger	1948–53
Vice President in Charge of Finance	Wallace P. Roudebush	1945–53
Vice President and Treasurer	Wallace P. Roudebush	1953–56
Vice President for Finance and Business Affairs and Treasurer	Lloyd A. Goggin	1966–82
	Edward Demske	1982–95
Senior Vice President for Finance and University Services and Treasurer	Edward Demske	1995–99
Vice President for Finance and Business Services and Treasurer	Richard Norman	1999–2006
Senior Vice President for Finance and Business Services and Treasurer	Richard Norman	2006–7
	Adolph Haislar (Interim)	2008
Vice President for Finance and Business Services and Treasurer	David K. Creamer	2008–
Provost	Clarence Kreger	1953–60
	Charles R. Wilson	1960–64
	Karl Limper (Acting)	1964–65
	Charles R. Wilson	1965–66
Vice President for Academic Affairs and Provost	Charles R. Wilson	1966–70
Executive Vice President for Academic Affairs and Provost	David G. Brown	1970–82
	C. K. Williamson	1982–85
	E. Fred Carlisle	1985–87
Provost and Executive Vice President for Academic Affairs	E. Fred Carlisle	1987–89
	Joseph T. Urell (Acting)	1989–91
	Ronald Henry	1991–94
	Robert C. Johnson (Acting)	1994–95
	Anne H. Hopkins	1995–99
	Joseph T. Urell (Acting)	1999
	Ronald A. Crutcher	1999–2004
	John H. Skillings (Interim)	2004–5
	Jeffrey I. Herbst	2005–

Vice President for Student Affairs	Robert F. Etheridge	1967–80
Vice President for Student Affairs and Dean of Students	Robert F. Etheridge	1980–87
Vice President and Dean for Student Affairs	Robert F. Etheridge	1987–89
Vice President for Student Affairs	Myrtis Powell	1989–2002
	Richard Nault	2002–8
	Barbara Jones	2008–
Vice President for Development and Alumni Affairs	John E. Dolibois	1967–81
Vice President for University Relations	John E. Dolibois	1981–82
	Douglas M. Wilson	1982–88
	Kenneth Burke	1988–2000
Vice President for University Advancement	Jayne Irvin	2000–2004
	Jayne Whitehead	2004–
Vice President for Information Technology	J. Reid Christenberry	2003–7
	Debra H. Allison (Interim)	2007–
Dean of the College of Liberal Arts	A. D. Hepburn	1902–8
	Raymond M. Hughes	1908–11
	Steven R. Williams (Acting)	1911–12
	Edgar E. Brandon (Acting)	1912–13
	Edgar E. Brandon	1913–30
	Howard Robinson (Acting)	1930–31
	Howard Robinson	1931–35
	William E. Alderman	1935–46
Dean of the College of Arts and Science	William E. Alderman	1946–59
	Karl E. Limper	1959–70
	C. K. Williamson (Acting)	1971
	C. K. Williamson	1971–82
	Joseph T. Urell (Acting)	1982–83
	Stephen Day	1983–90
	Karl Mattox (Acting)	1990–91
	Karl Mattox	1991–99
	John Skillings (Acting)	1999–2000
	John Skillings	2000–2004
	Steven DeLue (Acting)	2004–6
	Karen Maitland Schilling	2006–
Dean of the Ohio State Normal College	Franklin B. Dyer	1902–3
	Harvey C. Minnich	1903–12
	Benjamin M. Davis (Acting)	1912–13
	Harvey C. Minnich	1913–15
Dean of the Teachers' College	Harvey C. Minnich	1915–28
Dean of the School of Education	Harvey C. Minnich	1928–29
	Ernest J. Ashbaugh	1929–50

	Freeman G. Macomber	1950–55
	Herbert I. Von Haden (Acting)	1955–56
	Douglas S. Ward	1956–59
	C. Neale Bogner (Acting)	1959–60
	C. Neale Bogner	1960–77
Dean of the School of Education and Allied Professions	C. Neale Bogner	1977–80
	Janet Branch (Acting)	1980–81
	Janet Branch	1981–84
	Janet Branch-Kettlewell	1984–95
	Julie K. Underwood-Young	1995–98
	Curtis W. Ellison (Acting)	1998–99
	Curtis W. Ellison (Interim)	1999–2001
	Barbara Shirmer	2001–4
	Sally Lloyd (Interim)	2004–6
	Carine Feyten	2006–7
Dean of the School of Education, Health and Society	Carine Feyten	2007–
Dean of the Division of Educational Services	Freeman G. Macomber	1959–61
Dean of the Division of Academic Centers and of the Summer Session	Earl Thesken	1961–65
Dean of the Division of Educational Services	Earl Thesken	1965–72
Dean of the School of Business Administration	Harrison C. Dale	1928–38
	Raymond E. Glos (Acting)	1938–39
	Raymond E. Glos	1939–54
	C. Rollin Niswonger (Acting)	1954–55
	Raymond E. Glos	1956–63
	D. R. Cawthorne	1964–67
	Bill R. Moeckel	1967–88
	James F. Robeson	1988–91
Dean of the Richard T. Farmer School of Business Administration	James F. Robeson	1991–93
	John Cumming (Acting)	1993–95
	Daniel G. Short	1995–2002
	Roger L. Jenkins	2002–7
Dean of the Farmer School of Business	Roger L. Jenkins	2007–
Dean of the School of Fine Arts	Theodore Kratt	1929–40
	Joseph W. Clokey	1940–46
	Gordon A. Sutherland	1946–52
	George F. Barron (Acting)	1952–54
	George F. Barron	1954–73
	Charles L. Spohn	1973–82
	Harold Truax	1982–83
	Hayden B. May	1983–98
	Pamela Fox	1998–2003
	Curtis W. Ellison (Interim)	2003–4
	Jose Antonio Bowen	2004–6
	Robert Benson (Interim)	2006–7
	James E. Lentini	2007–

Dean of the School of Applied Science	George Bowers	1966–83
	Roscoe Ward	1983–88
	David Haddad (Acting)	1988–90
	David Haddad	1990–99
	Donald L. Byrkett (Acting)	1999–2000
Dean of the School of Engineering and Applied Science	Marek Dollar	2000–
Dean of the Western College of Miami University	Myron J. Lunine	1974–78
Dean of the School of Interdisciplinary Studies (Western College Program)	Myron J. Lunine	1978–80
	Curtis W. Ellison (Acting)	1980–81
	Curtis W. Ellison	1981–96
	Judith de Luce	1996–97
	Curtis W. Ellison (Acting)	1997–98
	Burton I. Kaufman	1998–2003
	William J. Gracie, Jr.	2003–8
Dean of the Graduate School	Harvard F. Vallance	1949–50
	William E. Smith	1950–59
	H. Bunker Wright	1959–69
	Robert E. Wolverton	1969–70
Dean of the Graduate School and Research	Robert E. Woverton	1971–72
Dean of Graduate Studies and Research	Spiro T. Peterson (Acting)	1972–73
	Spiro T. Peterson	1973–76
Dean of Graduate School and Research	Spiro T. Peterson	1976–82
	Gary Knock (Acting)	1982–83
	Herbert Waltzer (Acting)	1983–84
	Leonard J. Simutis	1984–91
	Gary Knock (Acting)	1991–92
Associate Provost and Dean of the Graduate School	Robert C. Johnson	1992–94
	Herbert Waltzer (Acting)	1994–95
	Robert C. Johnson	1995–2003
	John M. Hughes	2003–6
	Jeffrey Potteiger (Acting)	2006–7
	Bruce Cochrane	2007–
Director, Middletown Campus	Carl Eugene Bennett	1966–76
Executive Director, Middletown Campus	Carl Eugene Bennett	1976–86
	Michael P. Governanti	1986–2005
	Marjorie M. Cowan (Interim)	2005–6
Regional Campus Dean, Miami University Middletown	Marjorie M. Cowan (Interim)	2006–7
	Marjorie M. Cowan	2007–
Director, Hamilton Campus	Bernard F. Phelps	1967–76
Executive Director, Hamilton Campus	M. Douglas Reed	1976–84
	Harriet V. Taylor (Acting)	1984–85
	Harriet V. Taylor	1985–95

	Jack Rhodes	1995–2002
	Lee Sanders (Acting)	2002–3
	Daniel E. Hall	2003–6
Regional Campus Dean, Miami University Hamilton	Daniel E. Hall	2006–
Director, European Center	Warren L. Mason	1968–70
	J. Bryan Collester	1970–72
	Leslie S. Brady	1972–73
	Leslie S. Brady	1973–77
	Pierre Sotteau	1977–79
	Charles E. Teckman (Acting)	1979–80
	Warren L. Mason	1980–82
	Ivan A. Lakos	1982–88
Director, John E. Dolibois European Center	Ivan A. Lakos	1988–89
	Ekkehard F. Stiller	1989–91
Executive Director, John E. Dolibois European Center	Ekkehard F. Stiller	1991–2006
Dean, John E. Dolibois European Center	Ekkehard F. Stiller	2006–
Dean of Research	Donald E. Cunningham	1967–70
	Charles Vaughn (Acting)	1970–71
University Secretary	Wallace I. Edwards	1966–69
	William G. Slover	1969–72
University Secretary and Affirmative Action Officer	William G. Slover	1972–74
Secretary of the University	William G. Slover	1974–82
Secretary to the Board of Trustees; Secretary of the University	William G. Slover	1982–97
Secretary of the University	William G. Slover	1997–98
	Karen K. Shaffer	1998–
Secretary to the Board of Trustees	Stephen D. Snyder	1997–
Librarian	William Sparrow	1824–26
	William H. McGuffey	1826–36
	John McArthur	1837?–41?
	James C. Moffat	1841–52
	Charles Elliott	1852–58
	Robert W. McFarland (Pro tem)	1858–59
	Charles Elliott	1859–63
	David Swing	1863–66
	Robert W. McFarland	1866–73
	Robert W. McFarland	1886–88
Chair of the Library Committee	William A. Merrill	1888–90
Librarian	William A. Merrill	1890–93
	O. B. Finch	1893–1900
	William J. McSurely (Pro tem)	1900–1901
	William J. McSurely	1901–9
	Samuel J. Brandenburg	1909–22
	Edgar W. King	1922–56

	Leland S. Dutton	1956–69
	Charles D. Churchwell	1969–72
	Donald Oehlerts	1972–87
	C. Martin Miller (Interim)	1987–88
Dean and University Librarian	Judith Sessions	1988–
Dean for Program Development	Naomi Brown	1973–80
Dean of Students	Robert F. Etheridge	1960–66
Executive Dean for Student Affairs	Robert F. Etheridge	1966–67
Dean of Student Life	William T. Hollingsworth	1973–80
Dean for Student Development	B. Derrell Hart	1980–83
Dean of Student Life	B. Derrell Hart	1983–87
Dean of Students	B. Derrell Hart	1987–89
Associate Vice President for Student Affairs and Dean of Students	B. Derrell Hart	1989–93
	Richard Nault	1993–2002
	Gerri Susan Mosley-Howard	2002–
Dean of Men	Carl W. Knox	1952–59
	Robert F. Etheridge	1959–60
	William T. Hollingsworth	1960–73
Dean of Women	Elizabeth Hamilton	1905–40
	Bertha Emerson (Acting)	1940–41
	Elizabeth Hamilton	1941–45
	Bertha Emerson (Acting)	1945–46
	Melva Lind	1950–53
	Helen E. Page	1953–60
	Jean Hinds	1960–61
	Ruth Warfel	1961–64
	Naomi Brown	1964–73

Source Notes

Unless otherwise noted, all text attributed to Curtis W. Ellison

OVERTURE

Myaamiaki neehi Myaamionki: The Miami People and Their Homelands—George Ironstrack

ACT ONE

Prelude

"At about midnight . . . ": James M. Rodabaugh, "A History of Miami University from Its Origin to 1873," unpublished manuscript, November 9, 1949, Miami Archives. Act 1 is significantly in debt to this work, cited below as Rodabaugh.

"Helen Lefkowitz Horowitz has written . . . ": Helen Lefkowitz Horowitz, *Campus Life: Undergraduate Cultures from the End of the Eighteenth Century to the Present* (Chicago: University of Chicago Press, 1987), chap. 2

"I for one, at least, freely declare . . . ": Robert Hamilton Bishop, quoted in Rodabaugh, chap. 3, p. 20

Scene One

"There shall be reserved the lot No. 16 . . . ": Rodabaugh, chap. 1, p. 4

"Religion, morality, and knowledge . . . ": Northwest Ordinance, Article III, 1787

"instead of two townships . . . ": Rodabaugh, chap. 1, p. 9

"a College Township in the District of Cincinnati . . . ": Rodabaugh, chap. 1, p. 16

"An Act to Establish The Miami University . . . ": Rodabaugh, chap. 1, p. 17

Designing Higher Education in Ohio and the Midwest—Andrew Cayton

"In 1800 Ohio's population was . . . ": Andrew Cayton, *Ohio: The History of a People* (Columbus: Ohio State University Press, 2002), 15

"known by the name of Oxford . . . ": Rodabaugh, chap. 1, p. 20

Early Nineteenth-Century Ecology of Southwest Ohio—David A. Francko

Early Presidents of Miami University—Robert F. Schmidt

The Origins of Miami University's First Library—Robert S. Wicks

Grammar Schools—Kate Rousmaniere

James McBride—Terry A. Barnhart

Comparative Enrollment, 1838–1839: Morgan Library of Ohio; Rodabaugh; William F. Russell, ed., *The Rise of a University* (New York: Columbia University Press, 1937); Transylvania University Archives; William S. Yeck, *Old Miami Enrollment* (Dayton, Ohio: Yeck Brothers, 2006)

Miami's Presbyterian Heritage—Peter W. Williams

Robert Hamilton Bishop—Peter W. Williams

Oxford Theological Seminary—Valerie E. Elliott

William Holmes McGuffey, "Schoolmaster to the Nation"—Stephen C. Gordon

John Witherspoon Scott, Educator—Robert F. Schmidt

"We have just this day had a glimpse . . . ": John Witherspoon Scott to Thomas E. Thomas, Thomas Papers, Miami Special Collections, quoted in Rodabaugh, chap. 5, p. 17

Oxford's Most Celebrated Couple—Valerie E. Elliott

Careers of Miami Graduates, 1824–1840: Yeck, *Old Miami Enrollment*, 31

The Career of Benjamin Harrison—Robert F. Schmidt

Scene Two

Travel in the Early Midwest—John Hoxland White

The Miami Triad—Christopher R. Minelli

"The Society of Inquiry on Missions . . . ": Robert Morrison, "Miami University and Missions," *Miami Student*, January 1899, 75–77

Oxford's Three Colleges for Women—Valerie E. Elliott

Margaret Junkin Preston: Stacey Jean Klein, *Margaret Junkin Preston, Poet of the Confederacy* (Columbia: University of South Carolina Press, 2007)

"a sin against God . . . ": David M. Fahey, "'Slavery Is a Sin Against God and a Crime Against Man': Alfred J. Anderson and Oxford's Black Convention of January 7, 1853," *The Old Northwest* 15, nos. 1–2 (Spring/Summer 1990): 3–19

Contesting Liberty and Power in the Literary Societies—James Patrick Ambuske

"ill concealed Dislike of the north . . . ": Robert W. McFarland, Daybook, April 10–15, 1861, Miami Archives

"somewhat more than fifty percent . . . ": Rodabaugh, chap. 10, p. 13

"David Swing would live well . . . "—Peter W. Williams

"The War Governors," in L. E. Grennan, *A Bunch of Wild Flowers* (Oxford, Ohio, 1908)

David Swing's War Eulogy for Minor Millikin—James Patrick Ambuske

The Miamian Who Spoke at Gettysburg (Charles Anderson)—Rob Tolley

"Spare us, O God of Jacob . . . ": John W. Hall, quoted in Rodabaugh, chap. 10, p. 4

"a dilapidated pile . . . ": Robert Livingston Stanton, quoted in Rodabaugh, chap. 11, p. 4

Interlude

The Miami Classical and Scientific Training School—Robert F. Schmidt

ACT TWO

Prelude

"entangled in the great national struggle . . . ": Bertha Boya Thompson, *The History of Miami University from 1873 to 1900* (MA thesis, Miami University, 1954), 194. Act 2 is significantly in debt to this work, hereafter cited as Thompson.

"was sharp cure for all our ills . . . ": William McSurely, quoted in Thompson, 179

"more than doubled": United States Census of Population table, Smith Regional History Library

"longest single-span highway bridge": Jim Blount, "Miami Bridge, Hamilton's First, Opened in 1819," *High-Main Bridge* dedication pamphlet, republished, *Hamilton Journal News*, May 6, 2007

"meant dust, lime, mortar . . . ": Robert White McFarland, "Opening Address," *The Oxford Citizen*, April 22, 1886, 1 "a procession of students and citizens. . . ": Thompson, 40

"administrator, professor, librarian . . . ": Thompson, 44–45

"long, laborious and complicated . . . ": Thompson, 54

"In all cases of executive action . . . ": Thompson, 59

"Mrs. Fullerton says Dr. Byers told her . . . ": quoted in Thompson, 172

"proposed that no applicant be refused . . . ": Thompson, 17

"On October 10, two women were admitted . . . ": Thompson, 67

"served for a time as chaplain to . . . ": Henrietta Hepburn to H. C. Minnich, April 27, 1944, Hepburn correspondence, Miami University

"suave and diplomatic . . . ": Thompson, 61

"too much Presbyterian church": quoted in Thompson, 184; the account of trustee actions is given in Thompson, and in Board of Trustee records, 1888, Miami Archives

"No effort has been spared . . . ": Ethelbert Dudley Warfield, quoted in Thompson, 197

Scene Three

Warfield and the "Dude Faculty"—Robert F. Schmidt

"dress suit": Thompson, 203

"He said that on occasion . . . ": Benjamin B. Warfield, quoted in Thompson, 207

"very acme of their indiscretions": Carl Richard Greer, *Old Oxford Days*, 1947, quoted in Thompson, 207

Western College for Women and New Miami: see Narka Nelson, *Western College for Women* (Oxford, Ohio: Western College for Women, 1967), chap. 7; hereafter cited as Nelson

"is open to both sexes . . . ": E. D. Warfield, quoted in Thompson, 225

"The Society of Inquiry . . . ": Thompson, 235

Alumnae Accomplished—Aaron Andrew Spetz

"It was on the first Commencement day . . . ": Nelson, 104

"to break up . . . ": Thompson, 219

"The first annual meeting . . . ": Thompson, 232

Ethelbert Dudley Warfield and "The First Football Game"—Edwin M. Yamauchi

"For there is no calling in modern life . . . ": Henry Snyder, quoted in Thompson, 221

"About a month before . . . ": Thompson, 242–44

"a frank, straightforward man": William McSurely, quoted in Thompson, 250

"President Thompson was a businesslike manager . . . ": Thompson, chap. 5

"The electric system . . . ": Thompson, 257

"Thompson was an effective political leader . . . ": Thompson, 261–62

"The growth of modern college life . . . ": *Miami Student*, quoted in Thompson, 263

Henry and Minnie—Robert F. Schmidt

"The Doctor is an all around man . . . ": *Miami Student*, quoted in Thompson, 292

"Miami University stands in . . . ": William McSurely, quoted in Thompson, 367

"Prexy"—Robert F. Schmidt

Freedom—Valerie E. Elliott

Train 41—John Hoxland White, Jr.

"the most remarkable piece of construction . . . ": Ralph J. McGinnis, *The History of Oxford, Ohio* (Oxford, Ohio: Stewart Press, 1930), 52

"A half dozen times a year . . . ": McGinnis, in Walter Havighurst, *The Miami Years, 1809–1984* (New York: G. P. Putnam's Sons, 1984), 202

The Centennial Celebration of 1909—Peter W. Williams

"unintentionally killed . . . ": *Miami University Alumni Catalogue Centennial Edition, 1809–1909* (Oxford, 1909), 137

Scene Four

Teaching Teachers and Changing Society—Kate Rousmaniere

"all persons, regardless of sex . . . ": Thompson, 277

Miami's Early African American Students—A Long Time Coming—Jerome U. Conley, Valerie E. Elliott

The School of Business—William McKinstry

The School of Fine Arts—Robert S. Wicks

Oxford and Miami African Americans, A Timeline of Change, 1885–1941, adapted from Miami University Libraries *African American Timeline*, Digital Resources

Scene Five

"A recent investigation . . . ": Raymond M. Hughes, letter to Hinckley Smith, January 28, 1910, Miami Archives

"A new Miami's risen . . . ": *Miami Student,* December 1902

"What if to the old Miami fellows": *Miami Student,* January 1903

Delta Zeta, 1902—Kate Rousmaniere and Mary Jane Gregg

New Homes for Women—Robert F. Schmidt

"The reconstructed Hepburn Hall . . . ": Board of Trustees materials, January 1912

"It is possible, I believe . . . ": Elizabeth Hamilton, "Annual Report of the Dean of Women," June 1910, Miami Archives

"It has seemed to me that we should use every reasonable effort . . . ": Raymond M. Hughes, *Annual Report of the President,* 1927, 31–32

"Since our University is a residential one . . . ": Helen E. Page, "The Report of the Dean of Women," May 1955, Miami Archives

Shaping a New Campus Culture—Mary E. Frederickson

Scene Six

"The women of New Miami would become . . . ": Thompson, 123–26

Tower Rush, Flag Rush, Tug-of-War—Bradley J. Mollmann

May Day—Robert F. Schmidt

Homecoming—Robert F. Schmidt

The Freshman Cap—Robert F. Schmidt

Alma Mater—Roderick E. Nimtz

Alfred Upham and Miami Traditions—Bobbe Burke

The Fellowship in Creative Arts—Robert F. Schmidt

Interlude

Planning and Building an Academic Village—Aaron Andrew Spetz

ACT THREE

Prelude

Oxford, December 7, 1941—Robert F. Schmidt

Wartime Miami—Allan M. Winkler

"A total of 400 WAVES . . . ": Douglas Garwood Weaver, "Through Their Eyes: Women and the Homefront at Miami University," Summer Scholars Paper, 1998, Miami Archives, p. 4

Miami University War Training Program: *Alumni News Letter*, June 1946, 11

Barbara Brown journal entry quoted in Weaver, 2, 22

"that year's marriage rate . . . ": Weaver, 12

"In 1943 the campus engaged in a 'blue jean debate' . . .": Weaver, 13

Scene Seven

"Joseph M. Bachelor . . . ": Walter Havighurst, "Bachelor Hall Dedication Recalls Miami of Old," 1979, Miami Archives

"In his will he gave . . . ": Lori M. Gramlich with Kimberly E. Medley, *A Landscape Guide to the Bachelor Reserve*, Molyneaux Foundation and Bachelor Reserve Endowment, 1996, 2

"The returned student veteran believes . . . ": quoted in Havighurst, 219

Miami Wartime and Postwar Civilian Enrollment, Registrar's Report, 1942–1943, 1944–1945, Miami *Catalog*, 1951, Miami Archives

"the federal government committed to paying for . . . ": James Surowiecki, *New Yorker*, August 13, 2007, 28

"On October 7, 1946 . . . ": Robert E. White, Jr., *Oxford and Miami University During World War II*, 37

"To respond to this crisis . . . ," Havighurst, 224

"Temporary housing for married students and their families . . . ": Martin Egelston, "Happy Valley: Fertile Vetville," unpublished manuscript, Miami Archives, 2006

"When the trustees chose Hahne . . . ": *Miami University Bulletin*, series 44, no. 4, December 1945

"The wartime gender revolution continued . . . ": Claudia Goldin, "The Role of World War II in the Rise of Women's Employment," *American Economic Review* 81 (September 1991): 741–56

"On February 15, 1935 . . . ": "Miami Broadcast—February 15, 1935," Miami Archives

"These were listed in . . . ": *Miami Student*, October 7, 1947; November 7, 1947; December 9, 1947

"In late 1949 a 20-foot antenna . . . ": *Miami Alumnus*, November, 1949, 11

"Just five years later WMUB. . . ": *Miami Student*, November 8, 1955; March 25, 1958

"By 1960 the Miami University Broadcasting Service. . . ": *Miami Alumnus*, February, 1960; July 1964

Alumni Affairs—Douglas M. Wilson

" . . . their mutual deep affection . . . ": Joanne L. Yeck, ed., "The Miami University Letters, 1953–1998," unpublished manuscript, Miami Archives, 2005, i–ii

Origins of the Murstein Alumni Center—Robert F. Schmidt

Residence Life—B. Derrell Hart

"As dormitories came to be considered . . . ": Evalou Middaugh, *Miami University Department of Residence and Dining Halls: 160 Years of Service to Students* (Miami University, 1981, updated 1989), 12–19

"By the middle 1960s . . . ": Middaugh, 8

Working at Tuffy's—Karl R. Mattox

Campus Climate—B. Derrell Hart

"It recognized the facts of change . . . ": Havighurst, *Miami Years*, 226

"Millett's Commission believed . . . ": W. H. Cowley, Review of Richard H. Ostheimer, *Student Charges and Financing Higher Education* (New York: Columbia University Press, 1953), *Annals of the American Academy of Political and Social Science* 291 (1954): 183–84

"Born on a farm . . . Robert F. Etheridge . . . ": Arthur Sandeen, "Robert F. Etheridge, Miami University," *Profiles of Successful Student Affairs Leaders* (Washington, D.C.: National Association of Student Personnel Administrators, 2001), 83–94

"At a time when many student affairs professionals . . . ": Sandeen, 87

"to create a graduate program . . . ": Sandeen, 8

Selectivity—B. Derrell Hart

Graduate Studies—Robert C. Johnson

"In 1972 observers were writing . . . ": Eldon J. Gardner, "Ph.D. Degrees in a Changing Scene," in *Graduate Education Today and Tomorrow*, ed. Gustave Otto Arlt, Leonard J. Kent and George P. Springer (Albuquerque: University of New Mexico Press, 1972)

Scene Eight

"Where there is no growth . . . ": "Hahne Calls for Oxford Growth to Meet Larger College Need," *Oxford Press*, September 29, 1949, 1

"One week before it reported . . . ": *Oxford Press*, September 22, 1949, 1

The International Style in Oxford—Gerardo Brown-Manrique

"Fürth had earned an engineering degree . . . ": "Four Decades of Designing in Fürth Retrospective Show," *Oxford Press*, May 9, 1963, 8

"In 1955 Ohio voters endorsed . . . ": Christopher A. Maraschiello, *Wallace P. Roudebush: Spirit of the Institution* (Miami University Alumni Association, 1993), 77

"On February 19, 1957, the *Cincinnati Times-Star* . . . ": *Cincinnati Times-Star*, February 19, 1957, 1–2

"Miami University for some time has adhered to . . . ": *Statement of Architectural Policy*, Board of Trustees, Miami University, Oxford, Ohio, Attachment A, Board *Minutes*, Approved by the Executive Committee, March 30, 1957, 1–2

Oxford: adapted from "A Short History of the Oxford Museum Association," OMA Web site, 2007, William King, adaptation of item by Robert T. Howard

"President John Millet loathed Vetville . . . ": Egelston, 6

Letter of Charles F. Cellarius to John D. Millett, August 15, 1957, Miami Archives

"A birthday is simply a marker . . . ": John Millett, cover statement, *Miami: Her 150th Year*, unpaginated booklet (Oxford, Ohio: Miami University, 1959)

Remembering Old Main, 1816–1958—John Hoxland White, Jr.

"Nothing that has happened thus far has made good . .": Millett, *Miami: Her 150th Year*

"a place where Christian principles . . . ": Arthur C. Wickenden, *Raymond M. Hughes: Leader of Men* (Oxford, Ohio: Miami University Alumni Association, 1966), 109

John D. Millett, *The Liberating Arts: Essays in General Education* (Cleveland: Howard Allen, 1957), 82

"In an August 1959 letter . . . :" John D. Millett to Arthur C. Wickenden, August 24, 1959, Miami Archives

"knows what it is": Anne H. Hopkins, Provost and Executive Vice President for Academic Affairs, 1995–99

"In the past century . . . ": "Walter Havighurst," *Toledo Sunday Blade Pictorial*, March 31, 1957, 11

"Walter Havighurst spent forty-one of his ninety-two years . . . ": "A Memorial to Walter E. Havighurst," William C. Pratt with John W. Altman, Edward M. Brown, John E. Dolibois, Robert T. Howard, Frank Jordan, Jr., Marilyn E. Throne, Miami University, 1994; see also Phillip R. Shriver, "A Tribute to Walter Havighurst," February 19, 1994, Miami Archives

"In 1988 Douglas Wilson . . . ": Douglas Wilson, ed., *Our Miami Heritage* (Oxford, Ohio: Miami University, 1988)

"To generations of Miami students . . . ": Shriver, "A Tribute to Walter Havighurst," February 19, 1994, Miami Archives

"In my view, Walter Havighurst's *The Miami Years* . . . ": Phillip R. Shriver, *Miami University: A Personal History*, ed. William Pratt (Oxford, Ohio: Miami University Press, 1998), 1

"The quest for understanding . . . ": Walter Havighurst, *The Miami Years, 1809–1984* (New York: Putnam, 1958; 175th anniversary edition, Oxford Printing Company, 1984), 252

"The Bishops Come Home to Oxford," *Miami Alumnus*, July 1959, 29; see also Walter Havighurst, "The Two Graves of R. H. Bishop," *The Miamian*, Winter, 1988, 9–11

Walter and Marion Boyd Havighurst—Frances McClure

"Biography"—Robert S. Wicks

"President Millett took many steps . . . ": Millett, *Miami: Her 150th Year*

"On April 10, 1959, Robert Frost . . . ":—William Pratt

"On the morning of September 17, 1959 . . . "—Robert F. Schmidt

"study of instructional techniques . . . ": *Miami Alumnus*, January 1956

"History class has me bluffed . . . ": student class diary, American History, W. E. Smith, instructor, March 14, 1951, Miami Archives

Applied Science—Osama M. Ettouney

"In both industrial arts and home economics . . . ": John Millett, in "Earl Valentine 'Red' Thesken, A life Well Lived," *Oxford Press*, December 22, 2006, A12

Origins of Wright State University, from "History of Wright State University," "Historical Timeline," Wright State University Special Collections & Archives Web site, 2007

"President Millett favored . . . ": Phillip R. Shriver, "A Memorial to John D. Millett," Oxford, Ohio, November 18, 1993

"Before John Millett . . . ": Shriver, "A Memorial to John D. Millett"

"A Class of 1926 Miami graduate . . . ": *New York Times*, December 12, 1986

"But this Middletown Campus . . . ": "Storybook Tale Brought MU to Town," *Middletown Journal*, August 22, 1976

"The 'Miami Family' was growing well beyond Oxford . . . ": dedication program, Hamilton Campus of Miami University, September 26, 1969

Miami University Luxembourg: adapted from Miami University Luxembourg Web site

Oxford and Miami African Americans, A Timeline of Change, 1941–1970, adapted from Miami University Libraries *African American Timeline*, Digital Resources

Recruiting Black Faculty and Staff—Heanon M. Wilkins

Black World Studies—Heanon M. Wilkins

Interlude

"As We See It: Vietnam '68"—Peter Magolda; Laura Rhoades

ACT FOUR

Prelude

"At 2:00 PM Wednesday, April 15, 1970 . . . ": Rachel Weidenger, abstract, "Space to Dream inside History, Events of Protest at Miami University, Spring, 1970," Western College Program Senior Project, 1997

May 17, 1970, Miami University Memorandum, Miami Archives

Stephen Clegg Rowan: see Jim Blount, "Rowan Commanded Most Powerful Civil War Ship," *Journal News*, July 28, 2004; and "Rowan Leader in Transforming Civil War Navy," *Journal News*, July 21, 2004, Smith Library of Regional History, Oxford

"At the Parents' Day football game . . . ": *Miami Student*, November 4, 1969; November 21, 1969; January 23, 1970

The Gentle Revolution, 1969, pamphlet, 26 pp., Miami Archives

Cartoon, Gary Beeber, *Miami Student*, December 5, 1969

"In October two thousand students rallied . . . ": *Miami Student*, October 3, 1969

"They marched to Lewis Place . . . ": *Miami Student*, October 17, 1969

"In November the Student Mobilization Committee . . . ": *Miami Student*, November 18, 1969

Quotations, Capt. Dwight Carey and Harold J. Carpenter, *Miami and U, Newsletter of The Miami Alumnus*, May 1970

"At 7:00 a.m. . . . ": *Miami Student*, April 16, 1970

"That evening students took a novel mass action . . . ": *Oxford Press,* April 23, 1970

"Then on May 4, 1970 . . . ": *Miami Student,* May 5, 1970

"To a considerable degree . . . ": *Miami Student,* May 17, 1970

William G. Slover announcement, May 7, 1970, Miami Archives

"'Rap' sessions involving students . . . ": *A Report of the President's Commission to Investigate the Events of April 15, 1970,* May 28, 1970, p. 26, Miami Archives

"that police not be called onto the campus . . . ": *The SCAR Report: The Findings of the Select Committee on the Abuse of Rights,* p. 26, Miami Archives

It Need Not Have Happened—Richard W. Momeyer

"The whole challenge of this development . . . ": "Alumni Gifts 50 Percent Behind," *Miami Student,* May 26, 1970, 1

Scene Nine

"Once I came here . . . ": Lloyd A. Goggin, *Miami Stories* Oral History interview, June 20, 2006

"I look at the position . . . ": *Miami Student,* April 14, 1970, 1

"At Miami we had the wholehearted support . . . ": John E. Dolibois, *Pattern of Circles: An Ambassador's Story* (Kent, Ohio: Kent State University Press, 1989), 235

"Phil would never step on any one of us . . . ": David G. Brown, *Miami Stories* Oral History interview, April 10, 2006

"I think one of the real achievements . . . ": David G. Brown, Shriver Cabinet Story Circle, *Miami Stories* Oral History interview, April 10, 2006

"John Yeck proposed . . . ": John D. Yeck, letter to Phillip R. Shriver, July 20, 1973, *Proposals: The Western College of Miami University,* Miami Archives

"Former President John Millett . . . ": John Millett, letter to Phillip R. Shriver, August 22, 1973, *Proposals*

"In retrospect it was an exhausting way to lead . . . ": Brown, *Miami Stories* interview

1971: The Institute for Environmental Sciences—Eugene E. Willeke

1972: The Rise of Women's Studies—Ann Fuehrer

1979: "The Greening of the Future": *The Miamian,* June 28, 1979, September 18, 1980; *The Miami University Report,* December 10, 1981

1981: The University Honors Program—Carolyn Haynes

1983: "The Cradle of Coaches"—Susan Cross Lipnickey

"Miami clinched the MAC football crown . . . "—Robert F. Schmidt

The Miami University Marching Band—David Shaffer

"The message is clear . . . ": Richard Moll, *The Public Ivys: A Guide to America's Best Public Undergraduate Colleges and Universities* (New York: Penguin, 1985), xi–xxiii

"It's a drab ride . . . ": Moll, *Public Ivys,* "Miami University of Ohio"

1987: Liberal Education at Miami University: A Statement of Principles, adapted from Robert C. Johnson, "A Critical Review of Miami's Reform Project, 1985–1989, July, 1989;" Curtis W. Ellison, "The Miami University Liberal Education Reform Project, 1985–1990: A Narrative Account," July 5, 1990; *The Miami Plan for Liberal Education,* Oxford, Ohio, May 1, 1989

"To me, the single most impressive . . . ": Eulalia Benejam Cobb to Curtis W. Ellison, September 16, 1991, Miami Archives

1995: Project *Dragonfly*—Christopher A. Myers

Scene Ten

"Near the end of the Shriver administration . . . ": "Miami Faculty Perspectives: A Compendium of Serious Thoughts by Selected Faculty about the Future of Miami University," June, 1980, Miami Archives

"I will invite and use . . . ": Paul G. Pearson, State of the University Address, August 21, 1981

"In five years Richard Moll would . . . ": Donovan Auble, "Reference Tables," Miami Faculty Perspectives

"Some faculty perceived this . . . ": *The Miami University Report,* January 12, February 9, February 23, March 2, March 9, March 23, April 6, April 20, 1989; *Miami Student,* April 14, 1989

Pursuing Multicultural Diversity—Morris Young

Oxford and Miami African Americans, A Timeline of Change, 1970–96 adapted from Miami University Libraries *African American Timeline,* Digitial Resources.

Demographics of Change—Kate Rousmaniere; C. Lee Harrington

President Paul Pearson Responds to Tiananmen Square—J. K. Bhattacharjee

No Cars—Peter M. Magolda; Laura Rhoades

Interlude

Mascot—Bobbe Burke

ACT FIVE

Prelude

Oxford, 1998—Randolph Runyon; Robert F. Schmidt; Valerie E. Elliott; Curtis W. Ellison

"Her tank was once the village pride": Anonymous, Smith Library of Regional History, Oxford Water Tower file

Scene Eleven

Customers—Andrew Cayton; Curtis W. Ellison

"In 2006 the most popular evaluator . . .": Miami Web site, 2007

Student Life in Oxford—Andrew Cayton; Curtis W. Ellison

"In Oxford, police cited 243 people . . . ": *Cincinnati Enquirer,* June 21, 2007, A1–13

"Oxford's League of Women Voters reported . . . ": *Oxford Press,* April 21, 2007, A14

"A study by an anthropology class in 2004 . . . ": Chaise LaDousa, "'Witty House name': Visual Language, Interpretive Practice, and Uneven Agency in a Midwestern College Town," forthcoming, *Journal of American Folklore*

"the largest undergraduate major in the United States . . . ": Louis Menand, "The Graduates," *New Yorker,* May 21, 2007, 27–28

High Academic Standards: *About Miami,* Miami Web site, 2007

Premier Student Organizations, 2007: *About Miami,* Miami Web site, 2007

"News and Information Office released a story . . . ": Miami *News Briefs,* February 13, 2006

Expectations for Residential Living—Andrew Cayton; Curtis W. Ellison

Miami University Recreational Sports Center: communication from Ron Silko, Director of Customer & Facility Services

"Wally Szerbiak, Class of 1999, became . . . ": official Web site of the Boston Celtics, 2007

"Ben Roethlisberger, who . . .": official Web site of Superbowl Champion Ben Roethlisberger, 2007

"In 1999, President Garland recommended . . . "—Susan Cross Lipnickey

Twenty-First Century Arts and Culture: Miami Web site

History for the Public—Michael L. Carrafiello

Miami's Journey with Diversity—Gerri Susan Mosley-Howard

The Havighurst Center and the Silk Road: Havighurst Center for Russian and Post-Soviet Studies Web site, 2007

Modern Scientific Achievements at Miami—John M. Hughes

Strike! Miami *"Students for Staff"* Web site

Domestic Partner Benefits—William J. Gracie, Jr.

"This cut, which will remain . . . ": James Garland, State of the University Address, August 16, 2001

"59 percent of incoming Oxford first-years in 2007 . . . ": "Did You Know? Quick Facts about the *Oxford Campus* Class of 2011," Miami University Assessment Brief no. 28, September 12, 2007

"In 1992 the Farmers provided . . . ": Farmer School of Business Web site, 2007

A Campus Planning Timetable—Robert G. Keller

Changes, Anxieties, Assessments—Andrew Cayton; Curtis W. Ellison

A New Facility for the Farmer School of Business—Raymond F. Gorman

Scene Twelve

Adopting the Mind of a Scholar: David C. Hodge, Inaugural Address, October 20, 2006

"We need to begin the process on the first day . . . ": David C. Hodge, *Top 25 Project: Proposals Sought,* Miami *News Release,* January 5, 2007

Documenting Effective Educational Practice (DEEP) Report, National Survey of Student Engagement, George D. Kuh, Director, Indiana University Center for Postsecondary Research and Planning, November 4, 2003

Stumbling into History—James Patrick Ambuske

The ILR and Retirement in Oxford—Richard V. Smith

"In a perfect world . . . ": "Facing East," *Miamian* 25, no. 1 (Fall 2006): 8–12

Interactive Media Studies: Miami Web site, 2007

Voice of America Learning Center—Roderick E. Nimtz; VOALC Miami Web site, 2007

Postlude

Education for the Twenty-First Century—Marcia B. Baxter-Magolda

CODA

A People With a Past, Not From the Past, Miami University and the Miami Tribe of Oklahoma—Bobbe Burke and Daryl W. Baldwin II

CHORUS

"A New Alma Mater"—Randy Runyon

Selected Bibliography

Bartlow, B. S., ed. *Miami University Alumni Catalogue: Centennial Edition, 1809–1909.* Oxford, Ohio: Miami University, 1909.

Baer, Elizabeth H. *History of the Miami University Libraries.* Oxford, Ohio: Friends of the Miami University Libraries, 1997.

Church, Martha F. "Student Life at Miami University in World War II." Master's thesis, Miami University, 1947.

Dolibois, John E. *Pattern of Circles: An Ambassador's Story.* Kent, Ohio: Kent State University Press, 1989

Elliott, Valerie Edwards. *Images of America: Oxford.* Chicago: Arcadia Publishing, 2004.

Flower, Olive. *History of Oxford College for Women.* Oxford, Ohio: Miami University Alumni Association, 1949.

Gorn, Elliott J., ed. *The McGuffey Readers: Selections from the 1879 Edition.* Boston: Bedford/St. Martin's, 1998.

Havighurst, Walter. *The Miami Years, 1809–1984.* New York: G. P. Putnam's Sons, 1958. Updated and reprinted by Miami University, 1969, 1984.

Havighurst, Walter. *Men of Old Miami, 1809–1873: A Book of Portraits.* New York: G. P. Putnam's Sons, 1974.

Hoyt, Phyllis. *Where the Peonies Bloomed: A Memoir of My Years at Western College.* Oxford, Ohio: Western College Alumnae Association, Inc., 2000.

Kurz, Bob. *Miami of Ohio: The Cradle of Coaches.* Troy, Ohio: Troy Daily News, 1983.

Maraschiello, Christopher A. *Wallace P. Roudebush: Spirit of the Institution.* Oxford, Ohio: Miami University Alumni Association, 1993.

Nelson, Narka. *Western College for Women.* Oxford, Ohio: Western College for Women, 1954, 1967.

Pratt, William, ed. *College Days at Old Miami: The Diary of T. C. Hibbett, 1851–1854.* Oxford, Ohio: Miami University, 1984.

Robb, Dale Willard. "Religion in the History of Miami University, 1809–1932." Master's thesis, Miami University, 1954.

Rodabaugh, James M. "A History of Miami University From Its Origin to 1873." Unpublished manuscript, 1949. Miami University Archives.

Rousmaniere, Kate. *100 Years of the School of Education and Allied Professions: Teaching the Teachers and Changing Society.* Oxford, Ohio: Miami University, 2002.

Shriver, Phillip R. *Miami University: A Personal History.* Edited by William Pratt. Oxford, Ohio: Miami University Press, 1998.

Thompson, Bertha Boya. "The History of Miami University from 1873 to 1900." Master's thesis, Miami University, 1954.

Tobey, Walter Lawrence, and William Oxley Thompson. *The Diamond Anniversary Volume: Miami University, 1824–1899.* Hamilton, Ohio: Republican Publishing Co., 1899.

Upham, Alfred H. *Old Miami: The Yale of the Early West.* Copyright Alfred H. Upham, 1909. Oxford, Ohio: Miami University Alumni Association, 1947.

Vogt, Peter J. "Guy Potter Benton—His Effect on Miami University." Master's thesis, Miami University, 1956.

White, Robert E., Jr. *Oxford and Miami University during World War II.* Oxford, Ohio: Smith Library of Regional History, 1994.

Wickenden, Arthur C. *Raymond M. Hughes: Leader of Men.* Oxford, Ohio: Miami University Alumni Association, 1966.

Index